HINDU-KOH:

WANDERINGS AND WILD SPORT ON AND BEYOND THE HIMALAYAS

BY

MAJOR-GENERAL DONALD MACINTYRE, V.C.

LATE PRINCE OF WALES' OWN GOORKHAS
FELLOW OF THE ROYAL GEOGRAPHICAL SOCIETY

WITH ILLUSTRATIONS

WILLIAM BLACKWOOD AND SONS
EDINBURGH AND LONDON
MDCCCLXXXIX

VIEW FROM THE NITI PASS, TIBETAN SIDE .

HINDU-KOH

TO

HIS ROYAL HIGHNESS

THE PRINCE OF WALES,

HONORARY COLONEL OF THE AUTHOR'S LATE REGIMENT,

THE PATRON OF ALL MANLY SPORTS, AND A

TRUE DISCIPLE OF ST HUBERT,

THIS BOOK IS,

BY GRACIOUS PERMISSION,

MOST HUMBLY AND RESPECTFULLY

DEDICATED.

PREFACE.

THE subject of Himalayan travel and sport is now so old a story, that an attempt to create further interest in it is an almost hopeless undertaking, especially for one who has been more accustomed to handling the mountain-staff than the pen. But, old though it be, the field it embraces is so vast, that it may still afford scope for variety even should it lack originality; and such the author would fain trust may be the case in this instance. The following pages, however, are in nowise embellished with a vein of romance, which, whilst perhaps rendering a narrative of this kind more attractive to the general reader, is apt to give a fanciful and overdrawn picture of the reality. Nor has their writer any pretension to being either an erudite traveller, or a mighty hunter to whom hairbreadth escapes and thrilling adventures have been common occurrences. Consequently he is well aware that he is somewhat rashly launching his frail craft, so to speak, on the ruthless waves of criticism, with a very great risk of its foundering. But he trusts that the friends at whose suggestion he has ventured to put these simple reminiscences into print, and his brother sportsmen—more particularly the younger ones, for whom they are in a great measure intended—may find something to divert them in this humble endeavour of an old member of the fraternity to portray a few scenes and incidents gathered from his *bona fide* notes of wanderings and wild sport among the fells and forests of the Himalaya mountains, and on the bare rolling uplands beyond them.

CONTENTS.

CHAPTER X.

CHAPTER XI.

CHAPTER XII.

CHAPTER XIX.

CHAPTER XX.

CHAPTER XXI.

CHAPTER XXII.

CHAPTER XXIII.

CHAPTER XXIV.

CHAPTER XXV.

LIST OF ILLUSTRATIONS.

HINDU-KOH.

—◆—

CHAPTER I.

THE bygone performances of an old "muzzle-loader" may
perhaps be considered rather obsolete by the young sportsman
of the present with his double "express." But as human
nature always has been, and, I opine, ever will be much the
same, the pleasure of studying the habits of wild animals
in their native haunts, the excitement of the stalk, and the
charming influence of grand and beautiful scenery, must be
little altered now from what they were years ago, when first
I tried my "prentice hand" with the rifle among the highest
mountains in the world.

Before proceeding to narrate these old-fashioned performances, let me account for the heading I have given this book,
as to some it may appear far-fetched. So many works had
already been produced on this same subject, with a "Hima-

A

layan" cognomen, that I was at a loss to find a new name
for such an oft-told tale. To quote Solomon, "There is no
new thing under the sun," so I selected as a title an old and
but little-known designation for the Himalayas—"Hindu-
Koh"; and an ancient name would, I thought, suit well
with a somewhat threadbare topic. Moreover, as every
high peak of this mountain-chain is to Hindoos an object of
more or less veneration, this term,[1] which signifies "Hindoo
mountain," is, I think, quite as apposite, though perhaps not
so pretty as *Himaláya*—derived, it is said, from two Sanskrit
words, *hima* and *ayala*, "abode of snow."

It is now generally accepted as a well-established fact, that
these great northern bulwarks of Hindustan, and their vicinity, contain hunting-grounds which may be classed among the
best that are known. For grandeur of scenery, the Himalayas
stand unrivalled. Dame Nature has, indeed, been more lavish
of her charms here than in any other part of the universe.
That these are not exaggerated assertions, the many interesting records that have already been written on the well-worn
though inexhaustible subjects of Himalayan travel and sport
bear ample testimony, and render the following humble attempt to describe some of my own unscientific wanderings
and experiences quite unnecessary for this purpose.

When out after large game on the mountains, the sportsman is, as a rule, constrained to content himself with his own
society and that of his native guides, if he has any idea of
being successful. Moreover, from the very nature of the
ground, it would be next to impossible for two men to hunt
together over the same tract of country, without materially
interfering and spoiling each other's sport; indeed, it is considered a point of etiquette among Himalayan sportsmen to
avoid intruding on ground on which anybody else has already

---

[1] *Koh* being the Persian for "mountain," this name probably originated with
the more western Asiatics. The range was known to ancient European geo-
graphers as *Emodos* and *Imaus*.

begun to work. Hence it follows that however much a man may refrain from egotism in the narration of Himalayan sport, he must either keep his experiences to himself, or describe the performances of that objectionable *Ego*. A sportsman in the mountains is wonderfully fortunate if he can so arrange his beats as to bivouac at night on neutral ground with a chum, with whom he may discuss a pipe at the camp-fire after dinner, compare notes of the day's doings, and separate again in the morning, "each to gang his ain gait"; but to attempt to work in couples is ruination to sport, and only vexation of spirit. Nor need one ever feel lonely amidst the grand and the beautiful. Fair Nature is always charming companionship, and—

> "Oh! she is fairest in her features wild,
> Where nothing polished dares pollute her path."

Long ere I was old enough to handle a gun, an innate love of the pursuit of the *feræ naturæ* found vent in trapping birds by the numerous means devised in the youthful mind, and in rambling in quest of their eggs; rat-hunting at the dismantling of a corn-stack, the wild excitement of which, I then thought, nothing could surpass; and suchlike ways of indulging juvenile sporting instincts. I doubt whether the keen delight felt on killing my first game-bird—a woodcock—has in all my shooting experiences been equalled. To my good fortune in having been a Goorkha, so to speak, during the whole of my service in India, is due the fact of my having had such opportunities of fostering this taste for wandering and wild sport as seldom fall to the lot of the sojourner in the far East. For the Goorkha battalions are generally quartered either in or near the Himalayas; and the Nepalese mountaineers, of whom they are composed, are second to no other shikarees, not to say soldiers, in the world.

The first three years of my service were passed at Peshawur, which, though an excellent school for a soldier lad, from the practical lessons taught in the frequent expeditions that took the field from it against the turbulent hill-tribes on the frontier, afforded little scope for sporting proclivities beyond good snipe-shooting and quail when in season, or an occasional chance of hawking the Oubara (small bustard), &c., in which sport the richer natives of the Peshawur valley often indulge.

Towards the end of 1853 we marched for Rawul Pindi, in the Punjab, a much better field for sport, owing to its proximity to the foot of the Himalayas—its neighbourhood being then well stocked with game—and the excellent mahseer-fishing which was to be had within reachable distance.

I was out after Oorial,[1] the wild sheep of the Punjab (*Ovis cycloceros*), and gazelles, here termed " ravine deer " (*Gazella Bennettii*), among the comparatively low but somewhat rugged hills, and the deep ravines in the western part of the Rawul Pindi district, when I was recalled from my leave and ordered to proceed with a recruiting-party to an outpost on the Nepal frontier, in the mountain province of Kumaon. I was sorry to have to forsake the game little wild sheep among which I was getting good sport. It was then the end of March, and I had two months of hot travel before me, as there were in those days no railways in Upper India. But the long journey was of little account, with a cool climate and such a fine country for game in prospect at its termination.

Marching through the plains of India during the hot season is by no means pleasant. I therefore resolved to avoid the heat, the dust, and their concomitant evils as much as possible, by diverging from the regular route and travelling for a part of the way through the outer Himalayan ranges. With this intent I made direct for Simla—that Indian Capua which, with its salubrious climate and social attractions, is,

---

[1] The Oorial is the almost exact counterpart of the Moufflon of Southern Europe. It is found plentifully distributed over the Salt-range in the Punjab, and among the lower ranges of Afghanistan.

like its ancient prototype, much favoured by the magnates of our Indian empire, who are wont to luxuriate there during a great part of the year. Thence, about ten days' stiff marching brought us to that other popular, but less ostentatious, mountain resort—Mussoorie. The scenery and climate on this portion of the journey were a truly delightful change after the dreary monotony and thick sultry atmosphere of "the plains." The clear bracing air of the mountains and the refreshing fragrance of pine woods instilled new life into one. Now our path would wind for miles through forests of noble deodar cedars, or of grand old oaks and rhododendrons, their gnarled and crooked branches all bedecked with lichen and orchids, or ragged with trailing beards of grey moss; and the rhododendrons (which here are not merely shrubs, but large forest-trees), although past the season of their flowering prime, were still gorgeous with a wealth of crimson blossoms. Now it lay along some bright green valley, beside a clear brawling brook dancing in the sunshine over its pebbly bed, and flanked on either side by wooded heights or steep grassy slopes. Sometimes, where it traversed a rocky eminence or an open hillside, a superb panorama of the distant range of perpetual snow would be disclosed to view,—the long irregular chain of grand frozen peaks and ridges rising sharply on the clear skyline, and stretching away right and left, their pale summits gradually becoming more indistinct as they sank towards the far horizon. The mists of early morning often lay in level white banks along the bottom of the deep intervening valleys. As the rising sun grew more powerful, the vapour would slowly lift, and, taking the form of fantastic-shaped cumuli, envelop the snowy crests in its heavy white folds, leaving in the profound hollows a soft blue haze which was fitfully darkened by the broad shadows of transitory clouds hovering above.

But mountain-roads have their drawbacks as well as their delights. And of this fact one is reminded by having to climb some heart-breaking hill, before reaching the top of which the weary climber loses much of his admiration of the scenery as well as a good deal of breath, and frequent stoppages are made, nominally on account of the former, but really in behalf of the latter, vulgarly termed "bellows to mend." Moreover, when the traveller least expects it, some of those beautiful masses of white cloud he has admired so much as they rested like huge piles of cotton-wool along the mountain-tops, have gradually crept up unnoticed until warned of their approach by distant rumblings and mutterings of thunder, when suddenly the storm-cloud bursts over him, and discharging its humid contents, drenches him to the skin. But even the storm has its wild charm should the wayfarer be fortunate enough to find some friendly rock at hand, from under shelter of which he can view its approach, and listen to the thunder rolling and reverberating among the surrounding crags and precipices—for a tempest in such mountains is truly a grand sight.

The greater part of a day was spent in crossing a deep, rapid river by a rope bridge, or "jula" as it is called. A stout rope is stretched from side to side, generally between two convenient rocks. Each man or bundle of baggage is placed on a short plank of wood, like the seat of a swing, which is attached to the main rope by a crooked bit of stick, forming a kind of running-block. The load, animate or inanimate, is sent sliding along down the rope as far as its weight will take it, and then hauled up to the opposite side by a guy-rope attached to the running-block. Although there was little or no danger, I was glad to find myself on *terra firma* again after being swung over, the more so as I had just seen the load of baggage that preceded me left dangling in mid-air above the roaring torrent, until the guy-rope, which had parted company with the block, was replaced by an acrobatic individual who clambered out on the main rope to repair damages. There is another kind of jula, made

DEHRA DOON AND SEWALIK HILLS.

of ropes formed of twigs, twisted and bound tightly together, which, though more elaborate in its construction, requires more nerve to cross. For the crosser has to perform a sort of dance on the slack-rope, with nothing to prevent his falling from it into the water but two smaller ropes for his hands to clutch on either side.

The crow of the black partridge (*francolin*) was frequently heard by the wayside, and pheasants of various kinds were said to be pretty numerous. But even had there been leisure for shooting, it was the nesting season.

Before descending from Mussoorie to the Dehra Doon, through which a portion of our route lay, the view of this beautiful valley, as we looked down on it from the heights abruptly rising 5000 or 6000 thousand feet above it, was singularly imposing. Some fifty miles long by about twelve miles broad, and over 2000 feet high, this forest-clad valley or "Doon" lies along the base of the mountains, its wide-spreading jungles interspersed here and there with open tracts of long grass, irregular patches of reclaimed land, and intersected by broad beds of shingle and sand, where the tortuous streams flowing along them shone afar in the sun-light like bright threads of silver. On the east and west it is bounded by the rivers Ganges and Jumna respectively, where they first issue from the vast mountain-gorges through which they roll down from their sources among the eternal snow; on the south, by the low but very rugged and wooded belt of the Sewalik hills separating it from the plains beyond, which fade gradually away in the distant heat-haze that blurs the horizon.

Our way next led through these dense woods, in which, one morning, I chanced to have a rather exciting interview with some of their wild denizens. Having heard pea-fowl calling hard by, I had left the road in quest of them, followed by a little Goorkha carrying my rifle. As we were skirting along a large patch of very tall reeds (called *null* or *nurkul*), a rustling noise, evidently made by the movement of some large animal, was heard therein. Our doubts as to what it could be were soon dispelled by finding the fresh droppings and tracks, or "mullen," as the latter are there called, of wild elephants, as well as by sundry snorts and rumbling sounds which were now and again heard. Loading my gun with bullets, and exchanging it with the Goorkha for the rifle, we stole cautiously through the reeds towards the spot whence the sound proceeded, and had not to go far ere I discovered the head and big flapping ears of an elephant a short distance from me. Suddenly detecting our presence, the animal cocked forward its ears, whisked round in an instant, and went crashing away through the reeds, followed by two well-grown calves, of which I just caught a glimpse as they disappeared. In my excitement I let drive at the old one's stern, which foolish example was followed by my companion. She merely gave a shrieking trumpet and continued her flight. Had I then been more experienced in such matters, I should have known the danger and folly, not to mention the cruelty, of so reckless a proceeding; and had it chanced to have been a male, he might have made our position rather hot.

Thinking we had seen the last of the elephants, we had cleared out of the reeds, and had been skirting along them for some distance, when again we heard a tremendous crashing amongst them. Each moment it grew louder as it rapidly drew nearer. Either the injured elephant, or one of her mates that we had not seen, was evidently making straight for us, with the intention, we imagined, of resenting our rash and random shots. The business now seemed about to assume a more serious aspect, for we were in the open, and not a tree of any size was near round which we might have dodged the animal; but the plucky little Goorkha stood firm as a rock as he quietly whispered, " Look out, Sahib! we'll give it her in the head when it comes in sight." However, perhaps fortunately, no head appeared, for just as we expected the elephant to be down upon us, with a loud snort it suddenly stopped short, and nothing more did we see or hear of it but the rustling of the reeds as it made off.

After three days' travel through the Doon, we quitted the hill-tracts for the open plains, where we crossed the Ganges at Hurdwar. The great holy fair at this place of Hindoo sanctity, where countless thousands of pilgrims annually congregate to purify themselves in the sacred river, was recently over, and the vast crowds had dispersed, carrying with them, far and wide, that terrible pest, cholera, which, as usual, had broken out amongst this sweltering mass of humanity in a fearfully virulent form. I firmly believe that those dreadful epidemics which sometimes almost devastate whole districts of Hindustan and its neighbouring countries, emanate principally from this source.

After ten days' weary travel through a fiery atmosphere, resembling the colour of pea-soup, myriads of flies, and with disease rampant around, we hailed with intense relief and joy our first sight of the outer hills of Kumaon, as they loomed through the murky haze. Our last day's march, before re-entering the mountains, was across the Terai. This belt of dense forest and swamp extends, as is well known, for hundreds of miles along the base of the Himalayas, varying in breadth. From June till November its climate is deadly. During the rest of the year it is comparatively healthy, when game of many sorts and sizes, from a jack-snipe to a wild elephant, may be found there, not to speak of the mahseer-fishing in its rivers. There is always, however, a feeling of restraint when boxed up in a howdah, as well as a certain amount of dependence upon the elephant that carries you and the mahout who drives it, which, in my humble opinion, detract much from the enjoyment of this style of sport; and from the close heat of the atmosphere and the thickness of the jungle, it can hardly be either pleasurably or properly

achieved in the Terai on foot. For my part, give me mountain work, with its freedom of action, glorious scenery, and
fresh bracing air, and with one's own wits and limbs only to
depend upon in pursuit of game.

After a rest at the mountain sanitarium of Nynee Tāl,
with its deep clear Tal, or lake, lying embosomed among its
beautiful surroundings of steep wooded slopes and moss-grown
crags, a few days more through the mountains brought us to
our recruiting-station, and, I may add, my first hunting-ground
in the Himalayas, after a long hot journey to it of about 750
miles.

Crossing a "jula."

CHAPTER II.

THE outpost of Shore, or Pithoragarh, as it is officially termed, at which I had arrived, is situated in a pretty, basin-shaped, green valley, about eight miles in circumference, at an altitude of somewhat over 5000 feet. The valley is encircled by high hills, except where a wide gap to the north-east discloses a beautiful glimpse of the snowy range. The post consists of a small British-built fort, and a stockade perched on an adjacent eminence; a few native shops; the huts for the detachment quartered there; and three dwelling-houses for the officers. The only benefit, probably, ever derived from the fort was by the individual who took the contract for building it, as it is completely commanded from higher ground, and there appeared to be no efficient arrangement for the supply of water. As for the stockade, I could never discover what was its builder's intention, even from the oldest inhabitant.

Black bears and other large game were plentiful at that

time on the neighbouring heights, and hill-tigers and leopards were not uncommon.   One grand hill, immediately
south of the valley, and rising about 3000 feet above its
level, was especially famous for game—the Thakil by name,
so called after a singular kind of palm-tree that grows on
it, and seemingly peculiar to that hill, as I observed it on
none of the neighbouring ones. Its bare straight stem, topped
with a bunch of feathery, fan-shaped fronds, has a rather
anomalous effect, shooting up singly, to a height of 30 or 40
feet, here and there among gnarled old oaks, rhododendrons,
and conifers, at an elevation of between 6000 and 8000 feet
above sea-level, and more especially in winter, when the hill
is covered with snow.

On the low ground feathered game was fairly abundant,
and a few hares, which were much larger than those of the
plains of India.   In the depth of winter, woodcocks (here
called *sim-kŏkra*—meaning rill or spring fowl) were to be
found.   Of the latter, I once in about a month bagged thirty-
seven in this valley and a neighbouring one, eighteen being
shot in one week. But such exceptional good luck was during,
and subsequent to, an unusually severe snowstorm, which had
driven so many woodcock down from the higher ranges, where
they bred regularly.   Most of them, however, were shot in
the other valley, which was always more or less favoured
by them in winter. I compared stuffed specimens of these
woodcocks with their European relative, and found them exactly similar in plumage, and apparently so in size.   On the
same occasion I shot several wood-snipe, which at first, on
being flushed, are apt to be mistaken for woodcocks, as they
rise in much the same manner, and, like the woodcock, carry
their bills hanging downwards when on the wing. I once
had ocular proof that the woodcock lifts its young from the
ground. I was hunting on the Cashmere mountains at the
time, when, on flushing a cock, I noticed that its flight was
retarded by something it evidently was carrying. As it

lighted, after flying a short distance, I followed it up. This time, when it rose, it flew off unencumbered. On examining the spot from whence it had last risen, I found its half-fledged offspring on the ground, where it had been left by the parent bird. The "chuckor" (very like the red-legged partridge) also afforded good sport on the broken bushy slopes around the Shore valley.

On the evening of my arrival I had been dining with the officer commanding the outpost, who was then the solitary European resident at the place,—and any of his contemporaries in the Bengal Presidency who may chance to read this, will wot how well and amusingly I was entertained by my host, poor Frank Crossman, who has long since joined the "majority." When bidding me "good-night," he laughingly expressed a hope that I might not be disturbed in the house where I had taken up my quarters, as it was reputed to be haunted. There certainly was a deserted, dismal look about the place, which was anything but inviting. Long rank grass and weeds grew in great profusion around it, and the walls, which in many parts were falling to decay, were green with damp and moss. Within a few yards of the house there stood an old dilapidated tomb, which, report said, had been desecrated by some ruffians who had exhumed the corpse interred long ago beneath it, in search of plunder. There were many other queer stories concerning the locality, one of them being of a quondam occupant of the house having, in a fit of "D.T.," committed suicide there; possibly the individual buried under the ruined monument. Altogether, from its lonely situation, the supernatural tales concerning it, its general woe-begone appearance, which was augmented by some funereal-looking pine-trees that grew hard by, and the fact of the natives being loath to visit it after nightfall, it might indeed have been considered a ghostly sort of place.

Not being of a superstitious turn of mind, I thought little more about the reputation of my abode; and, being rather tired after my day's journey, was not long in turning into bed, and was soon soundly slumbering. I must have been asleep some time, when I was awakened by a hand, as it were, touching my foot. The room was dark as Erebus, and I had no matches at hand wherewith to strike a light. Nor was there anybody within hail to bring one, for I was alone in the house, all the servants having left it for their own quarters, which, as is usual in India, were outside; so there was nothing for it but to lie still and try to collect my somewhat confused ideas. My first thought was of the last words of my host at dinner regarding the reputation of the house; my next was that perhaps he might be playing a joke, for it was well known how dearly he loved one. Meantime I could feel fingers, as I imagined, moving slowly and stealthily up my leg and on to my body. I must confess I now underwent that most unpleasant flesh-creeping sensation which most persons at some time or another have experienced. And when the seeming fingers at last reached my head, and I felt them stirring my hair, which by this time was assuming an upright position, I could bear it no longer. Throwing off the clothes, I sprang from the bed, but only to hear a rustle on the floor matting as my nocturnal visitor pattered off in the dark. Little more sleep did I get *that* night, for the unearthly noises which went on through the house were enough to have awakened the seven sleepers of Ephesus. The place was haunted, and no mistake, in one way at any rate; but after that night never a ghost did I hear or see there—nothing but the rats, with which it was prodigiously infested, rampaging about it; and to these, after a time, I got quite accustomed. Next morning at breakfast we had a good laugh over my mysterious experience; but whether ghost or rat was my visitor that night, I have never to this day been able to determine.

The natives of the Himalayas, like all mountain races, are very superstitious, and particularly so about hunting. If a man is a successful shikaree, his luck is attributed to his practising some magic charm. They also have an idea that the wild animals are sometimes protected from harm by the deity of the mountain, for every prominent hill or accessible peak, where the people of the country are of the Hindoo persuasion, has its rudely-built little temple, or cairn of stones, dedicated to the particular "deota," as they call it, which is supposed to preside there.

Having sent off my men to their recruiting beats along the Nepal frontier, there was little to be done in the way of military duty until their return, which might not be perhaps for months. Neither was there much to do in the shikar line before September; for the rainy season had now fairly set in; and its heavy showers were almost incessant. Moreover, the steamy heat not only made hill work unpleasant and toilsome, but also unhealthy, and caused rank vegetation to spring up with astonishing rapidity, rendering it almost impossible to find game. Leeches, too, at that season are very abundant in the Kumaon hills. These little wretches will penetrate to one's feet and ankles through almost anything. On taking off tightly-laced boots after a walk, even along beaten paths, I generally found that one or two had managed to reach my skin. Besides, it was what *ought to be* the close season for game, although, I regret to say, in India this is not always considered. In September, however, black bears might be expected to come down from the neighbouring wooded hills into the valley, there to make their nightly raids on the Indian corn and other crops which would then be ripening.

The Himalayan black bear, called *bāloo* or *reech* by the natives, is common everywhere on the middle and lower ranges. Why it is termed *Ursus Tibetanus* in natural history I never could quite comprehend, as it is distinctly a forest-loving beast, and most unlikely to be found on the bare table-lands of Tibet, where it is never heard of.

It was early in the month of September when one morning

news was brought in of a bear that had been committing depredations in some corn-fields a few miles off. There happened at the time to be several sportsmen at Shore, all eager for shooting of any kind; so we at once proceeded to beat up Bruin's quarters.

On reaching a deep, broad ravine filled with thick brush-wood, to which the raider had retired to digest his morning meal, the various guns were quietly posted in the most likely places on each side, and at one extremity of the cover, whilst across the other end were ranged a number of villagers who, on all being ready, were to commence beating through it.

At last the appointed signal is given, and is immediately followed by a hideous chorus of yells, whoops, and whistles, as the beaters dash into the covert like a pack of fox-hounds. But there is little doubt that this ostentatious display of zeal results more from the idea that the greater row each man makes the less chance will there be of the bear's coming near him, than from eagerness in its pursuit. Presently a loud "wugh," "wugh," is heard above the clamour, and conflicting exclamations of "Kubberdar!" (look out), "There he goes!" "Here he comes!" are heard from the beaters in every direction; so that, at first, it is difficult to form any idea as to where the brute really is.

"Crack" at length goes a rifle, and a responding "yeeough" from Bruin sounds as though something more than the report had caused it. Other shots follow, accompanied by cries of "lugga!" "lugga!" (he's hit), "maro!" "maro!" (shoot), uttered by the villagers in their half-frightened excitement. Gradually the rumpus approaches my station near the extremity of the jungle, where each moment I expect the animal to bolt. But he breaks away on the opposite side of the ravine, and fully a hundred yards off. I take a snap-shot at his great black carcass as he gallops clumsily along between the bushes, its effect being to elicit another grunt and make him roll over. This may perhaps result only from fright, as, on recovering himself, he appears to go faster than ever. Having thus far run the gauntlet of the guns, he takes his way down the rocky bed of the stream, along the bottom of the ravine, which becomes narrower and more free from bushes.

The business now gets pretty exciting, and not altogether free from the danger of stray bullets, as we all go scrambling along over the rough, uneven ground on either side, firing shots whenever an opportunity offers, but seemingly with little effect. At last I manage to get a fair chance at the brute's broad back, about twenty yards off, as he attempts to climb the opposite bank, when a bullet between the shoulders brings him rolling down into the water. At the same moment my foot slips into a deep hole hidden by long grass, and down I go, giving my knee such a painful wrench that I take little more heed of the bear. Even had he been able to show fight I was almost *hors de combat*. But this shot had finished him, which was some little compensation for being laid up for many days after.

In localities where oak-forests abound, perhaps the pleasant-est if not the best time for shooting these bears is in the month of December, when they wax fat on acorns, which are then ripe. They generally commence feeding about sun-set, when they climb up the oak-trees and gorge themselves with acorns all night, often not betaking themselves to their lairs—which are generally either caves or thickets near their feeding-ground—until some time after sunrise. Their where-abouts is easily discovered from the broken branches showing distinctly against the dark foliage of the trees, the back of the leaf of the Himalayan oak being white. At the commence-ment of the acorn season their attention is so much engaged with their feast that usually they are easily approached. But on suddenly finding themselves "treed," their astonishment is sometimes ludicrous to behold.

Early one morning I was strolling along a ridge command-

ing a view of a wide deep hollow, filled with oaks and thick
underwood, keeping a sharp look-out for sign of Bruin, and
occasionally stopping to listen for the snap of a branch.
Suddenly the wished-for sound was heard away down in the
hollow. After a careful study of the trees, a patch of black
was detected among the leafy branches near the top of a very
high one. Having carefully noted the spot, I stole quietly
through the heavy jungle towards it—Kurbeer Goorung, my
Goorkha henchman and shikaree, following closely with my
second gun. Every now and then we stopped to listen and
to examine the trees, but nothing could we either see or hear.
We were beginning to think the beast must have winded us
and decamped, for Bruin's olfactory powers are exceedingly
acute, when we were rather startled at hearing a sort of humming moaning sound close to us. Kurbeer, in a whisper,
suggested that it might possibly be a tiger, for we had observed the fresh tracks of one in the vicinity. Instinctively
we both placed our backs against the trunk of the nearest
tree, and anxiously peered around into the thick dark jungle.
We had been standing thus but a few seconds when something wet came dropping on to my head. On looking upward,
there, in the very tree we were under, was the object of our
search—

> " In shape o' beast ;
> A towzie tyke, black, grim, and large,"—

like a spread-eagle among the branches, gazing wistfully down
at us, and looking the most absurd picture of astonishment
and concern at being thus disturbed at his breakfast. We
were not long in standing from under *that* tree. A shot from
each of us, for the lad was too excited to withhold his fire,
brought the brute straight down, with a thud, to the ground,
where, after one or two whining grunts, he succumbed to his
fate.

A bear, when up a tree, even if only slightly wounded,
never attempts to clamber down. It invariably flops straight

on to the ground from any height whatsoever. I once saw a bear I had shot at roll over and over like a ball down an almost perpendicular declivity for several hundred feet, and seemingly without much inconvenience from its tumble, as it was nowhere to be found at the bottom.

When two or more bears are found together, on one of them being wounded it will sometimes show its resentment by savagely attacking one of its companions. In illustration of this, I may relate an amusing little episode, as told to me by that well-known old Indian sportsman, Colonel E. Smyth.

"My friend Mr Beckett once stalked a large she-bear feeding in some open ground with a half-grown cub at its side. He could not get a shot at a vital place, and so instead of waiting, as he ought to have done, he fired and hit the animal in the hind-quarters. He might just as well have hit her with a lady's riding-whip. The animal turned round to see what was the matter, and seeing nothing but her own cub feeding quietly by her side, came to the conclusion, I suppose, that the cub had bitten her in the hind-quarters, for she at once rushed at the cub to punish it for its presumption, and the two rolled over and over and disappeared in the jungle. My friend was too much amused at the incident to get another shot."

The black bear of the Himalayas is not so pugnaciously inclined as its concoloured relative the sloth-bear (*Ursus labiatus*), which inhabits the hilly districts and jungles of "the plains" of India, the Nilgherries in Madras, and other high ranges of hills. The latter animal is a cantankerous brute that will often attack on the slightest provocation, and sometimes seemingly out of mere "cussedness." Whereas the former generally tries to escape if possible, even when wounded, and seldom shows fight except as a last resource, or in defence of its cubs. Colonel Smyth told me of many adventures he had had with bears. I may give one of his experiences in his own words,

" I was out with a friend after bears in the jungles near
Burdwan in Bengal. We had formed a long line with some
thirty or forty beaters about five yards apart from each other,
and were walking quietly along, when I heard the grunting
and a kind of scuffling noise of bears in front of my part
of the line. I thought that two bears were on foot in front
of us, and, frightened at the noise we made, were beating a
retreat; so I rushed on ahead of the line by myself with one
rifle, and presently I caught a glimpse of a bear running
away in front of me. The jungle was very thick, and I only
saw him for an instant. He disappeared, and I went on by
myself, and presently heard a great noise in front, and in a
moment three bears appeared, all running towards me, about
ten yards off. I had just time to aim and fire my remaining
barrels at the front one, and then turned and ran as hard as
I could, with all three bears after me. I ran for 100 or 150
yards, but found I did not increase my distance from them,
so I caught hold of a little tree and swung myself round, and
went off in another direction at right angles. In swinging
round, my hat (a large *sola-topee* or pith hat) fell off, which I
expect saved me from getting a terrible mauling, and perhaps
my life. After running another 100 yards, I found I was
not pursued, and I soon reached my friend with the coolies,
and the man who was carrying my other (loaded) rifle. We
then went to the spot where I had swung myself round the
tree, and I found my hat smashed to pieces. The bears, not
able to catch me, were satisfied with the hat! I found a blood
track, which showed I had hit one of them as he charged
me. We followed the tracks for some distance, but eventually lost them. The very day before this, in the same jungle,
I had wounded a large bear which I was following up, when I
came suddenly and unexpectedly upon him. He saw me at
the same moment, and came down upon me like a thunderbolt.
I had just time to aim at him and fire. My bullet struck
him in the head, and he rolled over dead within two yards of

me. If I had missed him, or only slightly wounded him, he would have been in the midst of ten or twelve poor coolies who were huddled together within a few yards of me, in great fear and trembling. This was a very large bear, and unfortunately the skin was spoiled. I had pegged it out in front of my tent; and all night long I was kept awake by the howling of jackals around my tent. In the morning I found the skin had been almost entirely eaten by them."

Colonel Smyth also favours me with a remarkable instance of his having killed a full-grown Himalayan black bear with small-shot. I give his own account of it.

" Once, while out after pheasants, I met a bear, and had just time to ram down a bullet, my only one, over the shot, and take a snap-shot as the animal was disappearing. The bear was wounded, but not badly; and I traced him down the hill for a mile or so, very circumspectly as may be imagined, for I had only a shot-gun loaded with No. 6 shot. After some time I lost all traces of him, and was about to return to my tent when I saw a kind of cave amongst the rocks. On going up to it to reconnoitre, my friend Bruin came out with a rush and a roar, when I fired my two barrels of shot into his face, at a distance of five yards, which caused him to drop back into the cave. I then bolted behind a rock to reload, and coming to the mouth of the cave I heard him inside; but as he would not come out, I got a long stick, which my guide, who was the only man with me, poked into the cave. This brought him out again, and two more shots in the face finished him. It proved to be a full-grown she-bear with cubs."

I have killed and wounded many a bear, but can only remember one instance, and that rather a mild one, to record of my having been regularly charged by a black Himalayan Bruin.

One evening I had discovered a she-bear and her half-grown cub up an oak-tree growing just below the brow of a steep hillside. But the old one had already detected me below, so, leaving her offspring to take care of itself, she quickly cleared out of the tree, and, before I could get a shot at her, had disappeared over the brow. The youngster, not being quite so knowing, took longer in getting down, and so gave me a chance of putting a bullet through his hide, which made him "tune his pipes" pretty loudly, and sent him scampering away down the hill. The cub's cries of distress soon brought its mother back over the brow to the rescue, when she came tearing down the steep slope straight for me, grunting out her wrath in a most savage manner. I waited until she was within fifteen yards or so, and then gave her the contents of the second barrel. This at once doubled her up, her impetus causing her to tumble heels over head close past me. After rolling some way down the hill, she recovered her legs, struggled on a short distance, and then fell to rise no more. I never found out what became of the bereaved cub, but in all probability it did not long survive its dam, as it was hard hit.

Villagers are not unfrequently seen with their faces fearfully disfigured from wounds inflicted by bears' claws. But this is easily accounted for, as, when they discover an old thief devouring their crops, they usually surround and attack him with sticks, stones, or any offensive weapons they can lay their hands on. The irritated and affrighted brute, in his endeavour to escape, charges wildly through the yelling mob, and the first man he meets in his headlong course sometimes pays the penalty by being blinded, scalped, or severely mauled about the head; for a bear, when attacking a human being, almost invariably goes for the face, whereas a tiger or leopard usually seizes a limb first, which is a remarkable and well-known fact.

On moonlight nights a shot may sometimes be got by watching places where the bears come to feed on the crops from a machān. This construction is a small platform of sticks, either raised on poles at a safe height from the ground, or on the branches of some convenient tree, where the villager is wont to sit on sentry with his matchlock, or as often to fall asleep at night, by way of protecting his crops from the ravages of wild animals. But the chances are so doubtful that "the game is not worth the candle." One of the many tales told by my native followers round our camp-fire, was of a villager who paid dearly for playing a practical joke in personifying a bear. Enveloping himself in his black blanket, and imitating the noise of a bear, this man one night entered

a corn-field with the playful idea of testing the courage of the tenant of the *machān*. The watcher promptly let drive with his matchlock, and inflicted a wound from which the practical joker died.

It is a marvel how a cunning old Bruin will sometimes contrive to hide his big black carcass in a tree, so well as to avoid detection. Of

"On sentry" in a Machān.

this I had a fair example when I camped out and spent Christmas-day with my shikarees among the *feræ naturæ* in the woods, there being no compatriot with whom to pass that festive time then within sixty miles of the outpost. Kurbeer and I had been trying to circumvent two jurrow deer, which, having got wind of us, made off. As they were trotting away past an oak-tree, I chanced to notice that some of its branches were violently shaken. Being just the end of the acorn season, we conjectured this phenomenon was traceable to a bear up the tree, so we stole quietly towards it in order to have a closer inspection. I had almost passed the

tree, having taken, as I thought, a quite careful enough survey of it to be able to discern a large black object like a bear,
when a low whistle from Kurbeer, who was following a few
paces behind, caused me to stop, and, on looking round, I saw
him pointing towards the middle of the tree. We moved
closer under it, and there, behind a thick part of the stem and
some closely interwoven branches, I discovered a patch of
black hair of the cunning beast, which evidently thought
itself well concealed. With a view to turning its flank, I
moved to the right and left of the tree, which was unassail-
able from its far side, where it overhung a deep drop. But
from nowhere could I get a better sight of the brute, which
kept quite still during all my manœuvres. I therefore decided
on risking a shot at its only vulnerable point, hoping to make
its resting-place so hot as to induce it to drop from the tree,
and then get a chance at it *en route*. I fired, and down came
Bruin in a monstrous hurry. There was no occasion for a
second shot, as the black patch was the neck of what turned
out to be a large she-bear that had managed to hide her body
so cleverly.

Never having tasted bear-meat, I suggested to my cook
that he might add a morsel of it to my frugal Christmas
dinner. But the horror and disgust depicted on his face at
the bare idea was such a caution that I refrained from pressing the matter, so it never appeared at table. Although these
bears are usually clean feeders, their food chiefly consisting
of grain, fruit, roots, and suchlike, they are decidedly carni-
vorous. They will sometimes destroy sheep and goats, and
will greedily devour carrion. Honey is perhaps their favourite
food, and to obtain this they are sometimes so bold as to rob
the village beehives, which are formed of short bits of tree-
trunks, hollowed out, closed at the ends, and slung under the
wooden eaves of the houses. Small blame to them for being
so fond of it, for the Kumaon honey is the purest and has
the whitest and thinnest comb I have ever seen.

Bear's flesh is never, so far as I know, eaten in India, except by the Doms (a very low caste of hill Hindoos—in ancient times the slave class), although tiger's flesh is often used as a charm. One of the wonderful properties the natives believe it to possess is that of its making their children grow up brave if they partake of it in their youth. The whiskers, too, are regarded as so potent for working evil with, that if they, and also the claws, are not carefully looked after, you are sure to find the former either singed off or plucked out and the latter extracted surreptitiously by your camp-followers. The following anecdote, related to me by an old Central India sportsman, is a curious instance of superstition respecting tiger's flesh.

A dead tiger had been brought into camp, and all the native followers, except one, seemed anxious to secure some of the flesh. The exception was an old shikaree of the wild tribe of Gonds. On being questioned as to why he did not wish to take his share, he replied, with an expression of disgust, that he never ate tiger's flesh, but would enter into no explanation as to why or wherefore. After a little persuasion, however, and the promise of a glass of grog, the old man at length agreed to join the party at the camp-fire after dinner and relate his story, which, being freely interpreted, was much as follows: " My grandfather and grandmother were once encamped on the outskirts of a jungle, near a great city, when one day they saw issuing from the city gate a grand hunting-party, riding on elephants with silver howdahs and gorgeous trappings, and escorted by armed retainers mounted on splendidly caparisoned horses. My grandmother, being struck with envy, exclaimed, ' Why should we Gonds, whose forefathers were the lords of this land, now be reduced to such poverty and live in the jungles, whilst this upstart race enjoys such wealth and luxury? I will change myself into a tiger and watch the city gate, and carry off every rich man I meet until I have amassed wealth enough to enable us to resume our former position, and then return and show you where I have buried my riches.' That night the old woman arose from beside my grandfather and went into the jungles, and as she has never since been heard of, she must still be amassing riches in the form of a tiger; therefore, if I eat the flesh of one, I may be devouring a bit of my grandmother."

Most probably the old woman did enter the form of a tiger that night, but as its supper. Anyway the old Gond did not seem to mind killing his grandmother, though he objected to eating her, for he said he liked slaying tigers, because the more of them he destroyed, the better chance there would be of one of them being his ancestress, who might then assume her original form, and return with her riches.

Fables innumerable about bears are common among the *pāhārees* (hill-men), and they are often amusing from their utter absurdity. The occasional abduction of women from the villages by bears is firmly believed in, as is also their being able to use a branch of a tree held between their paws as an offensive weapon, and suchlike nonsense.

Before concluding this matter-of-fact dissertation on black bear shooting, I would venture to offer the young hand a hint which may save him the loss of many a wounded bear; for Bruin's vitality is such, that unless he is struck in the proper place, the amount of lead he can carry away is astonishing. A bear, after being skinned and decapitated, looks very like a corpulent man with short muscular limbs, and its vitals lie in much the same region, with regard to its shoulders, as those of a human being. It is flat-chested, and its forequarters are straight and placed far forward, so it is necessary to plant your bullet a good span behind the shoulder, and pretty high up. This, of course, only applies when there is time for a deliberate aim and a good position for taking it from. These can generally be got if the animal is not approached from windward, for Bruin is as dull with his visual organ as he is sharp with his olfactory one. I have lost many

a bear by shooting *at* its shoulder, but seldom or never since
I learnt from experience where the most vital spot lay—provided I was able to plant a bullet there.

Shooting black bears, though sometimes rather exciting, is,
to my mind, the least interesting of any Himalayan sport;
for the beasts are not often found in the open, and therefore
seldom afford the pleasure of a stalk. And when you have
secured your bear, its skin is of little value as a trophy, as
the hair is coarse and wiry. But in killing a bear you have
the satisfaction of knowing that you are doing the villagers
a service, not only by ridding them of the greatest enemy to
their crops, but in providing them with bear's grease, which
they consider a most efficacious emollient for rheumatism.

Village beehive.

CHAPTER III.

THE MAHSEER—MONSTER FISH TAKEN WITH THE ROD—THE MAHSEER COMPARED WITH THE SALMON—SALMONIDÆ NEVER FOUND IN INDIA —A FISHING - RIVER IN THE HIMALAYAS—THE SURJOO VALLEY— ITS WILD DENIZENS—THE JURROW—BARKING-DEER—THE GOORKHA "KOOKERIE"—TEMPTING PROVIDENCE — A DAMP COUCH—JURROW-HUNTING UNDER DIFFICULTIES—A HEAVY FISH LOST—THE WAY WE INVEIGLED THE WILY MAHSEER — JUNGLE FARE—DENSE MORNING MISTS—A FORENOON'S SPORT IN THE SURJOO — BEST MONTHS AND BEST FLIES FOR MAHSEER-FISHING IN THE HIMALAYAN RIVERS— FISHING THEORIES—THE KALABANS—COLLECTING CATECHU.

THOSE who have fished both for salmon and mahseer will doubtless agree with me in thinking that they are nearly on a par as far as sport is concerned. In its habits the mahseer much resembles the salmon, except that it never migrates to the sea, but in appearance it is very different. The mahseer (*Barbus Tor*) of Himalayan rivers, which is said to belong to the carp family, is a beautiful fish both in form and colour, but in flavour it does not approach the salmon. Yet its firm white flesh is by no means to be despised for the table. On the back its hue is a dark olive-green, shaded off, on the sides of a well-conditioned fish, into a golden orange, which merges into pale pink and silvery white below. It has rather large toothless jaws lined with a very tough membrane, so it requires to be struck pretty hard to be properly hooked. When I say *struck*, I mean that after the fish has hooked itself, as it will do by its own weight, a good pull, without a jerk, is necessary to drive home the barb into its leathern jaws.

Owing to this toughness of mouth, a mahseer when fixed is seldom lost unless it breaks the tackle. This a big fish often will do in its first plunge, when it sometimes has a way of lashing its tail over the line. That crisis being safely over, if your tackle is trustworthy, landing your fish is usually only a matter of time and patience. Its strong teeth are set far back in its gullet, and the stoutest tackle has a poor chance if it gorges your lure beyond them. It cannot be easily clipped, as its large round scales are so hard that the sharpest gaff will glance off them. When running a mahseer after it has been fairly hooked, I have never known it leap from the water, and I think it rarely does so, but its long and rapid rushes quite equal if they do not surpass those of any

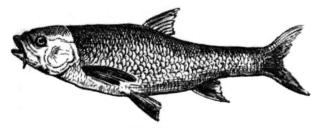

The Mahseer.

salmon of a similar size. As regards its weight, I am well within the mark when I state that the mahseer reaches nearly, if not quite, 100 lb. The largest mahseer I ever heard of as having been taken with a trolling bait, was 93 lb.; and with fly, one that turned the scale at 62 lb.[1] But such monsters as these are very seldom landed with the rod.

My reason for drawing comparisons between the salmon and the mahseer is chiefly because the latter is sometimes termed the "salmon of Indian rivers." It might just as well

[1] The 93-pounder was killed by Mr H. Vansittart, C.S., in one of the rivers of the Dehra Doon ; the 62-pounder in the Pooneh river in the Punjab, by the late General Sir Herbert Macpherson, who was as keen a sportsman as he was a good and gallant soldier.

be called a cod, for in truth it more resembles one, barring its scales, both in appearance and in flesh. It does not even belong to the same family, for I may safely assert, on good authority,[1] that no fish of the Salmonidæ tribe exists in any of the Indian or even more northern waters south of the river Oxus, although there are fish very much resembling trout taken in Indian streams. But let us now try and catch our mahseer.

Towards the end of September I started with a brother sportsman and keen fisherman, Lieutenant F——, who has since become one of my truest and dearest friends, to try our luck in the Surjoo, a fine fishing-river within easy reach of Shore. There was also a possibility of getting a shot at sambur, here called "jurrow"—the big deer termed *Rusa Aristotelis* in natural history—which were plentiful in the heavy jungle that covered the steep hillsides flanking the river. It was rather doubtful whether the water would be in good fishing order so soon after the periodical rainy season, then barely over, and during which the Himalayan streams are in a perpetual state of muddy spate. The long, rank vegetation, too, would still be so luxuriant there as to make our chance of being able to see even a big beast like a jurrow in it most uncertain. But we were so weary of the monotony of indoor life that we resolved to take our chance, either of sport or fever, whichever it might be, the latter being most probable at that season in these low-lying jungles.

After a hot tramp of about twelve miles, ending in an abrupt and rough descent of several thousand feet, we reached the Surjoo about noon. It looked a perfect fishing-river. Here it surged and foamed among rocks and huge boulders, there it widened into swirling expanses of deep water, forming a succession of the most splendid streams and pools a fisherman could desire to behold. From its shores of sand,

The late Dr Oldham, Superintendent of the Geological Survey of India.

gravel, or rock on either side, rose steep lofty acclivities clothed with dense jungle. This gradually changed its tropical character to that of the more temperate and higher altitudes, as it spread far up the mountain-sides to where they became more craggy and steep. Here the fir, the oak, and the rhododendron took the place of the Kyer (thorny mimosa), the bright-green Sāl tree, and the luxuriant tropical under-growth that flourishes below. The tiger and leopard found a safe harbour in the lower jungles, but from their being able so easily to slink away unobserved in the long grass and dense underwood, they were very seldom met with; although the deep-toned voice of the former, or the succession of hoarse grating sounds—like the sawing of wood—made by the latter, might often be heard through the still night air. There also the jurrow-deer sought refuge from the fierce noonday heat, among tangled masses of the gigantic creeper called "maloo" or "maljoon," beneath the impenetrable shelter of which it delights to ruminate. The crags and precipices above were the haunt of the "gooral," or Himalayan chamois as it is sometimes called.

After an *al fresco* repast, for which our appetites had been sharply whetted by a refreshing dip in the river, we prepared our tackle under the grateful shade of the trees, before pro-ceeding to business later in the day, for the sun's rays in this low-lying valley were overpowering.

Towards evening, when the heat became less intense, we commenced proceedings in a splendid pool where the Surjoo forms a junction with another fine stream. But our hopes of success that evening were small, for the water was too big, and in colour too "drumlie," as they would have said north of the Tweed, and "the fush wadna force." We, however, plied it most perseveringly with every kind of fish-lure we possessed, until darkness brought our fruitless efforts, for that day, to a close.

On our return we found that one of the Goorkhas we had

with us had been more successful on the hillside than we were on the river. He had taken one of our rifles and had managed to bring down a good jurrow. This fine large deer is identical with the "māhā" of the Terai, and the "sambur" of other parts of India. It affects heavy forest or its immediate vicinity, and is widely distributed over Hindustan from the higher ranges, close to the perpetual snows, to Cape Comorin. The colour and texture of its pile, which nature has adapted for the various climates of the localities where this animal is found, differ considerably. The prevailing hue of the stags is, however, a dark slaty brown, the throat and neck being covered with long wiry hair. The colour of the hind is of a lighter brown shade, and she has less of the long hair, resembling a mane, on her neck. The jurrow of the higher Himalayas has a darker and thicker coat, and it is also provided with a close undergrowth of very soft pile, called pushum, which in winter is common to all the quadrupeds of those high, cold regions, even to the dogs and horses. Having shot all the so-called three varieties, I am certain that, in point of appearance, this is the only difference between them, and in habits they are the same. Though not unlike the British red-deer in shape, the jurrow is very much larger. But it seldom or never has more than three regular points on each horn, though occasionally it may have one or two extra snags. I possess a pair of jurrow horns which measure forty-two inches in length, with an average girth of beam of eight inches, and a span of a yard inside the bend. But such a jurrow head as this never fell to my rifle, and seldom, I imagine, to that of any one else. The eyepits in this deer are always large, and become much more open and protuberant when the animal is in an excited state.

The little barking-deer (*Cervulus aureus*), also termed rib-faced deer, from the peculiar formation of the frontal bone, and called "kakur" by the hill-men, was common in these forests. It is found in most Indian jungles, and, like the jurrow, from the higher ranges downwards. In Madras it is known as the "jungle sheep," and I believe it is identical with the muntjac of the more eastern parts of Asia. It is rather smaller than a roe - deer, and bright red like that animal in its summer coat. Its head is curiously shaped, that of the buck being surmounted with two continuations of the V-shaped ribbed bone of its forehead, about two inches long and covered with skin and hair. From these grow the horns, which in a full-grown buck are three or four inches in length, curved inwards at the top, and with one short prong just above the burr, projecting to the front and slightly upwards. Although I have seen numbers of this curious little deer at all seasons, and killed many of them myself with horns of divers lengths, from a little sprout above the burr to their fully developed size, strange to say, I have never found them in velvet. From this I am inclined to think they do not shed their horns regularly like other horn-bearing Cervidæ (excepting the "cheetal" or spotted deer—*Axis maculatus*—which drops its horns very irregularly, as I shall hereafter endeavour to show), even if they do so at all. But upon this point I cannot speak with certainty. The upper jaw of the buck is provided with a pair of sharp canine teeth, which sometimes project quite half an inch over the lower lips. For what use they are intended is uncertain. An old shikaree, whose veracity I had no reason to doubt, told me that he had once come upon two bucks fighting; one of them was soon left disabled on the ground, when he observed it had a deep cut in its back, evidently made by the tooth of its opponent, but whether purposely or accidentally he could not tell. This pretty little animal is most frequently found in thick cover interspersed with patches of cultivation. In the latter it may often be found feeding very early in the morning or late in the evening, but generally so close to the cover that in the grey dawn or twilight it is often not detected until the white of its stern is seen bobbing away into the

bushes, from whence its short sharp bark comes at intervals,
as if deriding its pursuer for not having kept a better look-
out. When hurrying off, it sometimes makes a succession
of clicking sounds, but whether with the teeth or hoofs I
have never been able to ascertain. The doe is similar to
the buck, with the exception of the continuations of the
frontal bone, the horns, and long teeth.

These short imperfect descriptions of animals are merely
intended as rough sketches to enable such as may be unacquainted with Himalayan fauna to form some sort of idea
of their general appearance and habits, and not as attempts
to delineate them scientifically. Their theoretic nomenclature
is, however, given, not by way of seeming erudite—for what
little knowledge of zoology I may have is more practical
than scientific—but in order that more exhaustive accounts
by those who are more scientifically conversant with the subject, may be readily referred to elsewhere, if required, and
also. because the names given by natives to the same animal
so often vary in different localities.

We had foolishly brought no tent with us, having intended
to get our men to extemporise some sort of shelter of boughs
and grass cut with their "kookeries,"—those useful national
weapons which the Goorkhas invariably carry, and use as
much for domestic as for fighting purposes. But we had
not even that to protect us from the heavy night dew, as on
our return from fishing we found that almost all the men
were away up the hill fetching the dead jurrow, and it was
too late when they returned to commence it. We, however,
indulged in a stiff jorum of hot whisky-toddy before we
retired to rest, as a precaution against the damp malarious
night air. When I say retired, I mean that we merely
rolled ourselves up in our blankets, and, in order to avoid
the heavy drippings that fell like rain from the trees, lay
down on an open patch of soft dry sand, in which, by the

way, we had noticed during the day the fresh footprints of
a tiger.   But—

> " Inspiring bold John Barleycorn,
>   What dangers thou canst make us scorn !
>   Wi' tippenny, we fear nae evil ;
>   Wi' usquabae we'll face the devil ! "

Consequently we thought little of tigers, malaria, or anything
else, and were soon wrapt in profound slumber.

On awaking in the morning, we found ourselves enveloped
in a cold damp fog, through which we could scarcely see
twenty yards, and with our outer coverings and even our hair
saturated with moisture.   Being down in this hot humid
valley at all in September, about the worst time of year
for malaria, was tempting Providence, as I learnt from subsequent experience.   But we were young and thoughtless,
caring little for any risk so long as there was a chance of
sport.

Having shaken ourselves up, we performed our ablutions
in the river, which ran within a few paces of our sandy couch.
After a cup of tea and a biscuit, we started each to our respective work ; my companion electing to try his luck at the
river, whilst I, wishing him " a tight line," took the hill after
deer.   Owing to the thickness of the undergrowth and the
dense mist, there was very little chance of seeing game, although the fresh tracks of jurrow were numerous.   And when
the mist was dispelled by the rising sun, the sweltering heat
was so oppressive as to make climbing about the steep jungly
hillsides, in such close steamy atmosphere, next thing to impossible, not to mention the attacks of myriads of biting
insects.   On returning I found my hungry chum clamouring for a late breakfast, and much disgusted at having lost a
very heavy fish after he had run it for about half an hour.

In the cool of the evening we were both at the water again.
After trying flies and trolling baits all to no purpose, we were

at last reduced to the more prosaic method of bottom-fishing with a lump of dough kneaded together with wool to make it adhesive. To this, at the suggestion of an old Goorkha whom we had brought with us, a great authority on mahseer-fishing, was added some turmeric and garlic. These pungent ingredients, he said, made the bait more attractive. With this odoriferous compound, I managed to inveigle two nice mahseer of seven and eight pounds. My companion also killed a fine fish in the same sorry way, which was better than nothing.

That evening we fared sumptuously on venison-soup, fish fresh from the river, savoury though perhaps slightly tough jurrow steaks, followed by hot whisky-toddy and a pipe, to both of which latter we doubtless partly owed our immunity from the effects of malaria. We turned in on the old spot, having this time taken the precaution to have a "lean-to" constructed to shelter us, and were soon lulled to sleep by the roar of the river close by.

We shouldered our rods again as the dawn was trying to struggle through the dense mist. For in the morning, during the autumn and winter months, a heavy bank of white vapour almost invariably lies along the bottom of every deep, narrow Himalayan valley where any considerable stream flows, until dispelled by the sun's rays. The water looked more promising, so our spirits as well as our chances of sport began to rise with the lifting fog, which at first was a decided damper to both. It requires but little reference to my old shooting journal to call to mind all the details regarding the killing of my first really fine mahseer.

"Take a rest for a little while, and try again when the sun gets higher." Thus suggested old Chundreea—a native of the valley, and fisherman by profession, who usually attended me by the river-side—as I was getting rather impatient with my bad luck, and my back was beginning to ache from chastising the water with flies, and spinning line baits the whole morning without having moved a fish. Following the first part of his advice, I reeled up, sat down on a rock, and pondered as to whether it would be worth while acting on the last part of it. After I had consoled myself with a pipe, and Chundreea had adjusted a fresh *chilwa*,[1] I again waded into the river, and loosening a good handful of line, dropped the bait as far across the swirling pool as possible. I have him at last! Hardly has the *chilwa* commenced spinning in the water when I feel a heavy pull, which is immediately followed by a splash and a boiling swirl. Bob goes the point of the rod, and "whir-r-r" out runs the tightened line, almost smoking in the rings as it flies from off the reel, which is whizzing and humming with an impatient, irregular cadence, as if angrily remonstrating against the rough treatment it is forced to undergo. Those few moments of thrilling excitement repay me in full for all my enduring patience. But it suddenly strikes me that I am between the two rivers, and only a short distance above their junction, beyond which I shall be unable to follow the fish; and I am fully aware that if he once reaches the heavy and broken flood of the combined streams, there will be but little chance of my ever landing him. Consequently I am rather nervous and anxious about his intentions, and feel considerably relieved in mind when he suddenly stops. After remaining almost stationary for a while, jerking and tugging away at the hook until each moment I expect to part company with him, he commences boring up-stream, and then takes to sulking in the deep water, where, for a long time, he feels like a log on the straining line, which is vibrating like a harp-string against the strong current.

All that can now be done is to get Chundreea to pitch stones in his vicinity. This soon has the effect of inducing the fish to alter his tactics, and the reel resumes its remonstrances as he recommences careering away in such a frantic

---

[1] A beautiful silver-scaled little fish—the minnow of Indian waters.

manner that I again begin to experience those qualms of fear
and hope which, mingled with intense excitement, make the
sport of angling so fascinating to its votaries. My tackle,
however, is stout and trustworthy, and this enables me to
take a hard and steady pull on him, in order, if possible, to
keep him above the junction; so much so that Chundreea, who
is anxiously watching the tussle from the shore, seeing the
heavy strain on the bending green-heart, begins shouting, "Let
him run, Sahib, let him run, or he'll break the rod!" But
under existing circumstances I well know that such a proceeding will be as likely to prove fatal as holding him too taut.
After several more mad rushes and plunges for freedom, his
cantrips become somewhat subdued, and ere long he begins
to show signs of submission. As I gradually reel him in, I
can, for the first time, catch an occasional glimpse of his form
looming largely through the water, and the sun glints now
and again on his golden scales as he rolls helplessly about.
At length I am able to tow him towards a good landing-place,
where, after his making some of those last desperate wriggling
efforts to get free, during which a fish is so apt to be lost
after all, Chundreea bestrides him, and carefully lifting the
struggling, shining beauty by the gills from the shallow
water, proudly carries him ashore, and throws him kicking
among the stones on the bank.

My scaly prize was at once weighed, and found to be 26 lb.
This restored my flagging hopes, and I was soon fixed into
another fish, which took out the line with such a swish and
fought so hard, that at first I thought it equalled the first one
in weight, and not until it had been on some time did I discover that it was little more than half as big. But not even
another rug did I get that day. There is nothing like
patience for fishing, and nothing like fishing for trying it.

Next day the river rose again from the effects of heavy rain
higher up, and somewhat resembled the colour of potato-
soup. We found, too, that it was not the best time for the

Surjoo valley, as the warm and steamy atmosphere, biting flies, &c., made sport there, at that season, more toilsome than pleasant. The months of March and April are, I think, the best for mahseer-fishing, as the climate is then more pleasant and healthy in these low valleys than during September and October—the best autumn months—and the fish in the mountain streams more readily take the fly, and are in better condition in spring. It is said that on the days which succeed moonlight nights, mahseer are not so readily taken as they are after moonless ones; and strange to say, they are generally more easily moved on bright sunny days than on dark cloudy ones. The flies that seem to suit their taste as well as any, are bright and gaudy ones that show well in the water, like the "Jock Scott" or the Dee "Gordon," of various sizes up to at least 2½ inches for big fish, and perhaps one with black wings tipped with white, and black hackle and body ribbed with silver, for a complete change. But, like salmon, they will take almost anything when they are in the humour, and will look at nothing when they are not. I have not implicit faith in fishing theories respecting either salmon or mahseer, for I have often killed both fish under circumstances which are ordinarily considered most adverse. For instance, in Canada one evening I was fishing when it had grown so dark that only by the bright flashes of lightning could I see where my line was; yet I fairly hooked and landed a salmon of 9 lb. whilst the thunder was rattling around like great guns. I should like very much to know why the salmon of the western rivers of North America are so difficult to kill with the fly, whereas in the eastern rivers they take it so freely. One thing, however, is quite as important in mahseer-fishing as in fishing for salmon—namely, the size of flies to suit the state of the water; but when the angler has constantly to be changing his fly, depend upon it there is something wrong—and that generally lies more with the humour of the fish than with the fly.

Another kind of fish common in the Himalayan rivers is that called by the natives "kalabans," dirty mud-coloured creatures which are found in immense shoals. On looking down from a height into the Surjoo, I have seen a shoal of them which must have numbered thousands, lying along the bottom in a dark motionless mass. Their flesh is soft, muddy-tasted, and full of bones, and they never afford sport for the angler. The natives, however, net them in large numbers; indeed the chief occupation of the natives of this low jungly valley seemed to be either fishing or extracting *kuttai* (catechu) from the Kyer (mimosa) tree. They chop the dark-coloured heart of the tree into small chips; of these they make a decoction, which, after being well boiled down, is allowed to set until it becomes a congealed mass. This is cut into blocks about four or five inches square, something resembling solid chunks of cold, pink-coloured custard-pudding, in which shape it is exported for sale.

CHAPTER IV.

NOWHERE can a finer or a more invigorating climate be found
than at an altitude of between 6000 and 8000 feet in the
Himalayas, during the three months that succeed the clearing
up of the rainy season—about the end of September. The
wild animals, too, are then in their best condition both for fur
and flesh. The males would of course be better for food a
month or so earlier; but as the natives highly prize venison
at any time, it is never wasted; and the trophies, which the
sportsman values more than the meat, are none the worse for
the delay.

The November mornings were crisp and frosty, and the
days bright and clear, when I set out on a short hunting-trip
of quite a different character to the one just described. My
small retinue consisted of Kurbeer and another Goorkha lad
carrying the guns, a cook, and four or five "coolies" (native
baggage-porters), laden with a little tent, bedding, and the

few requisites for a short sojourn in the wilds. We reached
our destination—a hamlet near the foot of the hill we intended hunting over—in time to get everything "fixed up"
before dark.

On making inquiries about a guide for the ground, the
village Nimrod—a comical-looking little man attired in an
old black blanket, with a bit of rope round his waist supporting a small "koolharee" (wood-axe)—presented himself, and
made his salaam. This bare-legged individual rejoiced in the

name of "Baloo Mar,"
literally meaning "Bear-
killer," which *sobriquet* had
been given him, I was told,
by some former employer.
Not that he had earned it
from the fact of his hav-
ing performed any daring
feats in the destruction of
Bruin, but from his having
the reputation of making
himself scarce at the first
symptom of any dangerous
intention on the part of
the said animal. How-
ever, as he was reported
to know the country and

Village Shikaree, with matchlock and rest.
Province of Kumaon.

the haunts and habits of its game pretty well, I employed
him, and found that in this respect at any rate he did not
belie his calling, besides being a cheery, amusing little man.

The Himalayan native shikaree is, as a rule, a perfect
cragsman, an excellent stalker, and an adept in woodcraft
generally. His power of vision, too, is marvellously acute;
and his capability for quickly detecting game, either in thick
cover or far off in the open, is sometimes astonishing. If he
errs, it is in his endeavouring to get so close to game that,

unless you are capable, as he is himself with his bare legs and feet, of moving as noiselessly as a cat, it usually precludes anything but a snap-shot; and should the ground be precipitous and broken, sometimes not even that before a beast, on being alarmed, can get instantly out of sight, and is often out of range ere it reappears, if it does so at all. For wild animals, when they suddenly detect danger very close to them, are so terrified that they make off like an arrow; whereas, if it is farther from them, they will often stand and gaze in doubt, giving ample time for a steady aim, or stop to look back after going a short distance.

After dinner, and a pipe beside the camp-fire, I turned in pretty early, as the "bear-slayer" had informed me that if we expected to see "gooral" we must be up near the summit of Dhuj *teeba* (hill) about sunrise. Before proceeding further in search of the *Nemorhædus goral* of natural history, a slight sketch of this "Himalayan chamois," as it is sometimes called, may not be out of place. The ordinary height of a full-grown buck is

Head of "*Gooral*," or *Himalayan chamois.*

about 28 inches at the shoulder. The colour of its short rough coat is usually a uniform greyish brown, with a white patch on the throat. Its legs are sturdy and goat-like, and of a darker brown than the body. Both sexes carry short black horns, those of the full-grown buck being sometimes 7 inches or so long, annulated from the base to about half their length, and slightly curved backwards. The doe is similar to the buck in appearance, except as regards her horns, which are thinner, smoother, and shorter. I once saw the skin of a pure albino gooral which was shot in the Kumaon hills. The natives who lived near its haunt had a superstitious idea that the killing of this animal would be attended with bad luck to the slayer. And, strange to say, the experienced and well-known sportsman who shot it, on the same day met with a serious gun accident. This curious coincidence is no camp-fire yarn, for the sportsman was an old and intimate friend, and I saw him shortly after the accident. The gooral is found all over the Himalayan ranges, from the higher to the lower and outer ones, but seldom below an altitude of 3000 feet, and always on craggy and precipitous ground, which may or may not be more or less clad with forest.

As the terms *lower* or *outer*, *middle*, and *higher* or *upper*, are so frequently used in these pages to distinguish the various mountain-ranges of the great Himalayan chain, when describing the haunts of game, I may mention that the first apply to those rising directly from the plains or from the Terai, the second to those more in the interior of the mountains, and the third to the spurs of the snowy range and the precipitous, either open or forest-clad, slopes immediately below it. The " snowy range " needs no definition. But to revert to our pursuit of the game little gooral.

I had seemingly been but a very short time asleep when my slumbers were rudely disturbed, and I was informed that Baloo Mar was waiting to accompany me up the hill. After the usual cup of tea and a biscuit, we were soon climbing the steep ascent, where our way led up through forest of oak and rhododendron, or over open grassy slopes which were white and crisp with frost. As we neared the summit, just before sunrise, I could not resist the temptation, or perhaps, from having " bellows to mend," I should call it the inclination, to sit down and cast a look over the succession of mountain-ridges and deep trough-like valleys stretching away far and wide between us and the mighty frozen barriers of the snowy range. Some of the highest pinnacles had already begun to flush up with that exquisitely beautiful but utterly indescribable tint of delicate rose assumed by snowy summits when touched by the first gleam of morning. Gradually the ruddy glow spread from peak to peak, and grew brighter and more yellow, until the whole jagged line became suffused with golden light as the sun rose over it in dazzling glory and threw its slanting beams across the profound misty depths of the intervening hollows.

The bear-slayer being of a decidedly practical turn of mind, and also blessed with a first-rate pair of "bellows," did not seem to appreciate these charms of nature, but kept reminding me that we should be too late for our game if we did not hurry up. As we resumed our ascent, we soon became aware of the presence of a gooral, by a succession of short, sharp, sneezing sort of sounds which we heard above. The animal had been watching us whilst I had been viewing the scenery. We caught only a glimpse of it ere it vanished among the wooded crags. A gooral, when alarmed, almost invariably emits this sound, which is something like that made by pronouncing the word "tschick." If in doubt as to what the danger may be, it will often perch itself on some prominent point, and remain there for a considerable time with its head turned to the suspected quarter, hissing out its note of alarm at short intervals. But when once fairly satisfied of its danger, you may bid good-bye to it. I do not think the sense of smell is so acute in the gooral, nor in any Himalayan animals of the wild-goat family, as it is in those of the deer tribe: this is, however, in a great measure compensated for by keen powers of sight and hearing.

But we have now reached the crest, and here we call a short halt for breath before examining the open precipitous ground on the south side of the mountain, where the shikaree says we shall be pretty sure to find our game. We are soon on the move again. As we near the brink of the declivity, Baloo Mar creeps stealthily forward and cautiously looks over it. By the careful manner in which he slowly with-

draws his head, and the self-satisfied look he turns towards
me, I can tell he has sighted something. Crawling quickly
up alongside him, on peering over I have the satisfaction of
seeing four gooral browsing unconcernedly on a grassy slope
among some broken masses of rock directly below us. Being
a tyro at mountain shooting, I am suddenly seized with a
severe attack of what, in the backwoods of America, I have
heard termed "buck fever"; so without taking time to judge
the distance, or to allow my fast-throbbing pulses to subside,
I raise the rifle and let drive at the nearest animal. The
result is, of course, what might be expected under such circumstances — a clean miss of an easy shot. The gooral,
however, from the fact, I suppose, of their not having been
recently disturbed, are only startled, and stand gazing about
them as if undecided as to what course they should pursue.
This serves only to augment my complaint, causing me to
fire the second barrel almost at random, when the animals,
being no longer in doubt, make off. The bear-slayer's look of
satisfaction now gives place to one of bitter disappointment
and ill-concealed contempt for my performance, and on his
face I can plainly read that which, if he could only have
given vent to his thoughts, in modern English might have
been, "Well, you *are* a duffer!" But there is still another
chance, for one of the beasts, a fine buck, not even yet seeming quite satisfied of his danger, bounds up on to the point of
a projecting crag, where he stands balancing himself on all
four feet planted close together, sneezing out his warning
note. Drawing back under cover, I recharge my old muzzle-
loader as quickly as my trembling hands will permit, whilst
the shikaree remains impatiently watching our game. On
again looking over, I find the buck has moved up nearer us,
and is now within fifty yards. This time I take a more careful aim, and on the smoke clearing away, I have the delight
of seeing the gooral rolling down the precipitous hillside,
until stopped by some rocks below.

Baloo Mar was not long in reaching the dead buck and bringing him up. He now proposed that, as it was getting late in the morning for the animals to be out feeding, we should return by a different way to the one we had come up, and on which there might yet be a chance of finding more game. After lightening it of its paunch, he shouldered our prize, and, notwithstanding his load, set off as fast as the rough ground would admit of, stopping now and again to rest, and to take a look round about for any sign of game. We had not gone very far before we started another gooral from where it lay reposing among the crags, after its morning feed. A whistle caused it to stop, as a startled beast often will do for a few seconds, to listen and look back on hearing any sudden and unusual sound behind it. Off it went again, but this time hard hit, and, as is the wont of animals of the wild-goat kind when wounded, took to some very bad ground, where it lay down. We did not attempt to follow it, for my guide wisely remarked that if we disturbed it again then, we might never get it; whereas if we let it alone, he would return to look for it in the afternoon, by which time it might be less inclined to move, when there would be more certainty of securing it. We therefore took a bee-line for camp down through the thick forest of oak and rhododendron that usually covers the northern slopes of the middle and outer ranges.

The evening was devoted to beating up some patches of cover in the vicinity of the terraced fields[1] near our camp, where I bagged a brace of Kalleege pheasants. The Kalleege is common in most parts of the Himalayas. The cock is black, with grey hackles and crest, and the hen brown. As several varieties of this bird can be seen in the Zoological Society's Gardens in London, it is needless to describe it more fully.

---

[1] In the Himalayas the villagers always cultivate their crops in small fields arranged in flat terraces, one below another, in such a manner as to allow of their being irrigated from some neighbouring stream.

The men who had gone after the wounded gooral returned with it at dark. They had had considerable trouble in securing it in the difficult ground where it had betaken itself to. As the night was bitterly cold and logs were plentiful, we lit a huge camp-fire. This was always done whenever wood was procurable. And many a pleasant hour have I passed beside it before turning in for the night, smoking my pipe, and listening to the marvellous tales and adventures related by the mountaineers, some of which were as amusing as they were incredible. One I remember, as having been told by Kurbeer, will serve as a fair example. From his account it appeared that a comrade of his had fired at and wounded a huge wild boar, when it at once turned and came at him. To avoid the enraged brute he dropped his gun and climbed up the nearest tree. But the boar rushed at the stem, making a deep cut in it with one of his tusks, and passed on. Again it returned to the charge, cutting the opposite side of the stem in like manner. The man now finding the tree begin to totter, descended from it, and, unperceived by the boar, got up another. On came the brute once more, and down came the empty tree. What became of this "mighty boar," I regret to say I never heard, for an outburst of the laughter I could no longer suppress brought this wonderful yarn to a premature close.

Next day we tried other ground, on which I made a clean miss at a gooral and lost one wounded. We came upon a sounder of wild pigs, but did not manage to circumvent them. The "bunneyl," as the hill-men call it, is frequently met with in these mountains, where "pig-sticking" being impracticable, it may be considered fair game for the rifle, and native shikarees think a solitary old hill-boar quite as ugly a customer to deal with as a tiger. The only game bagged was a "cheer" pheasant, a handsome bird something resembling our own hen-pheasant, but lighter in plumage and larger. It is generally found on the higher hill-tops of the middle

and outer ranges, among wooded crags. Although cheer are
never very plentiful, they are, as a rule, easily shot when
found, but they sometimes lie very close among long grass or
bushes. On coming by chance across a brood of cheer, when
after larger game that I did not care to disturb by firing, I
have even flung stones at them as they sat among the rocks,
before they flew. But they are not always so easy to find
when wanted, as I know from the time and trouble it once
cost me to secure a single good specimen, which I was very
anxious to shoot for a collection of Himalayan game-birds I
was trying to make before I left Shore.

There was a craggy hill-top a few miles off, known as the
Drill-peak—so named, it was said, from an eccentric com-
mandant of the outpost having been in the habit of punishing
his defaulters by sending them, in heavy marching order, to
the summit and back, whilst he watched their ascent, with a
telescope, from his quarters. This hill was reputed to be an
almost certain find for these pheasants about dawn; so one
morning I turned out several hours before daylight, and
started with Kurbeer for its summit. On reaching our ground,
just as morning broke, sure enough we heard the cheer calling
loudly, and seemingly quite close below us. But after searching for them among the long grass for hours, we had to return
without having seen a feather. Next morning we repeated
the experiment, with the same result. I was, however, amply
repaid for my trouble by a most singular and beautiful sight.
As the grey morning dawned, there appeared, stretching away
below us, a perfectly level and unbroken expanse of mist—
except where some craggy hill-top, like a rocky islet, protruded — completely hiding everything beneath it, until it
was, seemingly, terminated by the irregular line of peaks and
ridges of the snowy range, which, in the dim uncertain light,
had the appearance of a rugged frozen coast abruptly rising
from the ocean. This extraordinary spectacle was of short
duration, and was succeeded by another almost as strange,

D

when the sun, after gilding the higher peaks, rose over the
sea of mist, which began to heave and toss itself into huge
billows, as it were, until it gradually wreathed itself about the
hill we were on, and enveloped us in its cold damp folds.

As I was sure the " cheer " must be somewhere on the hill,
I was determined not to be beaten by them ; so the third morning I took two or three men with me to mark the birds from
below, in case they flew downwards before it was light enough
for us to see them from above, as I thought they must have
done on the previous mornings. I had in some way mistaken the hour, and reached the ground much too early ;
consequently we had to wait there shivering with cold until
daybreak. As the first streak of light appeared, the cheer
began their whistling call as usual, and still our search for
them was fruitless. When it grew light enough to communi-
cate with the markers, we learnt from them that the whole
brood had flown from the top of the hill, and had lighted in
some broken bushy ground below. We had beaten all over
this, and I was just about to give up the pursuit as hopeless,
when one of the men flung a stone into some bushes where we
had marked down a black partridge, and out flew a cock-cheer.
The sly old rascal gave me a long shot, but a single pellet in
the head at last secured me my troublesome specimen. A
good dog, had I then possessed one, would have probably done
in an hour what I took so long to accomplish without one. I
may here, by way of parenthesis, remark that dogs kept in
these mountains very frequently end in becoming food for a
leopard. I have known a leopard so bold as to take a dog
actually from the doorstep of a room in which his master was
dining, and the table attendant passing constantly to and
from the kitchen outside through the doorway. This happened at the travellers' bungalow at Ramgarh, in Kumaon.

Another bird of the pheasant tribe is the "koklass." It is to
be found in almost every oak-forest, where its loud crow may
often be heard in the early morning. The handsome plumage

of the cock is grey and dark-brown. The female is something like our own grey hen, and, I should judge, about equal in weight. On the same kind of ground, the mournful whistle of the wood-partridge comes at times from the dense thickets and bushy dingles it affects. The " pewra," as the natives call it, is a game-looking bird, of a general dusky olive hue, from which it gets the name of " olive partridge," as it is sometimes termed.

Having made such a long deviation after one cock-pheasant, let us return once more to our hunt after better game.

On the third morning, the bear-slayer having mistaken the star by the rising of which he determined the time for our start in the dark, aroused me much earlier than was necessary. Being thoroughly awakened, I turned out, stirred up the log-fire, and made the best of it until it was time to set out. We had got about half-way up Dhuj, when there was a sudden stampede of heavy animals near us in the forest. At first we could see nothing in the deep gloom under the dense dark foliage of the oak-trees — for the morning had not as yet dawned, and there was only the pale dim light of a waning moon. "Hist! there's a *mirrig*,"[1] whispered Baloo Mar, as the form of a jurrow loomed indistinctly on the crest of an open knoll close above us; but whether a stag or a hind we were unable to make out, owing to the background of dark trees beyond it. Although I could not discern the sights on the rifle, I chanced a shot without them, and heard the unmistakable sound that a bullet makes when it tells on flesh. The rest of the herd went thundering away through the wood where it was too dense and dark to see them, although they must have been within fifty yards of us. It was useless to look for the wounded beast before daylight; so we continued our ascent. We had reached the top of the hill, and had been examining the precipitous craggy slopes on the south

---

[1] *Mirrig* is a term applied by the natives to any large game-animal except bears, tigers, and suchlike.

side for gooral, when one of my companions suddenly crouched down, and, pointing with his finger, in an excited whisper ejaculated the word *bāloo!* On looking in the direction indicated, there, sure enough, was a big black bear clambering about among the rocks and grass about a quarter of a mile off. He had evidently come out of the forest on the north side, and as he was not far below the crest of the ridge we were on, if he remained there only for a short time, I saw he could be easily stalked for a near shot. We therefore retired quietly into the wood, and made our way round through it as fast as the broken nature of the ground would allow of. After some rough scrambling and climbing, we reached the spot we had marked on the ridge, where we judged we should find our friend Bruin pretty close below us. I had crawled on to a ledge of rock to look over, when I almost met the brute as he was scrambling up the rocks *en route* for the wood, fortunately without his seeming to observe me. I tried to cock the rifle, but the hammers refused to move. Kurbeer and Baloo Mar were endeavouring to make themselves as small as possible behind me, and the brave slayer of bears, seeming neither to like such close proximity to Bruin nor to understand my delay in firing, kept urging me, in a trembling stage-whisper, to shoot. Meanwhile the bear had reached the crest, and was moving along within a few paces, just below us, beside the ledge of rock we were on,—and still, strange to say, without detecting us, or the consequences might have been unpleasant; for we were now between him and the precipice, and a tussle with Bruin under existing circumstances would have been decidedly in his favour. At this juncture it suddenly struck me that in my flurry I had forgotten to remove those worse than useless old appendages, the so-called "safety"-bolts, from the hammers. I had only just time to withdraw them, and to give the brute a slanting shot behind the shoulder, before he disappeared, with a grunt, down among the trees on the back slope of the hill. "*Ne lugga*" (not hit), exclaimed Baloo Mar, jumping up most pluckily, now that all possible chance of danger was over. Kurbeer and I, however, thought otherwise; so after reloading, we commenced tracking, and soon found the long grass bespattered with blood, which increased in quantity until we found the bear, a large male, lying stone-dead about three hundred yards down the hill. But the bear-slayer was determined to make sure that there was no possibility of doing harm left in the animal; for he flung several stones at its carcass, and also took the precaution to repeatedly prod at it with his long stick, at arm's-length, the while heaping a variety of abusive epithets on the defunct beast, before venturing to go nearer it.

After covering the dead bear with boughs and long grass to hide it from the eagles and vultures, we made for the spot where I had wounded the jurrow. But after tracking it for a long distance, we eventually lost all sign of it in the thick forest to which it had betaken itself. The afternoon was spent in skinning the bear, and removing and boiling down the grease, of which the beast had a pretty thick layer on its broad back.

The early part of next day was devoted to the gooral. The only one I shot at fell down a considerable distance among the crags, so I sent Kurbeer after it. On his return with it, he told me that whilst below he had seen a surrow. As I shall have more to say about this curious animal hereafter, I shall now merely describe its appearance as being something between a donkey and a big billy-goat, with short black horns. We returned rather early, as I intended to organise a drive for the jurrow, which I felt sure was lying wounded somewhere in the wood into which we had tracked it.

We beat up for volunteers in the neighbourhood, and soon had enough of willing hands for our purpose. The village dogs of all sorts and sizes were also, at Baloo Mar's advice, put into requisition. Some of these mongrel curs, queer as they looked, were quite up to the business on hand, for the

villagers often use them for hunting down jurrow, especially
during winter, after severe snowstorms, when these heavy
deer, from being unable to travel fast in the deep snow, are
easily driven down to the foot of some deep gorge, and there
mobbed by their pursuers, who despatch them wholesale, regardless of sex or size, with axes, sticks, and stones, in default
of better weapons. Although the hill villager never loses an
opportunity of killing jurrow in defence of his crops as well
as for food, they have an equally inveterate foe, in common
with most Himalayan game-animals, in the wild dog, *Cuon
rutilans* of natural history. The "bhowsa," as it is here called,
usually hunts in smaller or larger companies, and will follow
its prey with most deadly pertinacity and cunning manœuvring, until the whole pack closes round its devoted quarry, of
which it makes short work. Even the striped king of the
forest is said to dread the presence of the bhowsa on his
domain. Should the hunter find that a pack of wild dogs
has been sharing the sport in the same locality with him, he
may as well strike his tent and make for other ground. But
we shall now see what the more domestic members of the
canine family can do in the same line of business.

Having mustered our small army of bipeds and quadrupeds,
we started for the wood, which soon rang with shouts and
whistles as the line beat through it. On getting about half-
way down, it was evident, from the increased uproar of the
beaters and the barking of the dogs near the centre of the
wood, that something was afoot there. On reaching the spot,
we found the wounded deer lying in a pool of water in the
steep rocky bed of a stream, with the curs baying around it.
The defenceless creature, a big milk-hind, was unable to rise,
for, in addition to a smashed leg from the bullet, she had
broken another among the slippery wet rocks, in her endeavours to escape from the dogs. I was stricken with remorse
at seeing the poor animal lying helplessly there, with her
large mild eyes turned reproachfully, as it were, on her per-

secutors. It was a cruel lesson to me, and never to be forgotten, and one from which much might be learnt in the cause of humanity. By this I do not mean that even here, where the predatory animals keep them down quite fast enough, hinds should never be shot—and good yeld hinds killed in proper season are not the worst of venison,—but I allude to the wanton, indiscriminate destruction of game at all seasons—an unsportsmanlike practice which, I regret to say, is by no means uncommon in a country where there are no strict laws in force to prevent it, and one which has ruined sport in many easily accessible and much-frequented places, where game was formerly abundant. With the smaller animals, such as gooral and kakur, it is not always easy to discern the gender to which they belong; but with jurrow and suchlike large game this can seldom be mistaken.

After the deer had been put out of its misery, I left the men to bring it down, and straightway returned to camp in a mood that was more thoughtful than elated, although I must confess to a pardonable amount of satisfaction at having found the wounded hind. There was a good deal of wrangling about the distribution of the spoil. But all was amicably arranged by my two Goorkhas, who divided it with their kookeries into small equal portions, and distributed it fairly as far as it would go.

Before returning to Shore I had another successful day at gooral, killing one of two animals I shot at right and left.

Gooral-stalking in the precipitous and broken ground on the middle ranges is, perhaps, the pleasantest, though not the grandest kind of mountain sport. The amount of stiff climbing it entails is quite enough to give it zest without making it excessively laborious. The sportsman can generally return to his tent to rest during the heat of the day, whilst the gooral are doing likewise, hidden away among the shady recesses of the rocks, and he can always get back at night to a comfortable bed. Moreover, in a good locality, one seldom has to

score the toilsome blank days that are not uncommon on the
upper ranges, and are frequent, I may say, beyond them, on
the bleak dreary uplands of Tibet. After the experience of
hunting every sort of Himalayan game, my own predilection
for this kind of shooting may be deduced from the fact of my
finding sixty gooral recorded in my Himalayan game-register,
as having been fairly stalked and shot with the rifle, which,
with the numbers I lost and missed, represent many a day's
genuine sport after these game little animals.

Shooting-tent.

CHAPTER V.[1]

BEFORE relating my own experience of it, I shall endeavour
to describe one of the methods of killing jurrow, which is
often resorted to by Himalayan native shikarees at the season
these deer make their nightly raids on patches of young corn
which may be situated near their haunts. The hunter first
finds out a "run" or track by which jurrow are in the habit
of making their way through the forest to their feeding-
ground or elsewhere. This is easily discovered, as it is usually well defined, from the animals so often taking the same
one. He then selects an open spot, on a ridge if possible,
over which the "run" leads. Here he digs a small shallow
hole a few inches wide, and in it moistens the loose earth by
a natural action. He sometimes throws some salt on the
wet earth, but he generally considers this an unnecessary bit
of extravagance. The deer, in passing, are attracted by the
odour, and, like most animals, being partial to anything of a

[1] The first part of this chapter, as also portions of chapters ix., x., xiv., xv.,
xvi., xvii., were contributed by the author, years ago, to the 'Oriental Sporting
Magazine,' published at Calcutta.

saline nature, finding this on their path, generally stop and partake of it.

This operation is repeated at intervals by the shikaree, until in a few days a hole sometimes a foot or so deep is eaten down by the deer. Each time he visits the *kar* (salt), as he terms it, he obliterates the footprints around the hole, so that he is generally able to ascertain about the number and the size of the animals from the tracks and their appearance.

Having in this manner discovered that a large stag has become a regular nightly visitor, he proceeds to prepare an ambush within a few yards of this artificial salt-lick, taking care, as far as possible, not to make it in the direction of the prevailing wind. He generally digs a hole in the ground, or in a bank should there be one conveniently near, and over the entrance makes a careful covering of grass-sods or earth, leaving only a small aperture to look and shoot through. By this arrangement the deer have not the means of so easily winding him as when merely hidden behind a screen of bushes or of cut boughs; and also, if there is no moonlight, an animal's body can be seen in dark relief above him against the sky. The result is what may be expected. As the native shikaree seldom wastes a charge of his precious ammunition, the lord of the herd, or at any rate the largest hind, generally bites the dust.

I have tried this artifice, but without much success, for, although I heard the deer come quite close enough to the *kar* to prove the efficacy of the plan, they generally managed to get wind of me in some manner which prevented my getting a shot. And it requires such an amount of patience, and sometimes endurance on a bitter cold night, that the doubtful result hardly repays one for the trouble, not to mention its being rather a *dirty* way of doing business. On one occasion, however, I had the luck to get a chance at one of the finest jurrow I ever had the pleasure of putting trigger on.

An old Goorkha, a shikaree whom I was in the constant habit of employing, was the first to initiate me in the mysteries of preparing òne of these artificial salt-licks for deer. Old Jeetoo was about the best shikaree I ever came across. He was one of those men who talk little and do much, and had such a quiet business-like way of doing things withal. He was like a steady old hound, for his voice was seldom heard without good reason, and from being somewhat deaf, he seemed to anticipate one's intentions from one's looks.

One day I was surprised to see his long grave visage and gaunt figure at the door, for he seldom left the vicinity of his home except for shikar. He had come to inform me that, if I cared to sit up for it, he could almost ensure my getting a shot at a large stag with horns "like trees," as he described them, that came and ate the *kar* every night, not far from his village. The few traps necessary were soon packed up, and, after a tramp of about twelve miles, we reached a little hamlet, on the hill above which the *kar* was situated.

On arrival, just before sunset, I heard that a leopard had the day before killed a cow within a few hundred yards of the place. As one of the villagers had rigged up a kind of ambush in the fork of a tree near the remains of the carcass, with the intention of sitting there for a shot, I promised him a *douçeur* for his chance of a shot, and at once proceeded to take up my post, to which I was followed by several men from the village. Against this latter proceeding I remonstrated, but Jeetoo set my mind at rest by informing me for what purpose they accompanied us. He said that as soon as we were ensconced in our ambush, they would set up a shouting as if with the intention of scaring any animal away from the carcass. This row they would continue to keep up until they got back to the village. The leopard, which was probably lying pretty near, hearing the noisy ones depart, and their clamour become fainter as it grew more distant, and thinking from this that all was now safe, would most probably return to its prey all the sooner, and more especially as it was beginning to get dusk. I at first laughed at the idea, but Jeetoo assured me that he had often been successful on former occasions when he had tried this ruse with tigers as well as with leopards, and I have several times since found it answer myself.

On arriving at the carcass we found that there was little of it left, save a few bones which the vultures had picked nearly clean; and I began to think that there was very little chance of our feline friend taking the trouble to come for so poor a supper. But as Jeetoo seemed confident that the beast would come—and he was seldom wrong in his conjectures regarding game—I determined to wait there, at any rate until dark. So, having mounted the tree, we dismissed our followers, who departed exerting their lungs to the fullest extent.

The bones were at the foot of a rock in a small wooded ravine on a steep hillside, and our position in a tree which grew a little below was almost on a level with them, and about twelve yards distant.

We had been watching for barely a quarter of an hour, and every minute darkness was growing apace, when I heard a slight rustle among the dead leaves, and felt Jeetoo gently pressing my arm. In a few more seconds I saw the leopard slink noiselessly up below our tree and look stealthily around. I might have fired at him then, but I waited until he reached the bones, making sure that I should get a more certain shot. On finding so little to eat, he commenced glowering about as if at a loss to know what had become of his leavings. Carefully I now began raising the rifle, but in doing so it touched an unlucky twig that chanced to be in the way. Slight as the noise was, it caused the leopard to start and look upward; and before I could close the stock to my shoulder, with one bound he reached the top of the rock above him and was out of sight. I sent a random shot after the brute, but never saw a sign of him again. I had "counted my chickens before they were hatched." My delay in shooting had lost me' my chance. This little incident with the leopard, which may have served to illustrate one of the many hunting stratagems used in these mountains, has caused me almost to forget the *kar*-eating stag we had come out to look for.

After making an unsuccessful search for any traces of the leopard, I started on the following afternoon with Jeetoo for the place where he had reported the stag was to be found, which was situated a short distance above the outskirts of an extensive oak-forest that spread itself over the northern slope of an adjacent hill. Our way led up over some broken ground, where I shot at and wounded a gooral which I lost.

We reached the *kar* a little after sunset. As the spot was unfavourable for firing from the ground, Jeetoo had constructed a *machan* in a tree about twenty yards from the *kar*-hole. From the fresh marks around this it was evident the stag had paid it a visit the night before, and as there would be a bright moon, I thought matters looked very promising.

We had soon arranged our blankets in the *machan*, and had settled ourselves there pretty comfortably—in fact so much so on my part, that after watching for several hours I fell fast asleep. Such was not the case, however, with my trusty old companion, who had evidently been keeping his eyes, and his ears also, notwithstanding their deafness, wide open, for I was awakened by his giving me a gentle shake. How long I had slept I had no idea, but when I awoke the moon had risen high, and threw her broad, tranquil light over the forest sloping away down below, and into the deep, misty valleys that lay one beyond another like mighty trenches between us and the distant rampart of perpetual snow, rising dim and irregular along the horizon. The night was bitterly cold, and so calm and still that one might have heard the fall of a leaf. I could hear my heart beating as I lay there, hardly daring to draw breath lest it might disturb the silence. No one but a sportsman can appreciate the feelings of a moment like this.

Suddenly a loud sound broke the profound stillness, and was so startling from its unexpected proximity that it almost brought my beating heart to my mouth. It was the short alarm-note[1] of the stag, and was followed by several impatient stamps of his hoof. These signs were unpropitious, and, I feared, indicative of his having either winded or heard us. However, I lay there motionless, straining my eyes in the direction of the *kar*, in momentary expectation of his emerging from behind one of the patches of tall brushwood which grew close around. The loud, short bellow was repeated at intervals, accompanied by stamping, which grew more and more distant, and at length ceased entirely. There was no longer any doubt about it,—the beast had detected us, and there was now little hope of seeing him that night, or in all probability for several to come.

At the first streak of dawn we clambered down from our airy lodging, benumbed and stiff from cold, and exceedingly mortified. But there was no help for it, so we took our way regretfully down the hill, hoping for better luck next time. I must say the sunrise over the snowy range, glorious as it was, had not the same charms for me that morning as it would have had under more cheerful circumstances. This, however, was not the last of the stag.

Thinking it unlikely that he would return to the *kar* for at least two or three nights, I shifted my quarters with the intention of, in the meantime, hunting gooral on some ground where I had often been successful. The locality was exceedingly wild, and the hillsides very precipitous and difficult to work over. And from the fact of there being no human habitation within miles, and village shikarees considering it

---

[1] A totally different sound from his prolonged bellow during the rutting season.

too far to visit often, gooral usually abounded. We hunted
there, however, for several days with little success. It seemed
as if bad luck were to attend this trip throughout, notwithstanding the small offerings of copper coins, &c., old Jeetoo
had thought it necessary to make, for propitiating the spirit
of the mountain, at one of the rudely-built little Hindoo
temples that are so common on the higher peaks of the
middle ranges. My thoughts were constantly reverting to
the big stag, so we packed up and started to revisit his haunt,
and the same evening saw my little tent pitched near some
huts situated a mile or two below the place where we had
watched the *kar*.

Next morning we were up with the dawn, and, after a stiff
pull, reached the upper edge of the forest, a short distance
above which the *kar*-hole was situated. Our intention was
to inspect this, in order to ascertain whether the stag had
resumed his nightly visits. Thinking it was now much too
late in the morning to expect him to be there, we took no
care in approaching the *kar*, when suddenly, from behind
the bushes close by it, out walked a lordly stag, followed by
a hind, and presented himself to our astonished gaze at little
over a hundred yards, neither of the animals, apparently,
having as yet seen or heard us. Another second and the
sight of my rifle was on the stag's shoulder, the report being
followed by a "thud," and before the echoes of the shot had
died away in the forest below, he had subsided in the long
grass, leaving only his splendid horns and the tips of his ears
above it. Thinking him secured, I commenced deliberately
reloading the rifle, being at that moment in as happy a frame
of mind as a mortal can ever hope for in this world. But
alas! I was doomed to bitter disappointment.

Perhaps it was the slight rattle of the ramrod in reloading
that attracted his attention, for his horns began to sway to
and fro, and almost immediately he jumped up and went off
at a lumbering gallop. I had just finished recapping, so,

taking a hasty aim, let drive, and in my hurry, with sorrow be it told, clean missed the great animal; but, being very sick, he soon pulled up in a small strip of wood that extended for a short distance down the hill.

I now took Jeetoo's advice, contrary to my own opinion, with respect to taking up a position whilst he proceeded to drive out the wounded deer. My idea was to post myself at the lower end of the bit of wood, thinking that, as the stag was badly wounded, he would most probably take down hill. But Jeetoo persisted that he would take upwards, so I gave in to his superior knowledge of woodcraft, in which he was seldom at fault; consequently I had the mortification of seeing the stag leave the cover almost at the spot I had intended posting myself. He made straight for the thick forest below, in which he disappeared from our sight. We followed at once on his tracks, feeling quite confident that, as he was so hard hit, we should soon overtake him. We came up with him several times, and got so close as to hear him crashing away through the bushes, but, owing to the dense cover, without getting even a glimpse of him. Here we had made another mistake, in following him up too soon instead of allowing him time enough to lie down, when in all probability he would have given an easy chance for a shot.

For the greater part of three days did we slowly and perseveringly follow him, often finding clots of gore where he had stopped to rest. Jeetoo's tracking powers were truly astonishing. Sometimes, after losing all traces of the slot for hours, where it had led over rocky ground, my sinking hopes would be revived by his drawing my attention to an almost invisible speck of dry blood on a twig or a blade of long grass against which the animal had brushed in passing. The stag, however, baffled all his skill, and we were at length most reluctantly obliged to abandon the pursuit, where the tracks were irretrievably lost among a number of those of other deer, with which they had got confused.

Many a cold night-watch did old Jeetoo and I have together for game, although they were not often attended with success, as such work is very uncertain.[1] Something is, at any rate, occasionally added by night-shooting to one's knowledge of the habits of *feræ naturæ.* For instance, I was under the impression that a tiger in its wild state always killed its food and never touched dead meat, until one of our nocturnal experiences proved that it will greedily devour even carrion.

There had been a dreadful murrain among the cattle throughout the district, and Jeetoo amongst others had lost many of his beasts. As they died he merely dragged their carcasses from his *gote* (cowshed) to a neighbouring jungly ravine, and there left them to rot, and, from fear of infection, without even stripping them of their hides. One day he came and reported that a tiger had been at them for several nights. At first I thought he might have been mistaken, and that the nocturnal visitor must be a bear. But he so positively insisted that it was a tiger, that I at once resolved to go and judge for myself.

On reaching the village, we forthwith proceeded to inspect the place where the dead cattle had been devoured, and there found the fresh unmistakable footprints of a large tiger. Jeetoo had already removed all the carcasses, except one, to some distance, in order that there might, for obvious reasons, be more certainty of getting a shot. As it was growing late in the evening there was no time to be lost. We hauled the

---

[1] For night work I have found the following a good method of aligning the sights on an animal. Stretch a broad bit of white tape along the rib of the barrels between the back and the fore sights, binding it at either end on the rib with a bit of thin twine whipped tightly round the barrels. Commence aiming with the tape well in sight, and with the muzzle end of it rather above your object. Then gradually depress the muzzle on to the point you wish to hit, at the same time lowering the eye until the tape is hidden from view by the back sight, on the required alignement, when at once press the trigger. By this means you can tell if the back and the fore sights are correctly aligned, whereas you are uncertain of this if, as is customary, the fore sight only is rendered visible by having a bit of white cotton, or any other dodge, fastened on to it.

carcass to a likely spot for our purpose, and tied it tightly to
a stake driven into the ground, so that it could not be dragged
away without giving time for a shot. Some green branches
were cut and stuck upright to form a screen about fifteen or
twenty paces from the carcass, and on slightly higher ground
than where it lay. All being ready, Jeetoo and I took up our
position in our ambush about dusk, hoping that the tiger
might put in an appearance before it grew too dark to be able
to see him, as unfortunately there was no moon. We waited
there until I could no longer see either my rifle-barrels or the
dead cow in the pitchy gloom of the ravine, but not a sound
broke the deep stillness except the intermittent "chunk,
chunk" of the night-jar, so we quietly left our ambush.
Shortly after returning to the village, we heard at intervals
the deep-throated "aowoongh" of the tiger on his way down
from a neighbouring forest-clad hill to his supper. How
wild and eerie it sounded in the silence of night! This was
another new experience, for I had always thought that a
tiger stole warily towards its prey. But in this case, the
prey being dead, it perhaps thought such precaution unnecessary.

As it would have been as rash as it was useless to attempt
to go after a hungry tiger in the dark, we waited until morning dawned, when we cautiously approached the carcass in
hopes of finding the animal still at work on it. To our great
surprise we found it had not been touched, though we discovered the brute's tracks close to it. We followed them for
some distance, until we came upon another dead cow partially
eaten, which the tiger had very recently left, as was evident
from the freshness of his big pug-marks round about it. This
was annoying, as Jeetoo had unfortunately overlooked this
carcass, which lay concealed among the dense brushwood
when he had removed the others.

As the shades of evening began to gather around, we
fastened the two dead cattle together and once more took up

our post. Whilst we silently watched there in the gloaming, the hollow moaning voice of the tiger was now and again heard on the hill above. Gradually the sullen sound drew nearer and nearer as the brute came prowling down, until it seemed to be quite close to us, when it ceased and was heard no more. It had now grown so dusky that we were only just able to discern the outline of the carcasses, as, with bated breath, we crouched behind our ambush, listening for the slightest sound, and straining our eyes as we tried to pierce the deepening gloom. My heart beat faster and faster each time the light evening zephyrs stirred the loose leaves of some bush in our vicinity, until the feeling of anxious suspense became almost intolerable. We remained listening there, as if spell-bound, for some time after it had grown pitch-dark, expecting each moment to hear the crunching of the bones. At length my trusty old companion, in a whisper, suggested that it might be prudent for us to retire as noiselessly as possible from the ravine, lest the tiger should chance to prefer live to dead meat for his supper. Next morning we were again much astonished at finding our bait untouched. The wary brute must have got wind of us in some manner when he had approached so near, for no sign was either seen or heard of him about the dead cattle after that night.

Man-eater tigers are not uncommon in the Himalayas, but one seldom hears of man-eating leopards, although they are common enough in Central India. A hill leopard, when it does take to that sort of thing, is generally a very devil at it. A brute of this kind infested the Shore valley during part of the time I was there. It had killed some seven or eight people, and was so crafty that it baffled all attempts to destroy it. In one instance it was bold enough to carry off a little girl from the hut in which she was sleeping. Her people were so anxious to avenge her death and to rid themselves of this pest, that they came to the outpost and reported their having actually left the par-

tially eaten corpse at the spot where the leopard had dragged
it to, in the hope of the brute's destruction by a shot on its
return to its victim. I was absent from Shore at the time, but
a sportsman who happened to be there went and watched
over the body, to which, as was the custom of this cruel and
cunning brute, it never returned.   Man-eating tigers and
leopards are often pale and dingy in colour, and mangy in
appearance. This, however, is not due, as is commonly supposed, to their diet of human flesh, but to age. These pests
are usually old and more or less infirm animals, which, finding human victims easier to obtain than more active and
wary ones in the shape of deer or cattle, consequently take
to habitually preying upon them.

On one occasion, during my sojourn in Kumaon, I had an
exciting hunt after a perfect feline demon. I was on a visit
at Almora, the capital town of the province, when a report
was brought in that a leopard had temporarily established
itself in some terraced rice-fields near a village about half a
mile off. It had that morning given a forcible proof of
its unwelcome presence there by maliciously attacking a
woman who was at work in a field close below the village.
Two or three sporting members of the small European community of the place were soon on the scene of action, and,
having collected a number of willing men from the village,
at once commenced beating up the enemy's quarters. We
had not proceeded far when several hoarse grunts, followed
by the piercing screams of a woman, apprised us of the brute's
whereabouts. It was standing on the edge of one of the terraced rice-fields, lashing its tail from side to side and looking
back defiantly towards us, and in the field immediately below
lay the victim it had just seized and left. The beast was
rather far out for the borrowed smooth-bore I was armed
with, and fearing lest I might injure the woman I aimed
rather high. At any rate the shot had the effect of scaring
the leopard away from her vicinity, for it at once decamped.

On reaching the poor woman, we found her lying there with her head and back all lacerated and bleeding, and speechless with fright and pain. Having arranged for her being carried to the village, we at once proceeded with the beat, all of us vowing vengeance against the brute for this its second cruel performance of the day.

After beating, as we imagined, most thoroughly through the rice-fields, we reached a bushy ravine, in which we all, with one exception, thought the brute must have concealed itself. The exception was a tea-planter who had joined the party. He was one of the best mountain-hunters, and about as cool a hand as I ever met, and quite a character in his way. Originally in the army, his predilection for wild sport had been the cause of his leaving it and taking to tea-planting and shooting in the hills. He now expressed his opinion that the leopard was still lurking somewhere in the rice-fields, and his intention of taking his chance alone of finding it there whilst we beat through the ravine. We had just begun driving it when I heard him shouting to us. Supposing he had seen the leopard and was calling us back, I at once ran up towards where he was standing with the butt of his rifle on the ground. To my astonishment and concern, on reaching him I saw that he was profusely bleeding from a wound on his face, and that his coat was all torn and bloody. With his characteristic coolness he quietly remarked, " He's boned me " ; but from the expression and pallor of his face, I could see he was more injured than he cared to allow. It appeared that after our leaving him he had but just commenced wandering about in search of the leopard, when it suddenly sprang on him from behind, making its teeth meet in the upper part of his arm, and driving one of its claws into his face within an inch of his eye, and before he had time to use his rifle, even had he been able to do so, the beast had bounded away and was out of sight in a moment.

After bandaging up the tea-planter's wounds and arranging

for getting him conveyed home, we renewed our search for
the leopard. Although we beat about until evening, all our
endeavours to find it were fruitless, nor was it again heard of
in the vicinity. The hero of this hunt was not long in recovering from his wounds, of which, if he be still living, he
bears the scars on his face and arm to this day. With his
usual erratic disposition, he soon gave up tea-planting, and
wandered away elsewhere in search of adventure and wild
sport. The last time I met the " Bhagee," by which *sobriquet*
he was well known, he was with an expedition against the
hill-tribes on the north-west frontier, where, as an amateur,
he had been " shooting plumb centre," as he termed it, at the
enemy with his six-shooter. The injuries to the poor woman
were, fortunately, more ugly than dangerous.

This has truly been a chapter of unsuccessful performances.
But as I am writing simple facts, they must be taken as they
actually occurred. Indeed, in making these extracts from my
old shooting-journal, kept regularly for upwards of thirty
years, I have endeavoured to select such incidents as may
tend to depict shady as well as sunny sketches of Himalayan
hunting in their true lights. And although it is certainly
more satisfactory to bag one's game, wild sport is, perhaps,
none the less exciting to its *true* votaries because it does not
always end in a kill.

CHAPTER VI.

HITHERTO my Himalayan experiences had been confined to
the middle and lower ranges, and I had regarded those aerial
piles and peaks of eternal snow as a sort of distant dreamland, which I hoped some day to find a substantial reality ;
and for those who are not cragsmen born, so to speak, it
may perhaps be as well to get accustomed and inured to
mountain climbing where it is comparatively easy and safe,
before attempting to hunt among the dizzy heights and dangerous snow-slopes of the higher Himalayas.

It was the beginning of April when I purposed visiting the
Chipla mountain, a gigantic rocky buttress, as it were, of the
great frozen wall it seemed to support, and a favourite haunt
of the " tāhr." This member of the wild-goat family—*Hemitragus jemlaicus* of natural history—is plentifully distributed

over the precipitous rocky slopes just below the snow-line, and is occasionally found on some of the higher parts of the middle ranges, where, however, it appears not to attain the same size as it does in the higher regions below the snowy range.   I have never seen a more truly wild-looking animal in the Himalayas than an old buck tahr, with his long frill-like mane and shaggy coat of dark greyish-brown, short sturdy legs, and almost black face.   His horns are from twelve to fourteen inches long, and about nine inches in circumference at the base, broad and flat, with their rough anterior edges rising in a line with the forehead till they abruptly curve backward to a very fine point.   When seen from the front, they somewhat resemble a high coronet.   An old buck stands over three feet at the shoulder.   The doe, called "tehrny," is smaller, lighter in colour, and less shaggy, with horns of the same shape, but much smaller than those of the buck.   The great old bucks herd separately during the summer until October, generally betaking themselves to the wildest and most unapproachable places.   Their colour is often so dark as, at a distance, almost to look black, more especially in the autumn.   The flesh of the tahr, or "jhārrel," as it is sometimes called, is considered by the hill-men to be great medicine for fever and rheumatism; and shikarees often dry the flesh and sell it, and even the bones, in places where fresh tahr meat is not procurable.

As it would be difficult to procure even the bare necessaries of life in the wild, thinly populated part of the mountains I was about to visit, my commissariat arrangements, &c., were this time made on a rather more extensive scale, and our party consisted of some nine or ten men all told, including Kurbeer.   In two days we reached the village of Askote, the residence of a native potentate styling himself a " Rajwār " ; and the third morning brought us to the Goree, a fine rapid river, which was then in a muddy state of flood from the melting of the snow-fields about its source.   The only noteworthy incident that had hitherto occurred on our way, was the destruction of an enormous wild cat of a light sandy-grey colour, measuring 46 inches from tip to tip.

Thus far our road had been fairly good for a mountain bridle-path 5 or 6 feet wide. But after crossing the Goree, where it was bridged by a few tree-stems thrown over it at a narrow place between two rocks, we left the road and struck up the left bank of the river by a mere track. In some places our path lay close to the water's edge, in others it overhung the stream, and sometimes at such a height as, at first, to make looking down at it, surging impetuously along, rather unpleasant. That evening we sheltered, coolies and all, under a huge beetling rock, from which retreat we had to eject, with the help of smoke, myriads of small black, biting flies, here called "peepsas" or "moras," very like the "black-fly" of the Canadian woods, and just as troublesome. Their bite leaves, under the skin, a small blood-spot, which is very irritable.

Our way now led up beside a torrent that leapt from rock to rock as it tore furiously down a very steep gorge. After several hours spent in fording and refording this ice-cold stream where its sides were precipitous and impassable, and in assisting each other in clambering up difficult places, we exchanged this rocky defile for a stiff but less laborious pull up a steep wooded slope of the Chipla.

At length we reached an open space on the mountain-side, where the sloping ground was cultivated in small stony fields arranged in terraces. In these the inhabitants of the few log-built huts that were scattered here and there over this plateau, raised their scanty crops of "phapur" (buckwheat), and other sorts of coarse grain of the millet kind called "mundooa" and "chooa," just sufficient for their own wants. The "chooa," which much resembles the cockscomb of English cottage gardens, at one stage of its growth assumes a deep crimson colour, sometimes varied with bright yellow, and the small patches of it that are dispersed over the hillsides have a brilliant and curious effect among their rugged surroundings of grey rocks and stones. The bread made from all these grains is black, coarse, and bitter to the taste. These people, however, seemed to thrive well on their frugal fare, as they all looked robust and hearty, and were of a finer build than the inhabitants of the lower and middle ranges. But they are evidently of opinion that water is only intended for drinking, most of them being literally coated with grimy dirt. And as for their clothing, I doubt whether it is ever removed, unless it be at the prompting of the parasites that infest it.

There are some curious specimens of humanity to be found dwelling among the forests about the Chipla, called "Razees," compared with whom the villagers are quite civilised. As they are few in number, and hardly ever visit the villages, I much regretted not having had an opportunity of becoming personally acquainted with them. The villagers described these "junglee admi" (wild men of the woods), as they termed them to me, as being almost on a par with the beasts of the wilds they inhabit, subsisting chiefly on what they can secure with their bows and arrows, and by snaring. I at first suspected their existence to be a myth, until I afterwards learnt on good authority that it was a fact. My old friend Colonel Fisher, senior Assistant Commissioner of Kumaon, gave me the following short account of these interesting barbarians. "They were the original indigenous inhabitants of the country about there, but the persecutions to which they were subjected by the Kumaon Rajas, and especially by their neighbours the Goorkhas, were so cruel, that they abandoned their hamlets and retired into the wildest and least inhabited parts of the country, and lived on wild roots, fruits, and fish, and game, and lost all recollection even of their language. They had a language of their own, but it is quite extinct now; in fact, I was told by the Rajwar of Askote, they themselves have entirely disappeared from Kumaon, though there may be a few yet on the banks of the Sarda in our territory, or the thick jungles on the Nepal side of the river. The last time I saw a man and woman of the tribe was at Askote in 1866, and they were caught for my special benefit. We gave them a few rupees, but they seemed to value them as much as apes! They would eat anything given to them; and both the man and the woman wore long hair down the back, and used leaves stitched together for clothing." From this, the condition of these remnants of an almost lost race appears to have been still much the same as, we may suppose, was that of Adam and Eve after the fall.

As we were pitching our little camp on the plateau, we were interviewed by several of the tenants of the log huts, who willingly offered to give us every assistance in the way of sport. Tahr they reported as abundant higher up on the mountain, and a few black bears and plenty of kakur (barking deer) in the forest close above the plateau.

Long before the sun had topped the snowy crests of the towering heights eastward of the plateau, we were afoot in the forest above, and were not long in coming across one of its ursine denizens. I gave him the contents of both barrels as he shambled away through the bushes. He went off hard hit with the second shot, to which he loudly responded. We tracked him for some distance by his blood, but eventually had to give up the pursuit, as we wished to be back in time to move up to the tahr ground that day. I had also snap-shots at two kakur, one of which got away badly wounded in the thick cover. Whilst forcing our way through some tangled bushes as we were returning to camp, a twig I had pressed back with my hand flew back and struck me in the open eye, causing the most acute pain, and quite blinding me for the time of that eye. Being the right eye, this little accident proved highly detrimental to rifle-shooting for several days.

About noon we commenced our ascent to the haunts of the

tahr. For a mile or two our way led through forest, and over ground that was rough and uneven owing to huge fragments of rock that had been detached by some bygone convulsion of nature from the heights above, and which now lay jammed together where they had here found a resting-place below. Such travelling was tiresome for our laden men, though they made nothing of the difficulty. At length we emerged on to a rocky ridge which ran up the left side of a vast amphitheatre. From the naked crags and snow-streaked summits that almost encircled it, deep rifts, gullies, and broad landslips of stones and *débris* ran down its precipitous sides, until they terminated in a wilderness of partially wooded, rocky ravines far away below. Some idea of the proportions of this huge natural amphitheatre may be formed when I say that as we clambered along we might have been compared to ants creeping over the ruined walls of the Colosseum at Rome. Here and there amidst this chaos were steep, verdant slopes on which several small herds of tahr were quietly browsing or reposing, looking in the distance like little brown dots. Altogether it was a wonderfully wild scene to gaze upon, though I had only one eye for viewing it, the injured one being bandaged up for the time.

As we picked our way along the ridge, I was much amused with the behaviour of a big sturdy inhabitant of the plateau, who, notwithstanding his load, which was not a light one, was skipping nimbly about from rock to rock in his anxious endeavours to point out the tahr. Fortunately the animals were so far distant below us, that there was little chance of their observing his excited movements. On examining the animals with the telescope, I could discern no great old black fellows among them, only tehrny or young bucks. Some of the latter, however, showed fair heads.

We soon reached a spot on the ridge where the aforementioned stalwart individual, who had constituted himself our guide, had informed me that we should find a sort of cave, under

a big overhanging rock, capable of affording shelter for us all.
It was rather an awkward place to get at, from its being
situated just below the crest of the ridge, in such a way as to
render it necessary to clamber down, one by one, on to this
covered shelf of rock, below which was an almost sheer drop
of at least a hundred feet, terminating with a very steep slope
of incalculable distance towards depths unseen from above.

Taking with us our burly but agile guide, Kurbeer and I
lost no time in making a start after the tahr we had seen
below. Difficult as the ground looked from above, we found
it fairly easy, although toilsome to work over. As it was
very favourable for stalking, I had not much difficulty in
getting several easy shots. But no sooner did I uncover my
right eye to take aim, than its sudden exposure caused both
eyes to water, blurring the sights of the rifle and everything
beyond them, which of course made my shooting rather
erratic. It was almost dark when we got back to our cave,
and, much to the regret of its occupants—who had been looking forward to a hearty supper of tahr meat—empty-handed.
Notwithstanding the general disappointment, the place looked
cheerful enough, and highly picturesque withal, as the fires
blazed and crackled away, shedding a warm ruddy glow on
the black, smoke-stained rock beetling above, and throwing
up the wild figures of the mountain men, either in dark relief or in high light, as they moved to and fro, or squatted
before their little fires, cooking their evening meal. After
dinner and a pipe, my blankets were spread on the softest
spot I could find on our stony floor. Fortunately I am not a
somnambulist, or, from the position of my couch, my ambula-
tion might have taken me down over the rocks below at a
pace I never could have dreamt of.

Next morning my eye was still so bad that it would have
been wiser to have given it a rest than to have gone out
merely to disturb the game as I did, by firing several random
shots. One herd which towards evening we saw, must have

numbered about five-and-twenty animals. All of them, however, were tehrny or very young males. Being alarmed, they had huddled up together and stood in a cluster some 200 yards below. Half blind as I was, I thought I could hardly miss such a big mark. On the bullet striking, with a smack, on a stone in their midst, it was a pretty and curious sight to see the manner in which the herd instantly split into two bands, which galloped off, each in an opposite direction. I should never have fired such an indiscriminate shot, and at such inferior specimens, had I not become desperate at having as yet got no venison for our camp, after losing so many easy chances of procuring it. Of course the natives ascribed my want of success to the protection from harm afforded to the game there by the deity of the mountain. I discovered one fellow who had accompanied me from Shore, smoking my rifle with some burning stuff that he informed me was a charm with which he was endeavouring to exorcise the evil spirit he thought must have possessed it—for, he added, he never had known it behave so badly when he had been out with me on former shikar trips. The following morning, however, my eye being considerably better, such ideas were dispelled from their minds by my shooting a fine buck tahr, and also a gooral. The tahr was one of a herd of seven; but owing to the broken nature of the ground, it was not until after we had stalked quite close up to and shot him, that we caught sight of his companions as they scurried helter-skelter away among the rocks. My satisfaction at being, at last, able to kill some game on this ground, was added to by the opportunity it afforded of providing my friends of the plateau with some venison in return for their civility.

The game here had been so much disturbed by my wild firing, that I now thought it advisable to try fresh ground. About noon the loads were all packed and hauled up from the rocky alcove. The laden men descended along the ridge until they reached the lower extremity, as it were, of the

amphitheatre, where the torrent that drained it rushed and
tumbled down its rock-bound channel towards the narrow
gorge we had, a few days before, ascended with so much
difficulty from the river Goree to the plateau. Kurbeer and
I took a more circuitous route down through the crags on the
chance of finding game, but were unsuccessful. In the evening we found the camp pitched beside some huts near the
stream, across which, and rising abruptly almost from the
water's edge, was a very steep and rugged hill-face we intended scaling on the morrow.

In the early morning we crossed the stream and commenced the long and arduous ascent, which must have been
some 5000 feet at least, and not a drop of water was
there to be found on the way up. It was past mid-day ere
we all had reached the top. The heat of the sun's rays, as
they beat on us through the clear air of those high regions,
had been intense during our toilsome climb. I was nearly
dead beat when I threw myself down in the shade of the
rhododendron bushes that grew in great profusion along the
ridge, and my mouth was as dry as a limekiln from thirst.
But the glorious view from the ridge was a more than
adequate reward for the trouble of getting up there. And
the rhododendrons! which were all in full bloom—never have
I seen anything to approach the colouring and quantity of
their gorgeous blossoms. Here, almost at the limit of vegetation, they grow in the form of large shrubs—not as forest-
trees, like those of the middle and lower ranges—and their
bloom is larger, fuller, and of more delicate and varied hues.
Some were white as snow, others of a salmon-red, whilst the
tints of many ranged from the faintest blush of pink to the
deepest rose. The bunches of blossom were very round, with
the flowers on each bunch packed closely together. To see
the rhododendron blooming in perfection of form and colour,
one must visit the higher Himalayan ranges where nature
alone has nurtured it.

After a short rest we trudged on refreshed and invigorated by the cooling breeze on the ridge. The rest of our day's work was comparatively easy, being more or less through forest and down hill. And how we did enjoy an ice-cold draught at the first sparkling stream we came to! As a rule, however, it is a mistake to drink water when out on the hill, for the more you indulge in it the more you seem to want, and you soon get inured to doing without it. It was late in the afternoon when we reached our destination—a hamlet situated below the ground we intended hunting over. Whilst dinner was being prepared, I arranged with the village Nimrod for his services as guide, and after quickly disposing of my frugal repast, at once turned in—for sitting up to promote its digestion was quite unnecessary after such a hard day's mountain work.

The fleecy cloudlets that flecked the deep-blue sky were just becoming tinged with gold as I stepped out of my little tent into the bracing morning air. All traces of yesterday's fatigue were gone, and much to my joy, the sight of the injured eye was almost as clear as ever. At the shikaree's suggestion we left most of the *impedimenta* at the village, only taking with us a man to carry our blankets and food sufficient for the few days we intended passing on the hill. In consequence of these little arrangements having to be made, the sun had risen over the eastern snow-peaks before we had started.

"Look, there's a gooral!" exclaimed one of my companions in a hurried whisper, as he crouched down and pointed to where a buck was perched among some rocks high above us, basking in the rays of the morning sun. As his gaze was not directed downwards, he had evidently not observed us. The ground was favourable, so we had little difficulty in circumventing him, when a bullet sent him scrambling helplessly among the rocks. The shikaree was not long in securing him, and after slinging him over the few things he already had on his back, again took the lead upwards. Before we had gone much higher, three or four more gooral sped away up the crags. I took a snap-shot at one of them, which I missed. As we were going through a small birch coppice we flushed a pair of large beautiful birds here called "loongees," and generally known as the horned argus-pheasant. Its habitat is always on the higher ranges, where its wild peculiar call— a kind of mewing sound—may sometimes be heard issuing from thickets in the pine-forests and birch woods near the snow-line. Being a very shy bird, it is seldom or never met with in the open. Its general colour on the back is a gamely marked greyish-brown. The neck, breast, and shoulders of the cock-bird are blood-red, and from its black head rise a pair of red feathery ears or horns. The whole body, from the neck downwards, is profusely covered with small white spots rimmed with black. In another variety of the same bird, the cock has a black neck, and breast spotted with white instead of the blood-red colour, and over its throat hangs a broad sky-blue wattle, from under which depends a bunch of bright, glossy-red, beard-like hackles. Its long thin horns are fleshy, and devoid of feathers. The hen, of both varieties, is uniformly brownish-grey, dotted over with white, and minus the colour and appendages about the neck and throat of the cock-bird.

About noon we reached a small kind of cavity among some steep rocks, where the shikaree proposed we should temporarily establish ourselves. After skinning and breaking up the gooral, I took a careful search over all the ground in view with the spying-glass. There was a small herd of young buck tahr far away above, near the sky-line; but the steep intervening ground was so open, that there was no chance of getting near them from below, and it was too late in the afternoon to attempt to approach them from the ridge above, even had it been possible to reach it; we therefore proceeded to try our luck elsewhere. Two moving objects

F

are soon descried on a distant grassy slope. Surely they must be great old tahr, for they seem almost black against the steep background of dried-up grass on the slope, which looks yellow and bright in the rays of the declining sun shooting athwart it over the high rocky ridge already in deep shadow behind us. On bringing the telescope to bear on them, they turn out to be wild pigs rooting about among the grass. As wild pork is more esteemed by the hill-men than any venison, we at once resolve to try for a shot. After a long, tiresome, roundabout stalk, we find, to our chagrin, our porkers vanished. It was now getting late, and our fruitless endeavour had taken us a long way from our lodging, so we made for it as straight as possible, lest darkness should overtake us on ground where travelling was by no means easy, even in daylight. By the time we got back, the shades of night had closed down on the mountains, their rugged crests rising black and grim against the clear starlit sky.

After rekindling the fire, our supper of gooral-meat was soon frizzling away on wooden skewers over the glowing embers. The small share of our airy lodging I had appropriated for the night was rendered somewhat uncomfortable from having a sharp immovable bit of rock sticking up in it, which, from the limited space, I was unable to avoid; but after a hard day's clambering, such trifling inconveniences do not interfere very much with one's slumbers.

The moonal pheasants were whistling loudly among the adjacent crags when we sallied forth in the grey dawn. My only shot was at an old cock-moonal, which offered so tempting a chance, as we suddenly came on him where he sat, whistling away on a point of rock below us, quite unaware of our presence, that I could not resist such a rare opportunity, even at the risk of disturbing better game, for on open ground these birds are usually very wary. A wire-cartridge sent him whirling from his perch so far down among the rocks that it was hardly worth while fetching him, as his plumage was destroyed in his fall, and he turned out to be as tough as an old shoe. Nothing else was seen except a few tehrny.

Specimens of the moonal or Impeyan pheasant are now so common that any description of it here is quite unnecessary. But looking at a stuffed cock-bird in a shop window, or even alive in captivity, is very different from seeing him in his native mountains as he sails away over the blue depths of some wild rocky gorge, where his loud whistling cry is echoed and re-echoed among the neighbouring crags and precipices. Then is the time to see his splendid plumage to its best advantage, as the sun glints on the brilliant metallic hues of his neck and the dark purplish blue of his outstretched wings— colours so strangely contrasting with the snow-white patch on his back and the deep orange of his fan-shaped tail, which he always outspreads when in flight. The hen is modestly dressed in her sombre brown but gamely marked feathers, the only bright colour in her attire being the sky-blue skin round her eyes, and a pure white mark on her throat. The quantity of these beautiful birds annually killed to meet the demand for the adornment of ladies' bonnets, &c., is so great that one might suppose the supply would soon be exhausted. But as the plumage of the cock-bird only is used for such purposes, the general decrease in their numbers has not as yet become very apparent.

Moonals are often a great nuisance on tahr ground, where they are almost invariably numerous. Sometimes an old rascal will, on observing the stalker, set up his loud alarm whistle, and thus warn the tahr of impending danger, making them restless and suspicious, and consequently more difficult to approach.

Towards the afternoon it began to rain pretty heavily; we therefore returned to our lodging for shelter. By way of employment we commenced digging out the lump of stone that had made my couch so unpleasant. This we found no easy matter, as it proved to be much larger than we expected. After a good deal of work we managed to loosen it, when, with the help of wooden levers cut for the purpose by Kurbeer with his kookerie, we launched it over the mountain-side, down which it went hurtling and crashing, smashing, and carrying away everything that impeded its headlong course, until it disappeared from our sight in a deep dark gorge far below, where, as it dashed against rock and tree, an occasional sullen boom was heard, the sounds and their echoes growing fainter and more faint until they were no longer audible.

After the rain had ceased it was too late to go up after tahr, so we tried for gooral lower down, returning at dark only to score in my note-book "a blank day."

At daylight next morning we sent down our spare man with the blankets, &c., giving him instructions to have the traps we had left at the village taken by a lower route to our next camping-place. At the same time Kurbeer, the shikaree, and myself started with the intention of hunting over the heights above, and joining the camp in the evening. Much of the ground we had to get over was decidedly bad. On some of the steep slopes we traversed the grass was, at this season, so dry and slippery as to make the foothold very precarious, and they, as often as not, terminated abruptly on the brink of a sheer precipice. I must say I was rather staggered at the look of one very awkward place we came to, which there was no means of avoiding. As seen from below, it appeared to me to be a nearly perpendicular craggy precipice of at least fifteen hundred feet high. But our guide said it was quite practicable, and as it had to be scaled, there was no use looking at it—for the more one looks the less one likes such a place,—we therefore commenced the ascent. It was not so difficult, however, as it at first appeared, except in a few places where one or other of my companions had sometimes to place a hand from below on the nearly vertical face of some smooth rock for a step; there were juniper bushes, too, here

"TO SAVE HIMSELF FROM FALLING, KURBEER WAS OBLIGED
TO LET GO."

and there by which we could hold on. On nearing the top, it was decidedly unpleasant to look back, and I was very glad when we reached it. I was then but a neophyte in mountaineering on the upper Himalayan ranges, or I should probably have thought little of such a climb.

"*Kustoora!*" suddenly ejaculated Kurbeer, just as we topped the ascent. A musk-deer had jumped up close to us, and was standing at gaze on the ridge. All breathless as I was, I fired, and felt sure the animal was hit, although it made off. We soon discovered it standing on a little ledge of rock below the brow of the ridge. I could easily have finished it with another shot, but if it fell from the ledge there was nothing to prevent its going to the bottom of the rocky steep below it, by a much quicker route than the one we had taken in coming up. As it looked very sick, Kurbeer volunteered to clamber down and try to secure it. The danger of such a proceeding did not strike me until I nearly had cause to repent having allowed him to attempt it. Climbing cautiously below the ledge, he seized the little creature by one of its hind legs. In its struggles to free itself it toppled off the ledge, the lad still holding on to it with one hand, whilst with the other he gripped the ledge above him. At last, in order to save himself from falling, Kurbeer was obliged to let go, when the animal went whirling down among the crags. Had he lost his balance or his footing in the struggle . . . I don't like recalling the feelings of those few anxious moments to my memory.

Rather would I describe my sensations during a somewhat similar episode, when, from being the principal actor myself, they were less poignant than when beholding another in imminent jeopardy without the possibility of helping him, and for which I felt myself to blame. I had wounded a gooral, and it had betaken itself to a steep bare slope, off which the dry grass had been recently burnt, where it lay down in a dying state on a shelving slab of rock. Not wishing to disturb the ground by unnecessarily firing another shot,

I proceeded to secure the animal if possible by creeping up behind it, and laying hold of one of its hind legs, which I could see was hanging helplessly over the edge of the rock. No sooner did the animal feel itself seized than it kicked itself off the rock with the other hind leg, and fell struggling on to the steep slope below it. I still held on to its legs as we both went sliding head-foremost down the slope. But finding the pace was getting too fast to be pleasant, I let go. Fortunately I soon managed to stop myself by turning flat on my face, and stretching out my arms and legs like a spread-eagle, just as I was unconsciously nearing the brink of a nearly perpendicular drop. Over this the gooral went headlong in company with my cap, which had fallen from my head in the struggle. It was afterwards recovered with the gooral, which was found dead at the bottom. I felt truly thankful at having escaped with nothing worse than my knuckles well barked and my clothes a bit torn by the sharp stones on the slope. But we must now try to recover our musk-deer.

The shikaree at once set off down the hill to look for it. And judging from the time we had taken in coming up, I concluded he would be a good while getting down and returning with it on his back; so I sat down and lit my pipe, Kurbeer doing likewise with one he had made by twisting a green leaf into a conical shape, which he filled with my cavendish, and smoked through his clasped hands by way of mouthpiece. The hill-men are decidedly ingenious in some of their extempore contrivances for smoking tobacco. The most primitive I have seen was a small hole made horizontally under the surface of the ground and left open at the extremities. At one end was placed the tobacco, whilst at the other each man in turn knelt down and inhaled two or three long-drawn whiffs of smoke into his lungs.

Waiting so long on the ridge was by no means irksome to me, for I was glad of the rest it afforded. Moreover, when situated on such an elevated spot, commanding so extensive an area of grand mountain scenery, one need never tire of watching the ever-varying effects of light and shade as some passing cloud floats lazily across the deep-blue firmament, temporarily darkening and seemingly altering the rugged features of the mountains beneath it. Sometimes a great bearded vulture (the Lammergeyer of Europe) would come slowly soaring round the wall-like face of a cliff, rising high away to our left, and, with outstretched wings, sweep past so close to us that we could hear the rustle of his pinions. We almost fancied we could see his inquisitive eye regarding our prostrate forms with a hungry, sinister expression, as we lay motionless on the ridge. There was interesting enjoyment, too, in observing, through the spy-glass, the movements of a distant herd of tahr, and charms for the ear in the faint murmur of rushing water far away in the depths of the valley below, and the wild whistling of moonals among the crags.

However, after waiting there for nearly two hours, we began to grow anxious lest some mishap might have befallen the shikaree. Mist, too, had been gradually gathering around the mountain-tops, the sky became rapidly overcast with dark driving clouds of a leaden hue, and the keen cold wind that accompanied them seemed to indicate an approaching snow-storm. At last, to our relief, the shikaree reappeared, and over his back was slung the musk-deer. Its skin was much torn and its bones were all broken from having been dashed from rock to rock in its fall.

The musk-deer (*Moschus moschiferus* of natural history), or *kustoora*, as it is here called, is a very delicately formed little creature, both in body and limb. It stands, at most, two feet at the shoulder, which is slightly lower than the croup. Its hind-legs are very long, and are thus well adapted for the agile bounds it is so capable of making amongst the rocks, and have the appearance of being bent under its body, as though always ready for a spring. The ears are roundish, erect, and set closely together. In colour it is a dark greyish-brown, which deepens on the quarters, and is slightly mottled on the sides with spots of a pale brown. Its pelage is thick, springy, and brittle, each hair having a crimped appearance about half-way along from its root. The hoofs are small and pointed, and the upper or false hoofs peculiarly long. The habit of this little animal of returning to the same spot to deposit its droppings, is curious; they are frequently met with in heaps, which must have taken months to accumulate. Some of these heaps are highly scented with musk, while others are quite inodorous, which leads one to suppose that each heap has been made by the same individual. This deer carries no horns; but the upper jaw of the male is provided with a pair of canine teeth, which grow to a length of quite two inches, if not more. As the buck only has these teeth, it is hard to say for what use they are intended, unless it be for fighting; but their rather loose setting in the jaw, and their fragile make, are against this theory. The does are so similar to the bucks in size and colour, that at a short distance it is almost impossible to distinguish any difference between them; consequently many of the former are destroyed unnecessarily. The musk is found in the male only, in a small bag under the skin, close to the prepuce. When fresh, the secretion is soft and moist, and of a brownish colour. Its smell is then rather offensive; but when it hardens and dries, the well-known odour of musk becomes so powerful as to be almost permanently transmitted to anything with which it comes in contact. On being taken from the dead animal, it is at once tied up tightly in a bit of the hairy skin that covers the gland, and is then called a "musk-pod." The musk-deer inhabits the high cold regions below the snow-line, where it generally affects thick rocky cover; but it is not unfrequently met with among bare crags, and occasionally about the highest tops of the middle ranges. The natives say it can travel over even worse ground than the tahr. Its cry of alarm is a kind of hiss. As musk is the principal ingredient used throughout the civilised world in the manufacture of most perfumes, a good musk-pod sells for sixteen rupees, or more. These little animals are therefore more sought after than any other game by the natives, who capture them mostly by snaring, in the following manner: A low fence is made of boughs, &c., along the ridge of a hill, sometimes a mile or more in length. At intervals of 100 or 150 yards are gaps. The musk-deer, crossing the ridge from one valley to another, come across this fence, and to save themselves the trouble of jumping over it, walk alongside until, seeing a little gap, they try to go through it. But in each gap a noose of strong string is placed on the ground, and tied to a stout sapling, bent downwards. The noose is so arranged that, when the deer tread inside it, the sapling is loosed and flies back, leaving the noose tied tightly round the animal's leg. The people visit these fences every two or three days, and secure the deer thus caught, and repair the fences and nooses, which are often carried away or destroyed by larger game.

The musk-deer I had shot was unfortunately a doe. Although not so good as a specimen, it was better for the pot than a buck, the flesh of which is apt to be tainted with the flavour of musk.

Snow now began falling in feathery flakes as we struck down into the dark forest of tall and straight black-looking conifers that almost invariably clothe the northern exposures of the higher ranges on the south side of the great snowy chain. Here the ground was thickly covered with old snow, in which the tracks of jurrow were numerous; but as the day was now growing old, and we had still a long way to go, there was no time to search for the animals that made them. It was tiresome work plodding through the snow, which in many places was knee-deep, until, lower down, we got clear of it. As we descended, the falling snow changed to sleet, and eventually to heavy rain. Although the rest of the way was comparatively easy travelling, darkness was setting in ere we reached our camp.

We had now descended again to the continuation of the beaten track used by the Tartar traders, which up here follows the course of the Kallee (or the Sarda, as it is also called) for a considerable distance farther up the deep tortuous valley through which that big impetuous river flows, forming the boundary-line between British and Nepalese territory.

Starting at daybreak, we followed the regular mountain-road for a few miles, until we reached a small village, built on a slope, near the foot of a spur of the Chipla, abutting on the Kallee. Here I breakfasted, made arrangements for replenishing our stock of supplies, and engaged fresh local guides and coolies for carrying the traps, preparatory to once more encountering the difficulties of the craggy heights of the Chipla, after tahr.

Farther up the valley of the Kallee, on the open grassy slopes just below the perpetual snow-line, are good grounds for " burrell" (*Ovis nahura*). But I shall leave these wild sheep and their haunts alone for the present, as we are now after wild goats.

CHAPTER VII.

ALTHOUGH the Chipla, as seen from a distance, appears to be
a huge solid spur abutting from the snowy wall behind it, on
a nearer acquaintance it is found to have, as may already
have been inferred, mighty spurs of its own, with noble
rocky amphitheatres and stupendous V-shaped valleys lying
between them. As you ascend these steep-sloping valleys
they gradually grow narrower, and their sides become more
precipitous until they reach the snow-fields on the heights
towering above them.

Up one of these steep spurs our way now led. To the left,
as we ascended, its southern face fell away abruptly, either
in a succession of irregular drops, like huge steps, or in rocky
rifts and gullies. As we mounted higher, these features
were exaggerated until they became broad and terribly steep
inclines, appalling precipices, and almost vertical rocky
gorges, terminating in landslips of rubble and *débris* running

far away down into the contracted depths of the valley below. To the right, the northern exposure was rough and rocky, and, as usual, clad with primeval forest.

We went ahead of the coolies up a kind of goat-track for a mile or two, when our village shikaree suggested that we might take a turn over the steep broken ground on our left, and look for gooral, which, he said, were likely to be found there. We had not to search long before one was started.

"Shoot quick! or he'll be away out of sight down the rocks," excitedly whispered the shikaree, as the animal he had suddenly detected, after going a short distance, stood for a few moments to gaze back at us. Although hurried snap-shots in mountain hunting are, as a rule, a mistake—for it is better to let an animal go free on the chance of getting another and better opportunity, than to risk missing and disturbing the ground by firing an unsteady shot—yet this one luckily told. The gooral which fell to it was fortunately stopped by some projecting rocks ere he had rolled down very far, which saved us much trouble in fetching him.

Rain, which for some time had been threatening, now began to fall. This made the steep slopes slippery and dangerous; we therefore thought it prudent to get back on to the ridge, where we soon overtook the coolies toiling up the winding track with their loads. Leaving the dead gooral in their charge, we again went ahead.

We were now nearing ground where, at any moment, we might chance upon tahr. For the wild animals in these high regions are very irregular in their feeding-times, and may be seen out browsing at all hours of the day, and more particularly in wet or cloudy weather, when there is no need for them to lie up for shelter from the heat of the noonday sun.

Some distance higher up on the spur we came to a kind of promontory that sloped down from it, and extended for some distance along the side of a rocky hollow scooped out of the steep mountain-side. In order to examine the precipitous depths of the hollow, into which we could not see from above, we crept cautiously down behind the promontory. As the shikaree, who was in front, slowly raised his head to look over, he suddenly drew back and whispered "tahr.". On the opposite face of the hollow, and slightly below us, not only were there five or six tahr on a narrow and steeply sloping terrace of short green grass that ran obliquely downwards across it, but there was also a small herd of gooral browsing unconcernedly not far from them, and both were within range for a longish shot. Singling out the tahr that looked the best, I waited until he was in a good position for taking him. As the report of the rifle rang out, his companions instantly made off, and scaling the impassable-looking rocks above them with the most marvellous agility, disappeared over the ridge on the opposite side of the hollow, without stopping to give a second chance. The one I had shot at seemed so badly hit, as he went hobbling away after them, that, feeling sure of eventually getting him, I at once turned my attention to the gooral. They looked very much perplexed, but did not move off until I had emptied my second barrel at one of them as he stood hissing out his note of alarm.

"He's hit too!" exclaimed the shikaree with great glee, as the animal contrived with difficulty to follow the rest of the herd over the ridge, some distance lower down than where the tahr had crossed it. Scrambling down the side of the promontory, we almost ran along the sloping terrace the animals had been on. In cold blood I should most probably have hesitated to cross it at all, for the incline was so sharp that a slip would have been fatal, and it was not until we were on it that I could see the profound depth of the abyss below.

The shikaree now climbed after the tahr, whilst Kurbeer and I took up the track of the wounded gooral. The ground, which would at any time have been bad, was now rendered frightfully dangerous by being very wet and slippery from the rain which was still falling. We had missed the track of the gooral, and I was carefully going along the brink of a craggy precipice, to which I thought the wounded animal might have betaken himself, with my gun ready to finish him with a buckshot cartridge, should I catch sight of him among the rocky ledges below. Kurbeer was some distance higher up, on a very steep incline of short grass rising immediately above me, searching for the lost track. Suddenly I heard a scuffling sound above. Looking upwards, to my horror I saw that the lad had lost his footing on the slippery wet earth, and was rolling and sliding down the slope, clutching frantically at the short grass with his free hand, for, notwithstanding his danger, he still kept hold of my rifle he was carrying with the other. At once I saw that his only chance lay in my being able to arrest his progress before he reached the brink of the precipice. I had scarce time to deposit the gun safely on the steep ground, in order to have both hands free, ere he was down within a few yards of me. Fortunately I happened to be almost directly below him, so I set my teeth, dug my feet as firmly as possible into the wet earth, and, holding my breath, stood ready to try and stop him, for I knew his life depended on my being able to do so. Another roll and he would have been over. Making a desperate clutch at him, I luckily got firm hold of his loose clothes, thereby checking his descent sufficiently to enable him to recover his footing, otherwise his weight and impetus must have taken us down together. All this, of course, happened in very much less time than I have taken to tell it; and my mingled feelings of horror and thankfulness at this narrow escape were such as to be not easily forgotten.

We now called a short halt to recover the tone of our nerves, which had naturally been rather shaken by what had occurred. But as any one who hunts properly over such mountains as these is often more or less exposed to dangers of this kind, it is best to keep the mind as much as possible from dwelling on them. We therefore were not long in resuming our search for the wounded gooral, and we shortly after came up with him where he had lain down, when I secured him with a shot-cartridge.

The shikaree soon rejoined us after having tracked the tahr into ground where it was impossible for him to follow farther. It was now getting late in the day, and we had still some very difficult ground to get over, so, the gooral being shouldered by the shikaree, we made the best of our way to the place where he had directed the coolies to make for. This was, as hitherto, a kind of open cave formed by the big rocks that overhung it. We reached this welcome haven just before dark, weary and wet through. The coolies had arrived some time before us, and there was a savoury odour arising from the cooking quarter, which was most grateful to us, tired and hungry as we were.

In the Himalayas, at this time of year, the atmosphere is often dim with a bluish gauzy haze, which gives the mountains, and especially the more distant ones, a beautifully soft and dreamy appearance. This effect is probably due to the air being permeated with thin smoke, caused by the old dry grass on the mountain-slopes being, at this season, so much fired by the villagers, in order that the young green blades afterwards springing up on the burnt ground may the sooner afford fresh pasturage for their herds. I have seen the same effect produced by the smoke from the forest-fires in the Rocky Mountains and the backwoods of Canada during " the fall," when a sudden change of wind will dispel it in an hour or two, and make the atmosphere as clear as ever.

This morning, however, when we made our early start, the air, from the rain of the previous day, was wonderfully bright and transparent, and every outline and feature of even the most distant ranges in sight stood out strikingly distinct and clear. And here I may remark that in these upper ranges, from being so close below the perpetual snows, you seldom get the same expansive panorama of the great frozen chain, even from a coign of vantage, as you have of it at a greater distance, when viewed from the middle ranges. But when you *do* get a glimpse of a colossal white mass towering above the black pine-forest and grey storm-swept crags, or through the rocky vista of some narrow gorge, or, best of all, an uninterrupted view from an open mountain summit, the prospect is far more imposing. In fact, a sensation something akin to dread is inspired on suddenly beholding the startling propinquity and overwhelming magnitude of so sublimely grand a spectacle as up here is often most unexpectedly presented to the wondering gaze. But let us resume our business on hand.

We had not gone much over half a mile from our cave when we descried some dark objects moving among the rocks away down below.

"They are bucks for certain, as they look so black," so say Kurbeer and the shikaree, as I proceed to adjust the telescope, using my iron-shod staff as a rest for it; and bucks they prove to be. Three or four only are visible, but others may be hidden by the rocks. If they remain where they are, we can pretty easily approach them unseen, though it will be more difficult to do so unheard. For when stalking animals from above on precipitous ground, be it ever so favourable as regards cover, there always remains the probability of detaching loose stones, and of making more noise in clambering downwards than upwards.

As my two companions, with bare feet, generally precede me in our down-hill stalk, they contrive to cleverly "field" the stones set in motion by my heavy nailed boots, and sometimes place a hand or a shoulder against a smooth rock, or drive the point of an alpenstock into the ground for a footstep below me, until at last we manage to get within easy range. The shot is a downward one; so aiming low, I let the best-looking buck have it. Off they all start, but the one shot at soon separates from the herd, and makes for the brink of a declivity just below. As he nears it he stumbles and totters, struggles to the edge, and toppling over it, disappears from our sight. Meantime the rest have stopped to look back, giving me a chance at another fellow with the second barrel, ere they take their final departure.

On our reaching the spot where the tahr had gone over, we find beyond a sheer drop of fully a thousand feet. As we crane our necks forward to look down, we can see what we suppose is the dead animal lying among a confused mass of broken rock and boulders beside the torrent at the narrow bottom of the valley, but from the colour being so similar to that of its surroundings, the aid of the telescope is necessary to make certain. There lies our tahr, but how to fetch him is now the question. As reaching him is impossible, unless by making a long round which would occupy many hours, we finally decide on leaving him for the present where he is, and straightway proceed to follow up the other buck I had shot at, and soon find plenty of blood on his track.

In the excitement of our stalk we had failed to notice that a scudding rack was fast overspreading the cloudless sky of the early morning. A heavy veil of mist, too, was now trailing itself up the valley, and rain soon began to fall. The traces of the wounded tahr were rapidly becoming obliterated by the fast-falling drops, and as the track lay over very bad ground, our experience of the day before made us rather chary of following farther in the wet, so we gave up the pursuit. The mist also had become so dense that we could hardly see a dozen yards around us, making it difficult even for our guide to find his way back to the cave, towards which we now turned our steps.

On the morrow the early morning again broke bright and clear, so our shikaree proposed that we should bivouac, for the night, higher up on the hill, where, after pointing out the

G

dead tahr to the men who were to fetch it, he was to rejoin us in the evening. As the way was rough and steep for laden men, and we might up there in some places find the snow lying deep, he recommended our taking only our blankets and ready-cooked food with us. It was late in the morning when Kurbeer and I started with one or two of the men who knew the way, to our quarters for the night. We had not proceeded far when one of those sudden changes, so common in the mountains, came over the smiling face of nature. The hitherto sunny sky became obscured with clouds, and our inveterate enemy the rain was soon falling heavily on us. We toiled upward, nevertheless, until we reached our destination, another cavity among the rocks. Here we made a big fire, for which we fortunately found plenty of wood at hand. At this we dried our wet clothes and blankets, and made ourselves as comfortable as we could under the circumstances for the night. The shikaree turned up before dark, and reported that the tahr had been recovered, but that one of its horns had been broken off at the root in its fall, and was nowhere to be found. This was a pity, but we were lucky in having got the animal at all, for the shikaree said the place above where it had fallen was such a tremendous "pakhān" (precipice) that it was as much as they could do to reach where it lay and get back with its spoils.

As soon as there was light enough to see our way, we were out next morning. The ground in this vicinity was covered with fresh marks of musk-deer, and the air was often redolent with the perfume from their droppings, although we failed to get a glimpse of the animals themselves. We flushed several coveys of snow-partridges, here called "zingooria," a bird something resembling a ptarmigan in summer plumage, and like it, in winter, I was told, becoming pure white. At this season it appeared, on the wing, to be a brownish-grey patched with white. Far away up the face of a bare acclivity near the head of the glen, we espied a herd of tahr. The intervening ground was for the most part extremely steep, but being craggy and broken, there was a fair chance, we thought, of our being able to get at them, so we resolved to make the attempt. We had got over more than half of the difficult stalk when the animals suddenly became restless, and soon moved hurriedly off over the ridge above. Possibly they had got a taint of us on the wind, which in the steep valleys and gorges among high mountains usually blows upward during the day, and downward during the night; but more probably they were warned of impending danger by their guardian angels, the moonals, several of which were whistling away as they sighted us from their commanding positions around. Their wild notes just then sounded anything but melodious, and our remarks respecting them were, I fear, rather uncomplimentary.

Having gone up so far, we thought we might as well continue our ascent to the ridge above, and prospect the country beyond it for game—as, being above the timber line, the northern exposure would at that elevation be as bare of forest as a southern one usually is at any height. Before we could reach the ridge, however, it was necessary to traverse an exceedingly awkward place. It was a very smooth slope at a fearfully sharp angle. Not the smallest excrescence was there on it for foothold. The ground was covered with a thin layer of fresh-fallen snow, just enough to make the footing slippery and treacherous. Below it the rocks fell away so precipitously that the consequences of a false step would have been too dreadful to contemplate. There were only some fifty yards of danger, but my nerves underwent a considerable amount of wear and tear before we got over them. Be it remembered, this was my first essay at hunting on the upper ranges. Hitherto I had thought something of my experiences on the gooral grounds of the middle ranges, until they were totally eclipsed by those of the vast heights of these upper regions; and such a place as we had now to negotiate might

certainly have been considered, to say the least of it, unpleasant, even by the boldest and most experienced of
cragsmen.

It is on these dangerous slopes where that trusty companion of the mountain hunter, the iron-shod pole, affords
such invaluable assistance, both as a support and for digging
notches for foothold in the hard ground or frozen snow. It
will be found more serviceable for the latter purpose if,
instead of the usual iron point, it is shod with a light
triangularly-shaped spud, having its lower edge about an
inch and a half broad. It is almost needless to suggest that
one of the party should always be provided with an axe of
some sort, and the common little "koolharree" (wood-hatchet)
which almost every hill villager, when out on the mountain,
carries in his girdle—usually a coil of rope to be used in case
of need—answers all hunting requiremeuts, as well as the
best of ice-axes. The sensation termed "giddiness" I have
never, in the literal acceptation of the word, experienced when
on dangerous ground; but I freely confess having felt what
is vulgarly called "funk." Perhaps, in this case, the terms
are synonymous. From constant practice, however, in mountain-climbing, one grows more confident in his feet, and more
callous in his nerves. But I have dwelt so long on the
danger of the mountain-slope, and the ideas suggested by it,
that, at this rate, we shall never reach the ridge.

At last we arrived at the crest, and found, as we expected,
that the northern slopes were, at this height, almost free of
wood, except some scattered birches, rhododendron bushes,
and broad patches of juniper; but the ground was in many
places covered with snow-fields. Soon, however, our view of
it became obscured by blinding snow-flakes that now began
whirling about us, so we struck down the ridge, which trended
towards our old quarters. There was still a chance of starting a musk-deer from among the birch and rhododendron
bushes, for their fresh tracks were numerous, but these were

soon obliterated by the falling snow, and not an animal did
we see.

Floundering down through the deep snow-beds was tiresome enough, but as descending the spur was much quicker
and less laborious work than ascending it, we reached our
cave much sooner than I expected. On arrival we found
most of its occupants in a complete state of prostration, and
suffering severely from the effects of having partaken too
freely of tahr-meat. The sky had cleared again, it was still
early in the afternoon, and being my last day on the hill,
after refreshing the inner man we once more set out.

We had made for the ground below, in the direction of the
place where we had lost the first tahr I had shot at in this
vicinity. Kurbeer was following me, carrying my rifle, when
suddenly I heard him hurriedly whisper, "There he goes! and
he's surely the tahr you wounded, for he's lame," as a big
buck jumped up from behind some rocks close to us, and
rattled off. Had I had the rifle in my hand I could have got
an easy running shot; and when I did lay hold of it, I waited,
thinking the beast would be certain to stand and gaze back.
But he had no intention of stopping, so I lost my chance.
Nota bene—always have your rifle in your own hands on
likely ground when you can, for many an easy chance is thus
lost by letting it be carried for you. We did not follow far,
for even had the tahr been our wounded one, there was now
no blood on his track. On our way back we saw a herd in
the distance, but the shadows were already deepening around,
rendering a long stalk impracticable.

At daybreak next morning, whilst the loads were being
packed preparatory to our descent to the village, I took a
stroll in search of moonals. These pheasants may often be
found, early in the morning, on steep open glades among forest,
scraping up the earth, probably in search of insects. By
stealing up under cover below them, a rocketing shot may be
got overhead, as they invariably fly downwards. In this

manner I bagged a brace of birds, and missed several others; and then, as it began to rain, we made direct for the village, without attempting to hunt on our way down.

We now commenced retracing our steps homewards. For several days our route lay along the valley of the Kallee. The roaring river surging along between steep forest-clad or rocky acclivities made the scenery wild and grand, but one's appreciation of its charms was considerably marred by the concentrated heat at that season in this low-lying narrow valley, and by the inclemency of the weather. A halt was made at a place said to be famous for jurrow and kakur. I saw many of the former deer, but all were hornless, the stags having just shed their antlers; I only shot a young male to provide meat for the coolies. I also killed a kakur, which was not found until the following morning, when, from the nature of the tracks in its vicinity, it was evident that a sounder of wild pigs had, unfortunately for us, discovered it first, and had made rather a *mess*, in every sense of the word, of its carcass. Had I then known that near this place there was a famous salt-lick close to the river, I might, had I cared to take advantage of it, have spared myself the trouble of perspiring over the baked hillsides of these low warm regions in quest of game.

These salt-licks, or *kar* as they are termed by the natives, which may be described as places where the ground is strongly impregnated with some sort of saline or alkaline matter, are here and there met with all over the mountains. In such spots large cavities may often be seen where the earth has been scooped out of the hillside by the animals partaking of the *kar*. In wild unfrequented parts where game abounds, I am told that animals can at times be actually slaughtered by watching these licks. An acceptable addition was sometimes made to our fare by Kalleege pheasants, which were plentiful along this route; although shooting them at that time of year was hardly fair. They generally, however, took good care not to let me kill many of them, even had 1 wished it. Close to the road I shot a hill-marten (*Martes flavigula*), called "chitrōla" by the hill-men. Its pretty skin is dark glossy brown on the back, head, and legs, and yellowish below. In length it is somewhat over two feet, including the tail, which is rather long and almost black. It was eating a dead bird, and even after being shot, it still retained its grip on a wing it had in its mouth.

We struck the route by which we had travelled upwards at the wooden bridge where we had crossed the river Goree. Here,- as I had brought my rod with me, I tried with a minnow for mahseer, but the water was far too big and dirty to be in fishing order. I might just as well have wetted my line in a soapy wash-tub.

One day we came across an encampment of Tibetan Lāmās [1] in their black blanket-tents. They were returning to their homes in "Hundés," as that part of Tibet lying beyond the mountain-passes of the Gurhwal and Kumaon provinces is called. A wild, queer-looking lot these Tartars were, with their flat, ugly, but good-humoured countenances, small eyes, pig-tails, and peculiar dress. The latter generally consisted of a loose garment of coarse woollen stuff of a dirty purplish hue, confined at the waist by a girdle of cloth or a belt. In this was stuck a tobacco-pipe, about 8 or 10 inches long, with a very small brass bowl, and mouthpiece of the same material. Depending from it was also a "chuckmuck." This useful appendage—which, together with the pipe, and a wool-spindle, these people are never without—is a steel attached to a small leathern pocket containing a flint and tinder. It is often ornamented with red cloth covered with open work of silver or brass, and fastened to the girdle by a leather thong or metal chain. The rest of their apparel consisted of long woollen boots, fastened below the knee, and soled with

---

[1] The sacerdotal class of Tibetan Buddhists are called Lāmās, many of whom are engaged as much in their temporal as in their monastic pursuits.

raw hide; and a small cap either of felt or woollen cloth, sometimes with fur-lined lappets for covering the ears. Some of these people were rather profusely adorned with rude ornaments, principally consisting of silver amulets, strings of large coral or other beads, and large lumps of rough amber and turquoise, either real or sham, worn round the neck.

The occupation of both sexes appeared to be spinning wool with their spindles, which, whether sitting or strolling, they kept perpetually twirling, even when tending their large droves of sheep and goats. These animals they use as beasts

Tibetan " Chuckmuck," for striking a light.

of burden, each carrying down from Tibet its little load of borax or salt in a small pair of bags, and returning with them refilled with rice or other grain. The heavier articles are carried on stout ponies, or on yaks — the bovine cattle of Tibet.

The women had very much the same dress and general appearance as the men, excepting a long narrow flap of cloth, extending from the top of the head down the back to below the waist, and ornamented with bits of amber, turquoise, coral, and cowry shells. They were strongly built like the men, but, as a rule, not a whit less plain in feature. The exceptions were two or three sturdy young girls, whose rosy cheeks and merry expressions gave their faces a pleasing look, which in a great measure compensated for their lack of real beauty.

In respect of the latter, the Tibetan lasses differ from their fairer but more frail sisters of the middle and lower Himalayas, many of whom are remarkable for their comeliness both of face and figure. The pretty style of costume worn by the Kumaon and Gurhwal hill-women at their "melas" (fairs) and other extraordinary and festive doings, adds much to their appearance. On such occasions they may be seen to the best advantage, decked out in their tight-fitting, bright-coloured bodices, and full flowing skirts, and loosely enveloped in a long piece of coarse printed muslin, part of which is wound round the waist and skirt, and the rest thrown gracefully over the neatly braided hair. Even when labouring in the fields, where they do as much as, if not more than the men, their dirty and work-stained appearance fails to detract from the rustic grace and beauty of some of these mountain damsels. It is rather strange that in the lower and middle ranges of the Kumaon district alone they should so much excel— though perhaps it may only be in appearance—the other sex, who are, in my opinion, physically as well as morally the worst specimens of humanity I have ever seen in the Himalayas. This is not surprising in a province where polyandrism is, I believe, rife amongst the inhabitants, and where leprosy and goitre are by no means uncommon. But I have still a word or two to say about our Tartar friends.

In mentioning their flocks, their canine guardians should not be forgotten. Two or three of the fine large dogs, known as Tibetan mastiffs, invariably follow the camp of these nomads. They are most excellent watch-dogs, and never seem to rest during the night, when, much to the annoyance of the weary traveller who may chance to encamp near, their deep-toned bark is incessantly heard. As some of these dogs are both bold and savage, a man or even a beast of prey would be rash in approaching a Tartar camp after dark; and, when protected by the strong iron-spiked collar they usually wear, they are quite fit to cope even with a marauding leopard.

Whilst resting and smoking my pipe beside a stream near this Tartar encampment, I was much entertained by watching a little by-play between Kurbeer and an old dame sitting there with a buxom, rosy-cheeked girl, who, I presumed, was her daughter, spinning wool. It was a fair example of the light-hearted character of these simple-minded people, which their droll honest faces do not belie, and of how they could enter into and appreciate a little fun.

As the women seemed familiar with the Goorkhali language, Kurbeer and they were able to converse freely together. From what I could gather of their conversation, and was afterwards told by Kurbeer, it appeared that the old lady, after satisfying her feminine curiosity as to whence we had come and whither we were going, among other things asked him if he was married. On learning he was single, she jocularly began recommending her daughter to his notice, telling him of all her domestic accomplishments and the advantages to be derived by taking her for a wife. At hearing all this the lassie in question at first looked rather coy, and would only occasionally take a sly sidelong glance at Kurbeer, who, having much the same Mongolian type of feature as herself, she probably thought a good enough looking lad in his way. However, on his addressing himself to her, she seemed nothing loath to reply, and they were soon on pretty easy terms, asking each other's names, ages, and suchlike questions. However this little flirtation might have ended, I was sorry to be obliged to interrupt it by proceeding on our way, for we had still far to go, and distant thunder and gathering clouds testified that a storm was brewing.

We reached the hamlet where we intended to camp, only just in time to seek shelter from one of those tremendous

thunderstorms, accompanied by big hailstones and a hurricane of wind, which are not uncommon at this season in these
mountains. The most terrific storm of this description I ever
experienced came on suddenly one afternoon, when I was out
after gooral on one of the middle ranges. Its approach was
heralded by a sullen and gradually increasing roar, until it
broke on the place where my village guide and I sat cowering
behind a rock to avoid its fury. The hail fell like bullets, and
the torrents of rain that succeeded it seemed to pour down in
sheets. The fierce gusts of wind were so strong, that had we
not been in some degree sheltered, I verily believe we might
have been blown down the steep hillside we were on. Vivid
flashes of lightning came in such rapid succession as to be
almost a continual blaze, and were accompanied by one incessant rising and falling roll of deafening thunder. The
latter, together with the howling of the wind through the
trees, the creaking of bending boughs, the hissing of falling
hail, and the roaring of water rushing down the steep gullies—
all combined to create a truly appalling din, such as none but
those who have witnessed a storm of the kind can conceive.
Next morning I came across numbers of large pine-trees that
had been uprooted and felled, whilst others were snapped in
two, like dry twigs, by this furious tornado, which lasted only
some twenty minutes, and yet within an hour or so after it,
the face of the heavens was as calm and serene as it had been
before it.

One more day's tramp brought this hunting-trip to an end.
It had certainly been an enjoyable one, notwithstanding the
inclemency of the weather and the comparative smallness of
the bag. But to the true lover of wild sport, who is always
an ardent admirer of nature as well, the mere slaying of his
game is certainly not what conduces most to his delight in his
work. For my own part, a feeling of regret has always been
mingled with my exultation, at seeing a beautiful animal I
have brought down lying lifeless before me, however incon-

sistent it may seem.   Nevertheless, it is very satisfactory to
make a good bag.   When I say a *good* bag, I mean one of
fine, and if possible, of varied specimens, and not made up,
merely for the sake of competition, of inferior animals, such
as a man of true sporting instincts would feel ashamed
to shoot at, unless he required meat for his camp.   I
have less sympathy with those who shoot only for the bag,
than with the downright old poacher; not the murderous,
skulking cadger of the present, who nets and snares for the
game-dealer, but a man of the bygone Highland stamp, who
stalked a fat stag or shot a brace of grouse quite as much for
the keen excitement of the sport as for providing venison for
his family and his friends.

Spring is certainly not the best time of year for tahr-
shooting.   The proper months are October and November,
when the old bucks have their shaggy hair much darker and
longer, and the toil in searching for them is lessened by their
being at that season lower down on the mountains, and asso-
ciated with the does.   The weather, too, is then sure to be
settled and fine, which, of course, adds so much to the pleasure
of hunting.   In fact, " the fall " is the best season for sport of
almost every kind in the Himalayas, as it is elsewhere.

CHAPTER VIII.

THE GOORKHAS AS SOLDIERS AND SHIKAREES—THEIR SERVICES DURING
THE INDIAN MUTINY—A BIG DRINK—GOORKHAS *VERSUS* TIMBER—
THE BHABER—SHOOTING THEREIN — JUNGLE FIRES — THE TĀROOS
—AN INQUISITIVE LEOPARD—HE PAYS THE PENALTY—A RIDING-
CAMEL — JUNGLE - FOWL — STRANGE BEHAVIOUR OF A LEOPARD—
MALARIOUS SWAMPS—FLORIKENS—THE NEELGHAI—RAVINE DEER
—BLACK BUCK—ENORMOUS BANDS OF ANTELOPE—THE HUNTING-
LEOPARD—METHOD OF USING IT—THE OUNCE—THE CLOUDED LEOP-
ARD—LEOPARD CHASING A WILD CAT.

A few words respecting the men who form a very small but
most valuable item of the army of the British empire, and
with whom it was my good fortune to serve for thirty years,
may not be out of place in these pages. As light infantry
soldiers the Goorkhas are second to none, and as shikarees
they are unequalled. Indeed their aptitude for the former
capacity is probably in a great measure due to their excel-
lence in the latter, for a good stalker must necessarily be a
good skirmisher.

On our return to the outpost I found that some of my
recruiting men had returned, bringing with them a lot of
wild-looking, sturdy lads, with round flat faces, small eyes,
bare feet, and hair hanging down to their shoulders. This is
the "Goorkhali," or Goorkha, as he is called in the service,
pure and simple—the rough diamond as found on the mountains of Nepal. When he has passed through the hands of
the barber, the tailor, and the drill - sergeant, after having

been cut, polished, and well set up by these regimental func-
tionaries respectively, he is turned out a smart little gem, so
to speak, of a soldier, with a sparkle of unpresuming swagger
about him, which is quite in keeping with his brave, independent spirit.

The men generally enlisted for the Goorkha battalions are
those inhabiting certain mountain provinces of the Nepal territory, a few only coming from the valley of Nepal proper,
which is chiefly peopled by the Newars, a race which was
originally conquered by the Goorkhas, and who are more of
a mercantile than a military class. The "Goorung" and
"Mugger" classes are those from which the best soldiers are
drawn. The Goorkhas show their Tartar origin distinctly in
their features, and they are almost invariably strong and stout-
limbed, but as a rule short. An idea of their stature may be
formed when I say that the average height of the battalion I
first joined was somewhere about 5 ft. 2 in. But their hearts
are as large as their frames are short and tough. Indeed,
their pluck and faithfulness to their "salt" have now become
proverbial. For example, I may mention their behaviour
during the Indian mutiny in 1857, when the Goorkha regi-
ments were among the comparatively few of the Bengal army
that were to be depended on. In that memorable year the
Sirmoor Rifle Battalion (now Prince of Wales' Own Goorkhas),
under the command of Major (now General Sir Charles) Reid,
was the first regiment, British or native, to take the field,
and the first to pull a trigger against the mutineers. And at
the siege of Delhi it formed a permanent portion of the main
picket on the "Ridge" in front of the camp, where it was
under the fire—morning, noon, and night—of nearly all the
enemy's heavy guns for three months and eight days. During
this period it assisted in repulsing twenty-six different attacks
upon the Ridge, besides taking part in two assaults on the
enemy's position, and had 327 men killed and wounded out
of 490 of all ranks that first took the field, as shown by the

regimental records. It was, indeed, a proud moment for the
Sirmoor Rifles when the Prince of Wales, during his Royal
Highness's visit to Delhi in 1875, addressed a few kind words
to them as they stood on the very ground the battalion had occupied during the siege. And had it not been for the stanch-
ness of the 66th (now 1st) Goorkhas, the European residents
at most of the stations in Rohilcund would, in all probability,
have met with the same sad fate as those at Cawnpore.

As the Goorkhas are encouraged to bring their families
with them from Nepal, many of them look upon their regi-
ments as their homes; and their sons, who, as they grow up,
are, if physically fit, always enlisted, know no other. These
lads, who are called "line boys," are often among the smart-
est-looking and sometimes the best men in their battalions.
Even when children, almost as soon as they have found the
use of their legs, they may constantly be seen marching about
in squads, with sticks for rifles, the band being represented
by one or two of the urchins, who have picked up some popular English tunes, strutting in front, and singing them at the
top of their voices.

The men join eagerly in all athletic sports and games.
Putting the stone is one of their national amusements, and in
this many of them excel. They are undoubtedly the best of
shikarees, numbers of them spending all their spare time in
hunting and fishing, of which they are passionately fond. On
one occasion I remember an old Goorkha commissioned officer
of sporting tastes entering his hack at some sky races, and
finding his own Goorkha jockey, who surprised the spectators
by cleverly winning his race.

I used to get up capital games at football with my recruits
at Shore. As some of these wild lads were rather hot-tem-
pered, their scrimmages were occasionally attended with slight
ebullitions of warm feeling. I once saw a lad with the head
of an opponent "in chancery," punching away unmercifully at
it with his clenched fist.

The Goorkha, although he enjoys his tot of grog, seldom commits himself by exceeding when on duty, but on festive occasions he may at times indulge rather freely. The amount of liquor some of their hard heads can stand, without being "overcome," is astonishing. In this respect, however, they are beaten hollow by the Bhotias—the half-breed (Himalayan-Tibetan) inhabitants of the high villages situated immediately below the snowy ranges of the mountain provinces of Kumaon and Gurhwal. I was told of a Goorkha having backed himself for a wager to drink against one of these half-bred Tartars—a trader at the Bagesur fair in Kumaon, where numbers of Bhotias and Tibetans annually assemble to barter their commodities. As far as quantity was concerned, the result was about a tie; but the Bhotia walked unsteadily off as the winner of the stakes,—which were the price of the liquor consumed,—apparently not much the worse for this big drink, from the effects of which the Goorkha never recovered. He had "caught a Tartar," and no mistake. On the winner being afterwards had up before the court that investigated the matter, and fined for the part he had taken in it, his defence was rather characteristic of the astuteness of the Bhotia trader. He said he considered himself to be the injured party, for it was hard enough on him to have lost his stakes, without being punished besides, as, the loser having died, he, the winner, had had to pay for the liquor.

With my long experience of the characteristics and merits of the Goorkhas, and the interest I consequently and naturally take in their welfare, I think I may presume to say that, with an army which must necessarily be composed chiefly of mercenaries, it behoves the Indian Government to make the Goorkha battalions as attractive as possible to such trusty and valuable soldiers. And one way at any rate, and an easy one, would be encouraging the men in their innate love for wild sport as much as possible, by allowing them free access to the Government forests, of course only during the proper season for hunting game. This would not merely add to their contentment, but from the fact of their being accustomed to using their own wits and weapons, and shifting for themselves when out in the jungles, it would also conduce to their intelligence and efficiency on active service. In the Dehra Doon, the Goorkhas have, for sixty or seventy years, been in the habit of wandering as they pleased in its forests, where they could always pick up a deer as a help for feeding their families, which, as I have said, they are encouraged to bring with them from Nepal. Now, I am told this hunting privilege has been virtually denied them by the forest department. The consequence of this arbitrary measure—which I know has been, to say the least of it, much deplored by the Goorkhas quartered there—will probably be an increase in the difficulty there always, more or less, has been in recruiting the already limited Goorkha ranks, not to mention the many evils that may accrue from the men being deprived of such healthy exercise and instructive amusement in their leisure hours. And, after all, what is the value of some sticks of timber, even though barefooted shikarees could possibly injure them, which I very much doubt, if they are to be conserved at the expense of losing the services even of ever so few of such excellent soldiers? Why, a single company of Goorkhas is, in time of need, worth more to the State than all the trees in the Dehra Doon forests.

As the Goorkhali is of very independent character, and is well paid and made much of in the army of his own country, he will naturally become averse to either entering or remaining in a foreign one if his tastes and usages are not equally well considered therein.

Trusting I may be excused for having made this digression in favour of the gallant little men who were my companions in arms and in wild sports for so many years, I will now resume my original subject.

Towards the end of October I left Shore with my recruits to rejoin regimental headquarters in the Punjab. It was with

H

much regret that I bade adieu to a country where I had passed such happy days among its forests and fells, for I then had no idea that I should eventually revisit it and enjoy a repetition of its wild sports.[1]

On arriving at the foot of the mountains, a week's halt had to be made, until the camp equipage for our march through the plains should arrive from the nearest arsenal. This delay I did not at all regret, as, through the kindness of my good friend the Commissioner of the district, I had obtained the use of an elephant, and thus had an opportunity, for the first time, of enjoying a little sport in the "Bhāber," as the vast forests of the Terai are here called. But at that season, from the undergrowth being so thick and high, game is much more difficult to find than late in the spring, after the long rank grass and tall reed-jungle has all been burnt down, except where patches of it, from being too green to ignite, have escaped the ravages of the conflagration.

It is in such isolated bits of cover, which are often wet and swampy, that tigers and other game may then be found, and more easily beaten out by a line of elephants.

This wild tract of forest and swamp, however, looked far more beautiful than had it been a blackened waste, as I have since seen it, after being devastated by the jungle fires, kindled by the Tāroos and others, to clear the ground for the young grass to spring up and afford fresh pasture for the large herds of cattle that graze there. Wild and impressive as these sylvan solitudes are, there is a monotony about them that, after a time, palls in a manner that mountain scenery never does.

The human denizens of the Kumaon Terai are, as a rule, an emaciated, wretched-looking set of beings, from the effects of malaria. And, strange as it may seem, if these creatures are deported from a climate which to most people is deadly, to a cooler, and, to others than themselves, a more salubrious one

---

[1] When I had the good fortune to be appointed to raise an "extra Goorkha Regiment" (now 4th Goorkhas) there, after the Indian Mutiny in 1857.

in the mountains, they generally sicken and die. These Tāroos, as they are called, from their knowledge of the ground and the haunts and habits of tigers and other game, are most useful to the sportsman hunting in these heavy jungles.

By dint of much ploughing with the elephant through this sea of long grass and dense jungle, I managed to slay some deer and wild pig; and shooting the latter there, where pig-sticking is impracticable, I did not consider poaching. I also bagged a fine leopard rather unexpectedly, in this wise : One evening I was on my way back to camp, jogging along a forest-road on the elephant, and was in the act of lighting my pipe, when I saw the animal creep stealthily across the road some distance ahead, and before I could dispose of the pipe and take up the rifle, disappear into the jungle. I naturally thought this was all I should see of him, and so resumed my pipe, when suddenly the elephant came to a dead stop. On looking over the howdah rail to ascertain the cause from the mahout, without a word he pointed to a patch of grass a few yards off the road. On following the direction of his hand, I could just see a small patch of spotted skin, but was unable to determine what part of the beast's body it covered. Losing no time, I banged straight at it, and at once had the satisfaction of knowing, from the savage growls of the brute, and his writhings among the grass, that I had inflicted a mortal wound. The elephant was driven close up to where he lay snarling at us, but quite incapable of doing anything else, when another bullet finished him. His curiosity had been fatal to him, for he had evidently stopped in the grass by the roadside to look at us as we passed.

As we jogged on campwards through the dusky forest, I once more lit my pipe, and this time finished it with a zest that was considerably added to by the satisfaction of knowing that I had the beast, which had twice interrupted my smoke, dangling behind the howdah.

I had purchased a riding-camel, as being very useful for antelope and other shooting along our line of march through the plains. Having returned one evening rather early from the jungles, I had mounted this animal with a view to testing its paces as well as my own power of adapting myself to them, for it was my first essay at camel-riding. I took my gun with me on the chance of getting a shot at jungle-fowl, as these game little wild bantams of Upper India are not only exactly like domestic ones in their appearance, but they also have a habit in common of scraping among horse litter on roads, or wherever they can find it.[1] I was returning in the gloaming towards camp, when I noticed the indistinct form of an animal, which, in the dim uncertain light, I took to be a deer, lying in the middle of a small open glade not far from the road. Telling the driver, who sat in front of me, to make the camel kneel down, I dismounted, and taking my gun, which was loaded with wire-cartridges, had soon crept along under cover of some bushes, until I imagined I must be pretty close to the animal, when I cautiously raised my head to reconnoitre. To my astonishment I found I was within twenty paces of a fine leopard. He was looking towards me, and whisking his tail from side to side. As I thought that a charge of shot would hardly do for a leopard, I slowly withdrew my head, and stealing back as quickly and quietly as possible to the camel, drew one of the cartridges and replaced it with a bullet. Although the brute must have been watching us all the time, strange to say he never moved until I had crawled up near him as before. I had cocked the gun and was slowly raising it, when, ere I had time to take aim, with a grunt and a bound he disappeared in the thick jungle close behind him. Jumping up, I ran after him; but it was useless, for I could see nothing in the impenetrable gloom of the

---

[1] This jungle-cock differs from that found in the more southern parts of India, which is of a general greyish colour, with the white-spotted hackles so valuable to the fly-dresser.

forest. As I remounted the camel, and bumped away on it back to camp, deep were my regrets at not having chanced a shot with the cartridge.

Along the outskirts of the forest, and between it and the cultivated plains, lies an extensive open tract of long grass and swamp. Here, besides other large and small game, florikens may be found in considerable numbers. But as that part of the Terai is, during the fall of the year, generally considered the worst for malaria (called "āwul" by the natives), we made a long day's march across this deadly belt and encamped beyond it; consequently, I was unable then to have a chance at these beautiful game-birds.

As my purpose in these pages is to confine myself to reminiscences of the pursuit of Himalayan game, I merely touch incidentally on the wild sports of other parts of India, concerning which, my experiences having been limited, I do not pretend to be an authority. With respect, therefore, to the shooting I had along our line of march, suffice it to say I got fair sport at antelopes, "neelghai," and sometimes gazelles, or "chinkara" as they are called, besides at many varieties of wild-fowl, snipe, and other small game.

The neelghai (*Portax pictus*), or "blue-bull," as the male is termed from his slaty-grey colour, and short, stout, bovine-like horns, gives but poor sport, except perhaps when he is ridden after and speared; for although he is a big clumsy brute, he is fleet enough to keep a horse going pretty fast to overtake him, sometimes even when wounded.

The little "chinkārā" (*Gazella Bennettii*)—which, from being generally found among broken ground and ravines, is commonly called "ravine deer"—affords excellent stalking, though it seems almost a pity to shoot such graceful little creatures. They are so delicate in form, and their colour—a brownish fawn—so much resembles the ground they usually frequent, that they look more like little phantoms than realities as they sometimes suddenly appear and skim away before you, and

often as quickly vanish in a ravine as though they had sunk
into the earth. A good buck's head makes a pretty trophy.
I have shot these gazelles in the Punjab, with horns close on
fourteen inches long; and, I believe, they rarely attain a
greater length.

The dark glossy coat with pure white trimmings, long
spiral horns, and elegant carriage of the male Indian antelope
(*Antilope bezoartica*), or "black buck," as he is usually termed,
makes him certainly the most beautiful of all Indian animals,
though perhaps he may be the most common—for these antelopes in some parts congregate at times in large bands, when
they may be counted by thousands together. But they are
usually met with in small herds, and often an old black
fellow is found alone.

By native potentates they are sometimes hunted with the
"cheetah," or hunting-leopard. The cheetah is conveyed to
the ground to be hunted over on a common native bullock-
cart, to which he is fastened by a strap round his loins, his
eyes being blindfolded with a kind of hood. The cart is
driven up as near as possible to a herd of antelopes. Should
the cheetah get restless on the cart, a lump of cheese or some
such stuff, with which his keeper is provided, is given the
beast to lick. On nearing the herd the strap is unbuckled,
his head turned towards his quarry, and the hood slipped off
his eyes, when away he goes. Should he fail in seizing an
animal after a few rapid bounds, he lies down and sulks,
making no attempt to follow it. If he has been successful,
his keeper bleeds the deer, catching the blood in a ladle.
Whilst the cheetah is occupied in lapping up the blood from
the ladle, the hood is slipped over his eyes and he is replaced
on the cart.

The hunting-leopard (*Felis jubata*) is quite distinct from the
common leopard (*Felis pardus*), or panther, as it is as often
called, and by the hill-men "cheetooa." The former animal
is more slightly made, lighter in colour, and its markings are

black spots—not rings, as they are on the skin of the latter—
and its claws are not so retractile as those of the panther.   I
have never heard of its being found in the Himalayas.   The
snow-leopard or ounce (*Felis uncia*), which is only found on
the higher ranges near the snow, differs from both the above
in having paler, softer, and longer pile, with its black markings less distinctly defined.   Another kind — the clouded
leopard (*Felis diardi*)—a very beautiful animal, which is, I
believe, found only on the more eastern Himalayan ranges, is
about similar in size to the common leopard.   Its black markings are more blotchy and irregular, and the ground colour of
its skin is darker and of a more greyish hue.

It may here be worth mentioning that I once, in the mountains, came suddenly upon a leopard in full chase after a
large sandy-coloured wild cat.   A feline animal hunting one
of its own species I considered rather singular.   Possibly its
intentions were more amorous than deadly.

Kookerie, or Goorkha knife.

CHAPTER IX.

" WHO has not heard of the Vale of Cashmere ? " Soon it may almost be said, Who has not seen it? for it is now becoming a regular resort of the tourist.

My first visit to the " happy valley " was during the reign of the Maharajah Gholāb Sing, to whom it had but recently been disposed of by the Indian Government, and it had then been only a few years " open to the public."

All arrangements in the way of travelling equipment, &c., for our trip having been completed, I started from Rawul Pindi in April, with a young brother-officer who, like myself, was an ardent lover of wild sport. My left arm had but a short time been freed from the bondage necessitated by a broken collar-bone, which I, however, hoped would be quite fit again ere I commenced rough mountain-climbing. There was little to interest us along the first part of our route, so we got over it as quickly as possible, our object being to reach our shooting-ground in the beginning of May, which is generally considered the best spring month for ibex-hunting. Earlier in the year, and particularly if it be a late one as regards snow, this sport is attended with considerable risk from the constant falling of avalanches; and the mountain-passes leading into the best ibex country are then difficult to cross, and sometimes not practicable before May. Later in the season, when the mountains are more free of snow, the ibex are higher up and more scattered on them, and consequently more difficult to find.

Every traveller by the Murree route to Cashmere must be as much struck as we were with the romantic beauty of that part of it between Uri and Baramoola, where, for the last eighteen miles or so before reaching the valley, the path winds through shady woods of deodar cedars, horse-chestnuts, and other grand forest-trees, or thickets of hawthorn and wild-rose bushes, where steep sloping acclivities and craggy pine-clad heights flank it on the right, whilst on the left the river Jhelum rushes by with a deafening roar, which resounds among the mountains rising lofty, and often snow-capped, on either side of the contracted and winding valley through which that splendid river here flows. The tremendous volume of water tears and surges along, in some places taking the form of a raging cataract, in others churning itself into broad sheets of seething foam. The Cashmerees have it that the beautiful Jhelum gives vent to these mad caprices by way of showing her wrath at being forced to quit their lovely valley, through which she flows so tranquilly. And should the wayfarer have an archæological bent, he can here find, half hidden among trees, and much overgrown by their gnarled old roots, some curious ruins—so ancient as to be of doubtful origin— to interest him as he rests by the roadside.

Nor can any one with an eye for the beautiful look unmoved on the charming scene that suddenly presents itself as he reaches the brow of the hill, whence the road slopes gently down to the pretty village of Baramoola.[1] How changed is the river Jhelum—now looking smooth and bright as burnished metal—where, as it winds tortuously over the green expanse lying below, it resembles a huge silver serpent issuing from the Woolar lake lying dark and blue along the base of the distant snow-crested mountains, among which square-topped Haramook towers like a hoary old giant above his smaller dependants.   And the numerous hamlets that are dotted over the verdant plain, what pleasing features of the landscape they present, as they lie embowered among groves of walnut and poplar trees, and grand old chenars (oriental plane), which latter, with their pale grey trunks, and summer foliage of brilliant green, constitute one of the principal ornaments of the Cashmere valley.

Before us, at last, lay the far-famed " Vale of Cashmere." There was music in the very name, which to our youthful minds conveyed ideas of the " nightingale's hymn," " love-lighted eyes," and everything enchanting.   And, truly, nowhere could a spot have been more aptly chosen for a poetic romance than the scene of " the feast of roses."   There is, however, a dark side to the picture of this lovely vale, for the fearful epidemics, famines, fires, and earthquakes with which, during my own recollection, it has so often been visited, and in some instances partially devastated, tend to show that it is not always a " valley of bliss."   But I am wasting time in thus descanting on the charms and woes of a country that is now so well known.

We did not give ourselves up very long to romantic ideas about the vale, as our thoughts were just then centred more in the ibex on its neighbouring mountains—so, having hired two of the picturesque-looking boats of the country at Bara-

---

[1] Since then earthquakes have, I am told, made sad havoc with this place.

moola, we at once started up the river, and reached Srinuggur next evening. At this quaint old wooden metropolis we made a short stay to complete a few final arrangements, and to engage shikarees before proceeding to Wurdwan—a wild, remote district eastward of the valley. The Wurdwan mountains, which are now so well known to sportsmen, were generally considered the best ground for ibex. Early in the spring, whilst the winter snows still lay low down, ibex might, at the time I write of, have been found on the hills rising immediately above, and north of the Cashmere valley; but the old bucks receded with the melting snows to higher and more distant solitudes.

With regard to engaging shikarees at the capital, subsequent experience taught me what a mistake I had made in doing so, as those worthy of the name seldom come there to seek employment, but remain at their homes, which are generally near the hunting-grounds, until sent for. But as the country and its language were then new to us, we were obliged to at once engage men as guides and interpreters.

And now a word regarding Cashmere shikarees in general, for I have no doubt most of them are no better at present than they were then. With few exceptions, even the best of them are an avaricious grasping set of men who are never contented,—in fact, the more you give them the more they want. But the arch-scoundrels are the fellows that pester the new arrival at Srinuggur with numerous testimonials they may have received from tourists or others who have managed to slay a few black bears under their guidance, which animals any ordinary villager might have shown them where to find. These pseudo-shikarees are usually "made up" in sporting costume, wearing *puttees* (woollen bandages) round their legs, *poolas* (straw sandals) on their feet, and belts covered with leathern pouches, hunting-knives, &c., round their waists. They are, or were, as a rule, the most unmitigated impostors in Cashmere, generally giving themselves all sorts of fine airs, and expecting the most exorbitant wages, besides food and presents of cash. In addition to this, they frequently use their employer's name for obtaining anything they require from the villagers, for which they usually forget to pay. The real good men, of whom there are comparatively few, are only to be got by making arrangements with them beforehand, either by messenger or letter. As such men are, of course, in great request, obtaining their services is not always easy. Should the sportsman, however, fail to get a well-known good shikaree, it is better for him to proceed to his ground without one of any sort, and trust to picking up a non-professional hand at some village in its vicinity, than to engage one of the aforesaid impostors, who, in any case, would get what guidance and information he wanted from a villager, whilst he, the impostor, pocketed the profits. Although these remarks may not be very entertaining, they may be useful to a sportsman visiting Cashmere for the first time.

Of course we were soon surrounded by these rascals wanting service, and as at that time we knew no better, engaged two. My companion was more lucky in his choice than I was in mine, as his man turned out to be a great acquisition; the one I engaged proved the very reverse. Again taking to our boats, we continued our course up the river to Islamabad.

For some distance above Srinuggur the windings of the Jhelum are so tortuous as to form a succession of pear-shaped loops, so to speak, of water. There is a legend in Cashmere that the idea of the loop-like pattern, so common in Cashmere shawls, was originally suggested by the appearance of the river thus winding through the valley, as viewed from the top of an eminence near the city, on which stands the ancient temple called Takht-i-Suliman (Solomon's throne).

Islamabad we reached next day, and after inspecting its tanks, teeming with sacred fish, and collecting men to carry our traps, at once went on to the village of Shangus, about eight miles distant. At this place we purchased a supply of rice for our followers, as we were told that food for them would not be procurable in Wurdwan. Here also I was lucky enough to secure the services of a well-known shikaree. This man's demeanour was totally different from that of the sham one I had had the misfortune to already engage. Ramzan Meer was a grave, taciturn, little old fellow, very much addicted to snuff, and was not, at first sight, either in appearance or costume, the sort of person one would have taken for the first-rate hunter he really was. He was dressed in the loose wide-sleeved garment of light woollen cloth commonly worn by Cashmerees, which reached almost to his feet. His waist was girt with a white *kummerband* (sash), without so much as the knife, invariably carried by Mohammedans, visible, and his head was loosely wrapped round with a huge white and very clean turban. But there was something about his eyes which spoke volumes. The Srinuggur man was, on the contrary, a noisy hulking fellow, got up in the conventional impostor style, with belt bristling with sporting appurtenances, and who was continually boasting of his exploits with his former employer, and what he now intended to perform with his present one. Nor was Ramzan, though a good man and true in many respects, quite " straight " where his own interests were concerned, for I learnt from a brother sportsman I afterwards met in Wurdwan, that he (Ramzan) had a prior engagement with him, by letter ; but thinking, I suppose, that " a bird in hand is worth two in the bush," he had taken service with me. I owe it in gratitude to this *true* sportsman (an officer then belonging to the 27th Foot), to record that, on my hearing the facts of the case, and offering to give the man up, he generously refused to deprive me of his valuable services. And here, as a sample of the dangers which sometimes attend mountain hunting, I may also chronicle a narrow escape that this same sportsman told me of his having made shortly before I met him. He and his men were after a herd of ibex, and had but just crossed a steep gully, when a tremendous avalanche of rocks and stones thun-

dered down it. Not many yards ahead was another gully
they would have to cross, but ere they had recovered from
their astonishment, to their dismay a similar avalanche rattled
down it also. Most probably both had been the result of a
landslip far above, which had, in some providential manner,
been diverted to either side of them in its descent, or they
must have been swept down by it.

Our next day's tramp was, at first, across a low range covered with wood, and then up the valley of Nouboog, to a little
hamlet consisting of a few log-built huts, much resembling
the ruder kind of Swiss châlets. The scenery of this long
narrow " strath," as it would have been called in Scotland, or
" nye," as it is here termed, is surpassingly lovely. Flanked
on either side by high hills, on which broad tracts of deodar
cedars and tall sombre-hued pines alternate with rocky steeps
or green sloping glades, it extends up towards the Mergun
pass into Wurdwan. Mulberry - trees, weeping and pollard
willows,[1] overhang the clear brawling stream that meanders
through it, between banks of velvet-like turf. Here and there
along the base of the mountains, picturesque groups of log-
built houses lie nestling among groves of grand old walnut
and chenar trees. Early in summer an additional charm is
lent to the beauty of this glen by the ground being carpeted
with both red and white clover, and by the wild indigo plant,
which grows there in great profusion, being in flower, its
purple blossom looking, at a distance, like luxuriant blooming
heather.

As we wended our way upward the prospect each moment
grew more charming. Over the dark pine-forest and green
birch woods rose the bald grey crags and snow-covered crests
of the range we were about to cross before entering Wurdwan,
their rugged features all softened by a delicate blue haze.

[1] Willow-trees, which grow abundantly in the Cashmere valley, are generally
cut down into pollards, the young shoots being stored and used as winter fodder
for cattle.

The lovely scenery of Nouboog Nye is the more indelibly impressed on my memory from my having, in after years, passed many a happy day hunting the " hangul " (Cashmere stag) in its forests, which were then, whatever they may be now, a favourite resort of this noble animal during the autumn and winter months.

Shortly after starting next morning, as we neared the head of the Nye our surroundings assumed a much wilder character, and the path became more and more steep. The latter now led close beside the stream, which up here took the form of a rushing torrent as it dashed over rocks and fallen pine-trunks that lay in and across it in the wildest confusion. After pitching our little tents on a small grassy flat a short distance below the pass, there being still several hours of daylight left, we took our rifles and sallied forth, each in a different direction, with our shikarees, on the chance of getting a shot at a deer or a brown bear, either of which animals Ramzan said might here be met with.

Judging from the fresh tracks, hangul must have been pretty numerous, although we saw none. And even had we found a stag, he would most probably have been hornless, as these deer have generally shed their horns by the end of April. As for brown bears, I had ocular proof of their being plentiful there, for I saw five. First we espied three together, but they had unfortunately got our wind, and were in full retreat. Just as it was getting dark we saw two others eating the green grass on an open space at the bottom of a gully flanked with birches. By the time we got near them, the light was so bad that I was unable to see the fore-sight of the rifle, but the loud response made by one of them to my shot, showed that it had told. The beast, however, made off with its companion, and it was too dark to follow it up.

As the snow on the pass would be easier for our laden men to travel over when hard frozen in the early morning, we were off again at the first break of dawn. The ascent to the

pass, though short and comparatively easy, was nevertheless
pretty steep and rough.   Silver birches now took the place of
conifers, and still higher, tangled masses of juniper bushes
spread themselves widely over the open hillsides, which were
craggy, broken, and here and there covered with patches of
snow.   On the pass, which is 12,000 feet high, where our
track was almost level for some distance, the snow still lay
very deep, and we often sank up to the knees in it.   Several
times we had to wade through a half-frozen stream, from
the cold of which our legs were tolerably well protected by
the *puttees* that were bound round them; but our feet, on
which we wore only *poolas* over our stockings, suffered
terribly.   Fortunately the sky was overcast with clouds, for,
on the higher ranges, if the eyes are not protected with a coloured veil or goggles, the sun's glare off the snow frequently
causes temporary blindness, which sometimes lasts for several
days.

We saw numbers of marmots, here called "drin," among
the loose fragments of rock that had slipped from the flanking heights, and were piled together in confused heaps, off
which the snow had partially melted.   The creatures, on observing us, would sit up on their hind-legs and utter their
shrill, chirping cry, like a loud dog-whistle blown sharp and
short, which sounded quite eerie as it broke the frozen stillness around.   They frequently let us approach within small-
shot distance, but if not shot quite dead, they instantly dived
down among the interstices of the rocks, from which it was
impossible to get them out.   These marmots are considerably
larger than the Alpine ones.   Their general colour is yellowish below, and reddish-brown intermixed with black above.

After crossing the pass, a little episode occurred which
shows the folly of two men attempting to hunt over the same
ground.   As it was still early in the day, Ramzan suggested
that we might take a turn down over some steep craggy
ground below our route, where he said we might at this early

season chance to find ibex. My companion and I therefore proceeded, as we thought, in quite different directions in search of them. Having discovered a small herd, Ramzan and I were attempting to stalk it, when, on peering downwards over a rock, to our surprise we saw that my chum and his shikaree were doing likewise. They were directly below, and between us and the ibex, which now, becoming alarmed, moved off without either of us getting a shot.

After a long and steep descent, where we had, in some places, to keep a sharp look-out for detached rocks and stones rolling down from the heights above, in the evening we reached the village of Unshin, in Wurdwan. Here we learnt that four sportsmen had already crossed the pass, and had taken up their hunting localities, with which we were in honour bound not to interfere. As three of them had gone up the main valley northwards, and only one had gone down it, we decided to proceed in the latter direction.

The following day, after proceeding about six miles down the valley, I struck up a steep narrow glen to the left, whilst my companion went straight on with the intention of hunting over the mountains above Mārroo Wurdwan further eastward. A rough walk of several miles up the glen brought us to the spot where Ramzan proposed pitching our camp for the night. Next day was Sunday, and never can a day of rest be more appreciated than when hunting among such mountains as these.

On Monday morning, as we were proceeding up the glen by the side of the torrent that tumbled impetuously down it, Ramzan, pointing upwards, quietly remarked in a casual sort of way, "There are bears up yonder." He evidently considered bears—which were in those days so very numerous among these Cashmere mountains—to be almost beneath our notice when we were after ibex. There they were, however, two of them, feeding on a green grassy slope some distance above, and I had no idea of letting them off without a shot if I could

I

help it, and more especially as I had not up to that time
killed a brown bear, or, as it is sometimes called, a snow-bear.
Taking care to keep well to leeward, we easily got up to
within a few yards of them; for although these bears, like
all their tribe, have a marvellously acute sense of smell, their
eyesight is comparatively defective—so much so, that when
occupied feeding, one might almost approach them behind the
cover of their own hairy bodies, if not to windward of them.
The first shot was planted well behind the shoulder of the
nearest beast, which went trundling head over heels down
the hillside, until it fell into the torrent below, where we
afterwards found it in a deep pool. Before the other fellow
had recovered from his astonishment, the contents of my
second barrel were into him. With a loud grunt he started
off downwards, but before he had gone very far we could see
that his race was nearly run, for he showed certain symptoms
of approaching dissolution. I was the more satisfied at having shot these two beasts right and left, because, even if a
lucky fluke, as it probably was, it impressed old Ramzan with
the idea at the time, however erroneous it might afterwards
prove, that his endeavour to show me ibex might not be quite
fruitless, and he, consequently, would be more likely to take
pains to find them.

The Himalayan brown bear (*Ursus isabellinus*) or " Kooneea
Harpat," as it is called in Cashmere, usually inhabits the
cold regions of the higher ranges near the snow. But being
omnivorous like the black bear (here called " Seeah Harpat "),
it is often found as low down as the Cashmere valley, which
is only 5000 ft., where it grows fat on fruit and grain, and
even carrion, for which latter it has a great predilection, when
it can find it. I once shot a big brown bear in the Cashmere
valley while the beast was in the act of devouring the putrid
remains of a dead cow. In spring, after waking up from its
winter snooze, it carries little or no fat, its food then chiefly
consisting of green grass, which may often be seen regularly

cropped down by bears as if cattle had been grazing on it. The colour of this bear is usually a yellowish or isabelline brown. In some cases the shade is very much darker than in others, and the long soft pile often has a silvery tinge on its extremities, but its colour and length vary very much with the seasons of the year. In the month of May the skin is in splendid order, but later on in the summer it is not worth the trouble of taking off. Although these bears often attain a large size, some of them measuring as much as 7 feet in length, and standing well over 3 feet at the shoulder, they are not as a rule very pugnacious, although a cantankerous customer may sometimes be met with. It is always unadvisable, however, to shoot at any kind of bear that may be directly above one on a hillside, for the first impulse of a bear on being hit is to rush or roll straight down-hill, and whether the beast means mischief or not, it is apt, in its flight, to claw anything it may come across. Bears used to be so common in the Cashmere mountains, and might be got with so little trouble, that, when after ibex or suchlike game, the sportsman seldom laid himself out much to shoot them.

We skinned the bear that had succumbed on the hill, and then descended to the stream. With some difficulty the other beast was extricated from his bath, and after a like operation had been performed on his wet coat, we went on to the place where we next intended to camp farther up the glen.

The night came on stormy and boisterous, and next morning the surrounding heights were so coated with fresh-fallen snow as to make stalking almost impracticable. About noon, by which time the heat of the sun had melted most of it off, we went out, and soon sighted a herd of eight or nine ibex, but none of them were large old bucks. We tried an unsuccessful stalk over some abominably steep snow-beds, where it would have been difficult to travel without straw sandals, which give wonderfully firm footing on steep rocky ground

or hard sloping snow. These sandals, or *poolas*, as they are
called, are made of thin rope of twisted rice-straw, and when
that is not procurable, of grass, or twisted strips of thin wet
bark. As they only stand at most one day's hard walking, a
great many pairs are worn out, but the Cashmerees can make
a pair in an hour or so.

For the next day or two the rain, snow, and thunderstorms
were so incessant, and the mist clung so constantly to the
mountain-sides, that hunting was impossible. One night the
lightning flashed so continuously, and was so instantaneously

followed by deafen-
ing peals of thunder,
that I sometimes felt
half inclined to get
up and remove my
guns from where
they usually lay
under my camp-bed;
and the sleet and
hailstones that pelt-
ed on my little tent
seemed almost as
though they would
be driven through

A pair of Poolas.

the canvas by the force of the keen cold blast that came
howling down the glen. We made an attempt next morning to go up after ibex, but were soon beaten back by a
blinding snowstorm. I wounded a bear that had wandered
close to our camp, but lost him. To add to our troubles,
I found that our stock of rice was getting exhausted, and a
man I had sent down to fetch more from Mārroo, the nearest
place where it was procurable, had returned without it.

A consultation was now held, when it was agreed that we
should make for Mārroo, by a way known to Ramzan over
the heights at the head of the glen we were in, hunting *en*

route, and after having there replenished our stock of provisions, return to our ground. We accordingly moved the camp on somewhat nearer this pass, intending to cross it next morning.

I fired several shots at a bear we came across on the way. Although the poor brute went off leaving the snow crimsoned with blood, he baffled our efforts to overtake him. We saw several others that we did not manage to circumvent. By this it will be seen how numerous brown bears at that time were; and before these hunting-grounds became so accessible to sportsmen, they had been much more so, and were then, I was told, the bane of the shepherds, amongst whose flocks they constantly committed depredations. Sometimes they even attacked ponies, large numbers of which are driven up from the Cashmere valley during the summer for the grazing on the higher mountain-slopes, which, on all high ranges, are often much less precipitous than the intermediate ones.

I once witnessed a rather curious proceeding with respect to these ponies at the time they were up on these grazing-alps. It was here the custom to administer, once or twice during the grazing season, a large dose of salt to each pony. As most of the animals, owing to their long freedom from all restraint, were next thing to wild, catching them was no easy matter. To accomplish this, some of the more tractable and most sure-footed beasts were mounted by men, who were each provided with a lasso. This they used very expertly, and their excitement was worked up to the highest degree by the sport. Real sport it was and no mistake, and somewhat dangerous withal, as the riders heedlessly rode their animals barebacked over such break-neck slopes after the semi-wild ones. On a pony being lassoed, it was at once thrown, and after about half a pound of salt had been crammed down its throat, it was again set at liberty. The reckless riding of these men over such a country, without coming to utter grief, was truly miraculous. I must say I had not such confidence

in my own horsemanship as to make me wish to join the
sport, exciting as it appeared.

The wretched weather had shown no signs of improvement,
until towards evening it began to clear up; so, whilst our
camp was being pitched, I started out for a stroll up the
bottom of the glen in hopes of getting a shot at an old Bruin.
We had not to go far ere we espied three in company, but
they managed to wind us before we could get within half a
mile of them. Soon, however, we find another—a monster
that looks like an ox as he grazes on a small grassy flat beside
the stream that runs down the glen. He is in a good place
for a stalk, and this time the wind is right. Under cover of
some detached blocks of stone strewn here and there about
the ground in his vicinity, we easily approach him within
twenty yards or so. The first shot, which is aimed, as I
imagine, well behind the shoulder, strikes, probably, too low,
for it only sends him off with a loud angry *wugh.* The second,
catching him in rear, has merely the effect of accelerating
his flight and making him grunt again. Away he shambles
across the stream, and then takes straight up a steep-sloping
snow-field, dyeing it with blood, until presently he begins to
show decided signs of distress. Without waiting to reload, as
I should have done, Ramzan and I start in pursuit with the
other rifle he is carrying. Under cover of a depression in
the snow - bed, running up parallel to his course, we soon
overhaul him, when I ply him with a third bullet. Loss of
blood now begins to tell, for this time he only makes a whining remonstrance, and after moving on a few paces again
pulls up. The contents of the remaining barrel elicit another
testy reply, as he slowly turns round and stands glowering
about him in a manner that seems to bode mischief. Luckily
for us, he has as yet neither seen nor got wind of us as we
crouch low behind the snow-bank. The business now begins
to get awkward, for we are very close to the brute, and below
him; both rifles are empty, and I have stupidly left the am

munition with the other shikaree, who has considered it prudent to remain below, and with whom we dare not com-
municate lest the bear may detect us—and judging from the
surly glances he casts around, he is quite prepared to make
himself exceedingly disagreeable should he catch sight of us.
Ramzan, in a smothered whisper, suggests that as the beast
looks "bobbery," as he expresses it, we should make ourselves
as small as possible behind our cover, and thus await the
issue of events. Like pancakes we, therefore, continue to lie
flat, merely raising our eyes carefully now and again for a
peep, until at length, as his strength fails him, he begins
sliding slowly down the slippery incline. Immediately he
reaches our level, up we jump, and with a view to getting
well above him, take to our scrapers upward, for we can see
he is now too far gone to charge up-hill after us, though he
makes abortive attempts to do so. We can now shout to the
man below to bring up the ammunition by a circuitous route,
so as to avoid the bear, which is still quite capable of doing
damage down-hill, and on its arrival a quietus is administered
to this tough and ugly customer—a huge male, and, I think,
the biggest brown bear of the many I saw in these mountains,
and I am certain I never killed a larger. We left the defunct brute as he lay, sprawling on the snow, it being now
too late that evening to perform his obsequies.

So much snow had fallen overnight, and was still falling,
on the heights above, that crossing the pass next day was out
of the question; so, by way of employment, I accompanied
the men who went to skin Bruin. We had hardly set out,
when on came the snow again heavier than ever. Nearly
two inches must have fallen ere we returned from our task,
during which we nearly perished with cold.

All day, and all that night, snow fell almost incessantly.
By morning it lay so deep that my little tent was half-buried
in it, and could scarcely support its weight. My native followers had contrived to make themselves pretty snug by con-

structing little huts of bent birch-boughs covered over with
birch-bark, and were doubtless warmer and more comfortable
than I was in my tent. Cashmerees generally manage to
keep themselves warm in the coldest weather with their
kangrees (small earthenware bowls covered with basket-work),

which they fill with red-
hot ashes, and, when
either sitting or lying,
place under the long
sack-like gowns, which
are invariably worn by
both sexes in Cashmere.
There was now barely
sufficient food for two
days left, and I was be-

Cashmere " Kangree" or fire-basket.

ginning to think that, if the snowstorm continued, we should
have to pay another cold visit to the dead bear—this time
for meat. Under such circumstances there was nothing to
be done but to retrace our steps down the glen, and make
for Mārroo by the lower route, for Ramzan said it would now
be as useless as dangerous to attempt the upper one.   Indeed,
from the ominous rumbling sounds which were occasionally
heard in that direction, we could tell that avalanches were
falling there; so we struck the camp, and commenced plodding down through the snow.

Although we started at daylight, and the distance was not
very great, we did not reach the foot of the glen until evening.
What a wearisome trudge it was, too, with the cold sleet
beating pitilessly down on us as we floundered through the
deep soft snow! The shikarees and myself had enough to do
in helping the coolies along with their loads, until lower
down we got clear of it.   Shortly before reaching our camping-place, we came across a fine brown bear, which I managed
to slay with one bullet. This was some compensation for the
hard day's work.

Next day we reached Mārroo, a cultivated little valley containing several villages, and surrounded by lofty, precipitous mountains, our way to it having led down beside the rapid broken stream which flows through the grand main valley of Wurdwan, and forms the principal affluent of one of the five great rivers of the Punjab, the Chenab.

Having found fairly comfortable quarters in the open wooden balcony of a house at Mārroo, I determined to remain there until the weather became more settled.. After a day or two it began to show signs of improvement, when Ramzan suggested our making a short move to a place farther down the valley, on the heights above which, he said, we should be pretty certain to find ibex at that season. Whilst fixing up our camp there under some fine old trees, we were apprised, by the sudden rustling of the leaves overhead, the oscillation of the ground under foot, and a mysterious rumbling sound, that we were experiencing a sharp shock of an earthquake.

By dawn next morning we were breasting the hill, and after a stiff and steady climb reached the ibex haunts about noon.

" Look! there are khel up yonder, just below the snow ! " said Ramzan, as his keen, practised eye soon sighted a herd of some six or seven ibex far away above us; and with the spy-glass we could see that amongst them was one patriarchal old buck. They were all taking a siesta on a rocky ridge that ran down from the bare crags and snow-fields on the upper part of the range.

" The *bundobust* (arrangement) will be very difficult, for there is no way of getting above them," remarked Ramzan, as he proceeded to gird up his loins with the skirt of his long woollen gown, whilst he carefully scanned the intervening ground. A sudden change had come over his usual listless air. His hitherto impassive countenance brightened up with intelligence and excitement at the prospect of circumventing an animal he considered worthy of a difficult stalk, or *bundobust* as he termed it, and he now became as active and wary as a wild cat, whilst we cautiously approached our game.

By means of his clever *bundobust*, then—for stalking ibex from below is always a difficult business—we at length got within what I imagined to be sixty yards or so of the big buck, as he lay on a small projecting ledge of ground almost directly above us, with his head and shoulders showing over it, his splendid knotted horns sweeping grandly backward against the sky. He seemed so close and so large that I thought it unnecessary to raise any sight. Cautiously placing my cap on the top of a rock as a rest for the rifle, I aimed point-blank at his chest, fully expecting to see him, the next moment, roll lifeless from his perch. But, to my amazement and concern, he jumped up and disappeared like magic, before I had time to think of giving him the contents of the second barrel. When we next sighted him, he was well out of range, though I chanced another shot at him as he now took his way slowly but steadily up the mountain-side.

My anguish at that moment is impossible to describe. An almost irresistible inclination to fling the empty rifle after him suddenly seized me, as I helplessly gazed at his retreating form. To make matters worse, my companions would keep repeating, " Oho ! what a pity ! he *was* such a big khel ! " accompanied by that well-known but indescribable sound made with the tongue and teeth, indicative of disappointment, thereby aggravating me to such a degree that I fear I must have used very hard language towards them.

Still clinging to the faint hope that the ibex might perhaps show symptoms of being wounded, as he had separated from the herd, we continued to watch him as he traversed a broad snow-field, on which, in the distance, he looked like a fly on a whitewashed wall, until he at length disappeared over the crest of the range, where it was to us inaccessible. My attention had been so much engrossed by the big buck that I failed to observe what had become of his smaller companions.

With a heavy heart I now climbed up to inspect the place where the ibex had been lying, when the distance to it was found to be much greater than it had at first appeared. The bullet had struck just under the spot from which the animal had risen, and, after perforating the ground he was resting on, had in all probability entered his stomach. This perhaps accounted for his starting off in such a hurry, and separating himself from the herd, such being very unusual with ibex that have not been much disturbed, if unwounded. I had misjudged the distance, owing to my having, at that time, but a vague idea of the size of a full-grown buck ibex. Such a misfortune as this would not, however, be likely to occur with the flat trajectory rifles of the present day.

The full-grown buck ibex of the Himalayas (*Capra sibirica*), or khel, as it is called in the mountains of Cashmere, and more eastward on the Himalayas "skin," stands about 3 feet 6 inches at the shoulder, and is very stoutly built. Its general appearance, haunts, and habits are much the same as those of the Alpine "bouquetin," or "steinbok," but it attains a much larger size of both body and horn. The colour of the ibex is not easily described, as, like that of most wild animals, it alters considerably at different seasons of the year, and some bucks are very much darker than others. In the spring it is a very dirty white, shaded off on the shoulders and flanks into a brownish grey, which merges into brown on the legs. A brown line runs along the back, ending in a very dark-brown short tail. The head and neck are reddish brown, and a nearly black beard, about 6 inches long, depends from the chin. Late in the season the dirty white becomes more decidedly brown. Under the rough outer coat grows a soft kind of down known as "pushum," which, like that of the domestic goat of these mountains, is used in the manufacture of the finest of Cashmere fabrics called "pushmeena," of which the shawls are made.

The general appearance of the magnificent curved and

knotted horns of the ibex are well known. But they are often misrepresented in drawings of the animal as sweeping high over the back, instead of merely curving over the shoulders as they in reality do. The doe is much smaller than the full-grown buck, and her colour a light reddish brown. She carries thin stumps of horns, which seldom grow longer than a foot, whereas those of the buck sometimes reach a length of 50 inches or even more, and a girth of quite 10 inches at the base. A crease round the horn denotes its yearly growth, not the knobs on its anterior surface, as is often supposed.

From what I have seen and heard of ibex, their sense of smell is not nearly so acute as their sight. But they seldom apprehend danger from above, so it is best to approach them, if possible, from that direction. During the spring and early summer, they may be seen feeding at almost any time of day, on the green patches of herbage, among the higher crags and snow-fields, only taking a siesta for a few hours at a time. In the dead of winter they are found much lower on the mountain-sides.

Provided they do not see the hunter, they are not always scared away by firing, probably from their being so accustomed to hearing the noise of falling rocks and avalanches. And sometimes they get so bewildered by the echoes of a shot, that they give time for several easy chances before making up their minds to be off. If one of them, however, catches only a glimpse of anything suspicious, a warning whistle at once sends off the whole herd, although they often depart very leisurely even after being shot at.

Ibex sometimes congregate in large numbers, but they are usually found in flocks of from six or seven to twenty or so, the older bucks often herding separately, except during the rutting season. Despite the quantities that are shot, killed by avalanches, and by those terrible foes to all Himalayan game, wild dogs, there appears to be little decrease in their numbers on the more sequestered hunting-grounds; for they are very prolific, each doe having as a rule a pair of kids every summer. The villagers sometimes train their dogs to hunt them down, when the ibex become so stupefied with terror that they are then easily approached and shot.

I asked old Ramzan if the popular legend about ibex leaping down from great heights and alighting on their horns was current in those mountains, and was much struck with the intelligence of his reply. He said that ibex, when hard pressed, would sometimes jump down almost incredible distances, and on their fore-feet touching the ground, their horns, from their great weight, were thrown forward, causing them to appear as if the animals had intentionally alighted on them. This, he thought, might perhaps have given rise to the idea.

Although ibex are so numerous, finding old bucks is often very chance work. Sometimes the sportsman may have to toil away for many days, or even weeks, without getting a shot at them. But if he is in luck, he may knock over four or five fine old fellows in as many days. The Himalayan ibex is tolerably plentiful in certain localities as far east as the province of Spiti, but is not found eastward of the river Sutlej.

Another variety of ibex (*Capra caucasica*), which I have never seen, inhabits some of the mountains of Western India, in Scind, but I am told it is very similar to the ibex of Western Asia, the horns of which are slighter and less closely knotted than those of the Himalayan kind; and the so-called ibex of the Neilgherry hills in Madras (*Hemitragus hylocrius*) appears to be totally different from both the above, with short horns more resembling those of the tahr.

But to return to the pursuit of the animal. The day after our disappointment with the big buck was devoted to hunting over another spur of the range, but nothing was seen except a couple of does. We had tasted no venison since entering Wurdwan, so I resolved to try for one of them to supply meat for camp use. As the stalk was rather long and

difficult, the trouble it cost us to get a shot was hardly repaid
by the flesh, which at that season is dry and tough.   In fact,
my instincts for the time being were like those of the man
who, as the story goes, whilst stealing up to some wild-duck,
regretfully remarked to his companion in the stalk, "By
Jove! we've got no lemons,"—more gastronomic than sporting.
Our work, however, had so sharpened my appetite that no
sauce was, in this case, necessary for assisting it.   So we
skinned and cut up the ibex where it had fallen, made a fire
of dry juniper sticks, and cooked some strips of the liver on
the embers.   This frugal repast was done ample justice to,
despite its having no seasoning but the wood-ashes that stuck
to the frizzled meat.

On our return to our quarters at Mārroo next day, we
found that all the supplies collected for me had, during our
absence, been appropriated by a man who was catering for the
similar requirements of some other sportsman in Wurdwan.
So we had to wait until more could be procured before proceeding to pastures new.

CHAPTER X.

THE mountains on both sides of the Furriabadee river, and around its sources, were at that time considered about the best of ibex grounds, and probably they are so still, for there are sanctuaries among them to which the ibex can betake themselves, and where no human foot can follow.

The Furriabadee, which drains the snow-fields and numerous glaciers about its sources in Sooroo, joins the Wurdwan river at Mārroo, whence we now directed our steps up its magnificently wild valley. After proceeding about seven miles, we pitched our camp beside a fine hot spring, in which I enjoyed the luxury of a warm bath. From the semi-civilised evidences about this wild romantic spot, I judged it must have been considered a sort of Leukerbad by the good people of Mārroo; for over the stone tank of steaming warm water, there was a construction of neatly-squared logs, with an upper half-open storey, where the invalid bather could rest after the bath, and enjoy the grand prospect and salubrious mountain air without feeling the cold. In fact, Ramzan informed me that such was the intention.

Although not an invalid, the refreshing effect of a warm bath certainly made me feel more fit to climb the steep hill-side next morning. After a long ascent, however, I was not sorry to sit down and search the ground with the spying-glass, when we soon discovered a herd of ibex about a mile off, and far above us. None of the animals were very big old bucks, but as some of them carried fairly good horns, we arranged for a stalk. By the time we neared the place where we had first sighted them, they had moved off into very precipitous ground, where they were masters of the situation, and were soon lost to view. As it was impossible to follow them, on account of a wide intervening chasm, we concealed ourselves among the rocks, and there waited for several hours, until they reappeared and commenced to feed.

As we lay there, hoping that they would shift their ground to where it might be more practicable for a stalk, it was interesting to watch them through the glass. Some were feeding leisurely on the patches of herbage among the rocks, whilst others lay resting their horns on the ground, or amused themselves by having a playful tilt. But I observed that there was always a sentinel, generally a doe, on the watch for danger. As the sun was getting low, and we were far from camp, I was at last most reluctantly obliged to shut up the telescope and leave them to their gambols.

Whilst descending we discovered two brown bears feeding on the opposite side of a deep wide gully. They were a considerable way off, but I longed to hear the "crack" of my rifle again, so, at the risk of getting benighted, we proceeded to look them up. They were on an open slope, but by dint

"ON THE WATCH."

of constantly tossing up bits of dry grass to try the wind, which, as is usual among mountains, was very shifty, we managed with some difficulty to keep to leeward of them. On reaching the place where they had at first been seen, there was only one now visible. To him I contrived to creep close up, as his attention was engaged in sniffing about and turning over the stones with his paws in search of insects, when a single bullet, planted well behind the shoulder, sufficed. After a few whining grunts and vain efforts to turn round and bite at his wound, he rolled over to rise no more.

Leaving one of the men to skin him, Ramzan and I now proceeded to search for his companion, which we concluded must be somewhere near, as she had not been seen to make off. We soon discovered her some distance farther down, and apparently quite undisturbed by the shot that had deprived her of her mate, for she was busily engaged grubbing after roots; and working on either side of her were a pair of cubs, which we had not before observed. As they were on very bare ground, and as we had this time the nasal and visual organs of three animals instead of one to take into account, it was impossible to get nearer than a hundred yards. At first I felt somewhat loath to disturb this interesting family party, which I continued to watch for some time, until its members began to show signs of uneasiness in their minds by every now and then sitting up on their haunches and suspiciously turning their noses towards us. As I considered the youngsters quite big enough to take care of themselves, I aimed deliberately at the old lady and let drive; she rolled a short distance down the hill, and, after a few struggles and grunts, expired.

The two cubs at first merely stood up on their hind legs and gazed about them with much apparent astonishment. But on seeing their mother lying motionless below, they at once ran down to her, when their behaviour was such that I felt quite sorry I had shot her. The anxiety they plainly

K

evinced,. as they ran grunting and sniffing about their
defunct parent, was quite touching to behold. Even on
observing us as we approached they seemed very unwilling
to leave her. When they at last made up their mind to do
so, they merely retired into an adjacent patch of wood, where
they continued their whining lamentations, occasionally venturing out a few yards to stand upright and watch us as we
ruthlessly stripped their dam of her hairy coat, and did not
take their final departure until we gave chase, thinking we
might capture them. Although they were too small to shoot,
they were quite knowing enough not to allow themselves to
be caught.

By the time we had finished skinning the bears, the short
twilight had deepened almost into darkness. As we had still
far to go, we got benighted on the hill, and had some difficulty
in finding our way down to a small hamlet. Here we procured torches made of bits of resinous pine-wood, and, with
their light, soon reached our camp about a mile farther on,
after having been on the hill for sixteen hours.

As I knew that my shooting chum and another sportsman
also were hunting somewhere higher up the valley, we could
not proceed much farther in that direction without trespass-
ing on their beats. After a consultation with Ramzan, he
recommended our moving only a few miles farther on to a
place where there were two or three log-huts, the highest
habitations in the glen, and then striking off on to the range
above them, where he thought we should be pretty sure to
find big bucks. Leaving the tents where they stood, some
blankets and other necessaries for passing a few days on the
hill were rolled up, and the same evening we reached the
huts. A fine brown bear, which we came upon shortly after
leaving the hot spring, was summarily disposed of.

Accompanied by a guide from the huts, next morning we
were far up the mountain-side ere the sun topped the multi-
form crests rising along the ridge of eternal snow and lighted

up such a sublimely grand prospect of fell, forest, and flood
as could hardly be surpassed.   Immediately on either side of
the foaming torrent that roared sullenly below and filled the
valley with a sullen resonance, the mountains rose in rugged
precipices, rocky amphitheatres, and abrupt spurs towards
the huge naked crags and shining snow-piles that stood out
in awful magnificence and with surprising distinctness
against the deep blue morning sky; two mighty twin-like
peaks, Noon and Koon, shooting up among their less lofty
neighbours to a height of over 23,000 feet above sea-level.
Glaciers lay in the hollows between some of the higher spurs,
whilst broad fields of glistening snow filled the head of the
main valley.   Farther down it the steep mountain-sides were,
above, bright with green birch-woods, below, dark with vast
tracts of sombre-hued pine-forest, which here and there
seemed as if rent from top to bottom, where long lines of uprooted and broken pine-trunks, masses of earth-soiled snow
and *débris*, marked the course of avalanches that had recently
swept down from the towering heights into the blue depths
beneath.   Not even among the finest scenery of the Alps
have I ever seen anything to surpass this view in beauty, or
to equal it in grandeur.

The traveller who visits merely the sanitaria on the outer
ranges, or even the Cashmere valley itself, beautiful as it is,
can have no conception of the magnificent scenery of the
higher ranges in close proximity to the perpetual snows.   In
fact, speaking comparatively, excepting a distant view of it,
he can hardly have seen true Himalayan scenery at all.

Early in May the Furriabadee river can usually be crossed
on natural bridges of hard snow.   Later in the season these
give way, when the torrent has to be bridged at some narrow
place by throwing a few tree-stems across it.

But whilst I have been admiring the prospect, Ramzan has
made good use of the glass, and has espied a herd of ibex far
away among the crags above.   After planning our stalk we

commence working towards them, but the ground we have to get over is in many places so difficult that we are several hours in approaching them. We are constantly employed in cutting steps in the hard slippery snow, where we are often obliged to cross steep fields of it, and on which the result of a slip might be unpleasantly doubtful. After a time, however, one gets accustomed to such places. Moreover, they often at first appear worse than they really are, for if the crust is hard and the notches well cut, a fair cragsman, with a little care, is almost as safe as though he were walking along "the shady side of Pall Mall," if his nerves would only allow him to believe so. But there are certain conditions of these snow-slopes when crossing them becomes ticklish work. I have never heard of the rope being used by sportsmen in the Himalayas, as game is not usually found above the limit of vegetation, unless driven to seek safety in higher and less accessible regions; therefore, being tied to your companions need seldom be resorted to as an absolute necessity in Himalayan hunting.

At last we get to within 150 yards or so of the place where the ibex are now reposing in a little corrie. But the best bucks are hidden from view, and we cannot get nearer without being detected. After waiting patiently there for an hour or more, and calculating with much satisfaction upon the certainty of, sooner or later, getting an easy chance, we are much surprised at hearing one of the beasts sound its alarm-whistle; for we are well hidden from them, and the wind is right. But we soon discover that the animal's keen vision has been attracted by something below, which it is intently watching, and after a few minutes we have the mortification of seeing the whole herd slowly walking away up the hill. Both rifles are emptied, and apparently without effect, for the animals still continue steadily to ascend without increasing their pace, until they disappear over the crags some distance above.

On turning our attention towards the cause of their disquietude, we descry a small white speck moving up the hillside, far away below. To our intense disgust, the spy-glass shows it to be the big white turban of the impostor, who had been left behind to clean and stretch the skin [1] of the bear I had shot the day before. The useless idiot was now following us straight up the hill, without the slightest attempt at concealment. If he could only have heard the Cashmerian " Billingsgate " applied to himself and his kindred by my two companions, they would not have felt flattered, and I did not bless him myself.

We now climb up to the place where the ibex disappeared, and are astonished to find one of them lying wounded among the rocks just beyond it, but on seeing us it instantly jumps up and makes off. I let drive a flurried shot after it, and miss. Whilst following this animal we find blood on the tracks of a second, and as they are larger than those of the first, we follow them up until the declining sun warns us not to risk being again overtaken by darkness so high up on the hill. We therefore descend to a small cave where Ramzan had proposed we should pass the night.

The greater part of next day was occupied in tracking the wounded animals, but they had betaken themselves to such bad ground that at length it became impossible to follow them any farther.

For nearly a month had I been perspiring over these heartbreaking hills, and I was now beginning to think that such profitless toil was only vanity and vexation of spirit, and that these infernal ibex were merely a delusive wile of some mocking demon of the mountains who was amusing himself at my

---

[1] The simplest way to temporarily cure a bear's skin is to peg it out on the ground and cover it with white wood-ashes from your camp-fire. These should repeatedly be rubbed into the skin with a rough stone. The paws, lips, and roots of the ears should have a little salt rubbed into them, and the cartilage of the ears should be skinned as far up as possible, otherwise the hair is apt to fall off.

expense. So disheartened had I become from persistent ill-luck and bad shooting, that it needed a good deal of persuasion on Ramzan's part to induce me to continue our pursuit of the beasts; for fatigue, disappointment, and bad weather combined, were beginning to tell on my powers of endurance and patience. "Try just a few more days, and our luck may change," said the old man. Indeed he appeared so anxious to cheer me up that it seemed almost as though he had some presentiment of coming good fortune.

Again we were toiling up the steep acclivities of the range which is known by the very appropriate name of "Dook" (trouble or pain). We had hardly been gone an hour when a herd of large old bucks was suddenly descried in comparatively easy ground for a stalk. In a second we were all prone on the earth; but there was a troubled look about Ramzan's face as he lay beside me anxiously watching the animals, and my spirits sank to zero when he whispered, "They've seen us." The glass was at once brought to bear on them, for they were a considerable distance above us. There were six, all of them carrying splendid sweeping horns, and to my inexpressible delight I discovered that, for once, the old man was wrong, as, after a short time, one of the beasts lay down, and his example was soon followed by his companions. Inch by inch we cautiously wormed our prostrate bodies backwards until we reached the edge of a gully, in which we were hidden from view of the herd, when Ramzan relieved his feelings of doubt by taking a huge pinch of snuff.

By following the long and steep windings of the gully, we at length got within easy range of the animals. My sagacious old companion, after carefully reconnoitring their position, then sat down, and with a most self-satisfied air again applied himself to his snuff-box, at the same time suggesting that, as the ibex would be pretty safe not to move for some time, I should wait for my nerves to get steady, and until I recovered the breath I had lost during our scrambling stalk. He then produced an apple from the capacious pocket of his long woollen garment and gave me it to eat, a practice common with him on such occasions.

How quickly my heart throbbed, nevertheless, as I cautiously peered from behind a rock at those six beauties, whose horns all looked so equally large that I was at a loss to choose which to shoot at. As the nearest offered the best chance, I levelled at his chest, which was towards me. The report of the rifle was instantly followed by a tremendous clatter as the six animals sprang to their feet and galloped away, apparently scathless, barely giving me time to take aim with the second barrel, which was emptied at one of them just as they were disappearing over a ridge.

I was speechless with vexation. No language, however strong and expressive, could at that moment have relieved my harrowed feelings. Even my Cashmeree companions seemed this time to respect my silent woe, for they gave vent to none of their usual confounded ejaculations either of disappointment or condolence. But the looks of contemptuous pity for my performance they cast towards me were just as hard to bear, making me feel half inclined to " loose off" both barrels—fortunately they were empty—at them, and then fling myself, rifle and all, headlong among the rocks below. I was very much younger and less experienced in human nature then than I am now. Poor innocent men! I should have known that they were only deeply lamenting the loss of the meat, and not pretending to commiserate my misfortunes.

When my frenzied state of mind became calm enough for me to think and act like a rational being, I came to the conclusion, judging from the tremendous pace at which the animals had made off, that either my chum or the sportsman in the Zaj nye ground, on the other side of this range, must have had something to say to them before me, and that, after all, matters might perhaps not be so bad as they seemed. Whilst I was impatiently reloading, Ramzan, who had run forward over the ridge to mark the herd, now reappeared on it, and, to my infinite relief and joy, shouted back that one of the ibex had dropped just beyond it. But, on getting up to him, I was again rather taken aback by the rueful expression of his countenance.

"Why, what's the matter?" said I. "It's all gone wrong," replied he, with a rapid succession of his exasperating interjections of disappointment. "What's all gone wrong?" I asked, with much anxiety and a little irritation, wondering what could possibly have happened now. "The khel, he's all spoilt," he testily answered. Not knowing what on earth to expect from all this, I proceeded, in a state of bewildered suspense, to where the buck had dropped. There the beast lay, stone dead, jammed between two rocks, and a bullet-hole in his chest testified to his being the first animal I had shot at. "Look!" said Ramzan, almost weeping, "he's quite dead, and all that meat is lost." What had happened began now to dawn on my perplexed mind. The ibex had expired before the old man had had time to bleed him. Consequently, according to his idea, the flesh was useless, for, of course, no good Mohammedan could eat of an animal which had not had its throat operated on by a follower of the Prophet with all customary form before the pulses ceased to beat, and Ramzan Meer was an extra-devout old Moslem.

My recovered energies were at once devoted to following up the second animal I had shot at, as, from the fact of our only observing four of the six bucks taking their way over the snow-fields far away above, we concluded that he too must have been hit, and so sorely as to be unable to keep up with the rest. But, unfortunately, we could find no traces of him to guide us, so we returned to flay the dead one.

A pleasing reaction now came over my feelings, and I really think that this was one of the proudest moments of my life, as I sat there smoking my pipe and admiring the massive and perfect horns. At last I had attained the object of my ambition and toil, and what I at that time coveted above everything.

After stripping the ibex of his head and skin, I reluctantly had to leave most of the meat for the bears and eagles—as the Cashmerees would not eat of an animal that had not had the "hullal" duly performed on it—and descended to a small sheltered plateau where we intended to bivouac for the night.

Towards evening, as we sat preparing the head, a man I had sent up to watch what remained of the dead ibex—in case of a bear getting a sniff of the meat—came tearing down the hill, gesticulating as he ran, and, on nearing us, breathlessly ejaculating "Khel! khel!" When his excitement became more subdued, we learnt from him that he had seen a large herd of ibex on the hillside above, and only about half a mile off. Sharp is the word. The covers are at once slipped off the rifles, and we are not long in reaching the place whence the animals had been sighted, when, sure enough, there they are, about sixteen in number, and two of them grand bucks; but the ground is bad for approaching them. As they are feeding towards us, we wait patiently there until, at length, a keen cold wind most opportunely begins to blow towards us, driving them all down for shelter into an intervening corrie, and bringing them within a longish range of our position. During all this time Ramzan, in half-suppressed pious expressions, keeps incessantly imploring the assistance of the Prophet. But now one of the does, becoming suspicious of danger, gives her warning note. There is no use in waiting longer, as the whole herd at once begins moving slowly off; so I single out the finer of the two big bucks, which in a few seconds falls rolling and struggling down the hillside. "Shabash!" (bravo) exclaims Ramzan. "Now for the other big one." A bullet speeds after him, but from want of "straight powder" he gets off uninjured. The men are determined this time not to lose *their* spoils, for they reach the fallen buck almost before the echoes of the last shot

cease rolling and reverberating among the crags and precipices, when they bleed him with all due form. Leaving two
men who had followed us to break up the ibex, Ramzan and
I descend to our bivouac, from whence we send them a flam-
ing pine torch to light them down after finishing their work,
for by this time it has grown almost dark.

It was with a light heart and a keen appetite I that evening despatched my frugal meal of broiled ibex - meat and
"chuppaties" (thin cakes made of flour and water). After a
"nightcap" of hot whisky-toddy and a few puffs of tobacco
beside the fire, notwithstanding very tough venison, and a
hard couch under no roof but the starlit sky, I was soon
ibex-hunting in dreamland.

We were astir next morning before the stars had ceased to
twinkle in the cold grey dawn. Leaving directions for having our limited amount of *impedimenta* taken down direct to
the hot spring, I started with the two shikarees, intending to
work over the hill above and rejoin our camp in the evening.
What a miraculous effect a little luck in hunting has on both
body and mind! How different were my feelings this morning as we climbed the craggy acclivities of Dook. There was
now not a thought of its toils or troubles; in fact, to per-
petrate a vile pun, it was no longer "dook" to me, and on
reaching our camp after a long day's hard work without
having seen a hoof of any kind, I felt as crisp as possible.
How delicious and refreshing was a draught of "lussee"
(butter-milk), and how I revelled in the warm water of the
spring, for truly I was in need of a good scrubbing. Ample
justice, also, was done to a more civilised repast than any I
had partaken of for some time, and to which I had brought
down an acceptable addition in the shape of wild rhubarb,
and several other esculents that grow on these mountains.

After ridding myself of the pesterings of the impostor, who
was perpetually demanding "backsheesh" for his worse than
useless services—by discharging him—we retraced our steps

to Mārroo. From thence I proceeded with Ramzau, and a couple of men carrying a few absolute necessities, up the south side of the Wurdwan river to a place called Passer, the heights above which were then considered to be a sure find for ibex. As we purposed to spend only a day or two there, the tents and heavier things were sent on to Unshin by the regular route on the north side, by which we had come down. In those days I used very often to "rough it" when there was no occasion for so doing, as was the case in this instance. Since then I have learnt that to court inconvenience at any time, when it can be avoided, is a grand mistake. In mountain-hunting, however, it may often be absolutely necessary to dispense for days together with many of one's comforts. Towards evening, on reaching Passer—a place represented by one log-built house picturesquely situated on an eminence near the river—it began to rain heavily. As it threatened to be a wild night we took shelter in this châlet, the kindly people to whom it belonged having done their best to clean up a small room in it for my accommodation. Never shall I forget the utter misery of that night. Oh, the rapacity of the myriads of fleas that infested the house! At daybreak I arose with my whole body covered with a rash as it were from their bites, and with my bones all sore from tossing and tumbling about on the hard uneven boards of the floor, as I vainly endeavoured to sleep. How deep and long were the— well, for brevity's sake I shall call them *regrets*, I gave vent to during that terrible night at my folly in not bringing my tent, which in this case I might easily have done. All next day the rain continued to pour, and the mountains were completely enshrouded in mist. To make matters worse, there was nothing for it but to choose between spending the night out in the rain, or again submitting to the torments of passing it among the F-sharps inside: of the two evils I chose the latter. Besides this, we had almost come to our "last split-pea," so we straightway took the route to Unshin. A tiresome tramp

it was too in the rain, along slippery slopes, and through
long wet grass and brushwood.

After a day's rest we recrossed the Mergun pass. The
snow had almost entirely disappeared from its summit, which
was now clothed with short green turf, thickly besprinkled
with buttercups, their bright colour presenting a strange and
pleasing contrast to the savage aspect of the bare grey rocks
and partially snow-clad heights on either side.

From the top of the pass I made a *détour* over the mountains, on the chance of finding a brown bear, as well as for
the purpose of visiting some curious tarns. The largest of
them, called Choar-nāg, must be nearly a mile in circumference, and from the look of its dark, sullen water, in which its
stern surroundings were reflected as in a mirror, I judged it
must be very deep. These mountain-tarns—or "nāgs" as
they are there termed—which are sometimes met with on the
Himalayas at very great heights, are regarded by the hill-men
with a certain amount of superstition, and usually there are
supernatural tales current concerning them. The Cashmerees
believe them to be the haunts of evil genii in the shape of
huge "nāgs" (snakes), which were at one time worshipped in
Cashmere. Early in the season, whilst the winter snow still
reaches almost to the margin of the evil-looking water, the
aspect of this wild mountain-basin is indeed eerie and lonesome enough for fancy to people it with any number of hobgoblins. And certainly, when contemplating the desolate
grandeur of such a spot, begirt as it is with a wilderness of
naked crags and stupendous snowy piles, which rear their
pale, spectral-looking crests solemnly aloft against the dull
blue-black sky peculiar to high altitudes, a vague sense of
mysterious awe steals over the beholder as he gazes on the
dreary waste around. The dead impressive silence, too, that
usually pervades these frozen solitudes is only emphasised
by being ever and anon broken by those intermittent blasts
of howling wind which are wont to come sweeping over them,

and gradually die away among the distant recesses of the mountains with a mournful sighing monody, which seems to the wrought-up imagination almost as though it proceeded from some sad invisible spirit lamenting over the utter desolation of its abode. But to return to the material denizens of these wilds.

The shaggy coat of another brown Bruin was added to my peltries. A long shot was also chanced at a friend that was with him. The bullet struck high, but it must have astonished his weak nerves, for the brute, much to our astonishment, gave a loud grunt of fear, and trundled itself heels over head several yards down the hill before continuing its flight.

On reaching our first camping-place in "the Vale," I was told that black bears were numerous in the vicinity, they having come down into the mulberry groves to feast on the fruit, which was then—the month of June—in full season. Although this kind of sport is rather tame after mountain work, it is by no means to be despised. I therefore determined to devote a day or two to looking up Bruin in his feeding-grounds. The first morning I failed to get a shot, although I was very close to one fellow, where he had ensconced himself among a lot of thick bushes, which effectually covered his retreat as he bolted. Next time we went out I had better luck, when I secured the only bear we saw, after putting several bullets through his black hide. The same evening we found another munching away quite at his ease in a mulberry-tree, when a ball sent into his back as he stood up stretching out his paws to gather the fruit, brought him down with a loud "yeeough" from the tree, at the foot of which we found him dead, his mouth full of mulberries, poor beast! A leopard was also seen at dusk by Ramzan as it slunk away through the bushes quite close to us.

After two or three days at this kind of work, I bade Ramzan good-bye for the present at his home, and made straight for Srinuggur, intending shortly to return to Wurdwan, as I concluded that a few of the sportsmen who had hitherto occupied some of the best hunting localities there would then, perhaps, have vacated them, thereby giving us a more un-limited choice of ground.

One of my first excursions on arrival was with a view to getting thoroughly cleansed at a hummām, kept by a queer character then well known in Srinuggur, as barber to the European visitors, and dentist, chiropodist, and general prac-titioner as well, among the citizens. As may be supposed, old Mirza's establishment was not fitted up with that luxu-rious elegance one finds in Jermyn Street. Indeed, on first entering the hot dusky hole of a place, which reeked with the vapour of stale warm water, it required only a slight stretch of imagination to fancy one's self in some dungeon of old, and that Mirza and his assistant—as they stood there in the dim steaming atmosphere, stripped naked, save a dirty rag round their loins, their swarthy skins streaming with perspiration—were the executioners ready to seize their vic-tim for torture. To further this idea, they both pounced upon me, laid me flat along the hot flagstones of the floor, and commenced what seemed to be vigorous attempts at dis-locating my joints and flaying me, accompanying their exer-tions with sundry grunts and startling exclamations that sounded quite fiendish as they rang through the stone-vaulted chamber. The only intermission in their labours was when old Mirza, whose ideas were inclined to be socialistic, would sometimes, by way of taking a short rest, begin breathlessly abusing the ruling authorities in rather unparliamentary language. After thus giving vent to his political opinions, he would resume the peeling process with renewed energy. Thus far I quietly submitted to their operations; but when the principal torturer, with a demoniacal grin, proposed im-mersing me in a dirty stone cistern full of scalding-hot greasy-looking water, I objected to further proceedings. After drying and dressing myself with the utmost expedition, I made my exit into fresh air with the least possible delay, vowing never again to try a hummām in Cashmere.

My companion returned from the mountains a few days after me, bringing with him, amongst other trophies, one of the most massive and altogether perfect pair of ibex horns I have ever seen. They were upwards of 4 feet long, with a wide and regular sweep, and their tips uninjured. Poor lad! he was not long permitted to enjoy their possession, for a short time after he fell a victim to that fearful scourge of India—cholera. He was a true sportsman and an excellent rifle shot; and his shikaree told me he had never been out with a more daring or surer-footed European cragsman. One of his last wishes on his deathbed was that his hunting trophies might be sent home to his father. Strange to say, he had a fixed presentiment, to which he often gave expression, that he should never see Almora, where our regiment had been ordered to shortly before he died; and sad to say, this was fulfilled.

Very fair fishing was to be had in the valley at certain seasons in some parts of the Jhelum, both for mahseer and silvery black-speckled fish, in appearance like trout, but wanting the second rayless dorsal-fin of the Salmonidæ. The former fish were comparatively small of their kind, those killed being seldom over 10 lb. or so. The latter were sometimes taken up to 8 lb. or more. The minnow was usually most successful for mahseer. The other fish took the fly pretty freely, and the fly that seemed as good as any was made simply with a bunch of white-cotton thread carded out and tied on to a naked hook. But the deadliest bait was a ripe mulberry, when the fruit was in season. The boatmen were rather clever at spearing small fish in shoal water from the bows of their boats.

Formerly, fishing was permitted anywhere in the river, but latterly it was prohibited between certain bridges in the city, for, as was alleged, the following ridiculous reason:—

The story went that, after the death of the Maharajah
Gholab Sing, his soul was believed to have transmigrated into
a certain very big mahseer in one of the sacred fish-tanks
near Islamabad, where, with many smaller companions, this
holy fish was well fed and cared for by the attendant
Brahmin priests.   One day a hungry sportsman, on his
return from the mountains, pitched his tent near this tank,
and seeing the fine fat fish it contained, straightway proceeded
to avail himself of the chance thus offered of so easily providing himself a savoury meal.   To the horror and consternation of the priests, he hooked the " Maharajah," and soon had
him cooking for his supper.   This catastrophe caused a tremendous rumpus, which resulted, I believe, in the author of
it being ordered to quit the valley.   Subsequently the spirit
of the defunct old ruler was supposed to have returned to the
capital, and to have been re-embodied in another big fish,
whose haunt in the river was said to be somewhere opposite
the palace, between two of the old wooden bridges; and so
it came about that fishing in that bit of the water was
proscribed.

The metropolis of Cashmere,[1] with its picturesque canal
communications, quaint old bridges, gondola-style of boating,
and bad smells, often reminded me of Venice.   Reclining
under the straw-mat awning of your Cashmerian gondola, or
" shikaree " boat, as this water-cab of the country is called,
whilst being paddled over the limpid glassy water of the
beautiful Dhal lake, through the *singara*[2] plants, and past
the large flat leaves and gorgeous red flowers of the lotus, or
among the floating gardens;[3] lunching *al fresco* on the Isle of

---

[1] Ozaka in Japan, with its canals and wooden houses, boats and bridges,
struck me as bearing a greater resemblance to Srinuggur in Cashmere than
any other place I have seen.   They differ, however, in respect of the former
being remarkably clean, whilst the latter is filthily dirty.   Indeed, I may say
in many ways Japan resembled Cashmere.

[2] The water-nut, much used for food by the poor class of Cashmerees.

[3] These floating gardens, so called, are considerable sized beds of earth, with

Chenars, or beside fountains and miniature cascades at the
Shalimar or Nishāt gardens, and returning in the bright moonlight, your boatmen keeping time with their paddles to some
wild Cashmere lay; or visiting the shawl-merchants' shops
and sipping spiced tea whilst inspecting their beautiful wares,

The Gondola of Cashmere.

—were all very delightful by way of rest after hard mountain
work. And here I may remark, with respect to the shawl
fabrics, that if some of their fair wearers could behold the
half-starved emaciated creatures who weave them, they would
not rest so lightly on their shoulders. I noticed that many of
these poor artisans had a permanent squint, acquired, I was
told, from being kept so constantly employed at their primitive hand-looms on this fine work.

Charming as the *dolce far niente* style of life in this be-
witching valley was for a time, I returned ere long to the
ibex and bears among the mountains. As I have probably
said more than enough about ibex-hunting, I shall not tire
the reader with a repetition of it, but commence another
chapter of wild sport in quite a different locality.

their foundations of matted reeds and grass so constructed as to be quite dis-
connected with the bottom of the lake. In order to prevent their being drifted
away, they are attached to long poles driven into the bed of the lake where it
is rather shallow. They are used chiefly for the growth of melon, cucumber,
and suchlike plants.

Before turning to it, however, I have a sorrowful episode to relate respecting my little Goorkha shikaree Kurbeer, who has on one or two occasions figured rather prominently in the preceding pages of this book. He had unfortunately been prevented from accompanying me to Cashmere, and of his sad fate I had heard during my sojourn there. It appeared that when out hunting with a comrade he had accidentally shot him dead. From the evidence of a little lad who was out with them, it was concluded that, either in a fit of remorse or from fear of what he thought might be the consequences to himself, he had committed suicide. His body was never found, only a spaniel I had given him, his empty gun, and his kookerie beside a rapid mountain-torrent, where the little lad said he had left him after the accident, whilst he ran to the nearest village for assistance. It was therefore supposed either that, after having shot himself, his body must have fallen into the torrent—which was in flood at the time— and been swept away, or that he had deserted. The latter seemed improbable from the fact of his dog having been found, and the little lad having heard the report of a gun at the place he had left Kurbeer beside the corpse of his comrade. There was a sad mystery about the whole affair that was never cleared up. Any way, I had to lament the loss of one of the stanchest and best shikarees that ever ac-companied me on a hillside.

I was up on the Kajuag range, north of the river Jhelum, below Baramoola, hunting that magnificent wild goat the markhor, when a messenger arrived bearing an order to re-join my regiment. Many military officers who were that year in the valley had thus to hurry away from it before the expiration of their leave, to join a field force proceeding on service against some of the hill tribes on the North-West Frontier. Of a merry circle of seven, five of whom belonged to my own regiment, who dined together one evening on our route to rejoin, poor Trotter of the Artillery—a fellow-cadet with me at Addiscombe—was drowned the very next day when rashly attempting to swim across the Jhelum; four went to their long homes during the Indian Mutiny of the following year; my valued friend, and at that time brother officer, John Tytler, fell a victim to the cold and hardships of the Afghan war, in which the brigade he commanded did such good service; and I am the only member of that party now left. *Sic transit gloria mundi!*

Let us turn to something less sad.

CHAPTER XI.

THE position and general features of the beautiful valley of Dehra Doon[1] have been mentioned in a foregoing chapter. As it lies within the Sewalik hills, which may be classed among the outer ranges, the sport to be had in its wild tracts of forest and swamp may, I think, be called Himalayan.

When I first knew the Doon, game of many sorts and sizes was abundant, from a button quail to a wild elephant, or from a minnow to a mahseer of a hundred pounds. From time out of mind it must have been a favourite haunt of wild animals, for many fossil remains of huge antediluvian creatures—the mastodon, for example—have been found in the Sewalik range, which bounds the valley on its south side.

From the beginning of June until the end of October the heavy jungles and swamps of the Doon, like those of the Terai, are deadly, but for the rest of the year they are comparatively free from malaria.

During the many years I passed at intervals in these

[1] I cannot bring myself to spell it Dún, according to the new-fangled method; it deprives the name of half its old romance.

" happy hunting - grounds," my shikar experiences were so numerous and varied that I shall endeavour to describe one or two only of those best suited to give a general idea of the wild sport of this locality.

The quantity of small game was formerly far greater than it was even within my own recollection, more particularly in the western part of the valley, where the ground in some places was pretty clear of forest, and where tracts of long grass, intersected by streams, were interspersed with patches of cultivation, sedgy marshes, and bush jungle, in which kind of ground the black partridge delights. Here were also to be found hares, pea-fowl, jungle-fowl, wild-fowl, grey partridges, plovers, several kinds of snipe and quails, and sometimes a floriken, a few sand-grouse, and occasionally a woodcock, &c.

When beating for small game, a sounder of wild pigs, or a deer, was not unfrequently driven from among the long grass and bushes, and I have known of a leopard, and even the striped king of the forest, having been disturbed in like manner. But as regards the two latter, such instances were rare, as feline animals, although numerous in the adjacent jungles, seldom ventured during the daytime into the open. Just before nightfall, however, they often prowled out after the village cattle. I remember, one evening when skirting along the margin of the forest after any game that might chance to turn up, coming unexpectedly upon a tiger as it was coolly taking its way down a wood-carting track towards the open country. This animal, when he saw our elephants slowly advancing within eighty yards, merely stopped short and slowly retraced his steps. The shot which I lost no time in letting go, was replied to by the deep guttural grunt which a tiger almost invariably gives vent to when a bullet tells on him. Wheeling suddenly round, he struck a heavy blow with his paw at a tree that stood in his way, and forthwith charged straight down on the line. Grunting forth his wrath, he dashed open-mouthed right in among the elephants, when a lucky bullet from one of the other guns caught him in the head and stopped his further progress *instanter*. The first shot was found to have gone clean through him, close behind the shoulders. This serves to show what a tiger is capable of doing after being mortally wounded. On another occasion, in broad daylight, I shot a leopard in a jungly ravine, within a few hundred yards of my house, where it had killed one of my servant's goats. In this case I left the dead goat, from which the domestics had but just scared the leopard away, as a bait, and tried the shouting artifice I have already described in chap. v. The shouters had hardly left me watching there a quarter of an hour ere the leopard returned to its prey. My first barrel, by some mischance, missed fire. The brute, on hearing the click of the hammer, turned his head towards my little screen formed of green boughs, as he stood with his fore-paws on the goat, within a dozen yards of the muzzle of my rifle. His wicked green eyes seemed to meet mine through the loophole in my ambush, whilst, without raising my cheek from the stock, I noiselessly cocked the other hammer and again pressed the trigger. A few gurgling grunts were his reply to the shot. On the smoke clearing off he was nowhere visible; but after reloading, I followed on his blood-tracks, and soon found him lying stone-dead at the bottom of the ravine.

Both the black bears—the Himalayan and the sloth bear —were occasionally met with in the valley, feeding on the fruit of the prickly "byer" (a kind of buckthorn) bushes when in season.

The prettiest sport of the Doon was the stalking in the Sewaliks. But the spear-grass that grows most abundantly there, as also on the lower ranges, is, when long and dry, dreadfully troublesome. The sharp barbed points of the thin hard seeds, from which it derives its name, catch in your clothes, and work themselves by myriads through them, and even down into your boots, until they reach your skin, which they often penetrate. In this comparatively low but rugged and forest-clad range of hills, the jurrow (called *māhā* in the Doon), the spotted deer (called *cheetal*), and the *kakur*, or barking-deer, were plentiful; and up about the jagged and precipitous sandstone summits of the range, *gooral* might always be found. Tigers and leopards, too, were numerous, though not often seen, and wild elephants were not uncommon. Shooting the latter, however, has now been prohibited by the Government, except in the case of a dangerous "rogue"; and very wisely, or *Elephas Indicus* might soon have become as extinct as *Dinotherium giganteum*.

But for many years pot-hunters, by indiscriminate slaughter at all seasons, have been doing their worst to exterminate the game in the Doon, and have so far succeeded fairly well in their nefarious work—for good small-game shooting, at any rate, is now a thing of the past.

I shall first try to recount the proceedings of a day after small game that I find recorded in my old shooting-journal. It will serve as a fair sample of many similar days' sport in the Doon.

It was on one of those fine sharp mornings which are the rule in this beautiful valley during the cold season, that a party of three guns, consisting of a travelling visitor to the place—vulgarly called a "Globe-trotter"—the Æsculapius of my regiment, and myself, after an early breakfast, lit our "baccies" and mounted our little equine quadrupeds, known in India as "tats." An hour's ride between thick clumps of tall feathery - foliaged bamboos—like gigantic ostrich-plumes— that sometimes flanked the road, or through umbrageous groves of grand old mango-trees, brought us to our ground, where a small crowd of beaters, gun-carriers, dogs, &c., had already preceded us. Our line being formed, we forthwith commenced business by beating up a few grassy fields and scattered patches of bushes, from which a hare, one or two grey partridges, and a few stray quails were transferred to the game-bag. I call them *stray* quails, because the common grey quail, being a migratory bird, is not found in any numbers except during a few weeks in the spring and autumn, although varieties called the rain-quail and bush-quail are met with at other times, the former only during the rainy season, the latter at any time, in bush jungle.

After quitting the fields, we beat through a sedgy swamp, where some long-bills, including several little jack-snipe, are picked up, whilst others twist away unscathed by our erratic shots. Our quota of snipe is added to by one or two of the painted variety, which rise from the longer reedy grass more like a big butterfly than a game-bird. On nearing a bushy corner of the "jheel" (marsh), the welcome cry, "Mark wood-cock," comes from Æsculapius on the right of the line; and we have the satisfaction of seeing this much-prized bird alight in a thicket some distance ahead, where it is again flushed and falls to the gun of the "G. T."

Our beat now leads through long grass, beside a clear pebbly stream called the Sooswa, that derives its name from its abounding with water-cresses, broad luxuriant patches of which might be seen extending along its bed, sometimes for fifty yards or more in length. We have not proceeded far when "whir-r whir-r" go a brace of black partridge (fran-colin), as they rise high over the grass and make away with the dashing straightforward flight which is their wont. "Bang, bang" on the right goes our medical adviser, before whose unerring barrels they are brought down in capital form, for he is as good a hand with his sporting implements as he is known to be with those of his craft.

A fair number of black partridges are accounted for ere we reach a more jungly part of our beat, when the cheery crow-ing of jungle-fowl and the musical cry of an old peacock advise us that we are likely to add variety to our bag. Pres-ently there is a "yap yap" from the dogs, followed by such a clucking and general disturbance among the little cocks and hens, as some flutter up into the trees, whilst others, older and more wary, either scurry off through the bushes, or wing their rapid flight as they betake themselves to a safer locality, that it seems just as if we are in the vicinity of a poultry-yard. One or two of the less crafty ones are rather shame-lessly potted on their perches, whence they fall almost into the jaws of the dogs that are barking at them below, by which diversion their attention has been distracted from us their more dangerous foes, as we approach them under cover of the bushes. The unusual row disturbs from its noonday repose a cheetal (spotted deer), to which our physician administers a dose of leaden pills, but at such a distance as to have little effect.

Our musical friend the peacock having betrayed his where-abouts by again raising his melodious voice—a practice usual with pea-fowl on hearing a shot in their vicinity, though they are otherwise uncommonly knowing—the old fellow is soon ejected by the dogs from his retreat among a tangled mass of elephantine creeper, where he has ensconced himself in the vain hope of concealment, and from which he ex-tricates his splendid long train with considerable difficulty and much flapping of wings, thereby giving an easy chance to one of the party.

Now came a very agreeable and welcome part of the day's proceedings, when we called a halt in a shady nook beside the stream, where it formed itself into a deep swirling pool. From this, had we come provided with a trout-rod, we might easily have added a dish of broiled fish to the cold collation that was being spread before us. Having done ample justice to the comestibles, and beverages cooled in the stream, after the usual pipe we prepared to make a fresh attack on the feathered denizens of the jungle. Although the quantity of ammunition expended was perhaps greater after lunch than before it, the amount of the bag, I fear, was, as it often is under similar circumstances, in the opposite ratio.

Towards evening my place in the line led me along a bank
overhanging the stream, when I suddenly heard an unearthly
skirling noise at the water's edge below me. On looking over,
I found it proceeded from two young otters fighting over a
fish. They were so taken up with their quarrel that they did
not notice me until I had jumped down and collared one of
them, like a ferret, round the neck. The other at once took
to the water; but this being quite shallow for some distance,
after depositing my gun, I was able to give chase, and succeeded in heading the little beast before it reached the stream,
and driving it back on to the shore, where I soon got hold of
it, like its companion, with the other hand. The difficulty
now was how to get rid of the struggling little wretches
without either being bitten by them or letting them escape ;
for although they were not much bigger than ferrets, they
were exceedingly strong, and their jaws were well provided
with sharp teeth. The only thing we could devise for carrying them was a kind of bag made of one of the beater's
turbans. Into this they were dropped, and slung over a
man's back; and judging from the noises that issued from
the bag, they seemed still to be carrying on their feud even
there. After beating back to where we had left our ponies,
we cantered home, well satisfied with our varied bag and our
pleasant day's sport.

It was some time ere the little otters could be prevailed
upon to eat, and all endeavours to conciliate them were at
first repulsed with vicious looks, peculiar humming noises,
and attempts to bite. But hunger at last had its effect, and
eventually they became tame enough to play about the house,
although they would never permit themselves to be freely
handled. They soon learnt to know their names, and would
come to me when whistled to. At breakfast they were always
beside my chair, and would sit up and beg like dogs, keeping
up an incessant whistling noise until they got something to
eat. Although I took every measure for their comfort by

having a water-tank for them, and providing them daily with fish, poor "Kelpie," the female, like most pets, came to an untimely end. She was seized with some affection of the loins, and died. "Brownie," the dog, also had an attack of the same kind, from which he recovered; but he grew so ill-tempered after his bereavement that I was obliged to part with him.

At that time I possessed another pet, in the shape of a tame pea-fowl, which always showed a strange animosity towards the otters. If it ever caught sight of them outside the house, it at once went straight for them, when they promptly beat a hasty retreat indoors. But let us hie to the wilder parts of the valley.

Although hunting on elephants in the forests and swamps of Dehra Doon or the Terai cannot, in my humble opinion, be compared with following your game on foot in the moun-

In the Doon jungles.

tains, it still possesses its own charms. First, there is the variety, and often the quantity, of game, large and small, met with in a day's shooting. When I say *quantity*, I do not, however, suppose that any one calling himself a sportsman would wantonly shoot at every hornless animal that gets up before his elephant. Then there is the free gipsy sort of life you lead—pitching your camp, which is provided with every comfort, at will in some beautiful forest-glade, where there is nothing to remind you of the more stern realities of life; where not a human habitation is to be seen, save perhaps, here and there, a grass-built shed, tenanted by herdsmen tending their cattle pasturing in the forest. And when the log-fire has burnt low, and the camp is all hushed in repose, what lullabies to the sportsman are the wild sounds that now and again break the solemn silence of night, as the echoes are aroused in the neighbouring woods by the "belling" of a startled deer, the deep-mouthed voice of some prowling tiger, or the distant trumpeting of wild elephants, which the tame ones at their pickets acknowledge by a low rumbling noise! How profound is your sleep under canvas, until awakened at the first flush of dawn by the shrill crow of the jungle-cock and the call of the pea-fowl!—when, after a comfortable breakfast, the elephants are brought up, their howdahs fastened on and furnished with all the necessary appurtenances, "baccies" are lit, and you are off for the jungles again.

Then comes the picnic lunch, which may occasionally be graced by the presence of some of the gentle sex who have been induced to trust themselves on elephant-back to see the sport. Baskets are unpacked, their contents displayed in the cool shade under the wide-spreading branches of some grand old banyan-tree, and the laugh and joke go merrily round.

Last, and perhaps not the least of the charms of this *quondam* El Dorado of wild sport, is the beautiful combination of undulating forest, winding stream, and adjacent mountain scenery. Moreover, the rivers afford the votary of the gentle craft ample scope for the successful use of his rod.

But alas! in the Dehra Doon at any rate, such halcyon days are, I fear, numbered; for its jungles are being slowly but steadily cleared, and with them their wild denizens must as surely decrease. Indeed it is by no means improbable that ere very long the whistle of the "iron horse" may replace the "bell" of the deer and the "trumpet" of the wild elephant— sounds which of yore were wont to be heard in sylvan solitudes which are now replaced by extensive clearings for the cultivation of tea.

It was about the middle of March 1860, when Colonel (now General Sir Charles) Reid, commanding my regiment, invited me to join his shooting-camp in the eastern part of the Dehra Doon. He had "padded" two fine tigers during the few days he had been out before I joined him. This was unusually good luck for the Doon jungles, where, although tigers are pretty numerous, they are difficult to find when beating for them with a line of elephants, from their being so easily able to slink away unperceived in the almost impenetrable thickets and swampy cane-brakes with which the eastern Doon abounds. If, however, intelligence can be got of a tiger's having just killed a buffalo or bullock, and the carcass reached before the "choomars" (leather tanners), who are always on the look-out for such events, have discovered it and stripped it of its hide and flesh, the chances of finding the animal at or near the "kill" are then pretty certain.

A delightful ride of about fifteen miles, chiefly through forest, brought me to an open spot where the jungle had been cleared, a few grass-huts erected, and the ground cultivated. Here I found the Colonel's camp pitched, and fortunately reached it just in time to escape a thorough drenching, as shortly after my arrival a terrific thunderstorm burst overhead, accompanied by high wind, which levelled one of the tents in no time.

When we mounted our elephants next morning the atmosphere was clear and cool, and our jungle surroundings looked

beautifully bright and green after the storm. In front of the
camp, over the irregular line of tree-tops, rose the precipitous
slopes and buttresses of the outer-range Himalayas, some
three or four miles distant. Rearward, in like manner, the
low serrated ridge of the wooded Sewaliks cut the deep-blue
sky-line. We beat over some excellent-looking ground, but
returned in the evening with empty pads—having agreed to
fire at no other game whilst there was a chance of finding a
striped jacket.

For the two following days we roamed through jungle
and swamp without success, as far as tigers were concerned,
although deer, wild pigs, and feathered game were plentiful
enough. Sometimes a porcupine would hustle away among
the long grass, from under the very trunk of one of our
elephants, the sudden rustle of its quills causing the huge
beast to shriek and shy as much as, if not more than, if it had
trodden on a tiger's tail. The amount of self-denial I had
to exercise in refraining from pressing the trigger was often
very considerable, as my rifle was brought to bear on the
shoulder of some fine cheetal stag, whilst he stood to gaze
for a few moments at the elephants steadily forcing their
way through the tangled jungle, when his sleek dappled
coat and long tapering antlers would slowly disappear in the
thick cover, as though the animal knew he had nothing to fear.

The manœuvres of an elephant whilst slowly forging its
way through heavy jungle are quite an interesting study.
The control its mahout (driver) has over the huge but docile
animal is truly marvellous, as he verbally directs it here to
tear down a tough obstructive creeper, or a projecting bough,
with its trunk, there to fell with its forehead a good-sized
tree that may impede its course in the line, or to break away
some precipitous bank of a nullah (water-course) with its
fore-feet, to form a path for descending into it, and then, after
the same fashion, to clamber up the opposite side. And if
its driver should chance to drop his *gujbag* (iron goad) among

the long grass, with what confiding sagacity does the animal grope about for it and lift it up to him with its trunk! In tiger-shooting, however steady an elephant may naturally be, its behaviour very much depends on the conduct of its mahout. I may mention a remarkable instance of cool pluck on the part of a mahout, which occurred during a tiger-beat in the Dehra Doon. Amongst some elephants attached to my regiment, as transport for our ammunition on field service, was a very fast and steady one which had had the honour of carrying the Prince of Wales when tiger-shooting in the Kumaon Terai. The mahout who drove Alice, as she was named, always wore in his girdle a hunting-knife, which he showed with much pride as having been bestowed on him by his Royal Highness. One day, during a scrimmage with a tiger, this knife dropped from the man's girdle. "Oh, my knife! my knife!" he exclaimed, and instantly slipped down off his elephant's neck on to the ground to recover it, at the imminent risk of being boned by the tiger.

On the third day we visited the scene of the death of one of the Colonel's tigers, in hopes of further success, as the place was considered one of the best finds in the Doon; but this time we drew it blank. It was a long narrow swamp filled with flag-grass (called "putteyr"), which grew nearly as high as the elephants' pads, and almost surrounded with tree-jungle,—altogether about as perfect a bit of ground for holding a tiger as could be desired.

On one occasion when beating through this swamp, we had a funny adventure with a crocodile,[1] which afforded us some sport, such as it was, and considerable merriment. The creature was lying among the flags, apparently taking a snooze, for it either paid no attention to or did not observe the approaching elephants, so I resolved to wake it up with a charge of buckshot on its cranium. On receiving the shot, it for the moment seemed stunned, but soon managed to wriggle

[1] The crocodile of India is usually but erroneously called an alligator.

its body into the soft mud among the roots of the flags, leaving only its tail visible, when a bright idea suggested itself to
one of the Goorkhas who were with us. Thinking the animal
was dead, or nearly so, he proposed that he should fasten a
rope to its tail, and then make one of the elephants haul it
out. He accordingly proceeded to carry out his plan, which
was more easily conceived than executed, for on his attempting to slip a noose over the tail, the creature gave it a
violent and an unexpected wag, which somewhat disconcerted
his arrangements and startled him considerably. At length,
however, after repeated failures, which elicited many jocular
remarks from his comrades, he succeeded in making fast the
noose. Having tied the other end of the rope to one of the
elephant's pads, we gave the word to pull, when away went
the elephant, dragging after it the saurian, which now, having seemingly recovered its wits, was struggling frantically,
and making abortive attempts to turn round and seize the
rope between the well-armed jaws it kept snapping together
with a loud noise. The creature was hauled on to an open
spot, and finished with a bullet through the head. It was
one of the "muggur" or broad-snouted kind (*Crocodilus
palustris*), and measured 7 or 8 feet long.

Pythons of very large size were sometimes met with in
these jungles, and I have myself shot several, one of which
measured over 21 feet in length, and in girth about 2 feet.
For the benefit of such as are fond of the marvellous, I shall
venture to here recapitulate the strange circumstances attending the slaying of this huge reptile, as contributed by me
years ago to the 'Oriental Sporting Magazine.' But those
who, from their inexperience of wild-jungle life, are always
inclined to be sceptical regarding "travellers' tales," had better
skip the rest of this chapter, for I warn them that the unvarnished facts it contains will almost require the powers of
deglutition of the creature in question to swallow. Nevertheless they occurred exactly as follows.

I was out in camp in the Eastern Doon with a party of
my regiment employed in cutting grass for barrack-thatching,
when one day I chanced to notice that one of the men at
work had adorned his head with a curious-looking turban.
A closer inspection showed it to be a portion of a huge
python's semi - transparent cast - off skin, which the lad, a
light-hearted Goorkha, had thus donned, much to the amusement of an admiring circle of his broad-faced companions,
who were regarding him with looks beaming with fun. On
questioning him as to where he got it, he told me he had
picked it up when out shooting in the neighbouring forest,
and that he had seen, close to the place where he had found
it, what must have been the snake that had shed it, as the
creature lay basking near the entrance to a big hole, into
which it had disappeared at his approach. As he said he
thought he could remember the spot, I proposed that he
should proceed there forthwith.

For a long way my sturdy little guide trudged silently
ahead through the forest, until at length he appeared to be
drawing up to something, after the manner of a pointer on an
uncertain scent, as he " gingerly " (excuse the slang, as being
the most expressive term for the movement) advanced each
bare foot through the long dry grass. Presently he motioned
to me to stand still whilst he proceeded cautiously to climb a
small tree, in order to get a better view of the ground in front
of him. After a careful survey, he beckoned me to advance.
Just as I reached the tree, a dark-brown object, which I
recognised at once as a big snake, glided across a bare patch
of ground about fifteen or twenty yards in front. In a few
seconds the reptile was helplessly writhing and twisting in its
death-throes, with a bullet through the thickest part of its body.

I now considered that I had secured the original wearer of
the cast-off skin, and that the business was at an end. But
the Goorkha positively asserted that this snake was not the
one he had seen before, which he declared was nearly twice

M

as large, and of a much brighter colour. This python was 13 feet long and about a foot and a half in girth, with dark-brown and black markings.

We now went to examine the hole, which was close by, and for which the snake must have been making when I stopped him. It had evidently been originally the den of porcupines, though now used as the temporary abode of snakes. Of its being the latter there was no doubt, for on looking into it we could see a bit of the tail-end of a second snake, which doubtless was the one the Goorkha had at first seen. We resolved not to meddle with it then, as we thought it would be pretty sure to be found basking in the sun some other day. We dragged the other to the nearest forest path and suspended it over a branch, where it could be easily seen by the men sent with an elephant to fetch it. Its body showed slight muscular action when brought to camp in the evening some six hours after being shot.

Business prevented my visiting the python's haunt next day. On the following morning, however, I went there with three Goorkhas who volunteered to accompany me. Cautiously we stole up to the place in hopes of finding the snake out sunning itself. But it was nowhere visible, so we proceeded to inspect the hole, and there found the creature's tail in almost exactly the same position as before. As no one seemed inclined to handle the tail, we poked at it with a stick, when it was merely shrunk a little farther into the hole. A fire was lit at the entrance and the smoke fanned into the hole, without the slightest apparent effect on the snake. Finding all our endeavours to rouse it fail, I sent one of the Goorkhas back to camp to fetch some tools with which to try and dig it out, and also an elephant for carrying the creature if we succeeded in our attempt to unearth it.

Meanwhile the other two men and I set to work by turns to enlarge the mouth of the hole with sticks, cut and sharpened to a point by the Goorkhas with their kookeries. From the ground being very hard, and the sticks having constantly to be resharpened, our progress was rather slow. After digging and scraping away for a long time, we had enlarged the mouth of the hole enough to admit sufficient light to enable us, by stooping and peering into the gloom of the interior, to see some of the reptile's huge coils, which looked as thick as, if not thicker than, a man's thigh. It was an enormous python, and we were surprised to find that it did not as yet evince the slightest signs of resenting our intrusion, although the creature must have been quite conscious of it; for we fancied we saw its eyes regarding us, as it lay with its great flat head resting on one of its coils.

Supposing the snake to be in a half-torpid state, we determined to try and draw it. We all three, therefore, proceeded—somewhat nervously I must own—to lay hold of its tail. To this familiarity it showed its objection by a decided inclination to wag its caudal extremity, which had such an electrical effect on our nerves that we dropped it like a hot potato, and—what shall I call it?—retired. It must have been very sleepy indeed, for immediately on its tail being released it desisted from moving it. This restored confidence, and again and again did we renew our futile attempts to haul it out. We had yet to learn the mighty muscular power of the creature, which had now withdrawn some of its coils farther back into the den, thereby giving them additional purchase. We had, however, so far succeeded, that several feet of its length were now exposed to view.

A shot would in all probability have induced it to relinquish its hold. But had I fired at random into the hole, I must have torn and disfigured its beautiful new coat (it was evidently the original owner of the cast-off one), which I wished if possible to secure uninjured as a specimen; and a wound near the tail might not have altogether disabled it. I therefore refrained from shooting until a more favourable opportunity should offer.

We continued to dig and scrape with our sticks and hands at the hole—our operations being sometimes interrupted by the startling presence of the creature's head, which it occasionally poked towards the entrance; and from the lively manner in which it kept darting out its little forked tongue, it seemed to be gradually awakening to a sense of its impending danger. It still, strange to say, allowed the few feet of its tail we had managed to expose to lie outside the hole—a fact for which I cannot account, except by supposing the snake to have been too sluggish to withdraw it.

At last the elephant and tools arrived, when a bright idea struck us,—we might draw it out with the elephant! Sufficient rope for the purpose was loosened from the elephant's pad. This rope, which was made of cotton, and about the thickness of a man's thumb, was hitched round the snake's tail, and its remaining length brought up again to the pad and fastened there, thus doubling its strength.

Now came the tug of war! A sudden jerk might have torn the skin; the mahout was therefore warned to put on the strain gradually. Little did we know what a tough and an obstinate customer we had to deal with. Tighter and tighter grew the ropes, when " crack " went one of them. Still the strain was increased, until again " crack "—the other had snapped also, leaving the snake *in statu quo.*

We were now at our wits' end as to how we should proceed to dislodge the creature without injuring its skin by shooting into the hole. After a short consultation and an inspection of the surrounding ground, we came to the conclusion that before resorting to this last resource there still remained one chance.

Situated on the other side of the den, and pretty close to it, was the abrupt extremity of a small ravine. By countermining from this we might be able to attack the place in rear. We accordingly turned-to once more at our excavating operations, which were now more rapid and easy from our having

proper tools to work with. Our perseverance was rewarded
by finding that we had luckily hit off the right direction from
the ravine, and we had soon succeeded in boring a hole large
enough to be able to stir up the creature with a long stick.
The snake, finding itself assailed both in front and rear, and
that its stronghold was becoming too hot for it, now began to
show symptoms of an inclination to quit it. I therefore,
·with one of the Goorkhas, took up a position that commanded
the front door of the den, leaving the other two to watch the
back.

The business was now becoming decidedly exciting. My
jolly little companions were getting quite wild with delight,
and were carrying on a hurried altercation, in their own
peculiar dialect, as to which way the creature intended
·making its exit.

"He's coming out on this side," shouts one of them from
the ravine. "He's not going out on your side, for here's his
head coming *our* way," argues the lad beside me. "Why!
we can see his head *here*," comes the reply from the others,
half frantic with excitement. "Then there must be *two* of
them," exclaimed my fellow, jumping up in a transport of
glee at the idea.

Such, indeed, proved to be the case. There was undoubtedly
a second monster in the den, and almost as large a one as the
first. As the snake on our side now thrust out its head
several feet, and was swaying it to and fro as if it meditated
·bolting (not my carcass, by any means, but its own) from its
lair, I retreated a few paces and planted a charge of buckshot in it, about two feet behind the head. This at once
doubled it up, literally, without much damaging its coat.

The scrimmage in the den, a portion of the interior of which
we could now see tolerably plainly, was tremendous, as the
huge coils of the stricken python, in its death-struggles,
became entangled, as it were, with those of its living companion. The latter, however, showed a decided disinclination

to quit its dwelling, where it remained screwing itself about,
seemingly in a great state of alarm, and seeking safety from
danger, like the " ostrich of the sandy desert," by attempting
to hide its head.   After just securing such a fine specimen of
the serpent family, killing this apparently harmless member
of it also would have been wanton butchery.

When the violent contortions of the dying monster had
somewhat subsided, we hauled it out and hoisted it on to the
elephant, not, however, without some trouble from its enormous weight, and the excessive slipperiness of its smooth
skin.   We left the remaining python in undisputed possession
of its now lonely abode, from which it still seemed loath to
depart.   A Goorkha, when out with his gun a day or two
after, came across it in the jungle not far from its old haunt,
and being unaware of my merciful intentions towards the
creature, shot it and brought it to me as a grand trophy.

I have already given the dimensions of the large one as it
lay unstretched.   It was beautifully and brightly marked
with yellow and black.   It is now a cleverly executed specimen of taxidermy by the late H. Ward of Vere Street, and
forms a prominent if not a very elegant addition to my small
collection of shikar trophies.

My own experience of Indian pythons is, that they are
not the fierce, bone-crushing creatures they are commonly
thought to be, at any rate with regard to human beings.
Indeed, from what information I have been able to gather
concerning them, they appear to be quite harmless; their
prey chiefly consisting of birds, hares, fawns, and " suchlike
small deer."   But I never have come across them during the
hot season, when they may possibly be more lively.   In
winter they always seemed to be timid, and usually sluggish,
on being disturbed.   This may account for our being able to
play such pranks with them as we did with impunity.

From this diversion let us hark back to the *putteyr* swamp.
This time when beating through it we saw neither tiger nor

reptile; nothing but some hog-deer (*Axis porcinus*), called
"pārāh" or "dhōter" by the natives—an animal about the
size of a roe-deer, and not unlike it in its grey winter coat.
The buck carries pretty horns, averaging about 14 inches
long, with two short upper tines on each horn, and one brow
antler, also short and pointing upwards. This deer usually
frequents open tracts of long grass and marshy ground, and is
very plentiful in the Terai and Dehra Doon. It affords capital
shooting from elephant-back, after the jungle conflagrations
in spring, when it can be beaten out into the open from the
unburnt patches of long grass. As the shots are almost invariably running ones, it requires sharp and pretty shooting
with the rifle to hit such a small mark.

The spotted deer (*Axis maculatus*), or cheetal, is very common in the same localities — in fact in almost all Indian
forests, from the base of the Himalayas to the sea-coast. It
affects thick cover in the forests, or tracts of long grass in
their immediate vicinity. In height it stands about 3 feet at
the shoulder. Its colour somewhat resembles that of the
fallow-deer, but the white spots are more clearly defined, and
on a darker ground. The ordinary length of its fully developed horns is about 30 inches. They have a very graceful
sweep, with three regular tines on each horn, and sometimes
an extra snag or two beside the brow antlers. The longest
pair I ever got were 37 inches before I peeled off the velvet
with which they were covered, and as the tips were quite
soft, they would probably have grown another inch. The
span was 30 inches, and 4 inches the circumference of beam
clear of velvet. They seldom, I think, grow much longer
than this, although sometimes slightly thicker. Spotted deer
appear to have no regular time for shedding their horns. I
have noted in my shooting-journal having killed them in
January with horns fully developed, but in velvet. I also
find one as having been shot with horns in exactly the same
state in April; and I shot one on 26th February—a date, be

it observed, about midway between the above two—carrying
long and perfectly clear horns with well-polished white tips.
Another killed in August had horns which, from their worn
and smooth appearance, were quite ready to be shed. Of two
stags I killed, right and left, in the month of March, one had
long clear horns with well-worn points, whilst those of the other
were in velvet and only half-grown. I could mention many
other instances tending to show the strange irregularity with
which this deer doffs its antlers. In the months of March
and April, however, I found the horns generally best developed. The cheetal stag is termed by the natives a
"jhānk," as are likewise the males carrying horns of all
the *deer* tribe.

The little four-horned antelope (*Tetraceros quadricornis*), or
"chousinghia" as it is called, is met with in much the same
sort of country, but rather sparsely, and usually singly or in
pairs. It is rather lighter in colour than the hog-deer, and
about the same size, but it seldom or never frequents marshy
ground. It is frequently found among bush jungle or near
the outskirts of forests. The front horns seldom grow longer
than an inch, and are more often mere nobs. The hinder
ones are about 3 or 4 inches long, and sometimes even more.
They are quite smooth, except a ring or two at the base, and
very slightly curved forward.

The swamp deer (*Rucervus Dauvancellii*), called "goen" by
the natives, which is plentiful in the open grassy swamps of
some parts of the Terai, is said to be occasionally met with
in the Dehra Doon; but much as I have hunted there, I
have never seen it in that locality. It is nearly the same
size as the jurrow, but paler in colour. It carries fine horns,
branching well forward, with many points along the upper
part of the beam, but only one brow antler on each horn.
In shape and paleness of colour the horns somewhat resemble those of the Virginian and the black-tailed deer of

North America, but the goen's horns grow considerably longer. This deer is never found on the mountains, and seldom in thick forests, although generally on its outskirts. A sketch of an exceptionally fine pair of horns of a swamp deer killed in the Oude Terai will be found at the end of the last chapter.

CHAPTER XII.

THE elephants having been fairly hard-worked during the past week, we gave them a day's rest. As our camp happened to be pitched not far from the junction of one of the forest streams with the Ganges, a place famous for mahseer, I got ready my tackle, with a view to trying a cast there in the early morning.

Leaving the Colonel and another sportsman who had joined us taking it well out of their blankets, I set out for the river as soon as it was light enough to find the way to it. The water was in good order, and the fish were rising well: not merely jumping and hogging their backs out of water, when—with mahseer—you may just as well reel up and go home, but with the boiling swirl that means business more than play. Consequently I was soon fixed into a good fish, and

before it was time to return for breakfast I had landed three
more.

Mahseer of enormous weight are often taken in the rivers
of the Dehra Doon and the Terai with trolling baits—phantom
minnows about 6 inches long, or even larger, being used for
big fish. Every Indian fisherman either knows or has heard
of the Raiewalla pool in the Doon, so famous for the monster
mahseer that are killed in it when the water gets into right
order after a heavy flood. But to fish it properly you must
use either a portable boat of some kind, or what is perhaps
better, and can generally be procured from the native fishermen—a *sernai*, which is a contrivance composed of three or four
big inflated skins, with a common native *charpai* (bed-frame)
fastened over them. On this you sit, with a man to paddle
you about. It need hardly be said that you must land to kill
your fish. Most excellent sport is also to be had in the
streams of the Doon with the fly, although the fish killed
with it are not, as a rule, so heavy. In proof of this I may
mention that on one occasion towards the end of October,
Major (the late General Sir Herbert) Macpherson of my
regiment and myself killed, in two and a half days' fishing at
the junction of the Āson stream with the Jumna, 221 lb.
weight of mahseer, averaging 6 lb. or 7 lb., the largest being
20 lb. Had we been working with the minnow instead
of fly only, we might in all probability have doubled this
amount and have killed much larger fish. The fly we were
using was a bright one, like the "Jock Scott," about 1¾ inches
long. I generally found this style of fly, of different sizes,
was successful with mahseer; but every disciple of Izaak
Walton has his own theories about the "gentle craft," and may
probably find a totally different one answer quite as well.
And after all, if the fish are in a regular fly-taking humour, I
am inclined to think that almost any combination of feathers
and tinsel will suit the taste of a salmon or a mahseer. A
well-known Doon fisherman of bygone days used to declare

he had sometimes fished for mahseer with a whole parrot! I must say, however, he was as celebrated for his exploits with the "bow" as with the rod. But, joking apart, I hesitate to describe some of the contrivances in the shape of flies I have known used with success for the huge fish in the Dehra Doon rivers, lest it should provoke a smile from the incredulous.

A propos of these big mahseer, a fisherman acquaintance of mine used to relate an amusing little anecdote of his angling experiences in the Doon. On one occasion he was out with a companion who was but a novice, and not quite such an enthusiast in the craft as himself. Observing his friend had got into difficulties with a monstrous big fish he had been for some time holding on to in a pool below, he proceeded to offer him his advice and assistance. Just as he reached him, however, the monster parted company with the line, when the novice, being unaware of the presence of any one so near him, was overheard to exclaim with a sigh of relief, " Thank goodness he's gone!"

A coarse shark-like fish called a "goonch" is occasionally caught when spinning for mahseer. A monster of this kind was landed from one of the Doon rivers by that keen all-round sportsman Mr Hercules Ross, B.C.S. (of rifle-shooting fame), which scaled considerably over 100 lb. Another member of the finny tribe which is sometimes taken in these waters is the "soulee," a smooth-skinned, dark olive-coloured fish, having a broad bull-head, and a fin extending round its caudal extremity, like a conger-eel — in fact it somewhat resembles an enormously thick and very short one. Unlike the mahseer, which loves a rocky or gravelly bottom, the soulee affects deep sandy holes. I do not remember ever having taken one with the fly, though I have frequently killed them, up to 8 or 10 lb., with trolling baits; and I do not think they often exceed this weight. The soulee always takes your bait near the bottom, and in its first rush frequently leaps once or more from the water, after which it gives in. It is, however, better on the table than on the rod, being richer flavoured and less bony than the mahseer. A good basket of small mahseer, and a trout-like fish called by the natives "golabee," which is as lively and strong as any real trout of equal weight, can often be caught with fly in the smaller streams of the Doon. I have taken dozens of both kinds combined in a day, averaging generally nearly half a pound, with an occasional fish (mahseer) of several pounds thrown in.

I have already drawn comparisons between salmon and mahseer fishing, which may have served to show that, as far as sport is concerned, they are about equal. But there are episodes attending the latter which occasionally make it more exciting—some might call it unpleasant—than the former. I know an instance of a tiger walking out of a jungle beside the river, coolly taking a drink at the pool and a look at the man who was fishing it, much to his astonishment, and doubtless consternation, and then, to his great relief, as quietly retiring. And once when I was fishing in one of the forest streams in the Eastern Doon, my two little dogs, which were hunting about after jungle-fowl, disturbed a tiger in a thicket not very far behind me. But such occurrences were rare.

Good as the fishing in the Doon streams is, it would be even better were it not for the wholesale system of poaching carried on by native fishermen to supply the markets of Dehra Doon and the sanitarium of Mussoorie in the hills close above it. The *modus operandi* which is most destructive, is placing a small-meshed net across the tail of some shallowish pool in any of the smaller streams where the fish run up from the large rivers to spawn, and then driving the fish with sticks and stones from a long way up-stream down into the pool thus netted. On the drivers reaching the head of this, a weir is made across it to divert the stream. The result is that the fish in the pool so drained remain stranded, the larger ones only being collected, while the small fry are left to rot in the sun. And as these poachers never take the trouble to break up the dam, a great stretch of water below it is ruined for fishing until the rainy season commences, when nature comes to the rescue with her flood of water, which soon levels all obstructions. The spots chosen for this nefarious proceeding are, of course, those which admit of a pool being easily drained by diverting the course of the stream.

The following day we made an early start, our intention being to ford the Ganges and beat up some swampy canebrakes on the farther side of it. As we moved leisurely on the elephants towards the ford, which was a mile or so distant, I diverged into a " null " jungle, along the edge of which we were skirting, in the hope of getting a shot at some jungle-fowl I heard crowing there. " Null " or " nurkul " is a long reed-like grass, common in the Terai and Doon jungles. It is generally a sure harbour for game of all sorts and sizes. I have frequently seen these reeds growing so tall that, when standing in the howdah, I was unable to reach their tops with my gun held up at arm's-length. Even an elephant looks comparatively small in a null jungle.

Well, my elephant had not got far into the null when I heard a deep angry growl, which was immediately followed by the shouting of men, evidently in a state of alarm. Pushing on to the place from whence the sounds came, I found two natives " treed," and hullooing away at the top of their voices. They said they were collecting wild honey, when they had suddenly come on a tigress and two cubs, and had at once climbed up the nearest tree. This information was not easily elicited from them, for they seemed to be as much frightened at the sudden appearance of the elephant as of the tigress.

I lost no time in getting back to inform the rest of the party, when we commenced a regular and careful beat round about the place where the tigress had been seen. But notwithstanding some of the elephants showing the usual and unmistakable signs of a tiger's proximity—in acknowledging the scent by smartly tapping the ground with their trunks, from which they at the same time emitted a peculiar metallic sound—and the noisy commotion among the jungle-fowl, and a troop of monkeys that were chattering and gibbering away as they swung themselves from branch to branch in the trees, which also betokened the presence of Madam Stripes in the vicinity, we failed to find her. The jungle was so thick and tangled that our progress was necessarily very slow, which delay she had evidently taken advantage of to slink away.

All hope of finding the tigress being at an end, we proceeded to cross the Ganges where it was fordable by the elephants, and commenced beating up the cane - brakes, or "bent jungles" as they are commonly called. The canes in these brakes have a remarkably beautiful appearance, growing in widespread tangled masses, or trailing in graceful festoons from the trees, their glossy dark-green fronds resembling drooping plumes of feathers. But of all bad ground for a line of elephants to get over, commend me to a bent jungle as being the worst. The canes are so closely interwoven, and so covered with strong hooked thorns, and the places they grow in are so soft and swampy, that it is sometimes quite impossible for an elephant to force its way through them. For dislodging tigers from such spots, a kind of firework called *anār*, which makes a deal of noise and smoke, is used. But even this often fails to drive them fairly out of these sanctuaries, in which they are very fond of lying up during the intense heat of the day.

It has been said that of the risks run in tiger-shooting from elephants, the danger from the tiger itself is the smallest. This is a matter of opinion. But there is no doubt about there being other dangers quite as great attending this sport—that from a timid elephant being about the worst; for if an animal of this kind gets thoroughly terrified and bolts among tree jungle, the consequences are likely to be disastrous. I once had my howdah and one of my guns smashed to bits by

a runaway brute of this sort. Fortunately I was not in the
howdah at the time.

A source of constant danger with us on this trip was a
vicious "mukna" (tuskless male) elephant. The brute had
already killed two men, and nobody but his mahout dared
approach him. Whenever any of us had occasion to dismount
from our elephants, the first question was always as to the
whereabouts in the line of Moula Buksh, as our dangerous
friend was named.

Getting badly bogged in a "fussand," as the natives call a
quaking morass, ranks about next in order. And an incident
that occurred in this day's beat will serve to show what it
means.

We had been beating slowly and with difficulty through
the patches of bent jungle, and plying the more inaccessible
spots with *anārs*, without having seen a sign of a striped
jacket, when, on reaching a more than usually swampy place,
Golab Soondrie (*Anglicè*, Beautiful Rose), the steady old
elephant I was on, showed a decided disinclination to entering it. Not wishing to leave my place in the line, I made
the mahout urge her forward, and she had not taken more
than a few steps when she was floundering about up to her
middle in thick black mud and water. The old lady finding
she had got fairly into it, continued to struggle bravely on
towards some firmer-looking ground a short distance in front.
But ere reaching this her body was almost entirely submerged
in the foul inky fluid, in which she rolled about like a dis-
masted ship in a heavy sea. It was impossible to leave the
howdah on account of the depth of water; and in such cases,
even when the ground is stable enough to admit of dismount-
ing, it has to be done with caution: for an elephant, on
finding itself in a fix of this kind, is said to be apt to lay hold
with its trunk of anything within reach, without respect even
to persons, to place under its feet for support. And the usual
method adopted, when everything else fails, for extricating an

elephant from a *fussand* (swamp or quicksand), is to throw branches of trees, bundles of grass, &c., within its reach. These the sagacious beast forces down with its trunk under its feet, until the footing thus made becomes tolerably firm.

At length, by dint of great perseverance and exertion on the part of Golab Soondrie, she reached the edge of this abominable quagmire, and having managed to get her fore-feet up on to some firmer-looking ground, was with difficulty dragging out her hind-quarters, when to my consternation the rotten bank gave way under her weight. Back she slid into the horrible slough almost perpendicularly—so much so that the guns lying in their sloping positions alongside me in the howdah fell back on to my outstretched arms, as I clutched the side-rails for support, and I for the moment feared she was going to roll completely over. Matters now looked serious; for the "kawās" (back partition) of the howdah was quite under water, and the black muddy fluid reached half-way up to my knees in the fore-part of it. The mahout was obliged to quit his seat on the neck of the elephant, and little else was to be seen of the animal save the top of her head and her trunk. Still the fine old creature continued to make the most prodigious efforts, until at last, thanks to her being a small and an active elephant, she managed to scramble out. Before we overtook the rest of the party—who, from the thickness of the jungle, had not seen our mishap—they had almost reached the tents, which were near at hand, when the dirty plight we presented after our mud-larking adventure afforded much merriment at our expense.

Finding there was no fresh "kubber" (intelligence) of tigers in this vicinity, we next day had a beat for game in general, of which the pads showed a fair amount, when, towards evening, we reforded the river on the elephants. As we were passing some grass-sheds on our way to camp, Moula Buksh displayed his evil disposition by chevying a wretched pony, which was heavily handicapped in the chase by being

N

hobbled. All the forcible persuasions of the mahout with his iron-hooked goad failed to stop him as he went straight for the pony. Just as his uplifted trunk was over his intended victim's back, the mahout, as a last resource, dropped his outspread turban down over the brute's eyes, and so saved the pony from being kicked to a jelly; for an enraged elephant generally vents its spleen on anything it considers obnoxious and can get hold of, by making a shuttlecock of it between its fore and hind feet. I once saw a Goorkha, who was out with us, have a wonderfully narrow escape from being thus kicked to death. A cheetal had with difficulty been padded on a timid unsteady elephant, which suddenly getting frightened at the dead animal's horns, which were dangling over the pad, touching her hind-quarters, began violently shaking her huge body with a view to getting rid of the objectionable load. This she succeeded in doing, as well as of the Goorkha, who was also on the pad. Before the man could regain his legs the elephant was on him, and playing football with his body. Fortunately the mahout soon managed to control the brute, though not before the man was left lying apparently lifeless. We were horror-struck, thinking the poor fellow was dead. Although he was terribly shaken and bruised, and the breath knocked completely out of him, strange to say not a bone was broken, nor was he otherwise very seriously damaged.

Although this visit to the eastern side of the Ganges was not attended with any unusual success, on a former one to the same locality, through the kindness of Major Baugh, who was then superintendent of the Government Elephant " Khedda " (Catching Establishment) in the Kumaon Terai, and whose camp we came across, our shooting-party enjoyed an exciting day's sport, the like of which it has seldom been my good fortune to witness. I may here transcribe my account of it, written long ago for the ' Oriental Sporting Magazine.'

There are several methods resorted to for capturing wild
elephants in different parts of India. These have been so
ably described by those who are much more conversant with
such experiences than I am, that I shall therefore only premise
my attempt to recount the incidents of an elephant-hunt witnessed by myself, by mentioning that the way the animals
were usually captured in the Kumaon Terai was by driving
them up from the level forest into some narrow mountain-
gorge, or *sote* as it is there called, the ridges on either side of
which having been previously lined with men provided with
firearms and blank ammunition, in order to prevent the elephants making their escape on either flank.

On the wild herd being driven into this kind of *cul de sac*
—an operation which was not achieved without considerable
tact and manœuvring—the entrance was guarded by some of
the largest and strongest male elephants being posted across
it; whilst other animals carrying the " phandetes " (noosers)
were ridden in among the herd, and the process of noosing
and tying commenced. This was very cleverly executed by
men trained to the work, assisted by the great sagacity of the
tame elephants. Before it could be effected, however, it was
occasionally necessary to subdue some mighty lord of the
herd by pitting a domesticated giant against him, when a
terrific combat sometimes ensued between these elephantine
gladiators, which usually resulted in the discomfiture and
eventual capture of the wild animal.

Intelligence of the proximity of a herd of wild elephants
having just been brought in to the superintendent by his
scouts, he at once prepared to go after it, and invited our
party to join in the sport.

The necessary arrangements having been quickly made and
orders given, each of us mounted an elephant, and seated
himself on a very small pad that had been substituted for
the usual large-sized one, as being less likely to get displaced
when moving quickly through tree jungle. A rifle or gun

was carried across the knees, but only to be used for defence in the event of a charge being made by a wild elephant.

As the Khedda camp was on the west bank of the Ganges, and the herd was reported to be on the opposite side, we at once proceeded to cross the river by the nearest ford. A truly fine sight it was to see some thirty elephants steadily ploughing their way through the water, which was running almost up to the pads, as the animals leant their huge bodies against the stream to resist the force of the rapid current.

All having got across the river, the first thing necessary before starting in pursuit was to carefully reconnoitre the exact position of the herd. This was done on foot by a few of the party, when it was ascertained that the animals were feeding among some thick clumps of bamboos, which were situated on so seemingly impracticable a position for elephants to reach, that it was difficult to conceive how such huge beasts ever got there; but it is almost incredible what steep and difficult places elephants can travel over. As the ground was found to be unsuitable for attempting to capture the animals by driving them up into a *sote*, Major Baugh's intention was, in this instance, merely to endeavour to drive them towards a more likely locality for circumventing them. At the same time, it was just possible that one or more of them might be noosed in the chase; at all events, he expected an exciting run.

The reconnoitring party having remounted their elephants, we all advanced slowly, and as silently as possible, towards the herd, which, apparently not as yet being much alarmed at the approach of the tame elephants, moved leisurely down through the jungle on the steep declivities towards the level forest below. Our progress was at first rather slow, our elephants using the greatest caution, whilst descending, in placing one foot firmly before venturing to move another. However, we at length reached more level ground, where we soon overhauled the wild herd, and a most exciting chase now commenced.

Immediately on viewing the animals, as some seven or eight of various sizes broke away about twenty yards in front from among some tall "nurkul" reeds, the phandetes shot ahead, balancing themselves, half standing, half kneeling, on their little pads, with nooses held ready to cast should they succeed in getting their elephants, which were being hustled along at a most astonishing pace for such unwieldy animals, alongside the wild ones. The latter, now becoming alarmed, began to increase their speed, though not even now to its full extent, from there being amongst them one or two calves whose retreat their mothers were anxiously endeavouring to cover, sometimes shuffling along half sideways as they tried to look back at their pursuers, who were gradually drawing nearer and nearer.

The wild excitement of the pursuit now reached its highest pitch. Our elephants, in addition to being driven half frantic from being urged along by the mahouts freely using their iron goads, and by their assistant "char khattas" (forage-cutters), who, as they clung on behind the little pads with one hand, with the other pummelled the poor animals most unmercifully in rear with short, heavy wooden clubs studded with a few iron spikes, had also become imbued with the general excitement, and had got their blood fairly up as they dashed ahead regardless of every obstacle.

Onward we go, and still onward, scrambling over prostrate trunks of trees, through dense underwood, thorny brakes, and tangled creepers, which snap like pack-threads before our elephants. Now we are bowling along across an open grassy glade, or rattling over the loose boulders in the dry bed of a water-course. Again we charge headlong into the forest, which resounds with the crashing of boughs and dry nurkul reeds —the shrill trumpeting and snorting of the elephants being mingled with the sharp ejaculations of encouragement or abuse of their beasts from the mahouts, as they vie with each other in their endeavours to keep the wild herd in view. We have plenty to do in perpetually ducking our heads and bending our bodies to avoid projecting branches.

There goes the first fall! An excited Goorkha is swept clean off the pad of an elephant near me by a tough creeper catching him across the middle, sending him sprawling among the bushes. There is no stopping to pick him up, but I glance back and see him on his legs again, he fortunately having fallen on a soft place. Now we are rolling and floundering through a quaking bog, from the black tenacious mud of which the elephants slowly and with difficulty drag their feet with a succession of squelchy sucking sounds. This causes a temporary check, and gives the fallen Goorkha time to scramble up on to his elephant, an acrobatic feat he accomplishes with the assistance of the animal's tail. But we are soon clear of the swamp, and still on and on we tear helter-skelter. How we, who are unaccustomed to such work, contrive to stick on to our small pads, and also to balance a gun across our knees, seems perfectly miraculous; but one does things in hot blood that one never dreams of being able to do in cold.

At last a nooser has managed to lay his elephant alongside the hindermost wild one. She appears only to see the elephant and not its rider, who, with ready noose, eagerly awaits a favourable opportunity for casting it; consequently she is unaware of her real danger until she feels the rope on her head. But now, with a shrill trumpet, she shoots swiftly on, slipping away from under the noose with a lift of her trunk and a toss of her head. Still her maternal solicitude causes her again to check her speed, for her offspring is beside her, and the phandete is once more up with her, and makes another unsuccessful attempt to noose her.

But the pace has been too severe to last, and some of our elephants are showing decided symptoms that such is the

case, by beginning to tail off. As they come straggling back
in groups from the chase, their excited riders have each some
wonderful tale of their prowess during the scrimmage to
relate, which they do with much gesticulation and true
oriental volubility.

Although Golab Soondrie, the elephant I rode, from formerly having been used in the elephant-catching line, was
well acquainted with the business on hand, she could not
keep pace with the noosers' elephants, which were of course
in a high state of training and condition for such work, from
constant practice. I was therefore unable to be in quite at
the finish, which resulted in the capture of one of the calves
only—its mother, after baffling all attempts to noose her,
having at length left it to its fate. The poor little creature,
which was scarcely bigger than a pony, was set at liberty, as
it was considered too young to be weaned from its mother.

The original intention of driving the herd towards a more
practicable locality for their capture having been effectually
carried out, we recrossed the Ganges as the shades of evening
were closing around; and this glorious day's sport was wound
up by a champagne dinner given by the Khedda superintendent, over whose hospitable board the exciting incidents
of the hunt were recounted and discussed.

The piteous cries of the little calf in search of its dam, as
they were borne across the river on the night breeze, and the
frequent low rumbling noises made by the still excited tame
elephants at their pickets, were the last sounds I heard ere I
fell asleep.

Next morning Major Baugh took us round his Khedda.
One or two of the more recent captures were bound fast by
their legs to trees, where they rocked themselves impatiently
to and fro, resisting all the blandishments of their attendants.
By way of accustoming them to the human presence and voice,
they were periodically stroked and brushed down with long
green boughs, the men performing this office the while singing

songs and talking to them. One magnificent tusker named
Scott attracted much of our attention. Although now the
principal gladiator of the Khedda, he had not been very long
in captivity, and still retained the proud free gait and high
carriage of head of his wild state. Major Baugh told us his
behaviour before tigers was splendidly steady, and that on
one occasion when a tiger had attempted to charge him, he
had actually lifted the brute with his trunk and sent it
spinning up for yards through the air.

The sagacity, and even enjoyment, which the domesticated
elephants evince in assisting at the capture of their wild
brethren is truly remarkable, and the more so as many of
the tame ones may themselves have been roaming free in the
forest only a few months before. For example, it is customary, on a wild elephant being captured, to conduct it
along to camp, or to lead it from one camping-ground to
another, attached by strong ropes to a Khedda elephant on
each side of it. These two warders hustle and jostle their
prisoner along, and should he show signs of becoming obstre-
perous, belabour him with iron chains, which they carry with
their trunks for this purpose. The captive, however, generally submits rather peaceably to his fate, and soon becomes
quite tractable to the will of his two custodians.

In Burmah I have watched elephants in the timber-yards
at Maulmain working with almost human intelligence.
There they may be seen drawing huge logs about the yards;
unhooking the dragging-chains with their trunks; lifting the
logs on to the piles of timber, and then adjusting them
squarely there; or launching them into the river with their
feet, to be floated away.

But to revert to our present doings on the banks of the
Ganges. The day after recrossing the river we were again
beating up the quarters of the tigress and cubs, when suddenly there was a cry of " Mukkee aya " (the bees have come).
Those who have never hunted in the Doon or Terai forests

can hardly imagine the startling effect this simple exclamation sometimes has on a line of elephants. And perhaps this will be best understood by relating what occurred in our case on hearing it.

In breaking through the underwood somebody had inadvertently disturbed a swarm of bees, which in these jungles suspend their combs from a branch, and often so low down that, if the nest is hidden by foliage, an elephant is very apt to run foul of it. This had in all probability happened in the present instance, for the infuriated insects at-

Wild bees' nest.

tacked both man and beast with such determined pertinacity, that the result was a case of *sauve qui peut*, causing the total disorganisation of the whole beat. Tigress and cubs were at once forgotten as the line scattered hither and thither in futile attempts to escape from the bees, which followed some of the elephants in clouds, plying their stings so viciously as to even leave many of them sticking in the leather that covered the iron rails of the howdahs. Strange to say, these bees, when thus disturbed, seem to devote their attention chiefly to certain elephants, and these they will follow for miles, only attacking the rest of the line occasionally and in small detachments. In this case the principal object of their animosity was the Colonel's elephant, which, though steady enough before a tiger, was quite unable to withstand this combined attack of little enemies. With a shriek of pain, she set off, tail on end, until pulled up by a tangled thicket of the huge "maljoon" creeper, into which she charged headlong, in the vain hope of eluding her persecutors.

Being on the extreme left of the line, with the help of a blanket and plenty of smoke, created by the Goorkha behind me in the howdah burning bits of rag torn from his turban, we managed almost to defy the more mild assaults made on our elephant.

On getting clear of the heavy jungle in which the bees had been disturbed, some sort of order was re-established, although many of them pertinaciously stuck to us, and we did not get entirely rid of the angry swarm for a long time. Notwithstanding each of us being provided with a blanket, which is usually kept ready for wrapping about one's head in an emergency of this sort, there was a visible change in the features of some of the party when we came to compare notes after our disorderly retreat.

But the excitement of this day's beat was not to end with the departure of the bees, for we had hardly got quit of them when a sound was heard, and not very far off either, that caused us all to prick up our ears. It was the deep guttural growl of a tiger, which, judging from the angry tone of its voice, was in a contumacious humour.

On we all push in line towards the spot from whence the sound had proceeded. Before reaching it, an unexpected obstacle occurs in the shape of a deep narrow nullah, with precipitous banks, and almost hidden by the long grass growing on both sides of it. Whilst I am pondering in my mind as to what could have induced the tiger to betray its whereabouts in this unusual manner, Golab Soondrie has been making a path for herself by breaking down the steep bank with her feet, and her fore-quarters are now in the nullah, the top of her head being about level with the opposite bank, when, with a succession of furious hoarse grunts, a big striped object comes rushing through the grass towards us. I only catch a glimpse of the charging brute, and cannot shoot, as the elephant, from being so much taken by surprise at this sudden and unprovoked attack, wheels sharply round with a jerk that is almost enough to send me out of the howdah. Quick as thought, Golab Soondrie has her fore-legs up the bank again, and our position becomes rather critical, for her hind-quarters are now in the nullah, and the howdah is on a level with the charging tiger. On comes the beast with a spring from the bank, just missing the back rail of the howdah, and falling with a splash into the shallow water in the nullah. The Goorkha in the kawas behind me scrambles over into my part of the howdah, to the side-rail of which the mahout is already clinging, he having jumped up from the elephant's neck at the first sign of danger. Altogether there is such a general scrimmage, and my hands are so fully employed in holding on to the howdah-rails, that it is impossible to handle a rifle ere the baffled tiger has slunk off and disappeared along the bottom of the nullah.

The bold behaviour of this animal was, under the circumstances, decidedly unusual; for an unwounded tiger, when disturbed, generally tries to steal off, if possible, unobserved, and seldom attacks a human being unless provoked. Even man-eaters, of which the proportion is fortunately very small, resort to the most cunning and sneaking methods for securing their victims. A female with cubs, however, is often an exception to this rule, and such our friend might have been, though in this instance we failed to find her offspring.

Meanwhile there had been some excitement in another part of the line, for as soon as I had time to look about me, I saw that the other elephants had got across the nullah, and were going ahead full speed, evidently with some object in view. The sound of a shot, followed by a "whoof," soon proved that such was the case. On overtaking the line, I found that a second tiger had been seen, at which the Colonel had got a snap-shot, but the beast had given them the slip in some heavy "null" (nurkul reed) jungle.

By this time it was getting dusk. In addition to this, one of the men, either accidentally or with the idea of trying to drive out the tigers, had foolishly set alight the long dry nurkul, and the fire, which now began roaring and crackling as the flames shot high in the air, was beginning to spread with such rapidity that, for the second time during the day, we had to beat a hasty retreat.

As we were a considerable distance from camp, we had a long and toilsome ride on the elephants, as they jogged slowly and wearily in single file through the dark jungle, which was ever and anon dimly lighted up by the red glow reflected on the clouds of smoke that overhung the fire raging fitfully behind us. The distance, however, would have been thought little of had there been a dead tiger on one of the pads.

We beat round about for the tigers next morning, and came upon one of them, but, owing to the thickness of the jungle, failed to get a shot. Being our last day out—after all chance, as we thought, of again finding the tigers was over—a general battue was commenced. It was just about sundown when, having badly wounded a fine stag cheetal, I left the line to follow him up; but failing to find him, I was jogging quickly and carelessly along, endeavouring to overtake the line. So little idea had I of seeing game of any sort on the ground which the other elephants had just passed over, that I had laid down my rifle in the howdah, and was not even on the look-out, when, by the merest chance, my eye fell upon an object the sight of which made my heart leap. A magnificent tiger was just on the point of disappearing behind some bushes about fifty yards in front of me. How the beast escaped being observed by the rest of the line was most strange, as the ground in the direction from whence it seemed to have come had been recently burnt, and was almost as bare as a billiard-table. Snatching up the rifle on the impulse of the moment, I foolishly let drive after the beast through the bushes, instead of first following it up. But, alas! there was

no responsive grunt to denote that the bullet had told; and
although I at once gave chase, the tiger had vanished in the
same magical sort of way it had at first appeared.

This incident may have served to show how necessary it is
to be always on the look-out when in the jungle for anything that may turn up, as a chance is often got when least
expected.

I was all the more disappointed at having lost such an
opportunity when, on reaching camp, some herdsmen told
us that this tiger had for a long time haunted the locality
where I had seen it, and had killed an incredible number of
their cattle. A cattle-lifter of this sort generally prefers
taking common cows and bullocks to buffaloes, as a herd
of the latter is always ready to resent an attack on one of its
community by a tiger, which often comes off second best. A
friend of mine, when out shooting in these jungles, came
across a Goojur herdsman instructing his buffaloes in the
noble art of self-defence. He had ensconced himself up a
tree, and was dangling among the herd below him an old
tiger skin attached to a rope, which the enraged animals
were fiercely attacking.

Thus ended a short hunting-trip in the Dehra Doon.
Although not so successful a one as regards the actual
slaying of tigers as others I might have told of, it is perhaps better calculated to afford a fair idea of the general
sport that was then to be had in that locality, and also to
show what chance work it is finding these cunning and wary
brutes in such heavy jungles, unless certain intelligence of
their whereabouts near a fresh " kill " has first been obtained.
Moreover, my experiences of tiger-shooting are comparatively
few, and in thrilling adventure they fall so far short of those
which have oftentimes been graphically recounted by more
practised hands at this noble sport, that any further narration of them would only be superfluous in a book which is
more intended for describing mountain work.

CHAPTER XIII.

ON the outer ranges and spurs of the Himalayas rising abruptly from the Dehra Doon, the "surrow" (*Nemorhœdus bubalina*), which is nowhere very common, was not unfrequently met with. This curious animal, which, like the gooral of the Himalayas and the chamois of Europe, is one of the links between the antelope and wild goat, might almost be supposed to have a strain of the donkey as well, for it has a decidedly asinine appearance, particularly about the head. It stands about 3 feet at the shoulder, which is an inch or two higher than the croup; and its build is so sturdy as almost to make its form look ungainly and its gait clumsy. The neck is thick, short, and black, and is surmounted with a bristling mane of coarse black hair extending back over the withers, which, with its almost black head and large mule-like ears, grey muzzle, short black horns, and dark fiery eyes, give this beast a fierce look which its character does not belie. Its general colour is a very dark kind of roan-grey, intermixed with black; black dorsal stripe, and tail which is very short;

flanks and fore-quarters reddish-brown, creamy-white from above the knees and hocks downwards; horns black, round, slightly curved, sharply pointed, sloping well backward, and roughly annulated for two-thirds of their length, which is ordinarily about 9 or 10 inches, with a circumference at the base of 5 or 6 inches; ears about 8 inches long; distinct but not very large eyepits, from which, I remember in one at any rate of the specimens I shot, a whitish-looking discharge rather freely exuded. The surrow is pretty generally, though sparsely, distributed over the whole length of the Himalayan ranges, and from the higher to the outer ones. Its favourite haunts are the wildest of craggy, precipitous, wooded gorges where dense "ringal" (a kind of long, thin, reed-like bamboo) jungle abounds, in the deep gloomy recesses of which it usually lies up during the day, seldom venturing abroad except in the very early morning and late in the evening to feed, and then usually only a short distance from its sequestered retreat. For it is of very shy habit, although its disposition is so bold that it is always ready to show fight when wounded, or even in defence of its wounded mate, with which, as well as with their offspring, sometimes it is found in company, though generally a solitary animal. Of its courage the following I know to be an authentic instance. A female surrow had been shot by a sportsman, when, on his native follower approaching to secure it, a male companion rushed out from the dense cover hard by, and going for the man, sent him rolling down-hill with a butt from its horns, making good its retreat ere the astonished shooter had time to remonstrate with his rifle. The doe is very similar in size and appearance to the buck, with horns of almost the same length and thickness. Its cry of alarm resembles a kind of sharp shriek, which, like the gooral, it emits at short and regular intervals. When suddenly surprised it sometimes shows a strange amount of stupidity. I have known it stand stock-still at gaze, even after being shot at, if missed. But once started it rushes off headlong regardless of every obstacle in the shape of rough precipitous ground, seldom stopping to look back. Its ordure, like that of the musk-deer, is generally found deposited together in large heaps. In the Kumaon district, and also, I believe, in Nepal, it is called "tāhr" or "thār"; the *tāhr* proper being there called "jhārrel." On the more eastern Himalayas a red-coloured variety of the surrow occurs, but even more sparsely, I am told, than its darker-skinned relative of the more western ranges.

In one of my many shikar trips among the mountains adjacent to Dehra Doon, I was exceptionally fortunate in coming across several of these rather uncommon nondescript animals. On this short excursion I started with a brother officer who, although not a sportsman, was an ardent admirer of nature. Our objective point was a singularly shaped craggy hill, called Gopee Chund *teeba* (hill), which formed a prominent feature of the outer ranges where it was situated.

Amongst the native folk-lore of this locality were many wild legends concerning this hill. It was said to have derived its name from a rajah of bygone days, who, with his boon companions of his court, used to carry on their revels and midnight orgies in his palatial halls, which were supposed to have once stood on the site of the bare grey crags and high cliffs formed by landslips, where the eagle now has its eyrie and the gooral roams free. But Rajah Gopee Chund having suddenly been stricken with remorse for his past vices and follies, resolved to become a *jogee* (religious devotee) for the rest of his days. On his turning *jogee* it appeared that he must in some mysterious manner have acquired supernatural powers, as prior to setting out on his lifelong pilgrimage he converted his castle and all its belongings into the rugged grey rocks that now form the hill.

When hunting over this ground, my shikaree, a native of a neighbouring village, was wont to entertain me with many a wild tale, and to point out objects of, to him, superstitious interest. Here he would draw my attention to a great chair-like rock, on which he said the rajah used to sit and hold his court; there, to some curious beetling crags, once the site of the royal stables, but now where gooral and other game had scraped out large cavities below the rocks, in partaking of the *kar* (salt) with which the earth there was strongly impregnated. Then he would relate how his grandfather had, sometimes during the dead of night, heard the neighing of horses, the baying of dogs, and the sounds of revelry borne down on the wind towards his village from the crags above, which my informant firmly believed were still haunted by the ghosts of the departed; and how, but a year or two before, the inhabitants of his village had been terror-stricken one night by a fearful noise caused by the falling of an enormous landslip, the roar of which sounded, he said, as if the whole hill were tumbling and going to bury them beneath it.

These big landslips are very common in the Himalayas, more especially during the rainy season, at times when the saturation of the mountains with moisture is excessive. The terrible landslip which occurred at the Himalayan sanitarium of Nynee Tal in 1880, when so many of our fellow-countrymen and an unknown number of natives were in a few moments hurled into eternity by the fall of a whole hillside into the lake there, is a matter of history. My wife, who was at the time residing in a house within only a quarter of a mile of the edge of the slip, has told me many a harrowing tale of this awful catastrophe. I may also mention a very extraordinary but less disastrous kind of landslip, of which the following is a description, as related to me by Colonel E. Smyth, who was for many years superintendent of the educational department of Kumaon and Gurhwal.[1]

[1] The late Pundit Nain Sing, the celebrated Asiatic explorer, who was awarded one of the Royal medals by the Royal Geographical Society for his valuable services, was originally one of Colonel Smyth's native schoolmasters, and was sent by him to Colonel Montgomerie of the Trigonometrical Survey of India, for employment as an explorer

"A very curious landslip occurred some thirty years ago, about a mile from Tapoobun, and between that place and Renee (in Gurhwal). The road to Malari goes up the left bank of the Dhoulee river, and about a mile from Tapoobun crosses a little stream which descends from the mountains on the right. Both banks of this stream were covered with thick forest at the time I first traversed this road. The year after, I came this way again, and found the whole valley of this little stream was on the move downwards, moving very slowly, perhaps not more than a few inches a-day. The trees were all crooked; some had fallen entirely—some one way, some another. The whole extent of ground thus on the move was perhaps, at its broadest part, near the Dhoulee river, about half a mile, gradually narrowing upwards. The road of course had gone, and we had to climb upwards for about 1200 feet of elevation, over perhaps one and a half miles of ground, until we reached the highest point of the slip, and we descended on the other side, along the edge of the slip, until we reached the road. Six years afterwards I again passed this spot: the landslip had stopped, but the trees were all uprooted and lying about, and the road had been re-made and carried over the rough ground left by the landslip."

By the natives it was supposed that the game on Gopee Chund hill bore charmed lives. Indeed I had almost reason for fancying that such was the case, for, plentiful as game was there, never before, when going over it, had I been able to shoot a single head. This time, however, I succeeded in breaking the spell by making two such wonderful shots, or flukes, and under circumstances so peculiar, that it seemed as though the spirit of the *quondam* rajah had transferred the favour hitherto conferred on the wild denizens of the hill to me.

We had reached the spot where we intended to encamp, which was a small saddle-like flat connecting Gopee Chund with another hill, and commanding a view of a mighty preci-

pice that extended almost from summit to base of the former
in almost a sheer wall of nearly 1000 feet high—the scene of
the recent landslip. We were resting among some rocks
awaiting the arrival of the men who were following us up the
steep track with our traps, when I chanced to notice two
brown objects moving among the crags above the precipice.
They were so high above us, and in the distance looked so
small, that we at first thought they were monkeys, as also did
some of our sharp-eyed hill-men, who had just arrived and
were depositing their loads; but on bringing the spy-glass to
bear on them, it showed they were gooral, so I lost no time in
trying to circumvent them. Leaving my companion seated
on the rocks below, from whence he could command a view of
the whole proceedings, I commenced working upwards along
the edge of the precipice, where the ground was favourable for
the stalk, until I got within what I judged to be well over 200
yards of the animals. Nearer than this I could in no way
approach them without their detecting me; so there was
nothing left but to chance a long shot, with little hope of
hitting such a small mark at so great an angle upward.
They were now standing motionless, apparently watching the
men moving about below; and their colour so much resembled
the ground they were on, that I again had recourse to the glass
to enable me, before shooting, to clearly distinguish their outlines from those of the rocks among which they stood. Steady-
ing my elbows on a convenient slab of stone, I took a careful
and deliberate aim at the larger of the two and let drive. It
staggered for a few moments, and then, toppling over, fell on
to a narrow ledge about 50 feet below it in the precipice, close
above the brink of which it had been standing. Off this it
shot down through space. I watched it almost with a thrill
of awe, as it went whirling through the air, until the latter
part of its descent was hid from my view by the crags
that projected over the profound depth below. So fascinated
was I by this extraordinary, I may almost call it appalling

spectacle, that at first I forgot to notice what had become of the other gooral. I now observed it climbing away over the steep rocks, so I chanced the contents of the second barrel at it. The bullet must have shaved, if it did not strike it, for it seemed to crouch down for a few seconds before finally disappearing.

I now got back to where I had left my companion below. He had been able to see the falling gooral for the whole length of its tremendous descent, during which, he said, it had only touched the rocks twice. I afterwards ascertained, with my mountain aneroid, that the drop was almost a sheer 1000 feet.

As we sat there watching our little tents being pitched, the noise made by the men who had gone down to fetch the fallen gooral disturbed another that had been reposing in some secluded niche beside the big precipice. Across the face of this the sure-footed creature took its way along an almost imperceptible ledge, which could only have been a few inches wide. When about half-way over it stopped, with its head craned forward to gaze down at the men, who had just reached the dead beast below.

I signalled to the men who were pitching the tents a short distance below where my companion and I were seated, to bring me up my rifle (which I had left there), with the idea of taking a sky shot at the beast, but without a notion of being able to hit it; for, although nearly on a level with us, it was fully 300 yards off. Sighting for that distance, I lay down and took my shot. Judge of our astonishment, then, at seeing the animal fall from the ledge and drop clear 500 feet, down almost beside where, on a steep sloping chaos of loose rocks and *débris* that had originally slipped from the precipice above, the first gooral lay, and nearly on to the heads of the men who were preparing to shoulder it. The mangled remains of the two goorals were soon brought up, when we were surprised to find them much less smashed and torn than might have been expected, owing probably to their having fallen so clear of rocks.

The rifle that served me so well on this occasion, as well as on many another—although seldom, if ever, with such astonishing results—is still in my possession: a ·450 bore, double, muzzle-loading Whitworth; and never was bullet thrown from a more trusty weapon. The dear old-fashioned thing, there it stands in the rack before me now as I write, and there it shall remain as a memento, nothing more, of many a happy day passed with it among the fells and forests of the grand old Himalayas.

In the evening I climbed up to the spot where the companion of the first gooral I had killed had disappeared, but found nothing on its tracks to show that it had been wounded.

After turning in at night, when all else was silent and still, we heard eerie sounds and a weird-like rustling of wings, as if the restless spirits of the haunted mountain were flitting through the air. But I soon discovered they proceeded from several nightjars that were flying to and fro close over the camp, having probably been attracted by the moonshine on the white tents. In the uncertain light, I at first took them for woodcocks, which, among the higher ranges, sometimes come hovering over the camp-fires after nightfall.

Speaking of the nightjar, or goatsucker, reminds me of a little fable the "paharees" (hill people) have about a small bird of the nightjar kind, which is very rarely seen, although its "too too" melancholy pair of notes may be heard at short regular intervals all night long among the oak and rhododendron trees. The legend runs that once upon a time the wild birds had a "mela" (fair) of their own, to which they all repaired. But this plainly attired little fellow, thinking his plumage was not grand enough for the occasion, begged a bright-coloured feather from each of his more gaily dressed companions and went to the fair bedecked with those borrowed plumes. When the fair was over the lenders demanded back their feathers, but their wearer, being much pleased with himself, objected to returning them. Upon this, the lenders snatched for their feathers, and in the scuffle the poor borrower was stripped, not only of them, but of most of his own as well. So this modest little bird has ever since been left lamenting its fate, and striving to hide its nakedness, which, they say, accounts for its mournful notes and its being so seldom seen. Often as I have endeavoured to catch a glimpse of this shy wee bird, by trying to follow it up when it commenced its piping notes at dusk, strange to say I always failed to discover it.

The commencement of our trip had been decidedly auspicious, and during the three following days I got some pretty shooting at the gooral in this neighbourhood, killing three more. One of them, however, which I wounded late in the evening, had been much torn by the eagles and vultures before what little they had left of it was eventually found by a goat-herd, whose attention had probably been attracted to it by the birds gyrating and swooping above it.

On the fourth day we shifted our tents a few miles, to a ridge that overlooked the Doon stretching away like a big green map far below. Early in the morning, whilst searching for game with my shikaree along a circuitous route towards our new camp, I noticed, away on the sky-line, the dark form of an animal which the glass showed to be a surrow. We waited until it moved out of sight beyond the steep-sloping ridge on which it had been standing, and then made the best of our way there. We were clambering round the rocky shoulder of the ridge, when I caught sight of the animal a short distance below me, but having got wind of us in some manner, it rattled away down the rocks, and before I could cover it with the rifle, was out of sight in a deep wooded "khud"[1] immediately beneath.

[1] "Khud," or "khālla," is the native term for a steep-sided, V-shaped

As I stood on a projecting crag, disappointedly gazing down in the direction the surrow had gone, the head and shoulders of another suddenly emerged from behind a rock not twenty yards below me. I was considerably out of breath from climbing, and the space I had almost to balance myself on was so limited and so directly over the animal, that I missed it, or at any rate made a shockingly bad shot. It must, however, have touched the beast somewhere, for I was close enough to hear it give a low kind of grunt, as it dashed off, like a rocket, downwards after its companion. We followed a short way on its bloodless trail, and then feeling much mortified at my muffish performance, made straight for our new camp, which had been pitched on the ridge running along the opposite side of the wide khud, in the dark silent depths of which the surrow had taken refuge.

After a late breakfast, as I sat deliberating as to whether it would be worth while turning out all our men to search the gorge below, on the faint chance of finding the surrow lying wounded there, one of them came running to tell me he had seen a surrow moving among the rocks and bushes far down on the opposite face of the khud. On taking a look through the glass there, I saw the beast, and, strange to say, not very far from where our two friends of the morning had been lost sight of. We watched it until it moved behind some bushes, and as it did not reappear, we concluded it must have lain down there; so I at once arranged for attempting a drive, the ground being rather unfavourable for a stalk. Sending some men round behind the ridge above the bit of cover the surrow had entered, I proceeded to take up a position commanding as much of the steep broken ground below it as possible, thinking that the animal would be certain to make for the dense ringals at the bottom of the gorge. At last one of the men appeared on the ridge, and pointing significantly towards

gorge, as "pākhān" is for a precipice, "khānta" for crags, and "pāhār" or "teeba" for a mountain or hill.

the bushes, soon drove the animal out by flinging down a stone. But the cunning brute must have detected me below, for instead of coming downwards, as I had every reason to expect, it took a slant upwards, and never stopped until it disappeared over the sky-line far away at the head of the glen; so I had once more to return dejectedly to the tents.

That evening one of the men reported his having seen, in the gloaming, a surrow moving among the oak-trees near the head of the glen, when fetching water for camp from a spring there,—probably the animal we had driven from its usual haunt returning to rejoin its companion. For surrow seem to be very domestic in their habits, with respect to their family ties; but as their homes are rather extensive and difficult of access, an interview with them is by no means easy to obtain.

Next day being Sunday, we gave ourselves and the surrow a rest. As we reclined on the grass near our tents, enjoying the cool evening breeze and looking down on the forest-clad Doon 4000 feet below, the prospect was singularly beautiful. The sun was sinking, like a fiery red ball, in the haze that dimmed the distant plain stretching away beyond the low irregular line of the Sewalik hills; whilst behind us, over the tree-tops, rose the pale full moon like a huge silver globe. Again the surrow was seen just before dark by our men who were fetching water, so I determined to organise a regular beat through the gorge on the morrow.

Early next morning I worked over some old landslips eastward of our camp, the long steep slopes of which, where not too rocky and precipitous, were now clothed with spear-grass and brushwood, interspersed here and there with oak and cheer trees.[1] On one of my previous visits to this locality I had killed a fine surrow there; this time, however, I saw

[1] The cheer-tree (*Pinus longifolia*) much resembles the Scotch fir, but with longer and paler-green spines. It is the commonest kind of pine that grows on the lower and middle ranges.

only one or two gooral and a barking-deer. I may here give
an instance, which came under my observation, of how wild
animals may recover from bad wounds. On one occasion
when hunting on this ground, I shot at a gooral—one of a
herd of five or six — which went off with its fore-leg so
smashed that I even found bits of bone on its track. The
following year I was shooting there again at the same season
—November—when I saw what was doubtless the identical
herd on almost exactly the same spot, and shot one out of it.
This animal was found to have a stiff knee-joint, the leg
having evidently been broken by a bullet, but the bones had
reunited in a long indurated lump; and I have little doubt
but that it was the same gooral I had wounded there just a
year before. I have the bone thus mended by nature now in
my possession.

In the forenoon all our forces were marshalled, and
most of them placed under command of old Hookmee,
the local shikaree, to be disposed in the manner he thought
best for driving the gorge below. Strict injunctions were
given that no other noise was to be made than an occasional tap with a stick on a tree stem, except by the scouts
posted on points of vantage to watch the gorge as the beaters
moved down it, and to signal by voice any movements of our
game they might detect therein. This precaution regarding
noise is always necessary when driving deer in cover, as the
beaters usually make such an infernal row, and the game
gets so bewildered by their echoing voices, that a beast is just
as likely to break back as to rush madly forward in its terror,
instead of moving on leisurely, as it otherwise would be pretty
certain to do.

Whilst Hookmee is proceeding with his small army of
beaters towards the head of the glen, I start off to take up a
position far down it, on a sort of promontory, overlooking as
much as possible the main gorge on the left, as well as a
smaller lateral one on the right, running into the main one

just below me, and up which offshoot Hookmee says the surrow may possibly take.

As I sit there expectant among the rocks, being half baked by the hot March sun, I can hear the beaters as they come slowly down through the ringals and trees in the khud, but only the sound of their tapping-sticks, for old Hookmee has got them well in hand. Presently a voice comes from high up on the opposite side of the glen. It proceeds from one of the scouts stationed there, calling my attention to two surrow he can see passing along the rocky face below me on the left; but the ground is so steep there, that to me they are invisible. Again he shouts that they have turned up the smaller gorge to the right, and I have not long to wait before a rustle among the dry fallen leaves apprises me that something is coming up it. But the beast keeps so well concealed in the thick cover, that it passes on without giving a chance for a shot. It is followed almost immediately by its companion, which suddenly detecting me, turns sharply round, and, under cover of the brushwood, makes for the opposite ridge of the ravine. More fortunately for me than for the surrow, it has to traverse an open bit of steep ground before it can reach the ridge; but a bullet from the Whitworth catching it in rear, turns it back. It stands for a few seconds as if bewildered, when another bullet causes it to totter back down towards the cover at the bottom of the ravine. A movement among the bushes below me now attracts my attention, and almost directly I catch sight of the first surrow, which, probably missing its mate, has returned in search of him, and is now standing broadside on, in a small open space among the brushwood, within fifty yards. The contents of my second weapon, a miniature ·360 express, sent into its shoulder, floor it at once in its tracks.

I now devote my attention to the other surrow, which I find is so sick as to be incapable of moving away. I have hardly settled it with the " pea-shooter," when again I hear shouts from a marker. He has seen yet another surrow, which, he says, has crossed the foot of the lateral gorge, and is now moving beyond it along the precipitous face on my side of the main one. I at once send several of the beaters, who have just joined me, round to try and intercept the animal, but the ground there is too steep and difficult for them to travel over. All they can do is to shell the place with big stones, so I am not surprised that he gives us the slip. Nor am I much disappointed either, being quite satisfied with the two animals secured.

One of the dead beasts had a half-healed bullet-hole in its ear, and was most probably the first surrow I had seen and shot at a few days before, not very far from where it had now fallen. Both were good specimens—a buck and a doe—and carried almost equally long horns.

As nearly all our manœuvres had taken place within sight of the camp, my companion on this trip had once more an opportunity of watching them almost from his tent. This was a very satisfactory termination to our pleasant week's holiday.

Village, Gurhwal Mountains.

CHAPTER XIV.

DESPITE its hardships and vicissitudes, the greater experience one has of a wild mountain life, the more does the passion for it increase. The craving for its roving freedom, in the temperament of some people, becomes such as at length to amount almost to a disease—as is known to be the case with Swiss mountaineers—when deprived of it. There is certainly nothing that tends more to invigorate both mind and body than the opportunities for studying the beautiful works of nature, the immunity from worldly worries, and the healthy exercise afforded by wild mountain sport. I have also ob-served that there is a kind of affinity between real sportsmen which attracts them towards each other, for among no other class of men does more good-fellowship exist. And I can affirm, from my own experience, that many a true and lasting friendship has commenced on a shikar trip.

Towards the middle of a very hot summer in the Punjab, I started for the Himalayas on two months' leave. From constant confinement indoors—where the sojourner in the plains of India during the hot season is constrained to shut himself up all day in a darkened room to avoid the intense heat and glare—I had been getting into that unhappy frame of mind which makes life almost a burden, and from want of sufficient light and fresh air, my face was rapidly assuming the blanched appearance presented by the inside of a tied-up cabbage. After this dreary monotonous sort of existence, it can easily be imagined with what keen delight I looked forward to being once more free to roam among the pine-forests and snowy regions of the Cashmere mountains.

My intention this time was to hunt markhor on the western end of the Pir Punchal range, above the sources of the Bonyar river. I chose this locality because I knew it had not been much hunted over for several seasons, although it had not as great a reputation for big markhor as other places I had visited.

If one wishes to have good sport in a foreign land, the first and most important thing to be done is to endeavour as much as possible to ingratiate one's self with the people of the country in the vicinity of one's hunting-ground. Acting upon this principle, which I have always put into practice, I proceeded to pay my respects to a nawab (native gentleman) who was the proprietor of part of the land I wished to shoot over. His residence was some six miles from Uri, on the Murree route to Cashmere, but he happened to be at Uri the day I reached that place. Shortly after my arrival, an individual of very imposing mien, and extensively arrayed in the sporting style of costume usually affected by the impostor class of Cashmere shikaree, swaggered up in the most confident manner and offered his services. On being informed that they were not required, he turned on his heel and stalked proudly away. He, however, continued to prowl about in the vicinity, and in the afternoon, just before I started, again presented himself, when, by way of getting rid of him, I pointed to one of the heaviest loads, and told him that if he chose he might carry it, which offer he treated, as I expected, with silent contempt, and disappeared. The next time I saw my friend, he had divested himself of most of his fine garments, and his fine airs also, and was toiling up a hill with the identical heavy load on his back. Finding I was not to be taken in, I fancy he had thought better of it. Though I have called him an impostor with regard to his capabilities as a shikaree, he was anything but one in his proper capacity as a weight-carrier; for, to do him justice, he afterwards turned out to be one of the most willing and hard-working men I employed, and whenever there was anything to be done that required more than ordinary strength and activity, Kazima was always to the front.

From Uri I was accompanied by the Nawab, who beguiled the time passed on our way with accounts of the kind of sport I was likely to get, and also with some of his own hunting experiences—for both he and his younger brother were men of sporting proclivities—and on our arrival at his village after dark, nothing could exceed his hospitality and attention to all my wants.

The following day was devoted to purchasing a stock of supplies for my men and making a few final preparations for our mountain work. The Nawab provided me with his two best shikarees—Gamoo and Hatha. The former was a very intelligent little man, with a bright good-humoured countenance; the latter, who acted under Gamoo's orders, was an active, willing fellow.

Before proceeding further, it may be as well to give a slight description of the noble animal we were about to seek. The markhor (*Capra megaceros*), or, in English, snake-eater, so called from his being supposed by the hill-men to be what his name implies,[1] is without doubt the finest animal of the wild-

---

[1] It may not be generally known that goats are ordinarily addicted to snake-eating,—so say the Highland herdsmen, at any rate.

goat tribe. There are several known localities in the northern Himalayas and in the mountains on the north-west frontier where it is met with, besides the comparatively unknown ones more northward, and in each of those known it differs slightly, principally in the shape of the horns. The horns of the variety found on the Pir Punchal and Kajnag ranges, west of the Cashmere valley, have three or four spiral curls in the shape of a cork-screw, and sometimes grow to an extraordinary length. I measured one that was 63 inches follow-

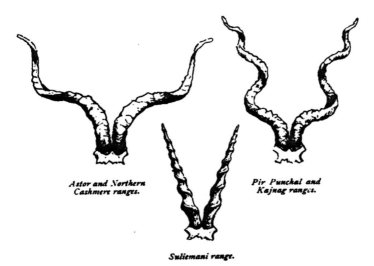

Astor and Northern Cashmere ranges.

Pir Punchal and Kajnag ranges.

Suliemani range.

Types of Markhor Horns.

ing the twist, and considerably over a yard straight. But this was an exceptionally fine specimen, and only a single horn, which was purchased at a village. The markhor found on the more northern mountains of the Cashmere territory are in colour and size much the same as those of the Pir Punchal, but their horns have fewer turns, although they grow equally long, and, as a rule, more massive. Markhor are there sometimes found on the same ground with ibex. In the Dehrajat country, west of the Indus, the markhor are

MARKHOR (PIR PUNCHAL).

sometimes attended with even more difficulty and danger than that of ibex—for the earth in such places is often so friable, loose, and rotten, and the short dry grass is so smooth and slippery, as to make the footing there most treacherous. Even in the depth of winter the old bucks seldom quit their fastnesses, where they are said then to subsist chiefly on pine-shoots.

The following extract from a memorandum by the late Colonel T. G. Montgomerie, R.E., on the progress of the Trigonometrical Survey of Cashmere, will give a good idea of the imposing appearance of the markhor: "Among the minor results of the expedition [1] was a great influx of presents to the Maharajah from all the chiefs between Gilgit and Kafiristan. Perhaps the most valuable in the eyes of the Curator of the Asiatic Society's Museum would have been a splendid live male specimen of the markhor, the greatest prize of Himalayan sportsmen. This animal was introduced into the full durbar, guided by four men with guy ropes. It was really a handsome animal, of a light fawn colour, with a capital pair of horns, and a fine long beard. The top of the markhor's head was, perhaps, 5½ feet from the ground, the horns towering up above all the men in attendance. The keepers of this animal evidently held him in the highest respect, though he had been a captive for at least two months. This markhor was a present from the chiefs of Kholi, Palus, on the Indus."

Trusting that my imperfect description of the "king of wild goats," as Gamoo called him, may have given some idea of his appearance and habits, we will now start for his wild domain.

Gamoo's intention was first to make straight for a remote and lonely tract of the mountains, where he thought the big old bucks were pretty sure to be found at that season—June —and which it would take us at least three days to reach.

[1] Maharajah Gholab Sing's expedition against Gilgit in 1860.

After packing off the men carrying the loads, with directions to pitch our little camp at a suitable spot, known to Gamoo, some distance down the other side of a lofty range that rose about a mile or two behind the village, I started at an early hour under the guidance of the shikarees. Although at that time of year great old markhor were not likely to be met with so low down, a chance might be got at a rind, a musk-deer, or a bear.

After several hours' hard climbing along rough stony beds of water-courses, up slopes of loose *débris*, and through steep pine-forests, we at length neared the upper part of the range. As we continued to ascend, the ground became more rugged and precipitous. Broad patches of melting snow, in many places very deep, still lay on the mountain-side, often forming a treacherous covering over gullies hidden by it, or to slippery branches of birch bushes that lay pressed down by its weight along the steep ground beneath, and on which our feet were continually either slipping or sliding.

Gamoo's sharp eyes were not long in discovering a single rind, as it lay taking its noonday repose at the root of a solitary pine-tree that clung to a small ledge of a precipice we were examining. It was a long shot, as there was no possible means of getting nearer, and the spot where the animal lay was almost directly below us. Consequently, on the smoke clearing off, I was not much surprised at seeing that the beast had disappeared; but whether it was hit or not, I could not tell. We continued watching there for some time, until at length the rind was again viewed climbing an opposite ascent, and apparently going pretty strong though not very fast, ere it disappeared in a patch of birchwood.

After a short consultation, Hatha was directed to make the best of his way, under cover if possible, round to the farther side of the bit of wood; for we now concluded that as the beast did not quit it, he must be wounded, and have lain down. Meanwhile Gamoo and I clambered up to a spot known to him, where, if the animal chanced to take upward, it would most likely, from the precipitous nature of the ground, pass pretty close to us.

Patiently we lay there for nearly an hour, anxiously watching the bit of cover, until I began to think that Hatha must have mistaken the spot. At last the rind quitted the wood without any apparent cause, until we saw Hatha, who had cleverly managed to circumvent the place without being seen, emerge from it shortly after. The rind continued to gallop across the steep hillside until he was lost to our sight among the crags far below. I gave a glance of mute disappointment towards Gamoo, who replied to it only by a sign to lie still. Presently there was a rattle of loose stones, detached directly below us, and almost immediately after I had the satisfaction of seeing our quarry, which now showed no signs of being wounded, springing nimbly up from rock to rock as he approached our place of concealment. Waiting until he was almost on a level with and about 50 yards from where we lay, I let drive, sending a bullet through his shoulders as he cantered past. After a wild spring and a vain tottering effort to gain the crest of a ridge close above him, beyond which he would have been safe, the poor struggling beast fell back and rolled down the steep declivity, disappearing from our sight in the abyss below. The next I saw of him was his skin and head, and as much of the meat as Hatha could conveniently carry, with which, after a considerable time, he made his appearance.

Although this animal was of little value save for food, securing it was so far satisfactory that it gave me confidence; for I have a firm belief, absurd as it may seem, in the luck that follows killing the first beast I fire at on a shooting-trip. At any rate, it gives the shikarees an idea that the trouble they may take to find game will not be fruitless, for first impressions always go a great way.

As it was getting late in the day, and the camping-place

was still a considerable distance off, we continued our ascent, and soon reached the summit of the range.

What a glorious panorama now presented itself as I sat down on the ridge to enjoy this magnificent prospect of mountain piled behind mountain, stretching away as far as the eye could reach! The day was one of those when, from the sky being overcast, the light was of that dull subdued kind, which gave to the more distant ranges an intense dark-blue tint, causing them to appear more solemn in their grandeur, and the valleys lying between them more profound in their depth, than had they been lighted up by the glare of a bright noonday sun. And the heavy pall of cloud that rested on some of the higher mountains threw a gloomy shade over their snow-clad sides immediately beneath, giving one a vague and an exaggerated idea of the height of their hidden crests.

A thin blue line of smoke curling lazily up from a sheltered spot among the pine-trees far below, showed us that the men with the loads had reached the place where it was intended we should pass the night. I was not, however, destined to reach it without the occurrence of a rather serious accident, which nearly brought my shooting-trip to a premature end.

The chilling wind that blew over the ridge, off the snow, reminded me, as I sat admiring the view, that it was not advisable to remain inactive. We therefore commenced descending towards the camp. The declivity, although very steep, would not have been difficult to traverse had not the ground been covered with a layer of half-melted slushy snow, which made the footing slippery and uncertain. I was walking rather carelessly, and happened to place one of my feet, on which I was wearing straw *poolas*,[1] on a smooth birch

---

[1] Hob-nailed boots I found safer, on the steep slippery slopes of dry grass so common in markhor ground, than *poolas*, which on these dangerous slopes become very dry, and consequently are apt to slide; so it is as well to be provided with both.

branch that lay hidden beneath the snow, when my legs seemed suddenly to fly from under me, and away I went slithering down the steep slope. Fortunately, I did not go very far; but when I picked myself up, which I did with the assistance of my two men, who ran down after me, I felt uncommonly sore all over, and there was a painful, partially numbed sensation about my left shoulder and arm that made me feel rather faint. On recovering from the shock, I soon became aware, from the position of my arm and my inability to move it, of the disagreeable fact that I had put my shoulder out.

Here was an awkward predicament to be in. I was sitting on a hillside, as steep as a house-roof, with a dislocated shoulder, and no surgical aid within at least four days' journey. Bad as matters seemed, I could not but be amused at the ludicrous picture of helpless concern presented by my two companions, more particularly by old Gamoo, who could do nothing but call on the name of the Prophet for help. Hatha was the first to regain his wits, he having acquired, more fortunately for me than for him, some knowledge of an accident of the kind by a similar one having formerly happened to himself; and from its occasional recurrence, which is, I now know by experience, often the case with dislocations, he had become rather expert in its treatment. Being fully alive to the necessity for immediate action, I directed the men to haul away at my arm, which they did for some time, with no better result than to make me feel very faint. This treatment having failed, with some difficulty I stood up on the steep slope, whilst Hatha made a lever of my arm, with Gamoo's shoulder under it for a fulcrum. My own weight on one side and a steady pull at the arm on the other, had the desired effect, for I could again move the limb; and on examination, Hatha, with a grin of satisfaction, pronounced it to be all right.

At the camping-place I found the Nawab and his brother,

who were carrying out the rites of hospitality to their fullest extent, by escorting me as far as the confines of their property. Their apparent concern, on hearing of my mishap, was almost as great as that of the shikarees, and many were the remedies suggested, which were about as useless as they were well meant.

I had considerable difficulty in getting out of my upper garments that night, and still more in getting into them again next morning; but as the Nawabs were bent on showing me a drive for game, I was determined to try and go out, even although I might be unable to use a gun, rather than disappoint them. Fortunately, the place where Gamoo, as the Nawab's head gamekeeper, planted me, was not far distant; so I sat down at the root of a pine-tree, there to await the advent of anything that might turn up. The only animal that put in an appearance was a half-grown black bear, at which I was able to "loose off" by supporting the rifle against the trunk of the tree beside me. I almost think I must have hit the beast, for with a loud "yeeough" it staggered back and disappeared down the hill. The Nawab and his brother, who were with the beaters, had seen two musk-deer, but nothing was bagged. My hospitable friends took their departure next morning, and I proceeded on my way; but I was forced to take matters pretty easily for a day or two, from my shoulder being stiff and painful to move.

We had now descended into the Bonyar valley, towards the head of which we turned our steps. At a cluster of huts through which we passed, the highest inhabited place in the glen, Gamoo picked up another assistant in a queer old image of a man named Sultana. His looks, however, belied his worth, for he turned out an excellent guide, and was thoroughly well acquainted with the haunts and habits of the wild denizens of his native mountains.

A great part of our way was exceedingly steep, and would have proved fatiguing in a hot June sun, had it not been for

the romantic beauty of the scenery through which it led.
Such grand forests of pine, and birch woods of gnarled old
trees; such green glades of brackens and velvety turf sloping
sharply down to the bed of the foaming torrent that surged
angrily past, as it dashed against masses of rock and huge
boulders which impeded its headlong course; such exquisite
glimpses of blue mountains and snowy peaks towering above
all; and at the end of our walk, such a surpassing lovely spot
on which to pitch our camp;—such an exquisite combination,
in fact, of nature's wildest charms, as to make one feel as
though he could be content to spend the rest of his days there.
But the weather was fine, and a good "square meal" had
been discussed *en route.* Had it been otherwise, as is very
frequently the case in such places, one might have viewed
things through a duller pair of spectacles.

The men pointed out a spot among the crags on an opposite
hill-face where, a year or two before, one of the Nawab's
shikarees had been killed by a fall when in pursuit of that
most dangerous, though perhaps most fascinating of all Himalayan sports—markhor-hunting. Indeed on this very evening
a little episode occurred which, lightly as we thought of it at
the time, might have been attended with serious results. We
had taken a turn upward to look for a bear, when our progress
was arrested by a very steep narrow gully. This we managed to cross by means of a sharp-sloping bed of old hard
snow that spanned it higher up. When we reached the same
spot on our return, a large portion of the identical snow-bank
we had trodden on had fallen in, leaving a dark yawning hole.
Our weight in crossing had loosened the snow.

A few miles more up the glen brought us to our first hunting-ground. During our short stay here I shot a young buck,
one of a herd of five that we found feeding on a very steep
and bare slope of short slippery grass. Down this declivity
the stricken animal went tumbling and sliding at a most
fearful rate, until it was lost to sight a thousand feet or

so below. Difficult and dangerous as already was the walking over such a smooth sloping surface, it was rendered even
worse by heavy rain which had fallen during the night.
Two black bears and a brown one had shown themselves
at long distances, and also some rinds and does; but as
there were no fresh marks of large bucks, we determined to
try other ground.

CHAPTER XV.

GREAT old markhor are always difficult to find, owing
chiefly to their usually affecting such inaccessible places, and
generally where the precipitous ground is tolerably well
clothed with pines and birches. Gamoo now proposed that
we should bivouac high up among the pine-trees on a neighbouring spur, on the farther side of which he was confident
we should find some old fellows. Accordingly, in the early
morning the little tents were struck, and directions left to
have them pitched wherever sufficient space could be found
beside the torrent at the bottom of the deep narrow valley
we had to cross, whilst the shikarees and I went on to the
new ground, taking with us two or three men to carry our
food and blankets.

After a long and tiresome descent, succeeded by a tedious,

hard climb, much of it being up a landslip, where the steep stony ground was so unstable as to make the foothold bad, we reached our destination late in the afternoon. On our way we knocked at the door of the residence of a bear in a hollow pine-trunk, our attention having been attracted to it by the fresh marks of claws on the bark, where the occupant had clambered up to the entrance-hole. Mr Bruin was, however, either "not at home," or too lazy to pay any attention to our summons.

The evening was spent in making ourselves as snug as possible for the night. It was dreadfully cold up here, the ground being partially covered with patches of snow. A lot of dry pine-logs were collected in a heap, and as the shades of night gathered in, a huge bonfire was cheerily crackling and blazing away, dispelling the surrounding darkness, as the ruddy glow was reflected on the nearer pine stems and branches, or penetrated into the gloomy recesses of the forest. A tin-can of soup was soon heating over the fire, and thick cakes were placed under the hot ashes to bake, first having been wrapped up in several layers of fresh birch-bark,[1] which gives them a nice flavour and prevents their being burnt. In this manner the evening meal was not long in being prepared, and discussed with a relish seldom experienced except under such circumstances. The fragrant weed was lit, and a lump of snow put into the kettle to boil, and a glass of "hot with" mixed, ere turning in on a soft couch formed of pine-branches so arranged that only the tender sprouts remain uppermost.

I may here remark that although a glass of hot grog is very grateful and comforting to the Himalayan sportsman after he has done his day's work, he will, I think, find cold tea far better than spirits and water, both for quenching his thirst and working upon during the day.

---

[1] Birch-bark is a staple commodity of commerce in Cashmere, where its thin under-layers almost entirely take the place of paper with the shopkeepers for wrapping up the purchases of their customers, besides for the many other useful purposes to which it is applied.

By daybreak we were on the move towards the wooded steeps and precipices above. After an unsuccessful morning's work, I took the spy-glass to have a final search over the ground before descending to our bivouac for breakfast.

There they are! I have them at last, a herd of eleven in all; and though they are so far off that we cannot distinctly make out the length of their horns, we can tell, from the white colour and size of their bodies, that the three foremost fellows are old markhor. They are slowly moving up to higher regions after their morning meal, and Gamoo says they will be pretty sure to descend in the afternoon towards the same feeding-ground. Under these circumstances it is useless attempting to approach them at present: we therefore continue to watch them until they are hidden from our sight, and then descend to our bivouac, intending, after breakfast, to make the best of our way to the spot where they were last seen, there to await their return.

Our meal is soon despatched, and we are off again. Our progress, however, is slow, for the ground is very difficult, and much time is taken up in digging footsteps across bad places. We take little heed of a buck tahr (here called "jagla "),[1] though he might be easily stalked were we not in pursuit of other game, which a shot might disturb; and after several hours of climbing and scrambling along, we at length reach our goal.

Dense masses of murky cloud and rolling mist have been for some time gathering about the crags above us, and distant rumblings of thunder herald an approaching storm. The rain, which soon begins to fall pretty smartly, combined with a cutting cold wind, almost benumbs my limbs—for, in my anxiety to be after the markhor, I have forgotten my usual precaution of bringing a blanket with me. Patiently we sit there huddled together, our teeth chattering and bodies

[1] On the Pîr Punchâl the tahr is frequently found on the same ground as the markhor.

shivering with cold, and I am just about to suggest the propriety of returning to a spot where we intended passing the night, when the rattle of a falling stone, detached somewhere far up in the mist, falls faintly upon our ears.

"They're coming down now," whispers Gamoo, followed by a suggestion that we should get more under cover of the ridge of the spur on which we have posted ourselves. Anxiously we crouch there, straining our ears to catch the slightest sound; but nothing more is heard save the soft patter of falling drops, the echoing claps of thunder, and the sough of the wind among the swaying pine-branches, until I begin to think the falling stone must have been loosened by the rain. But listen!—again the rattle of loose stones, and this time much nearer. Oh for a break in the dense mist that is scudding past, to give us a sight of the markhor, which, there is now no doubt, are on their way down to where they fed in the morning! At last fortune seems to be going to favour us, for the rain ceases, and the pall of cloud is gradually lifting, as rock and tree above begin to loom indistinctly through the flying vapour.

"Look!" again whispers Gamoo, his voice trembling with excitement, as he points in the direction of several tall pine-trees on a ridge some distance from and considerably higher than the spur that conceals us. About a couple of hundred yards beyond two of their massive stems—which form, as it were, a kind of huge rustic framing—such a truly wild tableau as seldom is witnessed becomes gradually disclosed to view. The undefined form of a stately markhor is emerging like a spectre from the mist, slowly wending his way downward. He is immediately followed by another, and yet another, equal in size to himself, whilst a string of smaller animals bring up the rear. As the leader reaches a broad ledge jutting out under a dark beetling crag, he wheels suddenly round and butts at one of his big followers, which, with lowered head, is ready to receive him. After a tilt or two, the leading buck advances to the brink of the ledge, where he gazes proudly about him for a short time, and then lies down with a listless confident air, as if quite satisfied with the security of his exalted position. How noble he looks, as he reclines there with his grand head towards us, his massive horns standing out in relief against the dark background of overhanging rock! I can almost count the hairs of his flowing beard as I watch him through the glass. The remainder of the herd have all trooped down behind him, and form an almost supernatural-looking group of wild beings, which seems to dissolve gradually away as the veil of mist again steals up and conceals them from our entranced gaze.

How to stalk them is now the question. The only place from which there is a chance of getting a fair shot is the ridge above, where the big pine-trees are, as the nature of the ground is such that the animals will be pretty certain to move down on the other side of it, and so out of our sight. There is only a short distance across to it, but should the mist clear off before we can reach it, we shall be in full view of the herd; and the slope is so frightfully precipitous, that it makes one almost shudder to contemplate what the consequences of a false step on the wet slippery ground might be. However, there is no time to think much about it, for the mist may lift again at any moment, when our chance of reaching the ridge unobserved will be gone; so, screwing up my nerves, I determine to risk anything rather than lose such an opportunity.

Slowly and carefully we plant the sides of our feet in the small nicks scraped out of the face of the hard, almost perpendicular slope, with the iron spuds on our long sticks, and luckily reach the ridge just in time, for we can hear the animals on the move again though we cannot see them. Sticking the points of my toes into the ground, I cautiously slip the long barrel of my single Henry rifle over the ridge, whilst Hatha lays hold of the loose part of my nether gar-

ments, for so precarious is the footing that even the recoil of
the rifle may cause a slip.   Once more the mist clears off and
discloses the whole herd, now coming straight down towards
us.   As Gamoo crouches beside me, ready to hand me my
second rifle, a double (not the Whitworth then, or it should
have had the post of honour), I can hear him praying to
Allah and the Prophet for help, and cautioning me not to fire
in a hurry, alternately.   The leading buck is within fifty yards
and broadside on, when Gamoo whispers, "Now, take a
good aim."

Can I have missed the beast ?—for he still holds steadily
on without a sign of being hit.   But another big fellow has
reached the same spot.   Quickly Gamoo hands me the other
rifle, and ere the animal has time to recover from his astonishment, a bullet smashes through his shoulders, his fore-legs slip
from under him, and he rolls headlong down the gully in our
front and disappears.   The third big buck now takes his
place, for there is only one way by which they can pass us,
and I am just about to fire when Gamoo directs my attention
towards the first, which has pulled up, and offers a fair chance.
Supposing him untouched, I empty the remaining barrel at
him.   He moves on a short way, stops again, totters for a few
seconds, and falls struggling down into a cleft between a
steep face of rock and a sloping bank of hard snow just below
him.   Both rifles being now empty, the remaining big buck
gets off scot-free, and vanishes with his smaller companions
long ere I can reload.

Numerous and loud are the expressions of delight indulged
in by the shikarees at our good luck.   But a shadow of doubt
arises in their minds as to whether they will be able to reach
the beasts in time to bleed them before life is extinct, as,
being good Mohammedans, without this ceremony being duly
performed the meat will be useless to *them.*   Hatha, and
Sultana at once start off down the gully to look after the
second buck, whilst Gamoo and I with some difficulty

clamber after the first. We find him still alive, but he has fallen so far into the cleft that we have considerable trouble in getting at him to give him the *coup de grâce*.

On examining the carcass, I found that my first shot must have inflicted a mortal wound. Had I known this I might in all probability have killed the third big fellow with the bullet I had wasted in firing a second shot at the first; for unless some large bone is broken, markhor, like ibex, when shot at, and even if mortally wounded, very often move off without increasing their pace from a walk. However, I had little cause to grumble at my luck.

It was too late to get the dead markhor out of the snow-cleft that evening; we therefore followed the other men down the gully to where they had found the other buck in time to bleed him. We had only to give his carcass a shove to start it rolling down several hundred feet, until it reached a long narrow incline of hard snow that covered the bed of a torrent which could be heard murmuring beneath. We were able to drag the beast easily down the slippery snow-bed for a long distance, fortunately in the direction we wished to go.

Leaving the men to skin and break up the markhor, I made the best of my way along a steep pine-clad hillside to the spot where we intended to bivouac for the night, the position of which I discovered by continually shouting and whistling on my fingers—a most useful accomplishment under such circumstances—until I was at length answered by the men who were there. It was dark when I reached it, so I at once sent off a couple of men with pine torches to assist the shikarees, who arrived some hours later with as much as they could carry of the spoils.

Koklass pheasants were crowing and the horned argus uttering its peculiar mewing cry when I awoke in the morning. Sending off a man with strict injunctions to mark the whereabouts of one of the *latter* beautiful birds, a good specimen of which I particularly wished to obtain, I hastily emerged from under my warm blankets, and performed my morning toilet, which consisted chiefly in donning my boots. The fellow soon returned, and after leading me a stiff pull up through the forest, pointed out one of the former birds, at which piece of stupidity my temper was considerably ruffled.

In the forenoon we shouldered our limited kit, and made for the camp, which was not very far off. I had directed some men to go and prospect the ground towards the head of the glen in which the tents were pitched. They now, much to my disappointment, reported it as being entirely blocked up with snow, and the torrent quite impassable; but being fully alive to the lazy and mendacious propensities of the Cashmeree, I was resolved to go and have a look myself. It was necessary, however, to remain where we were for a day, as the greater part of one markhor had still to be fetched, and the whole of the other was still lying in the snow-cleft where it had fallen. This delay afforded an opportunity for a general washing-up of dirty clothes. What a luxury it was to have a bath, and to turn in again on my camp-bed and be lulled to sleep by the resounding din of the torrent, that hurried down impetuously within a few feet of the tent! And as morning dawned, how pleasing to hear the black-birds (just like our old friends at home), which were numerous here, mingling their notes with the rushing sound of the water. As there was an icy blast coming down the glen, and it began to rain heavily, and most of the men were away after the venison, I thought I could do nothing better than take another turn in my warm bed until a pretty late hour.

On the arrival of the meat, my Goorkha servant Kirpa at once proceeded to cut quantities of it into long strips, with a view to jerking it for future consumption; and ere long, yards and yards of it were hanging in festoons from frames of sticks, constructed over smoky fires lighted all around.

A terrific thunderstorm, accompanied by hail and rain,

prevented our moving early next day, and after the storm was over the mountains were so enveloped in mist that stalking was impossible. During our stay here Kazima brought me a fine pair of markhor horns he had picked up somewhere near. He was much perplexed at my not caring to possess such a trophy, merely because I had not shot their wearer, and said he should keep them himself, to dispose of to some other person who might not be so particular as to how they had been obtained.

When the weather had cleared enough to allow of a move up the glen, I found, as I expected, that it was by no means so impracticable as the men had reported. For the first mile or so it certainly was very difficult travelling; but the huge piles of hard snow which blocked the contracted and precipitous gorge up which our way led, were rather an advantage than otherwise, enabling us to cross and recross the torrent by natural bridges formed of them. Higher up, however, the valley became more open, and was pretty free of snow. A more likely country for sport there could not have been, and it did not belie its looks; for we soon found the fresh tracks, as big as though they had been made by heifers, of a herd which must have fed there that very morning. Matters looked so promising that I sent back a man with directions to have the tents brought on; for we had only taken with us kit sufficient for passing a night or two under the best kind of protection from the weather we could find.

We were not long in selecting a snug spot for spending the night under some splendid pine-trees, which were almost impervious to rain. Here we sheltered from a heavy shower, which lasted several hours. Towards evening it cleared up; so I started with Gamoo and Hatha, intending to prospect the ground on either side of a steep, craggy, and partially pine-clad ridge, that ran up towards the snowy heights far above.

Q

First we sighted two rinds, which were not worth the risk of disturbing the ground by firing at, even could we have stalked them successfully, or had cared to do so. Three or four fairly large bucks were also made out among the crags on an opposite hill-face, but they were evidently not the big fellows that were "wanted"; and a deep precipitous-sided valley that lay between us and them, with a roaring linn at the bottom of it, precluded any possibility of our getting near them that evening. We therefore began descending the ridge we had come up, in the hope of finding them again at some future time.

Hardly have we gone a couple of hundred yards when, hark! something has detached a stone up on the steep hill-side to our left, and we have barely time to crouch down among the rocks on the ridge ere a hoary old buck, with a huge pair of cork-screws on his head, shows himself for a second or two, as he crosses a bare spot among a lot of birch bushes some three hundred yards distant. Five or six others of equal size follow closely in his wake. These must certainly be the beasts whose heifer-like tracks we saw below, and they are evidently on their way down to feed.

The ridge is so craggy and steep that it will take all we can do to clamber down and intercept them before they get near our bivouac, where they must certainly detect the men left there, for the beasts are making straight downwards in that direction.

Off we start under cover of the ridge as fast as the ground will allow of, passing the rifles from hand to hand down the more precipitous spots, and every now and then peering over at the markhor, upon which we do not appear to gain an inch, but if anything lose distance. Presently we reach a bit of more practicable ground, where we are able to travel faster, and when we again reconnoitre the animals, we find we have succeeded in getting a little ahead of them. There is no time to lose, however—for, as far as I can judge from the direction

they are taking, they will pass us at about 130 yards, and if
we let this chance slip they are lost.

I have scarcely got into position for a shot before they are
abreast of us; but the birch bushes are so thickly scattered
over the steep hillside, that we only catch occasional glimpses
of the animals as they move amongst them. Taking advantage of a convenient bit of rock for a rest, I let drive at the
first buck that shows himself. He fortunately happens to be
a beauty. To my intense concern, he only acknowledges the
shot by a spasmodic movement of his short tail, as he turns
round and slowly retraces his steps up through the brushwood. Quickly exchanging the empty single rifle for the
double, another bullet speeds after a grand fellow, as he
appears traversing a small opening between the bushes.
This time a decided wince follows the shot in addition to
the shake of the tail; but he moves steadily upward with
the rest, until they file slowly over a bare bit of ground, all
of them now in view, but almost out of range. In despair I
give them a parting salute with the remaining barrel before
they become hidden, one by one, from our sight.

A feeling of helpless disappointment seems to pervade us all
as we sit mutely there gazing up to where the animals have
disappeared. So disgusted am I with my performance that I
hardly care to reload the guns. At length Gamoo breaks the
silence by expressing a decided opinion that, from the fact of
their "wagging their tails," as he put it, on receiving the
shots, one buck is hit, if not both. Whilst he is speaking, a
clattering noise is suddenly heard far up in the direction the
beasts have taken, and to our great joy we soon see it is
caused by one of them coming toppling and rolling down
until it lodges among the bushes below. After intently listening for some time, in hopes of another following suit, we
jump up in great glee, and proceed to examine our prize.

I certainly ought to have been satisfied with my success
in securing such a magnificent trophy, for the horns were

almost a yard in length, measured straight without the twist, and were nearly a foot in girth at the base; but there is invariably one bitter drop in one's cup of happiness. We now discovered that my first two shots, both of which turned out to be deadly, had unluckily been at the same animal, which I had mistaken for a different one when I fired the second time as he moved up with the others among the birch bushes. We sighted a black bear in the distance as we were descending to our shelter. It was much too late to go after him; and what cared I for a bear then, compared with the noble animal I had just shot!

Besides the superstition respecting the snake-eating propensity of the markhor, there is another entertained regarding a small, smooth, dark-green stone[1] which is sometimes found among the entrails of very old bucks. My attention was drawn to this when, before starting for the hill in the early morning, the shikarees made straight for the spot where they had, the night before, carefully deposited the gralloch of the markhor. They rather unwillingly informed me, with the utmost gravity, that they were going to search for the said stone, which, amongst other properties they believed it possessed, was that of its being an infallible antidote to the poison of snake-bite if applied to the wound. Whether they found this talisman or not I failed to discover—and in all probability, had they done so, they would have kept it "dark," from fear of my depriving them of it.

As we proceeded upward we started a musk-deer, at which I was very nearly "letting loose," and glad I was that she escaped, for on getting up to the bed from which she had risen, we found her suckling offspring lying on it. After following far on the tracks of our friends of the previous

---

[1] *Bezoar*, a calculous concretion sometimes found in the stomach of certain animals of the goat tribe. The term comes from a Persian word meaning antidote, which this substance was absurdly supposed to be, and is still by Orientals, to the fatal effects of poison.

evening, seeing nothing but a few does with kids at foot, we returned to camp, which had been brought up during the day.

Ticks were numerous and troublesome up here, as they usually are at that season in such places, where the winter snow has but recently melted off the old withered grass. When out on the hill, we constantly had to stop and unfasten our nether garments in order to get at tender spots where the little flat wretches had buried their heads so deeply as to require a painful tug to extract them. A much more agreeable production of the ground in a similar state, at the same season, is the "goochee," a growth of the mushroom kind, which is often found springing up in a conical shape through the snow-flattened dead grass, like a dirty bit of sponge. The natives string these fungi together and dry them, but they are much better when eaten fresh, seasoned with pepper and salt, and fried or stewed.

To enable us to reach the ground where we had, the first evening, seen bucks on the opposite side of the deep rapid torrent, over which, up here, we could find no convenient blocks or beds of hard snow for crossing on, the following morning was devoted to constructing a bridge of thin tree-stems, cut down and thrown across between two suitable rocks. It was rather a rickety concern, and slippery as well, from being wetted by spray dashing over it.

We were not successful in finding the bucks again, though their traces were fresh and numerous, a male musk-deer being the only thing brought to bag. Once we unexpectedly found ourselves within about eighty yards of four or five markhor does, each with the smallest of little kids at foot. As they were quite unconscious of our presence so near them, an opportunity was afforded me of watching their gambols for some time. Any one who could have spoilt such an interesting family party must have been dead indeed not only to all sportsmanlike feelings, but also to those of humanity.

I did not, however, feel so kindly disposed towards a big brown bear whose repose we rather abruptly disturbed. The brute turned round and looked at us so saucily that I could not resist the temptation to put a bullet through his shaggy hide, even at the risk of disturbing markhor. And the loud angry language he made use of on being struck, as it echoed and re-echoed through the rocky glen we were in, was, I am sure, quite enough to strike terror into any other denizens the place might have contained. So certain did I feel of his being done for, that I did not think it necessary to add to the rumpus he was making by firing another shot, as with much difficulty he struggled up towards the top of a rise just above him. Over this he nevertheless contrived to scramble, and although we followed on his blood-tracks for a long distance, we failed to come up with him. Bruin is an uncommonly hard customer to deal with when not struck in the right place, and that place I evidently had missed.

It now seemed as though the good luck we had hitherto enjoyed were about to desert us, for the last day we spent on this ground was fraught with " grief."

Early in the day, as we were clambering across a break-neck place, I was startled at hearing a sharp exclamation, as if. caused by pain, from Hatha, who was following at a short distance behind. In climbing along the rugged face of the steep slope we were traversing, he had in some way managed to wrench his shoulder, which, being weak from former dislocations, had now slipped out again. As he objected to the rough treatment adopted in my case, there was nothing for it but to sling up his arm with a turban and return to camp. The poor fellow bore the pain he must have suffered during our long and rough trudge most pluckily. On reaching the tents, my cook, in whose surgical skill he placed more confidence than in mine, at once took him in hand, and, aided by the patient's own directions, soon replaced the dislocated joint.

Some men who had gone off in the early morning to search

for the wounded bear had returned without having found a trace of it.

As the day was still young, I proposed to Gamoo that we should take a turn in an adjacent birch wood, on the chance of finding a musk-deer or a bear. Hatha, who seemed quite hurt at the idea of being left behind on account of his mishap, insisted on accompanying us. Thinking there would be little or no chance of seeing markhor in the direction we were going, I took with me only the short double rifle, as being more handy than the long Henry in the event of getting a snap-shot at anything in the wood.

After beating through the wood, we emerged on to a gently sloping bed of hard snow, about a hundred yards broad, that extended far up between steep, rugged, and partially pine-clad acclivities, until it terminated among a wilderness of bald grey rocks and huge snow-capped crags that towered aloft at its head. Although the sun had sunk behind the high sky-line of the mountains, it was still early to turn our steps campwards; so I suggested a stroll up this long stretch of snow, in the hope of meeting with some old bruin out for his evening promenade.

We sauntered carelessly along for some time, taking an occasional glance up towards the wooded slopes and crags on either side, when, with a suppressed exclamation, down crouches Gamoo on the snow, and in a second Hatha, Sultana, and myself are prostrate beside him. Not a syllable is spoken as we crawl on all-fours over the snow-bed, until we get close under the steep hillside rising from its margin, when Gamoo points in the direction of the grey rocks ahead, and whispers " Markhor ! "

As the rocks are a long way off, I am unable at first to make out what Gamoo's keen sight has detected; but at length my eye rests upon a motionless V, which, even far away as it is, looks gigantic. I am afraid, however, from the jabbering whispers and doubtful glances that are exchanged between my companions, that they are rather perturbed in mind as to the issue of the business. On the spy-glass being put into requisition, it shows me that their anticipations are likely to be verified, for I distinctly see that the beast is gazing straight in our direction; but it also shows two others, quite as large as himself, that are browsing unconcernedly in his vicinity.

We lie silently watching him for what seems to my impatient imagination an endless time, as he remains standing there as still as the rocks around him. At length he turns slowly about and is lost to view; but he soon reappears walking leisurely across the snow-bed, his companions following at short intervals, until they all are hidden behind a high projecting crag. Our only chance—and a poor one it is—lies in our being able to reach that crag in time for a long shot as they ascend the hillside beyond it; for although their movements appear slow, they are evidently on the alert, and in all probability will not stop again until they reach some distant sanctuary.

Up we jump, and set off at our best pace along the snowy incline. It looks easy enough to travel over, but we get dreadfully "pumped," for the more rarefied air at this height —at least 12,000 feet—soon begins to tell on our wind. At last, panting and almost broken-hearted, we reach the crag. There is no time to wait for breath, as two of the markhor that are still in sight are just about to move over a brow nearly two hundred yards above us. Oh that I had the long Henry with me now! for I have not much faith in the short double rifle at such a distance. With my chest heaving, and my pulses throbbing as if ready to burst, I thrust my alpenstock into the snow to form a rest—for my arm is still weak —and taking a hasty aim, fire, and of course miss.

Alas! for that useless random shot, which I shall never cease to regret, although I have often since profited by the lesson it taught me.

Hardly has it left the barrel when there is a tremendous

clatter close above us, as the third markhor, which we imagined had preceded his companions over the brow, starts
wildly up from where he has been standing unnoticed in the
deep shade of the crag behind which we have approached.
So utterly astounded am I at this unexpected apparition, that
I actually miss the monster at about eighty yards distant, as,
with his splendid horns thrown backward, he springs nimbly
up from rock to rock until he vanishes with a bound over a
ridge rising just above the crag.

Here was a nice mess I had made from firing that long
random shot; and how often are good chances thus stupidly
lost! But "there is no use crying over spilt milk," so we
climbed up to examine the spot where the buck was when I
shot at him. He must have had a very close shave, for there
lay a lock of his long beard, which had evidently been cut off
by the bullet. We followed him over the ridge and down
into another deep valley, where his tracks led across a steep
snow-bed, on which, had he been wounded, we could not
have failed to find traces of blood, however small; besides,
it was now getting late, and we were a considerable distance
from camp, so with much reluctance and regret we gave him
up as lost.

Gamoo, lively under any circumstances, now proposed a
glissade down the snow-bed, as our way home led in that
direction. So we had soon almost forgotten, for the time, our
disappointment as we all went sliding, and I being less
expert at it, as often rolling, down the steep slope, much to
the amusement of my companions, who shouted with laughter,
in which I heartily joined. The shock to my nerves, once
experienced on beholding this easy and rapid method of
descending a steep snow-field, I shall never forget. I was
hunting ibex at the time on the mountains north of the Sind
river in Cashmere. One day, when shifting our ground, we
had to traverse a long sloping *aréte* of snow, the crest of
which was so sharp and hard that we had at times to cut

steps for considerable distances. Smooth snow - fields extended down on either side for tu _ a thousand feet, and
sometimes at an ngle of considerably less than than 45°.
After a long and tiresome descent, my shikarees and I sat
down '   ourselves, and to wait for our laden followers,

A Glissade.

who, as we watched them coming slowly along the ridge,
looked in the distance like small black dots moving on the
sky-line of snow. A sudden exclamation of horror escaped
me, which rather startled my companions, as I saw the leading man come tumbling, as I thought, down what seemed,
from where we sat, to be an almost perpendicular wall of
snow. My horror was mingled with astonishment at seeing
another and then another man follow the first, until all had
slid down to where the snow was less steep below, from
whence they leisurely continued their descent, when it at
once struck me what a mistake I had made in my unpleasant
surmises.

We moved next day to another locality, but fortune's favours had departed with those three big bucks. Such extraordinary luck in seeing, in so short a time, so many large markhor, which are usually very difficult to find, could not possibly last; and during the several days we continued to hunt for them, not another pair of good horns did we see.

It was with much regret that, at the termination of this short but satisfactory trip, I bade adieu to the shikarees and others that had served me so well on the mountains, and amongst them Kazima, who had turned out such a good fellow, and had made himself so generally useful. He had now entirely dropped his grand airs, and on being discharged had not even conceit enough left in him to ask for a testimonial as to his sporting qualifications. A short time after, when encamped in the Cashmere valley, I observed coming along the path which passed my tent a stalwart, sportingly got up individual, with a pair of markhor horns hanging from the mountain-pole he carried over his shoulder. As he drew near I was delighted to find it was my friend Kazima, and the horns were the identical ones he had picked up when with me on the Pir. As he had not as yet succeeded in "sticking" any one with them, he bore them as an emblem of his would-be calling. The pleasure of meeting seemed mutual, for on recognising me he ran forward as if about to embrace me, and pulling out a scrap of paper, exclaimed, "See what I've got since I left your service!" Taking the paper, I read: "The bearer of this, Kazima, has shown me a number of bears, and I can highly recommend him as a capital shikaree,"—to which was appended the signature of the fortunate man with whom our friend had been shooting bears among the groves of wild fruit-trees in the vale. When I had finished reading, he covered his face with his hands and laughed immoderately. It was the first shikar testimonial he had ever got. He informed me he was then on his way to Baramoola to try and pick up another sahib

of the same sort as his last employer. I wished him good
luck as he went on his way rejoicing.

Several years after, I chanced to meet him again in
Srinuggur, looking a mightier swell than ever. He was
then in service as a shikaree, and begged me not to divulge
his antecedents in that line. His gratitude was freely expressed when I told the good fellow there was little chance
of my so doing, and all the less since, for aught I knew, he
might now have become quite a proficient in the art of
venery.

CHAPTER XVI.

STAG - SHOOTING IN CASHMERE COMPARED WITH DEER - STALKING IN SCOTLAND — THE "RUNNING" SEASON — A MOUNTAIN "DANDY"— THE LOLĀB VALLEY—WE LOOK UP BRUIN AMONG THE PLUM-TREES —A SHOT IN THE DUSK—ON THE SCENT—THE "AWAZ KE WAKT"— THE "BARA SINGHA"—TAPPING FOR FLYING SQUIRRELS—WATCHING FOR A STAG—A LOVE-SONG—A ROYAL HART—HUMAN VULTURES— A MISS IN THE DARK—AN INQUISITIVE HIND—SPLENDID VIEW OF "THE VALE"—OUR REVERIES ARE DISTURBED—WILD MUSIC—RAM-ZAN'S STRATEGY—A RATHER MEAN ADVANTAGE—REMORSE—A CHAL-LENGE AND A REPLY—RECKLESSNESS OF STAGS DURING THE RUTTING SEASON—AN ARTIFICE FOR ATTRACTING THEM—WITH WHAT SUCCESS WE TRIED IT—A NATIVE PRACTITIONER—FORCED TO SUBMIT TO HIS TENDER MERCIES.

SHOULD the following account of the pursuit of the "hangul," or Cashmere stag, chance to meet the eye of any one who, like Leech's "Mr Briggs," has been "made free" of a Scottish deer-forest, he may contend that stag-shooting in Cashmere is inferior to deer-stalking in the Highlands. Well, in point of numbers he is perhaps right. But he must take into consideration that a forest in the Himalayas is very different from a forest in the Grampians. The former is a *true forest* in every sense of the word, where the deer are at all seasons liable to be disturbed by beasts of prey as well as by hunters, and where, in its vast wooded depths, they are often very difficult to find; whereas the latter, as is well known, is nowadays usually one only in name, so far as trees are concerned, where the cervine denizens, from being tended,

254 THE POETRY OF WILD SPORT.

as it may almost be called, for the greater part of the year, and sometimes even fenced in, like domestic cattle, to prevent them from straying, are consequently more numerous and less really wild, though during the stalking season they become just as crafty as their *confrères* of Cashmere. But to the keen sportsman and lover of nature the pursuit of the noble Cashmere stag in wilds where its protection from constant danger depends entirely on its own instinct, the grand and varied character of the mountains, the perfection of climate, the superiority of the trophies,[1] and, last but not least, there being no " march " beyond which the stalker cannot follow his quarry, are all charms which more than compensate for want of numbers, and make hangul-shooting in Cashmere the poetry of Himalayan, or, I may venture to say, of any other *mountain* hunting.

Far be it from me, however, even to hint that Highland deer-*stalking*—in wild and rugged tracts of country that are suitable for no other purpose—is not right royal sport. In fact, the Highland stag, from the open nature of the ground he usually frequents, requires more skill in stalking than does the Cashmere hangul. Still, there is not the same romantic charm about the pursuit of game that has been preserved, as there is when you know it is in every way wild; and in this I feel sure all real sportsmen, both at home and abroad, will agree with me. Indeed, for my own part, I much prefer circumventing a few wary old black-cocks in a day's walk over a bit of wild ground, to standing at the hottest corner of a preserve, even were I an adept at pulling down the rocketers, which I am not; for much rifle-shooting is not conducive to improving one's form at such sharp practice as that. But tastes differ.

[1] Few deer, if any, except the wapiti of North America, carry finer horns than the hangul, and hunting the "elk" (as it is termed) in the Rockies, I found to be, during the "running" season, very similar to hangul-shooting in the Himalayas; but the ground is much steeper in the latter mountains than in the former.

In the autumn of 1866, our regimental Æsculapius, after carefully attending me through a severe bout of illness, succeeded in persuading the ruling military powers that my return to the sunny plains of India from sick-leave to "the hills north of Dehra"—as the *mightiest of mountain-ranges* was then styled in official parlance—would be unadvisable before the end of November. Thus an opportunity was afforded me of hunting the Cashmere stag at the best season for finding him—the month of October and early in November.

Here I can quite imagine the fortunate holder of a Scottish deer-forest exclaiming—"Shoot stags so late in the season! What a poacher!" But I would crave his patience whilst I further explain to him that I once hunted indefatigably after hangul from about the middle of August until towards the end of September, over what was considered to be excellent ground, but, owing to the denseness of the undergrowth, without so much as seeing a single stag, even in velvet; and the constant rain and mists at that season were very detrimental to this kind of work. A circumstance over which I had no control—namely, the termination of my leave—obliged me then to quit Cashmere, just as the deer were beginning to rut, which is the only time that there is any certainty of finding stags, except when the winter snow drives them down almost into the valleys. During the rutting season they betray their whereabouts in the dense tracts of forest they affect, by their intermittent roarings[1]—strangely wild sounds which, when once heard echoing through those grand pine-woods, continue to haunt the ear for many a day. At that season, too, the gallantry of the stags in escorting the hinds from out the thick forest on to the open green slopes and glades, where they are wont to feed morning and evening, and their inclination, at that season, for a roll in their

---

[1] Whistling is the term applied to much the same noise made by the wapiti stag of North America; but something between a prolonged roar and a whistle perhaps gives a better idea of the sound.

soiling-pools, which are well known to the hunter, often cost them their lives. Moreover, the weather and climate there in October and November is simply perfection.

Although convalescent, I was forced, from inability to make proper use of my legs, to submit to the indignity, as I considered it, of being helped along by a *dandy*[1] for the greater part of the journey through the mountains between the sanitarium of Murree and Cashmere. My tottering steps were therefore at first turned towards that lovely locality, Lolāb, in the " Kamraj " or western end of the Cashmere vale, there to recruit strength before undertaking mountain work, by quietly looking up Bruin among the wild plum-trees, which were at that season loaded with ripe fruit.

The beginning of September found my little tents, and also those of a companion who joined me at the Cashmere metropolis, pitched in a grove of splendid old walnut-trees close to the picturesque hamlet of Sogām. It would be difficult to find a more pleasant spot for a convalescent to rest in, than amidst the pastoral scenery of the beautiful little valley of Lolāb. There was a calm dreamy repose about its broad green glades, its clear purling brooks, it shady groves of grand old deciduous-foliaged trees, and its gently sloping woodlands of pine, that could not fail to act as a soothing charm for restoring health and strength.

A garrulous old fossil of a villager volunteered to show Bruin's favourite feeding-grounds in the vicinity. The evening we—I mean the fossil and myself, for my companion did not shoot—first paid them a visit, my rifle was loaded with hardened, hollow, ·450 bullets, filled with detonating powder. I mention this trivial circumstance because the mistake made

---

[1] For those who have never seen a *dandy* of this kind, I may explain that it consists of a sort of canvas hammock slung from a pole. You sit sideways on the hammock, with a strap supporting your back, whilst two mountaineers, bearing the pole on their shoulders, carry you merrily (supposing you are not a Daniel Lambert) along. A *dandy* can always be extemporised, in an emergency, with a blanket, a bit of rope, and a stick cut by the wayside.

in using, in a small-bore rifle, such uncertain jimcracks against large game, will, I think, be demonstrated hereafter,— not, however, in any *sensational* account (I mention this at once, lest such might be anticipated) of an encounter with a savage wild beast.

An opportunity for testing the powers of these missiles soon presented itself in the shape of a big black bear, in whose hairy carcass I planted one of them as he shuffled past me among the bushes. His behaviour on being fired at was not such as is customary with Bruin on being hurt, for he went off without deigning to make the slightest reply to the shot. There was no doubt, however, about his having been hit, and sorely too, for he was broadside on, and certainly not more than twenty-five yards distant. As we could find no blood on his trail, and my old guide said we were certain to see other bears, our stroll among the plum-trees was continued. We had not gone far when we came upon what must have been a party of two, if not more, judging from the way in which we heard the fruit branches being broken. An occasional glimpse showed them to be black bears, but owing to the denseness of the thicket they were in, none of them offered a fair chance for a satisfactory experiment with the shell before they got wind of us and decamped. Another bear was also heard moving among the bushes close by us on our way back to the tents, just before nightfall—probably a brown one, for brown bears, from not being such good climbers as black ones, are often found feeding on fallen fruit, or what they can reach from the ground.

Next evening, on visiting the same locality, nothing was met with until dusk. We were skirting along a tangled thicket on our return to camp, when we became aware, from the sounds which issued from it, that a bear was taking his supper there. Owing to the uncertain light and the thickness of the underwood, from nowhere could we catch a sight of the brute. We therefore concealed ourselves among the

R

bushes in a dark corner of the thicket, with the intention of there patiently watching, in the hope that the bear might show himself on open ground if he chanced to shift his quarters. By this plan, too, I thought we should be better able to see him against the light outside. The success of our stratagem seemed doubtful, but we could lose nothing by giving it a trial.

For some time the sounds of cracking branches and rustling leaves were continued at intervals, as each moment the waning light became fainter, until at length I could scarcely discern the sights on the rifle. The fossil, not seeming to care much about such close proximity to Bruin in the gathering darkness, was just suggesting the propriety of a stealthy retreat, when we detected the object of his solicitude shambling towards us along the outskirts of the thicket. In the dusky gloaming the huge brute loomed even larger than he really was, when he suddenly pulled up within some fifteen yards of us, as if to listen, thereby adding considerably to the disquietude of the crouching fossil, who, in smothered whispers, began saying his prayers, interlarding them with ejaculatory suggestions to me to shoot. The brute was so close that he could hardly be missed, even in so bad a light. On receiving the shot he fell flat in his tracks, gave two or three convulsive sobs, and expired. The satisfaction of the fossil was very great as he now proceeded to relieve his pent-up feelings by calling the defunct animal every shocking bad name he could think of, in a manner that was highly entertaining.

We left the bear, a very large brown one, as he lay, until next morning, when my companion, who was a medico, made a *post-mortem* of the carcass with a view to ascertaining the effect of the shell. The results, in this instance, chanced to be so thoroughly effective as to give me a misplaced confidence in the infallibility of its destructive powers. The beast's vitals had been literally blown to pieces.

The accidental discovery of the bear I had first shot at was the only incident worth mentioning that occurred during the remainder of our sojourn in Lolāb. When I was out one evening for a quiet stroll, my olfactory organ was suddenly assailed by a most abominable stench, which seemed to be wafted from the direction of the locality where I had fired at and lost the black bear. It was too late to trace its origin that evening, but thinking it might very probably have been caused by the putrid carcass of the bear, my companion the medico and I took our walk next morning in that same direction with the intention of prosecuting the search. On reaching the place not the slightest taint of the odour could we detect. Either the night air had dispelled it, or the wind had changed. However, on the chance of again picking up the scent, we proceeded to make a cast by crossing over a low wooded spur, towards the other side of which the bear's trail had led after I had shot at him. Still not a vestige of a dead bear or its scent was there to be found, so we turned our steps campwards.

Scarcely had we gone a furlong when the medico, who was leading, suddenly pulled up. "There it is, and no mistake!" exclaimed he, as we both freely indulged an inclination to expectorate, which is common to most people on inhaling a foul effluvium; we therefore at once harked back. Away we went, scrambling through the thick covert as we followed up the hot scent, sometimes catching a stronger or a fainter whiff as we quartered the ground. At length it grew so burning that we could easily hold it by simply crossing and recrossing the wind, until finally we ran straight in on the object of our search. There was our bear, lying on the broad of its back, stark and stiff, and not very far from where we had tracked it to after I had shot at it. But it was in such an advanced stage of decomposition that we were obliged to leave it, with merely the satisfaction of knowing that the shell had proved fatal.

Before parting with the old fossil, I, strange to say, casually discovered, during our nightly palavers at the camp-fire, that he was the father of my old friend Kazima. The fond parent never tired of proudly describing his son—who, he said, was now in service as a shikaree—as being as mighty a hunter as he was a fine-looking fellow. But to turn to the pursuit of the hangul.

The time when the stags commence their roarings—the "awaz ke wakt," as the Cashmerees call it—from about the 20th of September till the beginning of November, was now at hand; yet, notwithstanding my sanguine anticipations of sport, it was with a pang of regret that I bade adieu to beautiful Lolāb, where time had passed so pleasantly, and also to my fellow-traveller, whose cheerful companionship had added so much to the enjoyment of my sojourn there.

At the capital I found old Ramzan awaiting my arrival. He looked more snuffy than ever, but was otherwise little altered by an increase of several years to his already advanced age. He proposed that we should try the forests on the hills above Nouboog Nye—which beautiful valley I have attempted to describe in a preceding chapter—although the general idea at that time was, that stags had become very scarce there. This, however, turned out to be one of the popular fallacies respecting the great decrease of all Himalayan large game. When I say this, I do not include the game in the more easily accessible localities, such as the Dehra Doon forests and parts of the Terai, where, from the indiscriminate slaughter of milk-hinds and calves, which are so often butchered from howdahs by those who call it *sport*, the decrease of game is a sad truth: I mean the animals on the higher and less accessible ranges. The real fact at that time was, that in the Nouboog forests, owing to the late grazing of the sheep there, the stags did not descend from their summer haunts on the higher mountains so early as was their wont in many other places—in fact, not before the time of year when the majority of sportsmen were, in those days, obliged to quit Cashmere. I therefore resolved to abide by the old man's decision, and had no reason afterwards to repent having done so.

The Cashmere stag (*Cervus Wallichii*), or hangul, as he is named in his own country, requires but little description, further than that he is merely an exaggerated red-deer stag. The horns of this noble animal are larger than those of any other Himalayan deer, except perhaps the "shou" or Sikim stag (*Cervus affinis*), which is found in some of the south-eastern parts of the Himalayan range; but I have never seen him. In weight I should say, at a rough guess, the hangul must be from 25 to 30 stone clean. Like the ibex and other large game of the higher Himalayas, he is provided during winter with an undercoat of the very fine and soft pile known as "pushum." I have seen a set of horns with seventeen well-defined points; but the usual number on a well-developed pair is from ten to twelve, those with ten often being more massive than those having a greater number. The three upper tines, or royals, are not so closely set together at their base, or "cupped," as it is commonly termed, as those of red-deer, and the beam is usually more curved. The hind is called "minnyemer" by the Cashmerees, the word "mooee" being applied by them to these deer collectively. This animal is customarily talked of as the "bārāsingha" (twelve-horned), which designation, as also "burrasingha" (large-horned), is given promiscuously by Europeans as well as by natives to all varieties of large-horned *deer* in India, but never by natives when they speak of them among themselves, only when describing them to foreigners. From this I conclude that the misnomer was originally coined by those who were unacquainted with their true local appellation, and thence adopted by shikarees and others for the large-horned Indian *deer* in general, though for none in particular. I have even heard the jurrow or sambur, which carries only six regular points, called a bārā-singha. But we will now proceed to the resort of this splendid brute, where I hope we may become better acquainted with him.

Our headquarters were at first established near the hamlet of Nouboog. It was rather early for the ground in that neighbourhood, very few stags having, up to that time, found their way down from their summer quarters on the higher ranges—for the lower woods were still full of tormenting flies, and the shepherds with their flocks had not as yet left the open pasturages above the forests. Other sportsmen, too, were at present in possession of the best shooting localities farther up the glen. The distant bellow of a stag was occasionally heard towards evening on some neighbouring hill. But on our reaching the spot where we hoped to have found the animal that had spoken, his voice would tell us that he had travelled far away to some other part of the dark forest. On such occasions Ramzan was wont to give vent to his disappointment by heaping abusive epithets on the innocent animal and its relatives, and expectorating towards it.

A certain amount of shikar was, however, afforded by "tapping" for flying squirrels, which usually have their domiciles high up in hollow old pine-trunks. The plan adopted was to scrape or tap with the end of an alpenstock at the bottom of any tree-stem in which there happened to be a hole aloft. The inmate, if there chanced to be one, generally answered this summons by poking out its head, when a charge of shot had, in most cases, the effect of making it kick itself out of the hole and bringing it to the ground. There were two varieties: the fur of one was a rich brown on the back, intermixed with grey and black hairs, and yellowish fawn beneath; that of the other was a general grey, like the colour of a rabbit skin. These animals are met with throughout the Himalayas, at elevations between 6000 and 9000 feet.

On one of the shooting-grounds farther up the "nye" (glen) being vacated by its occupant, we left our depot of supplies at Nouboog, and at once took his place—for we learnt that he had been but a short time there, and had not much disturbed the deer.

Our first ramble in the forest was made more with the view of reconnoitring the ground than that of shooting. Although no deer were seen, it was satisfactory to find that their tracks were both numerous and fresh. Next morning, after a long ascent, we found an open grassy hill-top, on which we expected to find deer out feeding, covered with sheep. Twice, however, I let off my rifle—once at a musk-deer (here termed "roos"), which was cleanly missed, and again, as we were descending in the evening, when I took a pot-shot at a splendid horned argus-pheasant of the black-breasted kind (here called "rungraol"), which flew away from its perch on a rock, minus a bunch of its beautiful plumage.

In order to avoid the trouble and delay entailed by the long climb each morning before reaching our ground, arrangements were made for sleeping out for a few nights high up in the forest, and that evening we found a snug resting-place under shelter of a big pine-tree in a deep sequestered gorge. The "roaring" of stags was now pretty often heard, but only in the thickest parts of the dense forest, where it was almost impossible to get even a glimpse of the animals that spoke. Nothing was seen except two brown bears, which were left unmolested, from fear of disturbing the deer, until the third day.

It was our intention, on the evening of that day, to return to our camp, with a view to again changing our ground. In the afternoon, during our descent, we found ourselves on a broad and gently sloping spur, on one side of which was a steep-sloping, fern-covered glade—on the other a dense pine wood. Here we found the tracks as fresh as they were numerous, and the beds in the long grass and brackens looked as though the deer had but recently risen from them. As we had, earlier in the day, heard a stag bellowing far down in the neighbouring forest, we determined to watch the glade from among the long brackens on the outskirts of the cover, in hopes of his taking an airing there in the evening.

The tall black pines were casting their long-pointed shadows over the glade as the sun sank slowly behind them. Still and silent we sat there, keeping vigilant watch, and intently listening for the note of a stag. At last comes the wild and welcome music floating faintly up through the forest. Louder and more harsh grows each repetition of the strain as it draws nearer and nearer, until there is no doubt of its being the animal's intention to visit the glade. Presently a hind comes tripping warily from out the wood. She is almost immediately followed by several others, until at last forth stalks a mighty stag wearing a splendid crown of horn. The hinds soon begin listlessly cropping the grass. They are jealously waited upon by their lord, who, with swelling throat and bristling neck, continues to bellow forth, at intervals, his love-song to his harem, his appetite being apparently much affected by his amours. Although comparatively close, he is much too far from our present position to risk a shot at him whilst there is a possibility of getting nearer. How my heart throbs between hope of a chance and fear lest I may lose it, as we worm ourselves along through the brackens towards the wood, and, on gaining it, creep stealthily on among the bushes towards our noble quarry! There are some who may say that an old sportsman should never get excited. To put it plainly, this is what is vulgarly called "gammon," or more politely, contrary to human nature. When the pulses cease to quicken at the prospect of bringing down a grand beast, slaying him in cold blood can no longer be called sport. The keener the sportsman the more intense his excitement, although experience may have taught him to keep it under control. But this is no time for moralising.

At last we get within easy range of the stag, now standing forth alone, snuffing the tainted air as though he had some inkling of danger. But little he recks of its being so near him as he stands there, his royal head held proudly erect, looking quite the "monarch of all he surveys." The bead-sight is on his broad shoulder; yet so fearful am I of missing him, large and near though he is, that I hesitate for some time before pressing the trigger. Off goes the shot at last, but, to my intense surprise and concern, without the slightest apparent effect on the stag. For a few seconds he stands stock-still, and then with a bound starts down the steep declivity in front of him. Oh, the agony of that moment! Fortunately for me, however, he has taken the open instead of the wooded side of the spur, thereby giving another chance as he rushes headlong down the hill. By great good luck, the second shot catches him high up in the hind-leg; but he still holds on, with the broken limb dangling loosely about, and disappears among the thick brushwood below. The track where his wide-splayed hoofs have ploughed up the ground in his rapid descent is easily followed, and we soon overtake him near the bottom of a steep rocky water-course, where he has lain down. He makes an effort to rise on our approach, but a shot effectually stops his farther pro-gress; and after a considerable amount of dodging to avoid his swaying horns and kicking hoofs, we at last succeed in giving him the *coup de grâce* with all due ceremony.

He was indeed a royal hart in every sense, with wide-spanning horns which measured six and a half inches round the thinnest part of the beam, and such brow, bay, and tray antlers as few stags can show. Yet I hardly deserved to get him, for we found that although the first shot had struck him just behind the shoulder, it was so low down that there was barely an inch to spare. We should certainly have seen the last of him had he not chosen the open instead of the wooded side of the spur for his line of retreat, thereby giving me a chance of spoiling his haunch as I did.

It was too late to make arrangements for carrying away the spoils that evening; so leaving our two spare men to keep up a bonfire for scaring off the bears, which would be certain to sniff the venison, Ramzan and I started for the camp. Night overtook us in the dark forest whilst we had still some way to travel, but our signals of distress were soon answered by our men below, who brought up pine-torches to light us down the hill.

Next day the villagers, who seemed to have scented the meat from afar, flocked to our camp from all directions, like so many vultures.

As the stags were reported to be now pretty constantly heard on the heights above Nouboog, we returned to our old quarters in that direction. During the next two or three days, although stags were frequently heard, nothing with horns was seen, until early one morning the spy-glass was brought to bear upon a solitary fellow carrying a splendid royal head, and roaring like a bull as he quickly ascended a steep open hill-face before disappearing over the ridge above it. After a hastily despatched meal we started to look up his domain, our blankets and supper being taken with us, as we purposed spending the night on the hill.

A stag, which we thought might perhaps be our friend of the morning, again "tuned his pipes" in the evening, as he moved up through the forest towards the open ridge above it. At length he made his appearance, but only when it had grown so dark that we were unable to recognise the shape of his horns as he stood bellowing there within what, in day-light, would have been easy range. As we saw nothing more of the beast after my random shot at him in the dim uncertain light, I scored what I might only have expected—a miss! Several distant stags began roaring in different directions as

we sadly took our way to where we intended passing the night
under shelter of a pine-tree; so I consoled myself with the
knowledge that, like the fishes in the sea, there were still as
good deer in the forest as ever came out of it.

Feeling pretty certain that in the morning we should find
one of these noisy fellows out on some open hill-top in our
neighbourhood, we were afoot very early. A milk-hind with
a well-grown calf, and what looked like a yeld hind, were
just retiring into the forest at one end of a glade as we entered
it at the other. I had no intention of molesting them, had
not the yeld hussey been so inquisitive as to turn back into
the open, where she stood gazing at us within little more than
a hundred yards. I felt sorry to do it; but as the stags had
been silent all the morning, and she offered such a tempting
opportunity of securing some good venison, I let drive. She
disappeared into the wood then, but a juicy portion of her
reappeared at dinner-time. After our morning meal we went
out again and followed up, for some distance, the track of the
stag I had shot at on the previous evening, but finding no
blood on it confirmed my idea that I had correctly scored a
miss. The prospect of sport on this ground seemed so good
that we determined to remain where we were for a day or two
longer.

That afternoon we tried the hill-tops that overlook the
Cashmere valley. Towards evening we took up a position behind a green knowe, whence we could watch a tolerable extent
of open ground, and listen for deer in the forest which bordered it. It had also the advantage of commanding an extensive view of "the vale," lying some 2000 feet below. Even
my native companions seemed impressed with the exquisite
loveliness of the prospect; for the Cashmeree, although small-
minded in many ways, still has in his soul a spice of romantic
admiration for his beautiful fatherland. At the foot of the
range we were on lay the dreary, treeless plateau, where, in
the centre, stands the massive old ruin of the Temple of the

Sun—" Martund " [1]—lonely and grand; whilst far beyond it, and all smiling in the mellow evening sunlight, stretched the broad green vale away towards the distant mountains rising blue

Ruins of the Temple of the Sun—" Martund."

and snow-capped on either side, its tortuous streams winding along like shimmering threads of gold until lost in the gauzy haze. . . . " Grrō-ō-ō-ō-ā-oo-ooā," nasally, with variations and *cadenza ad libitum*, goes a stag in the forest behind us, rudely interrupting our reveries. He is not very far off either, and Ramzan says there is just a chance of the animal's coming to have an evening roll in a small muddy pool, or "trag" as it is here called, that he (Ramzan) knows of in the vicinity.

We soon reach the pool, which is situated near the border of an undulating grassy glade immediately above the forest where the stag was heard. At the edge of an opposite wood, and about a hundred yards from the pool, Ramzan

[1] This noble old structure—by the natives called "Pandoo lurrie" (Pandoo house)—is, I believe—like the ancient ruins I have mentioned as situated between Uri and Baramoola, which, on a larger scale, it somewhat resembles—of doubtful origin. From the symbolical figures it contains it is, however, pretty certain that it was at one period dedicated to the worship of the Hindu triad—Brahma, Vishnu, and Siva. A noteworthy feature of its architecture is the keystone of the arches, which is formed of a solid T-shaped block, such as I have endeavoured to depict in my little sketch of this ruin.

selects a spot for an ambush, which merely consists of a few green branches stuck into the ground; but our view of the pool is quite obstructed by some rising ground on our side of it. This flaw in the position cannot, however, be avoided, owing to the direction of the wind; and Ramzan, from former experience, confidently predicts that the hangul, if he should visit the trag, will, after quitting it, be pretty certain to show himself on the said rising ground. The old man seems so satisfied of his conjecture proving right, that he goes so far as to divest his head of its big white turban—a precaution which he seldom thinks necessary in close country unless he really means business.

The bellowing, although now much nearer, is only heard at long intervals, until at last such a time elapses without its being repeated that my hopes of a chance are fast subsiding. But listen! a low sort of groaning sound comes from the direction of the pool. Again we hear it, this time in short subdued grunts, and there is no longer any doubt about its proceeding from the stag as he wallows in the mud, although we cannot see him owing to the rising ground that intervenes. My companion, as he sits silently by, exhorts my patience by intelligent glances, as I anxiously await the issue of the business. We have not long to wait, however, before a pair of broad-spreading horns with ten beautiful tines rise gradually over the grass, until at length their owner, all soiled with wet mud and quite unconscious of danger, stands in full view before us. A few seconds more and he is stretched on the grass, kicking furiously in his death-throes.

Dropping the beast on the spot was indeed a bit of rare luck, and was accounted for by a splinter of the shell, which struck him rather high behind the shoulder, injuring his spine. I only give my good old shikaree his just due when I say that getting a shot at this beast was entirely owing to the thorough knowledge of his calling he possessed. I have sometimes met sportsmen in India who affect to scorn the assistance and advice of a native stalker. But in doing so I think they are mistaken; for with their limited knowledge of the ground it stands to reason that they cannot work it with the same advantage as the native shikaree who has known all its features and peculiarities since his youth. I have known others who imagine they can walk down the paharee in his native mountains. With his oriental politeness he may flatter them into such a belief; but given any distance from five miles to a hundred over a rough mountainous country, with a good reward for the hill-villager at the end of it, and then see who will win the race—the bare-footed, agile mountaineer, or his white competitor, however athletic, in his boots?—the paharee, and even a very ordinary one, " I guess." Few shikarees are, however, of much use to an experienced hand except in their native neighbourhood.

My satisfaction, as I stood admiring the grand proportions of the fallen stag, was slightly mingled with remorse when I thought of the rather mean advantage we had taken of the unsuspecting animal in our method of circumventing him. The beam of his horns was only 5½ inches in girth, but this was compensated for by a span of 33 inches within the bend. We bled and gralloched him then and there; but as darkness was fast setting in, we left two men to guard him at night from those hirsute thieves the bears.

During the night I was awakened by the hoarse bellowing of a stag in the direction of a "trag" on an open spot within a quarter of a mile of where I lay. This time it must have been more of a challenge than a serenade, for it soon called forth a loud response in the echoing wood from a rival forest king, who seemed to draw nearer the challenger until their voices suddenly ceased. From this I divined that the rivals were fighting it out on the grassy arena beside the pool. Darkness, however, prevented my interference with their quarrel.

Early next morning one of the watchers came and reported

that during the night another hangul had actually come and
rolled in the mud beside the pond, within about twenty yards
of which the dead one was lying. This sounded rather improbable; but, as I intended hunting again in that direction,
I resolved to go and examine the place myself. There, sure
enough, was the fresh impression where a second stag had
rolled in the wet mud and had left some of his hair sticking
to it. Of one thing there was no doubt—both the watchers
must have fallen asleep and let their fire go out, although
they stoutly denied having done so.

These ponds or "trags" are used by the herdsmen for
watering their cattle when up grazing on the hill-tops. They
are always favourite resorts of the stags for soiling themselves
in during the rutting season, when the animals become very
restless, and often so reckless that when following a stag in
thick forest you may sometimes even attract him towards
you by breaking a dry twig, the slight noise of which the
stupid beast, in his love-sick imagination, supposes may be
caused by a hind.

Shortly after leaving the pond, a hangul raised his voice in
a thick pine-wood below us; so we determined to try and
follow him up there, for it was too late in the morning to
expect him to show himself outside it. As the roaring was
not continued, we adopted the following plan: after carefully testing the wind in the usual manner, by tossing up
scraps of dry grass, Ramzan and I moved stealthily towards
the place where the bellowing was last heard; whilst the
other two men of our party made a wide circuit below to
search for tracks, should the deer have moved downwards.
Each time we stopped to listen, the twig-breaking trick was
tried, but with no effect. On reaching the supposed position
of the deer, not a trace of any sort could we find to direct us,
when "too whoo," "too whoo-oo," comes the hoot of an owl
from among the dense dark pines some distance lower down.
This time, however, it proceeds from no bird of ill-omen, for

in it we recognise a preconcerted signal from the men below
for calling us down to them. It is at once answered by a
like sound, made by blowing between the hands clasped together in a certain way, and is repeated at intervals until we
find our scouts. They have ascertained by the tracks that
the stag has moved downwards in company with several
hinds. Keeping well on the alert for any movement in the
brushwood, we follow cautiously on the broad trail. Suddenly
a stampede is heard, and we get a momentary glimpse
through the trees of one or two of the brown hides vanishing
into a dell a short way ahead. As the animals have become
alarmed, our only plan now is to run forward to the place
where they disappeared, on the chance of getting a snap-shot
ere they get too far beyond it. Fortune is so far kind, for on
our reaching the desired spot, all breathless from running, I
catch sight of one of them—a stag, and a good one too—
through a vista in the trees, as he stands looking back within
easy range below me. The hanging smoke prevents my seeing the effect of the shot, but the sound of the striking bullet
seems to denote meat. "He's down!" breathlessly exclaims
Ramzan, as he feels for his knife. But this remark is succeeded by a much less exultant one. "No, he's up and away
again! Oho! tzh! tzh! tzh!"—usual interjections of disappointment made with the tongue and teeth. No venison,
however, do we find on going to look for it, although my old
companion positively declares to having seen the animal on
the ground, toes up, after the shot. All attempts at following the tracks for any distance are frustrated by numerous
fresh and large ones here leading in all directions, and there
is no blood to guide us. So I turn my steps campwards
lamenting, followed by Ramzan and the other Cashmerees
"tzh! tzh! tzhing" in the most aggravating manner all
the way.

Again the villagers flocked up from below to our bivouac,
where they gorged themselves and wrangled over the distribu-

tion of the meat until late in the afternoon, when we packed up and started for the tents below.

As we were descending in the gloaming, some hinds, followed by a stag with longish prongs, moved past us across a glade. Several rounds of ammunition were expended, only one apparently with effect, and that probably slight. Anyway, we failed to find the beast when we returned next morning to search for him. My spleen at losing him, which was considerably augmented by my having bad toothache, was vented on an unfortunate flying squirrel, whose abode in a dead pine-tree we chanced to come across as we were returning, and out of which we "scraped" him.

The camp was again shifted to a fresh locality farther up the glen. The fine weather we had hitherto enjoyed was now exchanged for wet and cold, which so increased my toothache that I could get no rest. Ramzan suggested that he should fetch a barber of his acquaintance, who, he said, had frequently operated on him under similar circumstances. This village practitioner was accordingly called in and consulted. Smiling blandly, he produced a barbarous implement about a foot long, and not unlike a very rusty old pair of carpenter's pincers, with a hook at the end of one of its handles to prevent the operator's hand from slipping. Even the sight of this terrible instrument failed to have the usual temporary effect of allaying the distracting pain; so I was forced to place my jawbone at the mercy of the hair-dresser, who, with the most cold-blooded indifference for my feelings, began deliberately washing his diabolical-looking forceps in a stream directly in front of my tent door, thereby hinting that he was quite ready to operate forthwith. After putting me to a protracted amount of torture, during which old Ramzan was praying audibly and devoutly behind me as he insisted on holding my head, the operator at length, to my infinite relief, both of body and mind, succeeded in extracting the proper tooth without fracturing my jaw. This, however, was not the end

s

of it. The excited dentist straightway dashed pincers, tooth and all, to the ground, and, energetically aided by Ramzan, frantically set to shampooing and " thrawing " my head to such a degree as to almost threaten my neck with dislocation, each of them accompanying their combined exertions with " Yah Peer! Yah Russool!" and suchlike hurriedly repeated pious expressions, until I at last managed to free myself from their tender mercies. A fee of a few " chilkees " (Cashmere silver coins worth about a shilling) sent the barber-surgeon home rejoicing.

CHAPTER XVII.

ALL Nature's charms looked more bright and beautiful when
the clouds cleared away after two or three days of almost
incessant rain, and we again took the hill. In the afternoon,
after a long ascent from the camp, we sat down to rest among
the brackens on a steep spur, and just outside a dense pine
forest that clothed its northern slope. Several stags were
bellowing away in a thickly wooded gorge far below. As we
sat there consulting as to how we should try to circumvent
one of them, a shaggy-looking animal suddenly bounced out
from the wood on to the open ridge, some 150 yards higher
up than where we were sitting, and after a few bounds downwards, again vanished into the wood. We were all quite
nonplussed as to what it could have been, for it certainly
was not a deer, and it had neither the gait nor the colour

of a bear. Whilst we were discussing the matter, a rustle was heard in the wood behind us. On looking round, to our utter amazement there we saw the long black visage of a tahr—not a surrow (termed "rāmoo" in Cashmere), which is sometimes in the more eastern Himalayas called tahr or "thār," but a veritable tahr. He was standing among the brushwood within twenty yards, and returning our gaze with apparently equal astonishment to our own. Snatching up the rifle, I blazed straight at him, letting him have the second barrel as he rushed away through the bushes. Being sorely wounded, he was soon overtaken, when another bullet finished him. He was a fine, dark, shaggy buck with good horns, and about the last animal we might have expected to see on such ground, where his appearance was most unaccountable, for there were no tahr haunts within at least thirty miles of it. Ramzan told me that he remembered only once before having seen a "krās," as he called him, on the Nouboog hills. This one was evidently a stranger in the land, and might perhaps have been chased from his own rocky fastnesses by wild dogs. It was the rutting season, however, and love is sometimes the cause of strange freaks.

Leaving the two spare men to skin and cut up the tahr, Ramzan and I tried to find one of the noisy stags which still continued their roaring, notwithstanding the firing. To one of them we got very close, but failed to get a chance at him owing to the thickness of the cover he was in. We hunted here for another day or two without firing a shot. Although the deer were plentiful, the woods were too dense for working them in. The villagers told us that bears had commenced their burglaries at night among the walnut groves in the neighbourhood; but the moon was then too young to afford light enough for looking them up. On dark nights, when the villagers detect an old thief committing depredations on their walnuts, they sometimes quickly surround the tree he is in, and lighting a big fire under it, set up a tremendous shouting, with drum accompaniment, thereby keeping poor Bruin a prisoner until it becomes light enough in the morning to make him pay the penalty of his misdemeanours. We heard them thus "treeing" a bear before daybreak one morning, but the performance was too far away for me to go and witness it.

The last of the sheep had been driven down from the higher pasturages on the hills towards the head of the Nouboog glen, and the shooting-grounds in that direction had all been vacated by their former occupants. Thither, therefore, we now turned our steps. Our little camp was pitched in a sheltered nook on the border of an extensive, undulating, grassy plateau surrounded with dense pine woods. As the place was about 10,000 feet high, the cold at night was quite keen enough to make a huge fire of pine-logs and a glass of "hot with" very enjoyable. In the morning I had to break the ice in my metal wash-basin, and the grass was all glittering with a thick coating of hoar-frost as we left the camp. That day we prospected the open hill-tops away up towards the Wurdwan range. Fresh evidences of deer were numerous, though we neither saw nor heard anything except some fine coveys of chuckor partridges. After nightfall a stag on an adjacent wooded eminence serenaded me with his stirring music whilst I sat in my tent at dinner. Another, or perhaps the same one, disturbed me at night as he awakened the multiplying echoes in the surrounding forest by roaring within what seemed, in the still frosty air, to be only a few hundred yards off my tent—almost tempting me to rise from my warm blankets and look after him. He had evidently come to visit one of the several trags on the plateau where we had noticed many fresh marks in the mud. The moonlight, however, was not as yet sufficiently bright for chancing a shot there at night; but all this augured well for sport in the neighbourhood.

The following afternoon, when we were far up on the hill,

ragged fragments of mist began to circle and toss wildly
about the mountain-tops, and snow-flakes soon commenced
drifting thickly and rapidly past us; so we sheltered under
the lee of some blocks of rock in a little birch coppice. How
we shivered with cold as the bleak chilling blast whistled
drearily through the birches and whirled away their withered
leaves before it! For several hours we sat dolefully there,
crouching over a little spark of fire, for we dared not light a
bigger one lest the smoke should alarm the deer. I had not
even the solace of my pipe, which I had stupidly forgotten to
bring with me; so I had recourse to Ramzan's snuff-box as a
substitute for a smoke. It was still snowing, and the lessen-
ing light warned us that it was time to be moving downwards,
when just then our drooping spirits were raised by the
welcome voice of a stag on an opposite hillside. The fire,
to which we had been gradually adding fuel as we grew
colder, was instantly doused. Exercise and excitement, however, soon warmed us up, and by the time we neared the
place where the stag had last been heard, it had almost ceased
snowing. But the dusk was fast closing in, and had it not
been for the fresh-fallen snow, on which we could distinctly
pick up the stag's slot, we should soon have lost the track.
Moreover, the beast was evidently now travelling pretty fast
and roaring very seldom.

We had tracked through a dark strip of pine-wood, and
were about to emerge on to an open undulating bit of grass
beyond it, when we caught sight of the stag standing there
some distance ahead. I was very anxious to "loose" at him,
for the light was fast fading; but as he had again resumed
his roaring at pretty regular intervals, Ramzan suggested that
we should try to get closer. Quickly we made a circuit
through some cover, and contrived to come up with the
animal as he stood for a few moments within some eighty
yards, slightly below us, and broadside on. But, alas! the
short Indian twilight had now failed us, and I could no longer

see the fore-sight of the rifle, for, unfortunately, it was not silvered, as the near end of the sporting fore-sight should always be; so I took the best aim I could at the shadowy form of the stag without it. The bullet told on him somewhere with a smart "thwack,"—a term, I think, better suited to the sound than the conventional "thud," which as often denotes *mud* as meat. The deer gave a sudden spring, turned short round, and plunging down the hill, disappeared in a deep wooded gorge. To follow him in the dark would have been worse than useless; we therefore made the best of a long trudge back to camp. Fortunately the clouds had broken, so we had some glimpses of moonlight to help us through the gloomy pine woods.

At peep of dawn we were off again, and spent several hours in trying to follow up the stag of the previous evening, as we felt certain he was hard hit. There was no blood on his track; but this might have been accounted for by the closing up of the small orifice made by a ·450 bullet, or by the shell hitting high in the animal's body, and bursting up without penetrating right through it. Ramzan, who was rather conservative in his ideas, had already suggested that the new-fangled "nasala ke golee" (medicine-bullet), as he termed my vaunted shell, might not be very certain in its effect, and I was beginning to think he was right.

The deer's track had been missed, and I was sitting down consoling myself with a smoke when a stag began bellowing on the brow of an opposite hill. I could see with the telescope that he carried at least a royal number of tines, as I watched him moving quickly down over a steep open slope, until he disappeared in the thick wood below it. Whilst still spying about with the glass, its field lighted on two more stags which were browsing among some bushes far away below. One of them carried good horns, but not to be compared with the royal set that had just disappeared. My

sage old adviser was away, casting about in the forest for the
lost track, or I should not have had to confess that in a
foolish fit of impatience I recklessly let drive a long random
shot. It was not only useless, but it lost me any chance I
might have had at the royal, which, but for my egregious
folly, I might possibly have got. There is nothing like con-
fessing one's mistakes, and they sometimes afford useful lessons. To abstain from firing random shots is a maxim which,
if followed, will gain the sportsman many a trophy, and will
save the humane shooter, and oftentimes his quarry, from
many a sore pang.

The cold at night had become so bitter up here that the
camp was moved to a warmer locality below. The stags,
too, had apparently gone lower down, for they were now less
often heard high up. We resolved, however, to take another
turn over the higher ground before descending in the evening to our new quarters. Our breakfasts had been discussed,
and we were all lounging lazily on a wooded spur when Ramzan, who was always on the alert, said he thought he heard
a hangul calling far away up on the hill above. So long a
time elapsed without a repetition of the sound, that I thought
he must have been mistaken. "Hark! there he is again," says
the old man, as this time the wild cadence, mellowed by distance, comes distinctly over the hill behind us. As the
ground above is pretty open, the chances of a stalk are in
our favour, so we at once commence working upwards. After
a long and stiff pull we reach a ridge overlooking a deep sort
of corrie full of dense brushwood, from whence the bellowing
now comes repeatedly in hoarse volumes. After intently listening for some time, Ramzan gives his opinion that, judging
from the approaching sound and the direction of the wind, the
beast will very likely cross the open hill-face below us. No
sooner has he given vent to his prediction than another lusty
roar comes from almost directly below, and the long, white-
tipped, upper tines of the stag appear moving among the

brushwood in the hollow. Onward they slowly come, until the mightiest stag we have yet seen is leisurely walking across an open slope below us, and within eighty yards. There is not much time for a steady aim, as in a few seconds he will again be out of sight. Feeling certain that the shoulder of a brute the size of an ox can hardly be missed at so short a range, I confidently let drive at him. He seems to half-stumble on faster for a few steps, and then resuming his original pace, slowly disappears behind some high bushes.

"Come this way, quick!" says Ramzan, starting off at a run; "he'll cross the ridge lower down, as he's making for the wood behind it." There is no stopping to recharge the empty barrel of my muzzle-loader, for we have only just time to run down the ridge and head the animal before the white tips of his horns are again in sight. How I gloat on those massive, wide-spreading beams and twelve long tines as they draw nearer and nearer! I fancy I can see those antlers now, as I write, swaying to and fro, as the seemingly wounded stag labours slowly up the hillside, until he is actually within fifty yards of where we are crouching low among the tall ferns. As I put up the rifle nothing is to be seen before its sights but a broad brown shoulder, and from the fact of there being only space for at least a mile beyond the deer, the loud smack made by the shell cannot possibly have told on anything but him. On receiving the shot he stops short, turns his head slowly towards us, and after standing for a few seconds steadfastly gazing at us, continues his course at a canter towards the ridge, and crossing it just below us, disappears into the wood beyond it, exactly as my crafty old companion had foretold.

"There's not such another hangul in all these forests," says Ramzan hurriedly, as he impatiently assists me to reload. "He's badly wounded, so we're sure to come up with him in the wood." Never before have I seen the old man so excited, and I feel quite confident myself that the stag is mine. But, alas! we are both mistaken this time. Although we follow the track until evening, never again do we set eyes on that monarch of the forest after his clearing the ridge.

It was some time ere I could realise the sad fact that I had lost this splendid brute. I now came to the conclusion either that the hardened detonating shell must have burst to pieces in the thick muscles of the shoulder without penetrating farther, or that the whole thing was an optical delusion. At any rate that stag must have borne a charmed life, for, as he stood looking at us after the rifle was empty—wae's me! it was only an old muzzle-loader—my gun, loaded with honest leaden bullets, was within arm's reach. But its carrier, who I had no idea was crouching quite close behind me, in his excitement had forgotten to hand it to me.

My frame of mind, as I plodded wearily down through the dark pine woods, was decidedly grumpy. For the best part of two days did we perseveringly search for the wounded stag, with only the doubtful satisfaction of finding here and there a few drops of blood on the trail. Fancy is often apt to picture the trophies one loses as the finest, but those magnificent lost antlers haunt my memory to the present day.

The moon being now near its full, Ramzan proposed that we should try watching beside one of the trags that was most resorted to by the stags. We therefore shifted our quarters back to the vicinity of the pool where, several nights before, I had imagined the tournament had taken place. Although this night-watching for stags is rather a "shady" way of doing business, there is certainly a wild charm about it on a calm moonlight night, as the sportsman—or poacher, as he may perhaps be considered—lies in wait, expectant for his quarry, beside some quiet pool, his senses all quickening at the slightest rustle of a leaf in the hushed forest.

The shadows of evening were deepening in the woods when we spread our blankets behind some bushes under the tall sombre pine-trees near the trag we intended watching. As night advanced, the occasional eerie hoot of a great horned owl, or the flit of a flying squirrel among the overhanging branches, where he nibbled the pine-cones, only made the stillness more impressive. Our surroundings, too, became more weird-looking as the rising moon shed a dim ghastly light on the gnarled and crooked stems of the silver birch-trees standing here and there like white spectres in the gloomy cloisters of the pine-forest that begirt the pool. Sometimes our flagging hopes would be raised as the far-off bellowing of a stag was intermittently borne towards us on the night breeze that gently rocked the pine-tops, but only again to sink with the sound as it gradually died away in the distance. This was all very romantic and exciting, until towards morning I grew so sleepy that I could no longer keep my eyes or ears open. And when, at grey frosty dawn, we returned, chilled and disappointed, from our night vigils, all my ideas of their romance had evaporated.

That evening about dusk I wounded a stag, which, though not a very fine specimen, would have been a welcome addition to our larder—which the villagers had nearly emptied—had we not lost him in the gathering darkness. We moved next day back to the locality where, amongst the numerous fresh tracks, we had lost those of the big wounded stag, our goods and chattels being sent round by an easier route. In the afternoon it was snowing thickly, when we heard the bellowing of a stag—evidently a traveller—on a hillside below us, and caught a glimpse of the restless, wandering beast—and a good one he was—as he quickly traversed some open ground. We ran round, and tried in vain to head him before he disappeared in some heavy forest where following him was hopeless. It was nightfall when we reached our camp, which had been pitched beside the dilapidated ruins of a shieling, long ago deserted by the herdsmen, and under some tall black-looking cypress-trees at the bottom of a silent forest-clad glen, where sunshine could have been but little known,

and solitude was now absolute. The monotonous babble and
plash of the brooklet which flowed past; the hooting of owls
echoing dismally around; the dirge-like sough of the cold
night wind as it rose and fell among the dark aisles of the
pine-forest; and the snow-clad heights looming stark and
wan above in the pale moonlight,—all served to augment the
idea of its being about as lonesome and elfin-looking a spot as
such a combination of depressing influences could make it.
At any rate, this seemed to be the opinion of my Goorkha
servant, who being, like most mountaineers, of a superstitious
turn of mind, next morning told me he had been all night
dreaming of hobgoblins coming down the glen to seize him.
He had most probably been partaking of a heavy supper of
venison, and listening to the wonderful legends told by
the Cashmerees as they sat round the camp-fire about the
wild haunted tarns of Choar Nag, which lie among the high
mountains at the head of this gloomy glen.   Poor Kirpa! A
few years later he was accidentally shot dead by a comrade,
with whom he was out hunting in the Dehra Doon forests. . . .

Whilst alluding to the superstitious tendency of the hill-
men, I may mention a little practical joke I was told of as
having been played on his shikarees by a sportsman when
ibex-hunting in days gone by on the Wurdwan mountains.
At that time the trigonometrical survey of Cashmere had
only been commenced, and the unsophisticated villagers
then regarded the scientific operations as a sort of "Mumbo
Jumbo" proceeding, which was quite beyond their compre-
hension.   One day this sportsman, whilst resting beside a
cairn of stones that had been erected on a hill-top to mark a
survey station, began questioning his shikarees as to their
ideas concerning it.   One of them replied that all he knew
about it was, that he had once ascended this very hill with
a Sahib (gentleman), who had set up a wonderful kind of
" durbeen " (telescope), through which he had looked in all
directions.   He had also made a great number of figures on a

bit of paper, and had then ordered these stones to be piled up. But what surprised him most was, that the Sahib before descending the hill had torn up the paper he had written so much upon into small pieces, which he threw on the ground. In fact he (the shikaree) considered the whole thing was some sort of "jadoo" (magic). The sportsman, thinking this a grand opportunity for practising upon the superstitious credulity of his companions, suddenly sprang to his feet, and with feigned terror exclaimed—"He strewed those bits of paper on this spot, did he ?—then *we* had better be off !" And away he ran down the hill, his terrified companions coming helter-skelter after him, as if Old Nick were behind them.

We hunted hereabouts unsuccessfully for two days, my only chance being at an old black bear, into which I one evening put a bullet, as he stood up on his hind-legs eating berries off a bush. He dropped quantities of blood, but as his trail led up through thick cover, and darkness was growing apace, we did not think it either prudent or worth our while to follow him far. The fresh-fallen snow, which now lay several inches deep on the open slopes above the forest, had evidently driven the deer lower down; so we left our cold gloomy quarter for the warmer and more cheerful one where I had shot my first hangul, and for which I had a lingering fancy. If the reader is not already quite tired of following me so often through the forest after stags, perhaps he will accompany me, just once more, in pursuit of one of the grandest of them all.

As we were setting up our camp, an old goojur (herdsman), who was grazing his beasts in the neighbouring woods, volunteered us the information that a very black-looking and big-horned hangul, which for several years had been known to visit this locality late in the rutting season, had, during the last few days, been several times seen about the head of the wooded glen in which he was then herding his cattle. As it was still early in the day, we decided upon at

once proceeding in quest of this famous beast. We had gone
about a mile up a burn that flowed through the glen, when
we heard a bellow in the wood above us; we therefore sat
down and listened. Soon it was repeated, this time lower
down in the wood and nearer, as though the stag were about
to cross the glen higher up; so we quietly moved on. We
had not gone far when I caught sight of a hind a short way
ahead. She was crossing the burn, and, from her nervous
behaviour, it was evident she had got wind of us. Just
then I felt a tug at my coat from the man following behind
me, who directed my attention to the head and shoulder of
a good stag which was standing, within easy range, among
the trees; but before I could cover him with the rifle he was
gone. He was a light-coloured stag, and certainly not the
beast we wanted to find.

My tent had been pitched close to a corn-stack, in consequence of which I was kept awake almost the whole night
by an invasion of rats and mice, that seemed to be amusing
themselves by running races over my bed. Next day our
search for the black fellow was again unsuccessful, the only
thing seen or heard being a stag with short horns, which we
"jumped" in the dusky twilight, and I missed.

The following morning we tried the ground where I had
killed the first stag, as the one we were now hunting for
was supposed to have his present haunt in the dense wood
below it. Towards evening we sat down among the tall
brackens to watch the edge of the wood from the old spot.
After waiting for an hour or more, we were almost startled
by a loud bellow, which was soon repeated quite close to us
in the wood. Presently a small beast with short prongs
emerged from the cover on to the open side of the ridge,
where he at once commenced feeding. But I felt quite
certain that this was not the animal that had just bellowed
so loudly, and as he kept looking back towards the wood, I
was equally confident he was not alone. As he fed gradually

up towards where we were lying prone among the brackens, Ramzan, who, excellent shikaree though he was, seemed to prefer a good chance of securing fat venison to the more uncertain one of securing a fine head but rank meat, insisted that this was the animal we had heard, although he must have known as well as I did that it was not. "Shoot, or he'll be off," whispered he impatiently, as the animal was drawing nearer and nearer—when lo! a stag, looking as dark as a "peat-hag," and carrying a huge pile of antlers, emerges slowly and hesitatingly from the wood. How my heart thumps against my ribs as the much-coveted black stag—for I have now not a doubt about its being the identical animal—stands before us within a hundred yards! There is no time to wait for my sudden excitement to abate, as the small beast has fed up very close to us, and the light evening wind is capricious. With trembling hands I slowly lift the rifle over the brackens, but it wabbles so much, as I try to cover the big fellow's shoulder, that I have to lower it. Again it is raised, and, holding my breath, I press the trigger. Off dashes the small beast down the hill; but the big one, although hard hit, merely gives a start, trots forward a few steps, and again stops, his grand horns thrown proudly back, as he quickly jerks his uplifted head round from side to side, as if at a loss as to what course he should pursue.

"Ne lugga!" (missed him), whispers Ramzan, testily followed by a rapid succession of his exasperating interjections of disappointment. But he is wrong again. Before the stag has time to make up his mind, another bullet—of good solid lead this time—smashes his shoulder. Still, strange to say, he scarcely moves. Gradually, however, his startled demeanour becomes more listless, and his proud head begins slowly to droop. But he is too far out to make sure of finishing him with a shot from the smooth-bore, which would most probably only send him back into the thick forest, where, although so badly wounded, we might as likely as not lose him; so I contrive to reload the rifle, fortunately without his detecting me. Once more it is raised: this time the bullet, passing through him, breaks the other shoulder, and brings him down on his chest. As we stand up and move towards him, the terrified brute, in his endeavours to escape, actually shoves himself along with his hind-legs down the steep grassy declivity before him. At the bottom of this we find him lying, panting and glaring wildly at us, as if quite prepared to make use of his ponderous horns, which he tosses in such a menacing manner as to make the orthodox rites rather difficult to perform.

Although not so fine a stag as the lost beauty, inasmuch as he had only ten points, yet the dimensions of his grand massive horns are, I think, worth recording. Length, nearly 42 inches; girth at the thinnest part of the beam, between the bez (or bay) antler and median tine, $7\frac{1}{4}$ inches; girth round the burr, $10\frac{1}{2}$ inches; round the bez antler, three or four inches from the beam, $5\frac{1}{2}$ inches, and brow antlers nearly as thick; span inside the beams, 33 inches. All the points were perfect. Although he carried such massive horns, he was not a very heavy-bodied stag; and Ramzan told me that these comparatively small dark-coloured hangul generally had the heaviest horns, and were the most noisy and pugnacious, or " bobbery," as he expressed it. His pile was in beautiful order, but the poor beast had rubbed all the hair off his chest, and had even excoriated a good deal of the skin, in his frantic efforts to escape down the hill. But his carcass looked as if he had not made a good square meal of grass for a long time, which was only natural at that season. No doubt the younger of the two stags would have been more appreciated by my Cashmeree companions.

It was now past sundown, so we merely took out the gralloch, and left watchers to perform a night wake beside the defunct, for bears were about. Next day, when the head was brought in, the old goojur of course declared we had got the right beast. But whether we had or had not, I felt supremely happy at having secured so majestic a trophy, and I hope I made the goojur feel equally so. A drop of gall, however, fell into my cup of delight, when next morning I was informed that my splendid prize had been mutilated during the night by a cat. On inspecting the head, I found that one of the ears had been taken off, not by a cat's teeth, but by a clean cut of a knife. I at once suspected foul play, and that it was just a spiteful trick perpetrated by one of my followers from a mean spirit of revenge. I had on several occasions found fault with the suspected culprit—who, I regret to say, was Ramzan's son—for the avarice he always displayed at the distribution of the venison. This time he had made away with it bodily, intending, as I was told, to barter it with the villagers for grain. On learning this I directed that both the culprit and the meat should be at once produced, when I rated the former well, and distributed the latter fairly among all hands. Next morning the ear was off the stag's head. I felt so convinced that the mischief had been done by this man—who was well aware how particular I was regarding the careful preservation of the heads—in revenge for the meat row, that I discharged him forthwith,—the justice of which sentence, I was glad to find, his father fully acknowledged.

From this place we returned to Nouboog. On reaching it we found that the dried-up grass on the heights about it had just been set fire to, which ruined all chance of further sport there. I had my suspicions as to who had raised this conflagration. At night the effect produced by the burning was truly grand, as the fire crept slowly on in long irregular lines, some of them many hundred yards in length. Here it shot up high in quivering tongues of flame as it ignited some dead old resinous pine-trunk and licked along its withered branches, casting a lurid glow on the murky clouds of smoke that hovered above. There, like streams of molten lava, it crept down the mountain-side, or flickered and smouldered in

T

isolated spots on the dark devasted expanse where the raging element had already spent its fury and passed on. One would suppose that such fires ought to utterly destroy every tree in a forest; but here, strange to say, comparatively little damage is done to the timber.

In Indian forests, after the trees have attained a certain size, they seem, as a rule, to become almost fireproof; for notwithstanding the annual burning of dry grass and brush-wood on the mountain-sides, you seldom or never see those tracts of charred and withered timber-skeletons so constantly met with in the American backwoods. I therefore very much doubt whether burning the undergrowth is here so pre-judicial as is generally supposed. In the forests of " sal " and other hardwood trees of the Terai and Dehra Doon, the ravages of white ants, especially where the undergrowth is left unburnt, are, I am sure, more injurious to well-grown trees than is the slight scorching of their outer bark by fire. More-over, the fire to a great extent arrests the progress of destruc-tion by the ants, and the clearance of useless scrub-jungle by burning gives freedom for the better development of the more matured timber. The exclusion of the natives, too, from the forests, in which, since the time when nature first planted the trees there, they have had the privilege of grazing their herds, has caused an amount of discontent, not to say distress, with which the doubtful advantage of such a proceeding is hardly commensurate. To this may be added the increase of malaria caused by the rank vegetation being left to rot on the ground from year to year. By all means protect the saplings up to a certain age; but would it not be better, after the timber has reached a fair size, that the villagers should be permitted to burn the undergrowth in order to provide fresh young fodder for grazing their herds on as heretofore ? The manure from the ashes and cattle ordure, and the clearance of the undergrowth, would tend to improve the trees, which would then be tall and strong enough to resist the ravages of the fire, though not those of the white ants, which would be

decreased by it. In order to justify my idea, let me remark
that I can remember the time when, notwithstanding the
annual conflagrations and the grazing of cattle in the forests,
the hardwood timber of Dehra Doon was of as fine a size and
quality as it is ever likely to be again with any amount of
conserving. I know of one instance in Scotland where a tree
was actually improved by being scorched. It was an apple-
tree, raised from Canadian seed, in a clergyman's garden in
Forfarshire. For years after it had attained a considerable
size, it never showed a sign of bearing fruit, until a pile of dry
weeds and garden refuse lying below it having been casually
set fire to, scorched it so much that the owner thought it was
dead. The following year, to his surprise, it again burst into
leaf, and for the first time yielded a heavy crop of splendid
fruit. However, the foregoing remarks are intended more as
suggestions than dogmatic assertions, for time alone can prove
their validity or their futility.

As the stags had now almost ceased their bellowing in the
forests, and were consequently very difficult to find, I took to
driving some of the densely wooded gorges for bears and
musk-deer; and driving is, in my humble opinion, not to be
compared with what our American cousins call " still-hunting "
in close country, or to stalking your game on more open
ground. The Cashmerees generally drive a gorge upwards,
the ridges on each side being guarded by men posted as stops
at short intervals along them, whilst at first, only a few beaters
advance slowly and quietly from below, giving an occasional
tap with their sticks against a tree. The line is augmented
by the flankers as it reaches their respective posts, until all
hands arrive at the head of the gorge, along which the guns
are posted under suitable cover. During the few times this
plan was tried, a good many hinds and calves were driven out,
but only one good stag was seen, and that broke back through
the beaters. Several black bears and musk-deer were also
beaten out: one of the former I shot. As I was unable to
secure another horned beast to furnish a new ear for the

mutilated head, I was reluctantly forced to sacrifice a good
hind for this purpose, as well as to provide venison for our
camp larder.

By this time I was getting near the end of the tether of my
leave, and was in daily expectation of the Cashmere Government authorities sending me notice to quit.   Indeed, I won-
dered they had not done so already, for all visitors were in
those days expected to be out of Cashmere by the 15th of
October, and it was now November.   Had I not taken the
precaution to keep on good terms with the head-men of the
villages by making small pecuniary gifts and sending them
haunches of venison, they doubtless would, long ere this, have
taken steps to rid themselves of my presence among them,
by informing against me.   Instead of this I had no difficulty
in collecting as many willing beaters as I required.   Moreover, they were always marshalled by a great hulking fellow
who, on my first arrival at Nouboog, with my full approbation
when I had duly inquired into the case, administered condign
punishment to one of my Hindustani servants for having
abused him.

On my return to "the vale," how changed in its aspect had
it become during the short period since I had left it!   A
dense smoky haze from the burning grass on the surrounding mountains rendered them quite invisible.   The bright
greensward was now all withered and dry from the effects
of frost, which made the ground so hard as almost to ring
under one's tread; and the few remnants of foliage that still
clung to the grand old chenar trees were sear and brown.
In fact, "the vale of Cashmere" was, at that season, quite
destitute of its romantic beauty.   At the first place I encamped in the valley, I was met by a *posse* of Government
officials.   I well knew for what purpose they had been
sent.   But their leader, who was a polite-mannered individual, on learning that I was about to leave Cashmere,
pretended to make a virtue of necessity by saying he had
come to inquire if he could do anything to assist me.

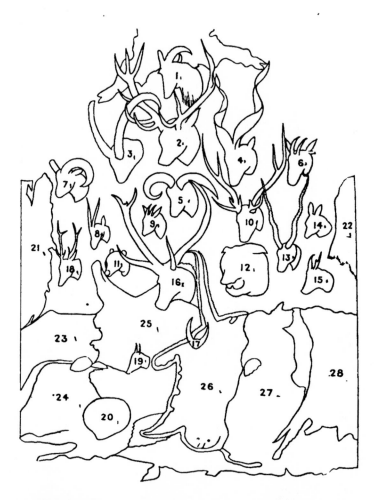

1. Tahr head and skin.
2. Cashmere Stag.
3. Ibex.
4. Markhor (Pir Punchal).
5. Burrell.
6. Surrow.
7. Oorial.
8. Indian Gazelle.
9. Gooral.
10. Cheetal.
11. Black Bear (Himalayan).
12. Brown Bear.
13. Black buck Antelope.
14. Musk-deer.
15. Barking-deer.
16. Jurrow.
17. Neelghau horns.
:   Hog-deer.
19. ..ur-horned Antelope.
20. Tiger.
21. Gooral skin.
22. Musk-deer skin.
23. Surrow skin.
24. Black Bear skin.
25. Tiger skin.
26. Leopard skin.
27. Brown Bear skin.
28. Burrell skin.

HIMALAYAN AND NORTHERN INDIAN GAME.

When my trusty friend Ramzan took leave of me for the last time, I think the regret was mutual, for tears filled the old man's eyes as I bade him good-bye. There never lived a better shikaree or cragsman in Cashmere than old Ramzan Mir.

My return to the Punjab was over the Pir Punchal pass and through the Poonch hills. This route is lovely almost throughout, but perhaps the most strikingly beautiful part of it lies between the villages of Poshiana and Barumgulla, a distance of about eight miles, on the south side of the pass. There the path leads along the bottom of a wild tortuous defile, which is so narrow and rocky that the rapid torrent that courses down it has to be constantly crossed and recrossed by innumerable little temporary bridges formed of rough tree-stems. At every turn a perfect study for an artist presents itself. Not even in Canada during the "fall" did I ever see anything that surpassed the harmoniously blended masses of colouring which were here presented by the gorgeous autumnal-tinted deciduous foliage, the dark ever-green pines, and the moss and lichen covered crags on the precipitous flanking heights. Here and there small cascades splashed and tumbled over the rocks, and, picturesquely situated close to Barumgulla, there is a really fine one, with a considerable volume of water and a fall of at least a hundred feet. But I am forgetting that this is now becoming a well-beaten track of tourists.

Such as I have attempted to describe was hangul-shooting at that time in Cashmere. Since then, I am told, the late Maharajah Runbeer Sing took to profusely decorating his palatial halls with stags' horns. The traffic in them, too, has of late years become much more extensive. And formerly, when the slaughter of a bovine animal was considered a capital offence in Cashmere, hangul skins were used for making the accoutrements of the soldiers, and this may be the case even now. At all events, the deer have decreased in numbers, and the sportsman may have to go farther afield to find them.

CHAPTER XVIII.

THE following endeavour to recount some hunting experiences in Tibet will by no means represent what may be termed a competition-bag of game, which, in these days of competition in everything, seems, sad to say, often to be thought almost the main object in shooting. Nevertheless, I trust it may afford the reader some idea of what the writer considered real wild sport in a very strange land.

On a first visit to the dreary inhospitable region north and east of Leh, the capital of Ladak, where, strange to say, very few of the scanty nomadic population seem to care much about hunting, the difficulty of obtaining reliable information respecting the haunts and habits of its wild fauna often makes game appear rather scarce there. Moreover, even had my companion on this trip and I found plenty to shoot at, we had no intention of turning sport and pleasure into cruelty and toil by striving to outdo our neighbours in our butcher's bill, regardless of the quality of the meat. The tyro, in his irrepressible excitement, may be forgiven for shooting at anything or everything; but he who persists in deliberately so doing, unless it be when food is absolutely necessary for his camp-followers, is no longer deserving of the name of sportsman. But let that pass as a well-meant, though perhaps rather caustic, digression in the interests of sport.

Once more I would invite the reader to accompany me to that "valley of bliss"—Cashmere. This time, however, we shall merely pass through its quaint old capital, and at once proceed up the beautiful Sind valley, with its coppices of hazel and hawthorn, its tangled thickets of honeysuckle and wild rose, and its picturesque log-built hamlets nestling snugly at the foot of the mountains amidst groves of walnut, apple, and mulberry trees, and grand old chenars. Much as we may wish to linger in such a romantic locality, we must not do so this time, for it is past the middle of May, and we are bound direct for a very different style of country—the remote, desolate wilds of Changchenmo—and a long tramp is before us ere we reach those haunts of the dong (wild yak) and the tsos (Tibetan antelope).

Passing through the unrivalled scenery of the higher reaches of the Sind river, whose verdant slopes, wooded steeps, and rugged precipices rise on either side of the rushing, roaring water, we find ourselves, after four days out from Srinuggur, at Sonamurg (golden meadow). Here the grassy undulating uplands are encircled with dark forests of pine, woods of silver birch, and grey snow-capped crags, and the clear bracing air is redolent with the perfume of innumerable wild flowers.

A long and laborious climb of an hour and a half up a very steep and savagely wild gorge filled with deep snow, takes us to the summit of the Zozzi la[1] (pass), 11,300 feet high, and flanked by glaciers and towering white peaks. Here the track leads for miles over almost continuous snow-fields, and for some part of the way beside a deep extensive tarn, which, when frozen over and concealed by the winter snow, is, we are told, the scene of many a fatal disaster from the treacherous crust falling in. Farther on, where the ground becomes more free from snow, we are often saluted by the chirping whistle of a marmot, sitting erect on some green knoll, ere he dives into his burrow at our approach.

What a sudden and marvellous change takes place in the aspect of the scenery as we descend gradually to the district of Drās, with its high sterile hills of the generally rounded form, and strangely bright and varied colouring, so characteristic of Tibetan landscapes! After crossing a narrow wooden bridge, where a few years later a British traveller, Mr Cowie, lost his life by falling into the wild torrent below it, when rashly attempting to ride over it, we encamp beside an old fort garrisoned by a small detachment of Cashmere soldiers.

At Lotsum we find a well-kept polo-ground, with a substantial covered stand for spectators, from whence the gentle sex of the land, we are informed, are wont to view the game of shuggrun as it is here called, which has from time immemorial been as popular here as it has lately become elsewhere. The palm of victory awarded by the fair dames is usually a good fat sheep.

Past Shargol, where we observe evidences of Buddhism in a quaint Lama hermitage, built into the perpendicular face

[1] "La" is the Tibetan term for a pass over a range of mountains, as "ghat" is the Himalayan.

of a cliff rising above the village. Here are also to be seen several oblong-shaped constructions like huge tombs, called chortans, on which the most uncouth and horrid-visaged deities or demons are depicted in the brightest of hues, vermilion predominating. They are intended, we are told, to mark the burial-places of sainted Buddhists.

At Moolbek we pitch our camp at an elevation of only 4000 feet, below an isolated eminence picturesquely surmounted by a gompa or Buddhist monastery. Over the Namika la and Fotu la, both more than 13,000 feet, but with easy gradients and not a vestige of snow, to Lamayuru. At this place the Lama monks, in full canonicals, turn out on the flat roof of their monastery and salute us with discordant music, performed on a variety of barbarous instruments, consisting chiefly of long brazen horns, gongs, and drums.

In the cool of the evening—for a Tibetan sun is scorching —we climb up to visit the monastery, which is perched high on a spur rising immediately above the village. The Buddhist monks show a considerable amount of taste in selecting sites for their gompas, which are often built on some picturesque eminence. At the entrance. we are met and ushered into the principal sanctum by a venerable Lama, who, we suppose, holds the position of abbot among the brotherhood. Here a most indescribable scene presents itself. About a score of Lamas, with shaven heads and attired in loose woollen robes of a dirty purple hue, are at their devotions. They sit in two rows facing each other. Some are blowing and thumping away on the afore-mentioned instruments, whilst others perform a monotonous chant in the profoundest of bass voices, as they tell the beads of their rosaries. Around are idols of every size, shape, and colour; rotating cylindrical prayer-wheels, from the size of beer-barrels downwards; and an endless variety of other articles used by the Buddhists in the performance of their religious rites. The walls are decorated with banners, confused hieroglyphics, and innumerable grotesque representations of figures, evidently belonging to the Chinese school of art. Two rows of rudely carved, massive wooden pillars, which support the dark smoke-stained roof, form the principal architectural features of the place.

It takes some time to become accustomed to the " dim religious light " from a number of brass oil-burners, and from a few little apertures near the roof, before we are able to discern all the wonderful paraphernalia contained in this monastic chapel. As a peculiar odour of joss - stick, or something answering the purpose of incense, combined with the smell of burnt oil and that perfume which usually emanates from unwashed humanity, pervades the close atmosphere of this ill-ventilated apartment, we are not sorry to be out of it and again breathing fresh air.

On the mountains in the neighbourhood of this place, a kind of wild sheep called shappoo or shalmar (*Ovis vignei*) is plentiful. As it is said to be almost identical with the oorial (*Ovis cycloceros*) of the Punjab, we do not care then to waste our time and tissue in its pursuit on such arid uninviting mountains as it here affects. There is, however, a slight difference between the shappoo and the oorial, the horns of the former being rather thicker and less circular in their curve, and the hair of the face and on the throat much darker than that of the latter. Yet it seems strange that animals so nearly similar should occur at such different altitudes and in such different climates, the one not usually above two or three thousand feet, and the other seldom below ten thousand. But let us resume our route.

Next morning a descent for some eight miles through the narrowest and wildest of defiles, where the path in many places overhangs the deep torrent rushing past below, and sometimes consists only of a few rough planks supported on poles driven into crevices in perpendicular faces of rock, brings us to the river Indus. After crossing the river by a wooden bridge, we encamp a few miles farther on in a small orchard of apricot-trees, where charming little double roses, of the most brilliant saffron-yellow, are blooming luxuriantly. This little oasis, like the few others we have passed here and there on our way, has been reclaimed from the surrounding parched wilderness by being irrigated with water carried for many miles in a small duct, cut along the bare mountain-side from some distant stream or spring.

After a weary tramp of twenty days from Cashmere, we reach the town of Leh. Its most prominent features are a fortified palace, so called, from the top of which we get a good view of the place and its environs; and a rather imposing bazaar, where furs, precious stones, and other commercial products of Eastern Turkestan freely change hands. In its immediate vicinity are a few poplar-groves and fruit-orchards, their vivid green contrasting rather strangely with the surrounding sterile plateau, which extends for miles towards the equally arid mountains that enclose it. Regarding this town, little more need be said here than that there, at an elevation of nearly 12,000 feet, the sun burns with an intensity that is truly surprising, the thermometer in summer often reaching 140 degrees or more in its rays; whilst the temperature in the shade is quite cold, and at night often freezing. The patient reader who may have accompanied me so far, had now better go no farther unless he is prepared to traverse some pretty high and rough country ere he reaches Changchenmo, which has little to recommend it beyond its being a favourite haunt of the wild yak and other Tibetan game.

Thus far I had had the pleasure of travelling from Cashmere with an old friend and schoolmate—Captain Basevi, R.E., —who was proceeding to carry out certain scientific observations on the highly elevated table-lands, which are among the principal geographical features of this part of Tibet, and were peculiarly suitable for his purpose.[1] But from Leh our

---

[1] These operations, which were intended, I believe, for determining the

routes and avocations unfortunately lay in different directions.

Here I met a brother sportsman, Major M., who was bound for Changchenmo; and as it is as pleasant as advisable to have a companion in remote uninhabited regions, we joined camps. We were rather disappointed, however, on hearing that two other members of the fraternity had already preceded us there; for in Changchenmo the wild yaks usually frequent certain localities, from which they are soon scared away if disturbed.

At Leh we engaged the services of an individual named Kurreem, a half-bred Tartar, who had, I believed, been converted to the Mohammedan persuasion. He willingly agreed to act as interpreter in the language of the country and make himself generally useful, on a salary of four rupees a-month and his food. The advent of a packet of letters and newspapers by the Maharajah's post to Leh was a matter of much rejoicing; but the pleasure it afforded was considerably damped by the tidings it brought of the death of my old Goorkha servant Kirpa, who had been accidentally shot by a comrade with whom he was out hunting.

After two days' rest we made a fresh start. For two marches our route lay along the right (north) bank of the Indus. We passed several of those curious oblong-shaped cairns which are so often seen by the wayside in Tibet, called *mānes*. They are formed of small slabs of rough stone piled loosely one upon the other, and vary in length from a

force of gravity under different conditions of the earth's crust, had been proposed by the Royal Society. They were carried out by means of pendulums swung at various geodetic stations in India, and for this work Captain Basevi had been selected. His investigations had necessarily to be conducted under circumstances which would have been most trying to any constitution, and doubtless were partly the cause of his death. The valuable services to science, and the mental and physical labours undergone by him in this arduous undertaking, were recorded by Colonel J. T. Walker, R.E., Superintendent of the Great Trigonometrical Survey of India, as a tribute to his memory, in a letter to the 'Times,' under date 19th September 1871.

few yards to sometimes several hundred. Each flat stone
has inscribed on it the words, "Om mani padmi hom"—
meaning, O God! the jewel in the lotus. We passed one
of these erections, which was some five or six hundred
paces long, and every stone of it had, I was told, this
short prayer engraved on it. All Tibetan Buddhists constantly repeat these words when twirling their little hand
prayer-cylinders, which contain a scroll inscribed with the
same mystical sentence, and each revolution is supposed to
represent a repetition of it. The Tibetans always pass these
mānes, or roadside shrines, on the right, whichever direction
they may be travelling,—thereby, I suppose, ensuring their
going round them should they return by the same route ;
circumambulation, as well as rotatory motion, being among
the ritual forms of the Tibetan Buddhist religion.

Across the Indus, opposite to where our path quitted its
valley at Khurroo, is the great Buddhist monastery of Hemis,
hidden away in a sequestered gorge. It is said to contain
several hundred Lamas. We now turned northwards up a
narrow glen leading to the Chang la (pass), and encamped at
Chimray, where there is another fine monastery perched high
on a hill.

The pass, although over 18,000 feet high, is easy to cross,
but we suffered somewhat from the rarefied air. Besides the
usual shortness of breath and the feeling of extra weight
and lassitude, more especially about the legs, in me it produced headache and nausea, which I did not get rid of until
the following day, when we descended to Tanksee. The south
side of the pass was quite devoid of snow ; the gently sloping
north side, however, was considerably patched with it, and
the cold at night was intense. And here I may remark,
that although the perpetual-snow line on the western side of
the main Himalayan chain is somewhere about 16,000 feet,
eastward on the ranges rising from the Tibetan uplands it is
nearly, if not quite, 20,000 feet. This difference may pos-

sibly be owing to the extreme dryness of the atmosphere on the Tibetan side.

Tanksee, a considerable-sized village, being the last place on our route where men, yaks (the domestic bovine cattle of Tibet) for carrying our baggage, and food were procurable, we made arrangements accordingly. Here I secured the services of a Tartar named Changter as guide, a pastoral inhabitant of the Pangong district, who was well acquainted with the haunts of the game there and in Changchenmo, and who had the advantage of possessing a very slight knowledge of the Hindustani language. He was accompanied by his son, a little lad named Norgie, who attached himself to my companion, the Major, in the capacity of gillie—and an uncommonly sharp one he made, notwithstanding his youth. Here I hired a pony—the Major was too proud to ride—by way of saving myself as much unnecessary toil as possible; and a few small sheep were purchased for our commissariat department, at one rupee (eighteenpence) per head.

The first evening after leaving Tanksee, by way of amusement as well as of making ourselves acquainted with our Tartar followers, we gathered them together around the camp-fire of sun-dried yak's dung—the only fuel procurable—collected in the vicinity, and got them to sing, dance, and perform on a musical instrument like a long, wooden penny whistle, from which they contrived to produce wonderfully dulcet tones. Great was their delight on the Major's passing round a snuff-box, and loud and boisterous their mirth at seeing one another sneeze.

How different are these independent manly fellows, with their good-humoured sociable ways, and droll merry faces, which are always ready with a broad grin, from their more sophisticated neighbours of Hindustan, with their austere castes and prejudices! And how infinitely superior to them, morally and physically, are these wild children of nature, who are, fortunately for them, not as yet corrupted by the vices and evils

consequent on a state of semi-civilisation ! Strange it is that
in a land whose bleak sterile appearance is calculated, one
would suppose, to depress the spirits, such a cheery race of
people is to be found. It seems as though their light hearts
were given them by a kind Providence as some compensation
for the dreariness of their country. But let us hie onward.

We noticed many pairs of the ruddy sheldrake, commonly
known in India as the Brahminee duck—evidently up here
to nest—where our way for several miles led beside a sluggish
stream flowing tortuously between banks of bright green turf,
which was quite a treat to behold in this desert land, where
green is conspicuous by its absence.

On the second morning we reached the western end of the
Pangong tso (lake), when, on emerging from a long glen
flanked on the one side by steep stony slopes, on the other by
beetling cliffs of a yellowish hue,[1] such a wonderful prospect
suddenly presented itself as to amply repay any one for the
long toilsome journey which has to be undergone to behold it.

Beneath a cloudless sky, the deep sapphire blue of which
was rendered extraordinarily intense in the rippling waves
that reflected it, lay this salt-water lake, at an elevation of
14,000 feet, stretching away for about thirty miles of its
visible length, its width being about five or six. From its
shores of pale-yellow sand, on either side rose barren heights
—some of them streaked and capped with perpetual snow—
whose brilliant yet harmoniously blended colouring of every
tint except green baffles all description. Here and there a
pure white glacier lay between the ridges that stretched down
towards the water, and sometimes jutted into it in fantastic-
shaped promontories and bluffs, their successive receding outlines growing more faint, until hardly distinguishable against

---

[1] These tall cliffs were entirely formed of a rather friable kind of alabaster
or gypsum, as we found from the snow-white blocks of it, recently detached
from above, that had rolled down below, the yellow colour on the surface
being caused by the action of the weather.

the purplish-blue of the snow-crested mountains that bounded
our view of the lake, where it takes a leftward turn for some
twelve more miles.

The strangely wild beauty of this scene was enhanced by
the extreme clearness of the air, which in Tibet renders surrounding objects, and their black clear-cut shadows, almost
startlingly distinct, and distances most deceptive. A natural
consequence of so transparent an atmosphere is, that the sun's
rays strike through it with the most astonishing power. Indeed, from the moment the sun appears over the horizon it
commences pitching into your face, and especially your poor
nose; and even although these may be shaded from its direct
beams, the radiation from the dry stony ground is so great as
to make some sort of covering for the face very desirable.
And oh! the merciless, marrow-searching wind that hardly
ever ceases blowing on these bare Tibetan steppes, except
for a few hours in the morning, and not always even then.
How it, combined with hard frost every night, parches and
cracks the sun-scorched skin on your face and lips, until
speaking becomes painful, to laugh is a torture, and to wash
is almost impossible. Day after day the skin peels off your
face and hands. There is no escape from this evil in Tibet;
it is *the* great drawback to a trip there. I generally wore a
kind of mask made of thin cloth, extending down just over
the nose, with apertures for the eyes, and always kept my face
well smeared with a salve composed of bear's grease and sper-
maceti, which acted like basting to roast-meat, inasmuch as
it prevented the skin from being quite frizzled up. A large
carriage-umbrella, which can so easily be carried by one of
your attendants, will be found most useful for setting up, to
rest and have your "bite" under, on those arid shingly uplands, where a spot of shade is so seldom to be found. How
often I wished I had brought one with me! Yet, with all its
inconveniences, the light dry air of Tibet is singularly exhil-
arating, and notwithstanding the sudden and extreme varia-

tions of temperature, highly salubrious. But at this rate we shall be a long time reaching Changchenmo.

A family-shot at a flock of rock-pigeons — a paler-coloured bird than the common blue rock, and slightly marked with white—and a wild goose of the bar-headed variety I killed in some marshy ground beside a stream running into the lake, furnished a welcome addition to our larder. The goose, however, was rather dearly bought at the price of a heavy fall among the stones, owing to the clumsy Tartar saddle turning as I dismounted to shoot. I felt the effects in the small of my back for more than a week after.

We camped at Lookoong, two miles north of the lake—a hamlet consisting of a few wretched little hovels, with about half an acre of irrigated cultivation attached. This was the last sign of any human habitation we should meet with until our return from the inhospitable region we were about to visit. From here two days more took us over the Marsemik la into Changchenmo. The ascent to this pass is so very gradual and easy, and there was so little snow lying even on its gentle northern slope when we crossed, that it was difficult to believe we were 18,600 feet above the sea-level ; but almost all of us, our Tartars included, suffered more or less from headache, and my nose bled slightly.

The best remedy for the unpleasant effects caused by rarefied air I found to be cold strong tea; spirits only increased them. The Tartars, however, drink quantities of *chung*, the weak spirit of the country, distilled from a kind of barley called *grim*, which, they say, answers the same purpose. It has a sweetish and not altogether unpleasant taste. In the more northern Himalayas, eating raw onions is said by the natives to mitigate these disagreeable sensations.

As we sat discussing our breakfast a mile or two below the top of the pass, previous to crossing it,—and here I may offer a bit of advice : never cross a high pass on an empty stomach, —we descried a flock of seven *Oves Ammon* (the magnificent

U

wild sheep of Tibet) on a sloping hillside far below us. The glass showed they were all rams, and two of them carried fine horns. But they were moving quickly, and the ground they were on was, at any rate, much too bare and open for a stalk ; besides, we had a long tramp before us to our next halting-place, which we did not reach until evening.

The following day we camped beside the Changchenmo river—a tributary of the Shyok—which flows over its wide shingly bed between bare, brown, stony slopes, surmounted with precipitous heights of the reddish and ochreous hues often so conspicuous in the colouring of the mountains in this strange land. Hereabout, growing on the sand-hills beside the river, we were surprised and delighted to find plenty of fuel in the shape of a kind of tamarisk called *oomboo*, which was so dry and inflammable that we had only to put a match to a big bush for the strong wind to at once set it ablaze and keep it smouldering away for hours, always taking care it was to leeward of our tents.

We now learnt from two Tartars left in charge of supplies belonging to the sportsmen ahead of us, that their masters .were, as we expected, in possession of the best hunting locali- ties. After a conference with Changter, he suggested that we should proceed up another long glen north of Changchenmo, named Kugrang, which he said was usually a pretty sure find for wild yaks. The Tartars had informed us that one of the sportsmen was hunting somewhere about the head of this glen ; but as Changter said it was more than twenty miles in length, and that there were one or two long lateral branches leading out of it, we considered that our each occupying one of these would not be poaching. The Major accordingly decided on taking up his quarters in one of them, whilst I did the same in another.

In order to reach our ground, it was necessary to cross the Changchenmo river. Fording this treacherous stream is always more or less unpleasant, and sometimes dangerous ;

for during the summer it can only be crossed at certain places, and at these only during the space of a few hours in the morning, after which a dirty turbulent flood of melted snow suddenly comes rushing down, and, spreading itself over the wide bed of shifting sand and gravel, renders it quite impassable.

As we pursued our way up the Kugrang glen we saw several small troops of kiang (*Equus hemionus*), the wild horse of Tibet, whose shy behaviour showed us that human intentions had not always been so harmless towards them as ours were. The kiang can hardly be called handsome, on account of its rather ungainly head, hog mane, and almost rat tail, which it always tucks in when it gallops; but it shows many good points. It stands about Galloway height, and its general colour on the body and head is a reddish dun, with a dark dorsal stripe. Its belly and legs are a creamy-white, as also is its nose. It is considered by some to be a wild ass. Its ears, however, are not large like those of a donkey, nor does it bray like one, its whinny being quite that of a horse.

We saw also two buck antelopes, which I attempted to stalk, but failed to get nearer than 200 yards before they decamped. Scanty as vegetation was everywhere, we found more of it here, strange to say, though at a considerably higher elevation, than in the main valley of Changchenmo, which accounted for game being more plentiful in this locality.

The Major now went on with his men to establish his hunting-quarters in an offshoot to the left, whilst I, accompanied by Changter, Kurreem, and a man leading my pony, turned up one northward to the right, our baggage-yaks following leisurely behind us. This offshoot of the Kugrang, Changter called Chang Loong Koongma. It runs up parallel to, and eight or ten miles west of, Chang Loong Yokma, leading to the desert plain of Lingzitang, averaging over 17,000 feet, across which vast elevated waste lies the route to

Yarkand. We had proceeded two or three miles when Changter detected some moving objects on a gently sloping plateau far away up the glen. The glass was soon brought to bear on them, when they proved to be a herd of seven antelopes, and two kiangs that were grazing near them. After watching for some time, we were glad to see the horses move off, leaving us a better chance of a stalk at the antelopes, amongst which I could discover several good bucks. As there was little chance of their noticing us at so great a distance, we moved cautiously on until we gained the cover of a high sloping bank, rising beside the stream that flowed down the glen. Here we left the pony, giving instructions to the man in charge of him to have the tents pitched, on their arrival, in a sheltered nook, whilst Changter, Kurreem, and I went on to try and circumvent the antelopes.

We had proceeded some distance along the stony bed of the stream, under cover of the steep sloping bank beside it, when we were suddenly brought to a stand-still by seeing a buck antelope moving in front of us down towards the stream, and a second soon followed. They were still a considerable way off, and, fortunately, did not detect us before we had crouched as close as possible under cover of the bank. Waiting until they were hidden behind some rising ground, we again moved cautiously forward. At length we reached the spot where they had disappeared, but, to our dismay, they were nowhere visible beyond it. Thinking they might have gone back again on to the higher ground, we crept up the steep bank and peered over it, when a single doe, that happened to be close by on the plateau above, catching sight of us, went away at speed. Still there was no sign of the bucks; and as the wind, which had hitherto favoured us, had now veered round, we made sure that they too had got intelligence of us and departed. As we lay there, uncertain as to what our next move should be, I noticed that old Changter's countenance brightened up, and his wandering

eyes suddenly became fixed. Turning his head slowly
towards me, he drew my attention to some animals near the
mouth of a small gorge some 400 yards off, and whispered
" Nian" (*Ovis Ammon*).

For the moment the antelopes were forgotten as the spy-
glass was directed on the nobler animals, but those in sight
turned out to be ewes; and as Changter assured me that at
this season there was little chance of finding old rams and
ewes in the same flock, my disappointment was considerable,
though I would fain have believed him to be wrong in this
instance. He was right, however, as was proved when the
beasts got our wind, and the herd, which consisted only of
three ewes, sped away up the gorge and disappeared.

As the sun was still pretty high, we decided upon moving
a little farther up the glen on the chance of again finding the
antelopes. We were descending the sloping bank with the
intention of getting back into the stream-bed, when we heard
a clatter amongst the loose stones. To our astonishment we
beheld a fine buck antelope coming galloping towards us
along the slope, and apparently so bewildered by something
that had scared him that he failed to observe us until he got
within fifty yards, when, suddenly detecting us, he wheeled
sharp round. I had only time to snatch my rifle from
Changter and take a snap-shot, before the animal disappeared
over the brow of the rise above us. Although he showed no
signs of being hurt, I thought from the sound that the bullet
had struck him. Quite forgetting the great height we were
at—well over 17,000 feet—I ran back quickly up the slope,
and on reaching the top saw the buck standing within twenty
yards, his drooping head showing how sorely he was wounded;
but I was quite incapable of using my rifle. There I was
obliged to lie down, gasping for breath, with my heart beating
as if it were ready to burst, whilst the buck moved slowly off,
gradually increasing his pace until he was lost to view in a
neighbouring ravine. My two men, who had wisely taken

it more quietly, reached the top of the brae just in time to
see the buck before he disappeared, much to their disappointment, which I think was equalled by their astonishment at
finding me lying panting on the ground without making any
attempt to stop him.

It was some time before I recovered breath enough to
follow the buck, which both the men said I had missed; but
as I was now quite sure he was hit, and badly too, I proceeded towards the ravine at a much more moderate pace.
As we neared it, I lay down, and gradually worming myself
along for some distance over the sharp loose stones, slowly
raised my head.   There, as I had half expected, lay the buck
about a hundred yards off in the ravine.   Before I could get
my elbows well planted on the ground and the rifle levelled,
he was up and making off again, when, to the great delight of
old Changter, who had crawled up beside me, the report of
the rifle was followed by the buck throwing back his horns,
tottering forward a few yards, and falling struggling on his
side.

Whilst the men were skinning and cutting him up, there
was ample time to note his general appearance; and as he
was a good average specimen of a buck tsos, a short description of the Tibetan antelope (*Kemas Hodgsonii*) may perhaps
interest those who have never seen this animal. He measures
from thirty-two inches to thirty-four inches at the shoulder;
thick and soft, almost woolly pile, of a very pale-yellowish
grey on the body, merging into white below the chest, inside
the legs, and on the stern; dark-brown marks down the front
of the legs, on the fore ones extending up to the shoulder;
an almost black patch on the face from between the eyes
downwards; muzzle very thick and coarse, with an odd kind
of puffy protuberance beside each nostril—possibly a pro-
vision of nature for assisting respiration at the very high
altitude this animal affects; another curious glandular protuberance in each groin; tail about four inches long and

tipped with white; horns black and lyrate, two feet long, set very erect and far forward on the forehead, and about a foot apart at the tips, slightly curved forward, closely knotted in front for two-thirds of their length from the base, and smooth behind. The does, or what I took to be does, for I never shot at them, appeared to be very similar in colour to the bucks, but hornless, and without the black patch on the face. I saw several herds of seemingly hornless antelopes whilst in this glen, and regretted not having shot a specimen, which I might easily have done, as I afterwards heard that it was then a moot point whether the does were quite hornless, or carried short thin horns like the female gazelle of India (*Gazella Bennettii*). But as these antelopes have now so often been shot by sportsmen in Tibet, this question has doubtless been settled. A unicorn animal is said to be found farther northward on these desert steppes, but I believe its existence to be as fabulous as that of the equine creature represented to the youthful imagination as fighting with the lion for the crown. An antelope minus one of its horns may possibly have given rise to the idea. It is also said that the camel is found in a wild state farther north, within the territory of Khoten. These antelopes usually frequent localities where the ground is more or less level or undulating, and are never found much below 15,000 feet, though they often ascend the sloping faces of the mountains to much greater heights, and particularly after being scared. Like all Tibetan game, their powers of sight and scent are extremely acute. Their flesh is tender and juicy.

During the first night or two up here, and especially towards morning, I experienced the uncomfortable sensation of being unable to sufficiently inflate the lungs, which may be described as a constant inclination to heave a deep-drawn sigh. This was not to be surprised at, considering our camp was at an elevation of 17,000 feet, calculated with a boiling-point thermometer I had brought with me. It gradually

wore off, however, as I became more accustomed to passing
the night in such intensely cold and rarefied air.

Whilst in this high valley, I, strange to say, never suffered
in the slightest degree from the nausea and headache I experienced on the open and tolerably level summits of the
Chang la and Marsemik, even when at as great altitudes.
Here I felt nothing more than shortness of breath when
ascending ever so gentle a rise, and a weight about the legs,
as if gravity were exercising an undue amount of influence
on them. On the upper ranges of the Himalayas, the natives
attribute the more unpleasant sensations to the exhalations
from certain poisonous plants[1] growing at great heights per-
meating the air; and my shikarees, when telling me about
shooting localities close under the snowy range, would describe some of them as being bad for *bhik* (poison), whilst
others which were as high, or higher, they said, were free
from it. Although this idea is generally ridiculed by
Europeans, it is so universally entertained throughout the
Himalayas by the hill-men, as to make one almost think
there must be some foundation for it. I certainly have seen
the deadly aconite flourishing luxuriantly on the higher
ranges, where the tall spike-like heads of its intense blue
blossom have a very striking and beautiful effect, shooting
up, as they often do, from some moist green spot, thickly
besprinkled with buttercups, amidst grey rocks and snow-beds.

At great heights I have always felt the effects of rarefied air
more on table-lands, or where the surroundings were comparatively level or undulating, than at similar elevations
where they were very steep, either upward or downward—and
I believe my experience in this respect is not singular. Moreover, it is remarkable that at Leh, which is under 12,000 feet,
but situated on an extensive open plateau, even the Tartars

---

[1] A Californian shrub, commonly called "poison-oak," is said by the
natives to have a noxious effect on those who inhale the air in its close
vicinity.

themselves are said to complain of shortness in breathing and headache. From this it would seem either that height is not the sole cause of, at any rate, the latter sensation, or the rarity of the air must vary considerably at equal altitudes, under different conditions. These ideas, which have been suggested to me not only by my own experiences, but also by those of other Himalayan travellers with whom I have talked on the subject, may perhaps be considered rather wild, so let us now turn from this long theoretical digression to something more practical.

Next morning we went up the glen in search of dong. There was a desolate grandeur about the mountains flanking it that was very striking, though perhaps not so charming to the eye as the forest-clad ranges of the Himalayas. The high arid hills to the right were rounded in form and of a general reddish yellow, like the colour of a half-burnt brick; whereas on the left they reared aloft in grey precipices, or in steep acclivities covered with large loose stones and shingle towards broad beds of snow, or serrated ridges of rock frowning grimly above. In some of the rifts and gullies running down into the glen lay beds of *névé*, terminating in abrupt broken declivities of pure white ice. Altogether it was a savage scene of utter loneliness, which language would fail to describe. And the silence!—during the lulls between the howling blasts of wind, the deep depressing silence that reigned over this desert waste was truly appalling. In most places one is accustomed to the buzz of insects, the rustle of leaves, or the "busy hum," though perhaps only as an almost imperceptible murmur. Even at dead of night the air is nearly always stirred by sound of some kind, however lightly it may affect the sense of hearing. Here, the stillness is as of a sepulchre—all Nature seems dead !

But I am forgetting that as so comparatively few of my readers can have seen the wild yak of Tibet (*Pœphagus grunniens*), the majority of them may wish to know what the creature is like. Imagine, then, a clumsy bovine animal,[1] standing from 16 to 18 hands at the shoulder, which is considerably higher than the croup, with a rough coat of a general rusty black inclining to greyish on the withers; a large, stooping head, slightly grey on the face and about the muzzle, and set on

Yak.

a rather lean neck; curly grizzled hair all over the forehead, almost concealing the eyes; thick round horns from 2 to 3 feet long, and about 18 inches in girth, growing outwards, curving to the front, and turning upwards near their points; an enormous bushy black tail, extending below the hocks; a thick fringe of long, matted, black hair hanging from the shoulders, sides, and flanks, and reaching about half-way down the short sturdy limbs,—and you have some sort of idea of a bull dong as he is here called. The cows have much the

---

[1] Dimensions of a wild bull yak shot by Colonel E. Smyth : circumference of horn at base, 18 inches ; length of ditto, 36 inches. Space between the eyes, 16 inches ; between the horns to tip of nose, 29¼ inches ; between horns to root of tail, 8 feet 5 inches ; length of tail, 37 inches. Height, 18 hands, or 6 feet (as far as it was possible to take it of a dead animal). Circumference of fore-foot, 21¾ inches ; ditto hind-foot, 19 inches. Girth round belly, 9 feet 8 inches ; ditto round shoulder, 10 feet 1 inch ; ditto round neck at thinnest part, 4 feet 2 inches. This animal (or else one shot at the same time, a little smaller) is now in the Leeds museum, very well stuffed and set up.

same general appearance, but are considerably smaller and less shaggy, and carry thinner and shorter horns than the bulls. Wild yaks generally congregate in herds, which may contain any number up to considerably over a hundred, but they are sometimes found singly. Their habitat is never lower than 14,000 feet.

Towards the head of the glen there were marks of these wild beeves that had been there some time before, but they had evidently shifted their ground. Doe antelopes—or what I supposed were does, for they all appeared hornless—were pretty numerous; but not a good buck did we see until we reached the almost level snowless summit of a very high pass—though it did not appear so from the great height we were already at—which terminated the glen. Here a fine fellow suddenly showed himself, and offered such a tempting shot that I could not resist the temptation to let drive at him, even at the risk of disturbing any dong that might have been in the vicinity. Of doing this there was, however, little fear, as the wind sweeping over the pass was quite enough to prevent a shot being heard at any distance.

The buck moved on slowly a short way, and then lay down. Giving him a wide berth for the present, with the intention of looking him up on our way back, when we should have a better chance of securing him, we went a considerable distance down the other side of the range, to a prominent spot which commanded an extensive view of the savage mountainous wilderness beyond. Even Changter, who had been exploring this wild country since his youth, said he knew little about the remote region across this pass. Every visible atom of ground which was only here and there patched with snow was carefully scrutinised through the spy-glass. Still there were no dong to be seen—only a couple of wild horses quietly grazing on an isolated green spot beside a little stream, more than a mile off and far below us; and a fine fox with a light sandy-coloured coat and a white-tipped brush.

He jumped up quite close to us, and turning round within an easy stone's - throw, stood gazing at us for some time as if with much wonder at our presence in this high solitude.

It was now late in the afternoon, and we were at least eight miles from our camp, so we returned to try and pick up the wounded buck. As I did not wish again to risk disturbing the ground by shooting at him unless absolutely necessary, he gave us a long chase before we caught him: fortunately he kept pretty straight down the glen.

I had not made a halt since leaving Leh; so, by way of taking a much-needed rest, the next day was devoted to dressing the antelope heads and working up some little sketches I had made.

On the following morning we started early to again try our luck after the wild yaks. This time I took the pony, to ride wherever the ground permitted; and I would advise any one who hunts in Tibet not to be too proud to do likewise, for the work that must necessarily be done on foot, when actually following game, will be found quite severe enough up here, where your legs always feel as if weighted with lead, without any extra and unnecessary toil when it can be avoided. In the inhabited districts of this part of Tibet a pony can generally be hired, which, as it seldom wants any food but what it can pick up for itself, will be much better suited for the work required of it than an animal brought with one; or a tame yak can be ridden with much comfort, and its paces are smooth and easy. But to proceed.

We had not gone far when five buck tsos were descried far away up on a sloping hillside; but I had determined to devote this day entirely to searching for dong, so we did not attempt a stalk.

Feeling much disappointed at again not finding any dong in the glen, I sat myself down about a mile below the pass, whilst I sent on a Tartar to prospect the country beyond it.

Nearly two hours went by without the reappearance of our scout. I had eaten my luncheon and emptied my bottle of cold tea. The sun was far too powerful to allow of my taking a nap to pass the time, and there was hardly a square inch of shade anywhere near to protect us from its almost vertical rays. Another hour passed, and my patience was getting exhausted, when Changter and Kurreem, who had been for some time lying dozing near me, suddenly lifted their heads, and said they thought they heard a shout in the direction of the pass. Hark to it again! There is no doubt about it now, as this time it is borne faintly towards us on the wind that comes sweeping down from the pass in true Tibetan style; and with the telescope I can distinctly see the Tartar signalling to us to come up. As the ascent is very gentle and easy, we are not long in reaching him, when, to our great delight, he reports having seen a single dong on the little green oasis where we had noticed the kiangs grazing two days before.

· Half running down the gradual and snowless slope on the other side of the pass, we soon reach our old look-out spot, from whence we can see our quarry, looking like a little black dot in the distance away below us; but we shall have to try all we know to circumvent the beast, for the ground is most unfavourable for a stalk. Our only chance rests in being able to reach the bottom of a deep wide valley between us and the dong, by scrambling down a steep stony gully which is in full view of the animal. If we can only manage to get down this unobserved and the wind favours us, the rest of the stalk appears to be comparatively easy.

Slipping the covers on the rifles to prevent the sun glinting on the barrels, and trusting to the great distance keeping our movements unnoticed, Changter and I commence the descent, leaving Kurreem to stop the man leading the pony, who has lagged some way behind us. Fortune is so far kind that we reach the bottom of the valley unperceived; but a serious obstacle here presents itself in the shape of a rapid swollen torrent of dirty melted snow. Up this we find we must make our way until we can discover a fordable place. Carefully watching the dong's movements, with our bodies bent nearly double, we move forward a few paces whilst it feeds with its head from us, crouching down motionless as the stones beside us whenever the animal turns towards us. Thus we slowly proceed for several hundred paces, until we gain the cover of a high bank on the far side of the stream. To my great relief, we can now walk upright until we reach a fordable-looking place some distance farther on. After wading pretty deep through the ice-cold, rapid-running water, we have to double back down beside it until we arrive at the foot of a narrow ravine, some distance up and to the left of which lies the little green flat on which we hope to find the dong. As we slowly proceed up the ravine, treading carefully to avoid rattling the stones, old Changter in a whisper cautions me to take time, and not to fire until I can get a shot at the animal's right side, which, he says, is more deadly than the left in a dong. He little knows the penetrating power of a hardened Whitworth bullet.

At last we reach a point which we judge to be about level with the animal. Here we stop to recover our breath, which has been pretty well pumped out of us by our recent exertions. Stealthily we crawl up the sloping side of the ravine, over the most abominably sharp stones, and on cautiously peering over the top, discover the yak within a hundred yards, now lying with its head turned from us. A slight rattle made among the loose stones whilst trying to plant my elbows steadily for the shot, at once attracts the beast's attention. Springing to its feet with the most wonderful alacrity for such a big brute, it stands broadside on, with its head turned towards us. Before it has time to think of making off, the sharp report of the Whitworth rifle rings out, and I can see the dust knocked up by the bullet ricochetting on the gravelly slope rising beyond the animal. Away the beast goes up the slope at a gallop.

I must by some mischance have shot over it. The contents of the other barrel are sent after it, but it still holds on. This time I feel certain I have missed, and my heart sinks within me. But there is yet a chance, for the beast breaks into a trot, and then into a walk, which becomes slower and slower, until at last it pulls up and turns its drooping head to look back. Taking the other rifle from Changter's ready hands, and quickly adjusting the sight for 200 yards, which in such rarefied air does for a much greater distance, I fire again. "Shabash!" (bravo), exclaims the old fellow, jumping up excitedly, as the dong totters for a few seconds, and then falling heavily on its side, lies kicking in its death-struggle.

On examining the carcass, we found that the first bullet had passed clean through behind the shoulder, and had afterwards knocked up the dust on the slope. The second had missed entirely, and the last had struck within a few inches of the first, but, taking a more forward direction, had actually perforated the heart, as was found on taking it out—a lucky shot!

It was rather disappointing to find that the animal was a female, for the head's sake; but I tried to console myself with the idea that cow-beef was preferable to bull-beef, and was certainly better than none at all,—and her fine bushy tail was, at any rate, a trophy worth having.

As the sun was now getting low, we could do little more that day than gralloch the dead beast. Whilst performing this operation, another dong suddenly emerged from a gorge below us; but catching our wind at once, it went off at a rattling pace, and was soon lost to view. It was dusk by the time we had recrossed the pass. Fortunately there was a splendid bright moon to light us down the glen, as the rapid stream flowing through it had to be crossed and recrossed several times at certain places, and fording it in the dark might have been a difficult, if not a dangerous undertaking. There is little risk, however, of getting belated in Tibet if the sky is cloudless, as the starlight alone, at such a high altitude, is broad enough to admit of surrounding objects being seen with unusual distinctness, and cloudy nights are exceptional. We were so late in getting back that our Tartars left in camp, fearing some mishap had befallen us, had started in search of us.

After sending off a couple of the baggage-yaks early next morning to carry in the beef, I went after the five bucks we had seen the day before on our way up the glen. We found them still on the same ground, but they were now on the alert, having winded us on our way up the hill; so our attempt to stalk them was fruitless. Later on in the day, we descried in the distance several black objects which we at first took to be dong; but, much to our disappointment, the glass showed them to be some of our baggage-yaks that had wandered miles away, on their own hook, in search of food.

Great was the rejoicing in camp that evening when the yaks returned laden with the meat; and a juicy beef-steak was a most acceptable addition to my own dinner—for, with the exception of there being little fat on it, the flesh of the dong is much the same as any other beef.

As Changter seemed to think there was now small hope of our finding dong in this glen, which, although usually considered one of their favourite haunts, they had this year apparently almost entirely forsaken, and the only other likely places for them in Changchenmo were occupied, and would probably be so for some time, I decided on retracing my steps to the Pangong country, where *Ovis Ammon* were said to be more numerous. By staying on here I might have killed many antelopes, and, by dint of excessive hard work, combined with much patience and luck, I might eventually have found a few dong on the ground beyond the pass; but my object was variety, not quantity, of Tibetan game. Moreover, I was particularly anxious to see as much as possible of other parts of this most remarkable land during my short sojourn in it. I therefore thought it waste of my limited time to remain longer in Changchenmo.

I had communicated my intentions by a messenger to the Major, and he agreed still to accompany me; so next day I rejoined him where he had moved his camp to the foot of the glen I was in. He had killed a fine buck antelope, but unfortunately some wild dogs had been sharing the sport on the same ground with him. It was rather late in the morning when we reforded the Changchenmo river, consequently one of the baggage-yaks had a mishap in the rapid water with its load, and my bedding, my shot-cartridges, and other things it was carrying got thoroughly wet. In the evening we were driven nearly distracted by myriads of almost invisible little sand-flies; and to add to our troubles, a pot of capital soup made of a hare I had shot, which we had been watching the preparation of with hungry eyes, was accidentally upset.

We had heard so much about the intense cold of this high region, that we were rather surprised at having hitherto suffered almost more from the scorching sun, although the wind was always cutting cold, and there was keen frost every night. We were not, however, to quit it without a taste of what the climate sometimes could be, even in the month of July. Next evening, after a long day's march, varied by grilling-hot sunshine and bitter-cold showers of sleet, we camped about six miles short of the top of the Marsemik, intending to cross it in the early morning. Towards dark, clouds began to gather ominously about the mountain-tops, and when we turned in at night snow was falling; but there was no appearance of it lying anywhere in the vicinity, except inside some small covered recesses of a kind of refuge built rudely of loose stones and earth. In these the drift-snow, from being entirely screened from the sun, lay in hard dirt-covered heaps, having probably been deposited there in winter.

In the morning I was awakened by an unusual sound of thumping and pulling at my tent. It turned out to be my

x

servant trying to effect an entrance through the fresh-fallen snow that had drifted up thickly about it, and on looking out, to my astonishment I saw nothing but one white waste of snow that had fallen nearly a foot deep during the night. The hillsides were shrouded in mist, and snow was still falling,—altogether about as cold and dreary a prospect as one could behold. Our poor yaks presented a most pitiful appearance as they stood helplessly chewing the cud of despondence, being entirely dependent for food—for they will not eat grain—on the small amount of vegetation which was now buried in snow. Even a pair of big ravens that croaked lugubriously about the camp, on the look-out for stray scraps of meat, looked more than usually sad, as they sat there with their sable plumes all ruffled from the cold.

Crossing the pass that day was completely out of the question, both on account of the thick mist and the snow that our men reported to be knee-deep on the track a short distance higher up. Fortunately for us, a quantity of *boortze*[1] had been collected here in readiness for Captain Basevi and his party, who were coming into Changchenmo, or we should have been wellnigh frozen.

The Major had pitched his little tent inside the stone enclosure of the refuge, where, although better protected than mine, it still was half buried in snow. Instead of turning out in the cold as I had done, he had more wisely kept under his blankets, where he snugly snoozed until breakfast-time. By way of trying to keep warm, I went into one of the stone-built recesses, where several of our Tartars were crouching round a small grass-root fire, and was considerably edified by watching them cooking and despatching their morning repast.

[1] *Boortze* is a kind of plant not unlike an exaggerated bunch of Alpine *Edelweiss*, with large, thick, dry roots. It grows in tufts, sparsely scattered over the stony ground, and is found almost everywhere where vegetation exists at all in Tibet, and is the principal, and often the only, fuel procurable.

To begin with, a very dirty copper vessel was put on the fire and filled with some green weed like nettles, barley-flour, and water. Whilst one of the men stirred this pottage round and round with a wooden ladle, another produced some raw meat—a bit of the dong I had shot. This he proceeded to tear up into small strips and throw them on the fire, every now and then popping a raw lump into his mouth and masticating it with the greatest apparent gusto. Even the bits on the fire were quickly disposed of after being merely singed. As soon as the pottage was considered ready, it was ladled out into little wooden cups, like the whisky "quaighs" of the Highlands, minus the handles, which each man produced from inside the breast of his dirty woollen coat, and gulped up from them with a prodigious amount of noise. After being replenished again and again until the pot was emptied, the cups were carefully licked clean, and redeposited in the place whence they had been taken. Another course of flesh was about to be partaken of, after the manner of the first, but a regard for my own appetite for breakfast prevented my waiting to see it discussed. These hardy Tartars are quite independent of any other dishes beyond their little wooden bowls. In these they mix their "suttoo" (meal made from barley) with a little water and salt, and make an expeditious repast of it whenever they feel hungry. Indeed this kind of uncooked porridge seems to be their staple food.

In the forenoon the sun broke forth, and some idea of its power up here may be formed when I say that by evening the ground about our camp was nearly free from snow, and next morning we were able to proceed without inconvenience over the almost bare earth, which was frozen as hard as iron. This time I felt no uncomfortable sensations from the rarefied air on the pass, nor did I again suffer from them on this trip, even when at considerably higher elevations, beyond the usual feeling of extra weight and lassitude about the legs, and the inclination—indeed I may call it the necessity—for constantly drawing a deep inspiration to fill the lungs, which I have already mentioned. I made a wide *détour* among the undulating heights on the south side of the pass, where we had seen the seven *Ovis Ammon* rams previous to our first crossing it. We found two flocks, one of nine ewes and the other of six ewes, with five lambs at foot, which, of course, were left unmolested.

At Lookoong we stopped for two days to await the arrival of Captain Basevi there, on his way to prosecute his pendulum observations on the highly elevated table-lands in Changchenmo. We took advantage of the halt to have a general wash-up of our dirty clothes in the stream that flowed past the tents, as also did old Changter to improve his personal appearance. For this purpose he came and borrowed one of the butcher-knives I used for skinning animals, to cut his hair with. Being curious to see the result of the process of hair-cutting with a knife, I was selfish enough not to suggest to him the use of a large pair of scissors I possessed. Some hours after, when he again turned up, his head, except where grew his pigtail and a few straggling locks beside it that had escaped the ravages of the knife, resembled the half-shaved back of a hedgehog, as likewise did his son Norgie's, upon which he had also operated.

Our men had caught a lot of excellent little trout-like fish in the stream beside which we were camped, by driving them under the banks and there "tickling" them. The largest were about 8 inches long, dark brown above, golden below, and had irregular black patch-like spots on their sides. We had also shot one or two fine hares, which are plentiful in many parts of Tibet. They weigh about 6 lb., and are not unlike the blue hare of the Highlands of Scotland in their habits and appearance, but a great deal more wild, and much lighter in colour. With these luxuries, a bit of antelope-

meat, and some wild-yak beef which were still to the fore
and in good order (as meat keeps for any time in Tibet),
some dried apricots from Skardo,[1] purchased at Leh, and a
solitary tin of preserved oysters I had by some chance
brought with me, we resolved to prepare a grand entertainment to celebrate our re-meeting with Captain Basevi. I
here give our *menu*, to show what may occasionally be accomplished in the way of *cuisine* even in these desert wilds,
with the help of the cooking-pot and the broiler invented
by Captain Warren, R.N., which I would recommend as an
essential part of a Tibetan sportsman's kit.

MENU.

Tibetan hare-soup.

Broiled Tibetan trout.

Beef-steak of wild yak and oyster sauce.

Broiled fowl
(*subscribed by our guest*)
and wild yak's tongue.

Green peas
(*canned, subscribed by our guest*).

Curry of Tibetan antelope, and rice.

Skardo apricots, stewed, with yak's-milk sauce.

Cheese.   Preserved butter.

Soda cakes.

Whisky-toddy.

Altogether a rare repast, such as even that world-known
restaurant, Les Trois Frères de Provence, in the Palais
Royal, would have found it rather difficult to provide—even
without the disadvantage of having the kitchen-roof fall in
during its preparation, as happened in this case, when the
servants' little tent, in which our feast was being cooked,
was blown down by a hurricane of wind and rain.

[1] The chief town of Baltistan or Little Tibet.

Here we parted from Captain Basevi—he proceeding on his way in search of scientific lore, we on ours in pursuit of the *feræ naturæ.* How little did the dear good fellow think, as, in excellent health and spirits, he cheerily bade us "Good-bye," that we were the last of his fellow-countrymen whose hands he would ever grasp! Sad indeed was his fate. In that inhospitable region to which his labours in the cause of science had led him, with not a friend near, and far, far beyond the reach of any aid save that of his native attendants, he was suddenly taken ill, and, after a few brief hours of suffering, passed away within eight days of his parting from us. He now lies at rest in the Christian cemetery in beautiful Cashmere, to which his remains were conveyed from Tanksee, where they had at first been interred.

Tibetan (hand) Prayer-wheel.

CHAPTER XIX.

IN hunting the *Ovis Ammon*, or Nian as in Tibet it is called, the sportsman must expect to undergo a great deal of fatigue and frequent disappointment, and to have his patience and endurance tried pretty severely; but should he have the luck to secure even one really fine specimen, he may think himself well rewarded for all his trouble. One may wander for days and days over known good localities without seeing large rams; and when they are found, their "cuteness" is in proportion to their size, for even then they may have to be followed for many a mile, and, as likely as not, without getting a shot at them after all. An old ram *Ovis Ammon* is certainly the most wary and restless game-animal that exists— even the crafty Highland stag is a fool compared with him; and the ground he frequents is usually so open and bare as often to make approaching him there next thing to impossible. The ever-blowing wind, too, which is so shifty among these undulating uplands and ravines, frequently baffles the best of stalkers; but all this only makes the pleasure of success the greater.

A full-grown *Ovis Ammon* (or *Ovis Argali*) stands about twelve hands. The general colour of its pile—which is short, soft, and close—is a kind of light brownish-grey, growing much darker about the withers and fore-quarters, and slightly so along the centre of the back. In autumn it becomes darker all over, and more glossy. Under the chest and belly it is much lighter—almost white, in fact. The legs, which are rather lanky and comparatively slight for a sheep, are also nearly white, with brown marks down their front. The stern and haunches are a pale yellowish-white. In old rams the hair in front of the shoulders is much longer than else-where, and stands out in a sort of greyish-white ruff. The muzzle is whitish and fine. Of tail there is hardly a vestige. The massive, deeply-creased horns are well arched upwards and backwards, their points curling round to the front beside the cheeks like cart-wheels. In weight the horns are not exceeded by those of any other known animal of the sheep tribe except the *Ovis Poli*, which inhabits the Pamir steppes and other more northern parts of Turkestan. The horns of the *Ovis Poli* are, however, not so thick, though they are very much longer, and have more curl and a much wider spread. About 40 inches long and 17 or 18 inches in cir-cumference at the base, may be considered a fair average size for a good *Ovis Ammon* ram's horns, though they often grow bigger; but in almost all large specimens the tips are broken, which takes several inches off what the horns would be in length if perfect. A head of about this size weighs quite 40 lb., yet it does not look disproportionately large, nor does the animal appear to be at all inconvenienced by its ponderous horns. The ewes are considerably smaller than the rams, and rather lighter in colour. They carry comparatively short and thin curved horns, and have no white ruff. Strange to say, they are much less wary than the old rams, which is

rather unusual with the females of the majority of gregarious
wild animals. They drop one lamb yearly in spring. Although *Ovis Ammon* usually affect open and more or less
undulating ground, they often ascend the sloping mountain-
sides to very great heights; but they are not much addicted
to nor adapted for climbing, like the other kinds of Himalayan wild sheep. In this respect the *Ovis Ammon* differs
from the animal nearest approaching it in appearance—the
" big-horn " of the Rocky Mountains (*Ovis montana*), which is
a good climber. During the rutting season the rams are
much given to fighting, and their whereabouts may sometimes
be discovered by the clashing together of their horns, which,
when the air happens to be still, can be heard at a great
distance, though the animals may be hidden from view. The
Ovis Ammon is strictly a Tibetan animal, but, as it sometimes
frequents the more gentle slopes on the eastern side of the
Himalayas, it may be included among the game of those
mountains.

This magnificent wild sheep, owing to the remoteness of its
haunts and the difficulty in circumventing it when you get
there, not to mention the grandness of its trophies when
secured, is perhaps more prized than any other Himalayan
game. In fact, the man who fairly stalks and kills his big
ram *Ovis Ammon*, may consider he has gained the " Blue
Ribbon," so to speak, of Himalayan sport.

My friend Colonel E. Smyth told me he had once the
wonderfully good luck to secure two of these grand trophies
with one shot. On this occasion he had crossed the Lipu pass
from the Byans district of Kumaon to the large village of
Tuklakar in the Hundés territory of Tibet. He had much
difficulty in persuading the authorities there to allow him to
go for sixteen days to hunt Hodgsonian antelopes in the
country eastward of the Mansorawar lake; for these Chinese
Tartars are very jealous of foreign intrusion, well knowing
that where the thin end of the wedge once enters, the thick

end will soon follow. To reach his ground from Tuklakar he had to cross the Yurla Mandrata range, at a height of 20,000 feet. One day he had sent his men back to camp with some game he had shot, and whilst alone he discovered four big rams feeding among some rocks, and stalked them success-fully. Their heads only were visible as they stood for a moment to look at him. He aimed at what appeared to him to be the largest ram, and rolled it over dead. The other three ran off, but one of them almost immediately fell dead also. The bullet had gone through the head of one of them and into the neck of the other. He cut the bullet out of the neck afterwards. Four large male antelopes also fell to his rifle during his short visit to this remote region. Several herds of wild yaks were seen in the same neighbourhood, principally cows; but as Colonel Smyth had in former years shot as many wild yaks as he wanted, he devoted himself more to the Hodgsonian antelopes, of which up to that time he had not killed a specimen.

Although I am a poor authority compared with others who have described the pursuit of these gigantic wild sheep, my success moreover, on this occasion, being small as regards trophies, yet I venture to hope that my humble quota of experience may assist in giving some idea of the real wild sport attending it.

On the 10th of July we left Lookoong for Chooshul, a fair-sized Tartar hamlet near some borax-mines, about eight miles southward of the Pangong tso, along the side of which the greater part of our three days' journey to it lay. Not a living thing was there to be seen, nor was there a sound to break the dead silence around this watery waste save the monotonous plash of the wavelets breaking along the sandy shore. From the unmistakable evidences about its margin, the water of this lake must be steadily receding; and Changter informed me that a long low rock which appears above water near its northern end was, within his recollection, quite invisible, and that each year it is gradually becoming more exposed. The water, although clear as crystal, is quite undrinkable, from having an intensely salt and bitter taste.

I had been told of a good locality for finding the big rams on the Chinese frontier eastward of Chooshul; but as the same ground had also been recommended to the Major, I relinquished my intention of hunting it at present in his favour. After replenishing our supply of flour and changing our baggage-yaks at the hamlet, the Major proceeded to work the undulating hills in the vicinity of the Pangoor tso, a more elevated but much smaller salt lake than the Pangong, some ten miles east of Chooshul. As I was feeling rather " out of sorts," I delayed my start in a more southerly direction for a few days. Changter recommended my taking two or three dogs and their owner with me from here, as being useful for hunting nāpoo (*Ovis nahura*)—the burrel or blue wild sheep of the Himalayas—which he said we might also find on the ground he recommended my hunting over for *Ovis Ammon.* They were ugly, half-starved-looking curs, but doubtless were well up to the work for which they were intended—being trained to hunt down their quarry as the ibex dogs are in the Cashmere mountains. It turned out, however, that I nearly had cause to repent having taken them, as will presently be seen.

After three days' rest I was fit enough to set out again, under Changter's guidance; so the baggage-animals were collected and packed. As yaks are sometimes apt to make free use of their horns, especially towards strangers, loading them is not always an easy job. The Tartars usually collect them in a ring, with their heads turned inwards, and their horns tied together until all are laden, when they are again set free and driven on their way.

Our route led over a low pass, or what looked a low one from the open level ground around Chooshul, which was already about 14,000 feet, but the ascent to it was pretty steep. On reaching the summit, a lonesome picture of flood and fell appeared stretching away beyond. About a mile from and considerably below us lay the Mirpa tso, an irregular-shaped sheet of dark, sullen-looking water, some four or five miles in circumference. Rising almost from its margin on every side were brown-coloured, rounded, and sterile hills, with nothing to break the dreary monotony of their appearance save a few patches of snow that lay near the top of some of their long stony slopes, and in one or two of the deeper hollows of the gullies that ran down between them. The scanty tufts of herbage that existed on the sides of this huge natural water-basin, as it were, were rendered almost invisible by distance, except in a few low and more level spots, where the moisture, derived either from springs or from trickling streamlets, had given the scraps of turf there a most vivid green, which was quite a relief for the eye to rest on.

After a short time spent in contemplating this joyless solitude, we descended to the shore of the lake. Not a breath of the usual wind was then stirring to ruffle its placid surface, which resembled a sheet of polished steel. The dull grey light of a cloudy day, and the solemn silence that reigned supreme, combined with the bleak and dismal aspect of the surrounding hills, were such as to induce a feeling of utter loneliness which was almost irksome. The men with me stretched themselves out on the dry white sand that bordered the lake, and were soon fast asleep. Even the pony seemed to feel the depressing influence of the profound stillness, as he stood listlessly there with drooping head and closed eyes. The only signs of life or motion to be seen were exhibited by the dogs as they tugged and gnawed at some dry bits of skin that partially covered the sun-bleached bones of a dead animal that lay close to the water's edge. If from this inadequate sketch the reader can picture it to himself, such was the ground in which I hoped to find the objects of my present search.

I was not sorry when my meditations, which under the

circumstances were not of the liveliest order, were interrupted by the sound of footfalls, and on looking round, I saw my cook approaching with the men who carried the *kiltas*[1] containing breakfast. After appeasing my appetite, which had not been so much affected as my spirits, we skirted along the shore of the lake, and camped at its southern end.

For the two following days we wandered high and low over these desolate hills, which I found to be a great deal steeper than they had at first looked. Carefully did I scan every hillside, glen, and corrie through the telescope, without a living thing appearing in its field except kiangs, or an occasional marmot as it sat basking near the entrance to its burrow. Not even a fresh mark of an *Ovis* did we see to encourage us. The animals had evidently shifted their ground, so we resolved to follow their example.

With this intent, next morning, leaving instructions for the traps to be brought on some distance behind us, in case of our meeting with game, we were on the move shortly after dawn. We had crossed a high ridge, and were descending a gentle slope beyond it, when one of the dogs, which, being little more than a puppy, his owner did not think it necessary to tie up, suddenly showed signs of more knowledge of his calling than he had been given credit for. This young beast, that answered to the name of Lukkur—or rather ought to have done so—was now drawing ahead, apparently on the scent of something, and neither the persuasions nor the threats of his master had any power to stop him. We had not proceeded many yards when, on the face of a low spur that had hitherto been hidden from our sight, we descried the cause of Master Lukkur's movements. A flock of seven male *Oves* were standing huddled together, evidently watching the dog, which had disappeared in a hollow lying between them and us; and almost immediately the sound of his bark was followed by the herd scampering wildly over the crest of the

[1] Baskets made for carrying loads on the back.

spur. My feelings at that moment can easily be imagined.
My anger and vexation were so great, that I could with difficulty refrain from shooting the confounded young beast as he
came trotting back after the mischief he had done. There
was, however, one chance left, though a very poor one. Fortunately the dog had not followed the animals far, and their
attention had been so much taken up with his movements,
that they in all probability had not observed ours. We
therefore resolved to follow them, on the chance of again finding them.

By the greatest good luck we overtook them about a mile
beyond where they had disappeared. Although some of them
had begun to feed, they were still in a restless state; so the
only thing to be done was to patiently watch them as they
kept slowly moving up the hillside. At last one of them lay
down, and the rest soon followed his example. Crawling
backwards until we were well under cover, we again got on
our feet, and as the wind was favourable, we resolved to
try and get above them. To effect this was by no means
easy, as the face of the hill we had to climb was awfully
steep, and composed of nothing but loose sharp fragments of
rock, that afforded most uncertain footing, and frequent stoppages were necessary to take breath.

On reaching what we considered a sufficient height to be
well above the place where the flock was lying, after a few
minutes' rest we had to resume the stooping and crawling
process for some distance. But notwithstanding all our
caution, the wily animals detected us in some manner, for
the next sight I got of them was at about 200 yards, as they
were galloping away up the sloping hillside. Sighting for
that distance, and making for a lump of rock a few yards in
front, that offered a good rest, I placed my cap under the rifle
and waited until they stopped, as I expected they would do
before going far, to look back. Taking a full bead on the one
I thought had the largest horns, I let drive. Away they

went in a cluster over the rise above them, leaving the lord
of the flock half dragging his hind-quarters after him as he
in vain tried to overtake the rest. I gave them a parting
salute with the other barrel as they topped the rise, which
compliment they failed to acknowledge. This was a lucky
chance and no mistake, as the distance must have been quite
250 yards. The poor brute dragged himself on his haunches
for fully a quarter of a mile down the other side of the hill
before his strength failed him, and on our approach raised
himself on his forelegs and menaced us with his horns. Although he was a full-grown ram, measuring about twelve
hands, his horns did not turn out to be so large as they had
looked at a distance.

By the time we got back over the hill, the baggage-yaks
had arrived at the place where we had left the pony and dogs
below. As the country about looked promising, and there
was water at hand, I decided to camp here for a day or two.
Good as it seemed, and although we worked hard over it, as
well as a more distant beat, to reach which we crossed a
rocky ridge that must have been considerably above 19,000
feet, our success was no better here than on our last ground.
We saw only four *Oves*, which the spy-glass spared me the
trouble of going after, by showing them to be either ewes
or very young males. How many a weary and useless mile
does a good telescope thus save! We also came across a black
wolf, but he was too far out for a shot, and his long slinging
trot soon took him out of sight. The only thing I emptied my
rifle at was a marmot, as it sat up whistling away, near the
mouth of its burrow, not far from my tent. It was somewhat
smaller than the Himalayan variety, and of a uniform yellow-
ish-grey colour, and appeared to be identical with the Alpine
marmot. The Tartars consider marmots excellent eating, and
probably they are so, though I could never bring myself to
try them. When we happened to encamp near their burrows,
of which there are generally a number together, like the

prairie-dog "cities" in America, our men would sometimes
secure them by smoking them out of their holes, and killing
them with sticks and stones. To cook them they were first
singed bodily in the fire to remove the hair, and then cut up
and boiled, skin and all.

The Major and I had arranged to meet at a place called
Numa, on the Indus, where it is fordable or ferryable, according to the season, as we should there have to cross it on our
way to the Hanlé country, where we intended to try our luck
after the goa (Tibetan gazelle). As my camp was at an elevation of over 17,000 feet, calculated by boiling-point thermometer, and was fearfully cold and windy, I was not sorry to
turn my steps downwards in the direction of Numa, which we
reached in two days.

Hearing no news of the Major at that place, by way of
keeping myself employed until his arrival, I moved up the
Indus valley to a locality where I was told we might find some
nāpoo.   I met him, however, at the place where I intended
camping for the night. He had seen a good many big *Oves
Ammon* on the ground he had been over, but unfortunately
had killed none, so we decided to go there and hunt it for a
few days longer, as he said there was plenty of room for two
guns.   He accordingly returned next morning to his old
ground, whilst I devoted a day to a search for nāpoo; but
finding no fresh signs of them, I moved on and camped within
a few miles of him.   There I engaged the services of one of
the occupants of some black yak's-hair tents that were pitched
close to mine—a Tartar herdsman who was well acquainted
with the ground in the vicinity.

In order to get to leeward of our first day's beat, as the
wind was blowing upward—which it almost invariably does
up here during the day, and downward at night—we began
the morning by toiling up to the extreme limit of the scanty
tufts of vegetation, which limit, in Tibet, is about 17,000 feet
—more or less. Above were steep bare acclivities of loose

rock, stones, and rubble, terminating in sharp grey crags, shooting up into the dark-blue firmament, whilst a broad tract of arid undulating hill and dale, scantily clothed with herbage, consisting of sparsely scattered bunches of boortze grass, sloped away for miles below.

Here I sat down to recruit exhausted nature by having my breakfast, and, after finishing it, was lazily reclining to promote its digestion, when my eye chanced to light on two moving objects on a bare distant slope. Drawing Changter's attention to them, he at once pronounced them to be "nian." On the spying-glass being brought to bear on them, they proved to be two fine rams; but they were in such an exposed situation that it would be utterly impossible to approach them unless they shifted their ground. Presently they began to quicken their movements downwards. This was exactly what was wanted, so we at once began a careful movement in order to get above them, and to leeward, if possible. We had gone but a hundred yards, and were descending the side of a shallow gully, when a brute of a kiang that was grazing farther up in it, and which we had, unfortunately, failed to notice, got wind of us. With his big ugly nose tossed high in the air, he galloped down the gully and away over the ground lying between us and our quarry. The glass was again put into requisition, to observe the effect of this *contretemps*. At first the rams stood and gazed, until I began to think that, after all, it was not of much consequence; but my experience of the ever wary and extremely suspicious nature of the *Ovis Ammon* was at that time very limited. Without much apparent concern they retreated slowly up the hill, until they disappeared over its brow.

How I *blessed* that kiang! I had a decided aversion to shooting these wild horses, as an utterly unsportsman-like thing to do, but I then felt as if I could have either slain or maimed that particular brute, not only without the slightest compunction, but with the utmost satisfaction.

Y

The only thing now to be done was to try and follow up the rams, as, to us, they did not appear to have been much alarmed. We had scarcely gone half a mile when Changter descried another flock of five more. They were a long way off and considerably above us, but they had already detected us, as they lay on the watch among the grey stones, from which, by reason of the way nature so often assimilates the colour of wild animals to that of their surroundings, they were hardly distinguishable until they rose and began moving restlessly about. There was one old fellow with a mighty pair of horns, evidently the guardian of the flock—and an uncommonly sharp one too, for I could see, with the glass, that his head was turned continually towards us. The other four, two of which also carried very fine horns, seemed to intrust their safety in a great measure to the extreme watchfulness of their big leader. I had got into the thick of them this time at any rate, but the ground was so open and undulating as to render a stalk there almost impossible.

For at least two hours did we lie on the bare stony ground, being half baked by the blazing sun, for we dared not move until the animals put some cover, in the shape of a hill-top, between us and them. When they at last did so, it took us at least another hour of hard work to reach the place where they had disappeared, and, after all, on getting there, nothing was to be seen of them in the wide valley beyond but their tracks. We, however, again made out our two first friends of the morning. But they were much too far off to follow that evening, so we left them undisturbed, in hope of being able to find them next day.

Find them again we did, but under such circumstances that I would rather have dispensed with their presence at the time, as will afterwards be shown. From the foot of the valley in which we had last seen the tracks of the five rams the evening before, I took a careful search with the telescope over all the ground within sight, and at length made out several rams reposing on an open slope near the head of it. We were rather puzzled as to our mode of procedure, for the morning was still boisterous after a stormy night of rain, and the wind was blowing in fitful gusts that veered constantly to different points of the compass. There was good cover for a stalk, at any rate for as far as we could see, along the boulder-strewn bed of a shallow stream running down from the direction in which the rams were lying, so I resolved to take advantage of it as much as possible and afterwards be guided by circumstances. Against this scheme Changter strongly protested, his idea being that we should make a wide circuit behind a spur to our left, in order to get above the animals. But I was obstinate; perhaps, too, a little lazy at the idea of a repetition of the long wearisome grind upward of the previous morning, and foolishly refused to take his sage advice suggested by long experience of the extremely shy and wary habits of the *Ovis Ammon*. Besides, I should myself have remembered that all mountain animals are more watchful of the ground below than of that above them.

The difficulties he had foretold commenced before we had gone half a mile, when we were detected by a flock of ewes that were feeding on a slope to our right. As they were at a considerable distance, we contrived to pass by without disturbing them more than to cause them to slowly move higher up the slope. After a long and tedious scramble among loose stones and boulders, we at length got within a few hundred yards of the point we first of all wanted to reach, when the Tartar herdsman that accompanied us—who, at any rate, possessed a very sharp pair of eyes—descried a large flock of rams moving down in our direction along a slope at the head of the valley. They were at least a mile off, and were, I supposed, the same I had made out with the glass from below, although there were now many more than I had at first seen. To avail ourselves of the cover of a big block of stone close at hand was the work of a few seconds. From this we could, at our leisure, watch the animals as they fed downwards. There were eleven, and most of them carried very fine horns. I almost thought I could recognise in the largest the wide-awake leader of yesterday's flock. Presently they all lay down, and as most game-animals are more vigilant when at rest than when feeding, we could do nothing with them in their present commanding position. Ten minutes had scarcely elapsed when they were again on their feet, with all their heads turned towards us. Although still at such a distance, they had evidently got some inkling of our presence, probably by means of the shifty wind. Led by the big and proportionately knowing one, they betook themselves to a higher but more approachable position on the slope, and after fidgeting about for a long time, again settled themselves to rest.

Now, I thought, was the time to try and circumvent them by means of a long ravine that ran up within what I judged to be shooting distance of where they lay. If we could only manage to reach the foot of this unobserved, by worming ourselves along for a considerable distance among the big boulders in the bed of the stream, which was up here nearly dry, our greatest difficulty would be overcome. But just as I was about to move forward, Changter called my attention to another ram that had suddenly shown himself on an adjacent eminence, well out of shooting range, to our left, and at once pronounced him to be one of our two big friends of yesterday. At that moment we wished them somewhere else, as the one in sight completely commanded the place where we were lying, not daring to move a muscle, lest he should detect us, and by his startled movements scare away the flock that lay above in full view of him. What was still more provoking, after a careful survey of the country in every direction, the beast lay down, leaving only his head and massive horns visible on the sky-line, in the most tantalising manner. This aspect of affairs was very exciting, no doubt, but under existing circumstances rather embarrassing,

for as long as he remained there we dared not budge an inch.
How bitterly I now repented not having taken my old companion's advice, for had I done so we should most probably
have been above our friend, and perhaps have got a chance at
him or his companion. At length, to my great relief, he
again rose, looked uneasily about him, and moved out of
sight.

We now lost no time in pursuing our tactics with regard to
the flock, which had not altered its position. Keeping an eye
in the direction where the single ram had disappeared, we
crept slowly along *ventre à terre* amongst the shingle and
boulders until we reached the ravine, apparently unobserved
by the animals, which continued to lie as still and almost as
indistinct as the stones beside them. After ascending the
ravine until we imagined we were about level with the animals, we turned to the left up its sloping side, near the top
of which I sat down to recover breath before taking the shot
I now felt pretty sure I was about to get. To my dismay, on
peering over, nothing was to be seen but the grey stones on
the spot where the flock had been lying, nor was there an
animal anywhere near it; but away in the distance an *Ovis*
was just disappearing over the crest of a distant spur. He
was immediately followed by six others, their horns looking
larger than ever, as through the spy-glass I could see each
ram in succession top the ridge and for a moment stand out
in relief on the sky-line. There was no accounting for their
quick and sudden retreat, as the wind had seemed favourable
during the latter part of our stalk—unless they had taken
alarm at the suspicious movements of the ram we had seen
below, or perhaps at the rather unusual sound in these
regions of one or two loud claps of thunder that had pealed
among the crags above them. It was just possible, too, they
might have been watching us when crawling among the
boulders; for wild animals, if you are at a considerable distance from them, and not to windward, will sometimes stand

at gaze whilst you are in sight, but directly you attempt to conceal yourself they at once take flight. I have often got a chance at beasts after they had detected me, by leaving a man for them to watch, whilst I stalked round under cover within shot of them.

Whatever had been the cause, in this case the rams had gone; but the sight of those magnificent horns on the sky-line had made me so keen to try and secure a pair, that, not-withstanding its being rather late in the afternoon, I at once continued the pursuit. On reaching the ridge over which the animals had gone, to my inexpressible delight there they were, not half a mile beyond it. Nine of them that were in sight were lying on the slope of a spur that diverged almost at a right angle from farther up the ridge we were on. Some lay resting their ponderous horns on the ground, whilst others kept strict watch over the open undulating country that stretched far away below. As I surveyed them through the telescope, I might have counted the creases on their horns, so distinctly could I see them; and my excitement was raised to the highest pitch, as I thought that at last I was about to reap the reward of all my patience and trouble.

A stalk would have entailed so wide a circuit that we feared lest darkness should overtake us before completing it, even were such a plan feasible, which was very doubtful; but as both the nature of the ground and the direction of the wind answered admirably for a drive, I proceeded to try the ex-periment with every hope of success, and, this time, with Changter's approbation.

The herdsman was directed to move as quickly as possible up behind the cover of the ridge we were on, and then down the far side of the spur, on the near side of which the ani-mals were lying. Strict injunctions were given him to be careful not to show himself until he had got well beyond them, when he was to move across and let them get his wind. Whilst this manœuvre was being carried out, Changter and I took up a position where we were well concealed among some lumps of stone, within twenty yards of which we felt pretty confident the flock would pass, provided our directions were properly attended to; for, immediately above us, the spur grew very steep, and was composed of a perfect chaos of sharp broken rocks, over which the *Ovis Ammon* would not be likely to climb when there was an easier way before them, and I did not expect they would take downwards when frightened. Besides this, we were evidently on their regular "run," as we could see by the numerous tracks.

Nearly half an hour had elapsed, and my heart was beginning to thump almost audibly between hope and fear, when the animals suddenly sprang to their feet and were all on the alert. But, instead of their looking to windward, as I expected, their gaze was directed straight up the spur, and ere a minute had passed they were galloping away into China, literally, for they had been lying on the very verge of Chinese territory. The cause of their flight soon became apparent. To our intense mortification, there, on the spur, and on our side of the spot where the flock had been lying, stood the figure of the herdsman. This was much worse than Lukkur's escapade, as I felt certain, from the terrified manner in which the animals had made off—this time from a man and not from a dog—that there was little chance of our ever setting eyes on them again; and the shades of evening, which were beginning to close, would, in any case, have prevented our following them farther that day.

One so seldom gets a chance at old rams, that it was hard indeed to have lost such a rare opportunity as this, and all owing to utter carelessness arising from the apathy regarding wild sport, and ignorance of everything connected with it, common to most Tibetans. Feeling half-wild with anger and vexation, I thought it best not to face the delinquent just then, so we let him follow us to camp by himself. As if to add to my anguish, whilst dejectedly plodding down the hill,

we saw what we felt sure were the two big rams that had
been the primary cause of our disappointment, disappearing
in the dusk. I suppose my bad luck had made me grow
callous to further excitement that day, for I merely joined
with Changter in giving them a parting malediction as they
galloped away at their best pace, seemingly in the same
direction the others had taken. Although I felt I had lost
my chance, on this ground at any rate, I spent some time in
a fruitless search among the hills in the vicinity of the Pangoor tso, which I had seen lying away to the north of where
the *Oves Ammon* had fled from, and towards which they
seemed to have gone.

The reader's patience will, I fear, have been as much tried
as mine was by this long and unsuccessful pursuit. But the
majority of Tibetan sportsmen will, I think, agree with me
when I say that its result was only what is very frequently
the case when stalking this most wary animal; and, as an
old shikaree once sagely remarked to me by way of consola-
tion on my missing my shot, " If we always killed our game,
there would soon be little left to shoot at."

On rejoining the Major, I found that his previous luck in
finding *Oves Ammon* must have been transferred to me, as he
had seen nothing but a small flock of nāpoo and a pack of
wild dogs. Amongst the latter he had observed two which
he described as looking quite black, with red or tan marks
about the head, and similar in size to the others, which were
of the usual red colour. I afterwards heard of black dogs
having also been seen by a sportsman in Changchenmo.
They could hardly have been mistaken for the Tibetan black
wolf, which is a much larger animal, and decidedly greyish
about the muzzle, and was not likely to be hunting in company with a pack of wild dogs.

CHAPTER XX.

SOUTH of the Indus, in the wild, almost uninhabited districts
of Hanlé and Rookshu, there are good localities for *Oves
Ammon;* but as Changter refused to budge an inch farther
than the river, and we were unable to get any one else who
was able or willing to show us where to find them, we resolved to make direct for the village of Hanlé, there to engage
a guide who had been recommended to the Major. Thence,
after hunting up the goa, or Tibetan gazelle, in the country
beyond it, we proposed returning with our new guide to again
try our luck at the big sheep.

Getting our traps ferried over the Indus at Numa was

rather a tedious business, which was accomplished by their being placed, a few at a time, on little rafts made of a rough framework of thin sticks tied over about a dozen small inflated goat-skins. Each raft was towed into the stream as far as possible, and then paddled across the deeper rapid water by a couple of sturdy Tartars in the costume of their most ancient forefather, minus the fig-leaves. After a considerable amount of splashing and exertion, the latter chiefly of the lungs, the raft reached the opposite shore several hundred yards lower down stream than the starting-point.

We had already seen some bright colouring on these Tibetan mountains, but nothing to compare with what we beheld along our desolate route between Numa and Hanlé. There some of the high rocky eminences looked actually blood-red in the reflected light of the setting sun. As the ground we traversed was in some places literally paved with fragments, large and small, of a kind of red jasper, which had evidently been detached from the heights above, we naturally concluded, from the colour of the latter, that they too were entirely formed of the same valuable material which here seemed so common. Among these red fragments I observed others of a dull black hue, which when broken presented a shining metallic surface. They were so extraordinarily heavy, that I concluded they must have contained either quicksilver or lead. How often I wished I could have wielded the geologist's hammer to some purpose up here in such a rich field for its use.

The hamlet of Hanlé, which we reached in three days, is the chief and almost the only inhabited place in the extensive district of the same name. Although so prominently marked in maps, it consists merely of some miserable-looking stone hovels situated at the foot of an isolated eminence surmounted by a big gompa. On our arrival we were received by the Lama Superior or Abbot of the monastery. This divine, who also acted as "Goba" or head-man of the pro-

vince, was attired in his sacerdotal robes of purple cloth, and
wore a profusion of ornaments and silver amulets about his
person,—a costume that contrasted rather oddly with a capital
pair of English shooting-boots with which he was shod. He
presented us with some rice and a little sugar, both rather
rare commodities in Tibet. In return we begged his accept
ance of a canister of gunpowder, with which he seemed highly
delighted. A similar interchange of civilities with some
other traveller in these wilds might account for his possession
of the boots.

Lama Monastery at Hanlé.

The hamlet presented a rather animated scene, as most of
the inhabitants, male and female, were bustling about packing their goods and chattels on yaks, preparatory to a sojourn
in their black blanket-tents in the wilderness, whither they
were about to proceed to graze their flocks on the nutritious
but scanty herbage.

To the south and east of Hanlé, stretching away for some
twenty-five miles to the confines of the Chinese dominions,
lies a desolate expanse of rolling uplands and ravines with an
exceedingly limited amount of vegetation scattered over them.
These stony downs, as they may be termed, the altitude of

which ranges between 15,000 and 17,000 or more feet, are a favourite haunt of the goa.

Standing from 22 to 24 inches in height, on most delicately formed limbs, the goa, or Tibetan gazelle (*Procapra picticaudata*), is perhaps one of the most graceful little creatures that exists. Its general colour is a pale brownish fawn; the head is light fawn, but in old bucks the hair on the forehead and about the roots of the horns is white. On the stern is a pure-white disc bordered distinctly with a yellowish-brown mark. The tail is dark brown, and very short. The horns, which in a full-grown buck are 11 or 12 inches long, are more curved than those of the Indian gazelle; they are closely annulated to within about 2 inches of their tips, where they turn slightly upwards, and sometimes inwards, and from being planted rather forward, and springing well upward in their curve, they give the beautifully formed little head a most jaunty appearance. The doe almost exactly resembles the buck, except that she carries no horns. In this respect she differs from the female Indian gazelle, which has small horns. I do not think the goa's sense of smell is quite so acute as that of other Tibetan game-animals, but this is compensated for by its wonderfully keen sight. The nature and height of the ground it frequents I have already described.

We were very glad to quit Hanlé, the immediate vicinity of which was next thing to a marsh, from the quantity of rain that had fallen during the preceding month, and was infested with hungry gnats. The periodical rains, which had been abnormally heavy all over India, seemed this year, contrary to custom, to have found their way across the Himalayas into Tibet. As regards the wild animals, too, this season was considered by sportsmen, and by Tibetans who were at all acquainted with the habits of game, to have been an exceptional one. Vegetation was, comparatively speaking, so unusually plentiful, consequent on the quantity of rain, that in many places the animals had deserted their regular feeding-grounds for others in which, this year, they found food equally abundant. This was more particularly the case with the wild yaks in Changchenmo, where they had almost forsaken their wonted resorts, and had appeared in great numbers more eastward, where in general they were much more scarce. This fact we afterwards learnt from the man who had been hunting near us in Kugrang. He, like ourselves, had seen hardly any dong, whereas his companion, who had been in another and, under ordinary circumstances, a more unlikely locality for finding them, had killed seven or eight, and without having to search far from his tent.

On the day we left Hanlé, as we were trudging along in advance of our baggage-yaks, we got our first sight of a buck goa as he beat a hasty retreat over some distant rising ground.

The following morning we were both afoot very early, each taking a separate line of country; whilst our traps were to follow direct to our next camping-place, in the vicinity of which the Major's guide said there was a chance of finding *Ovis Ammon*.

Phœbus was just waking up as I topped the brow of a rise and carefully looked over, when I noticed that the light of his countenance was shed on two small objects that stood on the face of an opposite slope. They did not look much like stones, though they were just as motionless. Pointing them out to a Tartar who was following me, he merely ejaculated " Goa!" and instantly squatted. On taking a spy at them through the glass, they turned out to be two fine bucks; but the sharp-eyed little creatures, notwithstanding the distance we were from them, had already detected our heads—for they could have seen nothing more—and were gazing straight towards us. Presently one of them went bounding and skipping away up the slope, sometimes turning round for a few seconds to look back, until he at length disappeared over its brow. His companion continued to gaze; but as we kept perfectly still, he at last appeared to think that he must have been mistaken in his suspicions, for he quietly turned round and began feeding. In a short time, however, he became restless, and after wistfully looking about him, as if he had suddenly missed his companion, trotted off in the direction he had gone, hardly stopping until his form appeared on the sky-line at the top of the slope, and after a good look around him, he too moved out of sight.

Up we jumped and followed at our best pace, which, in the thin air of an altitude of well over 16,000 feet, could not be very fast, although the ascent was quite gentle. On nearing the brow I made for some large stones, from behind the cover of which to view the ground beyond, and at the first glance had the satisfaction of seeing both the bucks feeding within 130 yards of where I lay. Singling out what I thought the better of the two, I luckily dropped him in his tracks. The other sped off for a short distance and then pulled up. If I hit him with the second barrel, as, from the sound, I thought I had, it must have been too far back in the body, for he galloped off and was lost to view in a dip of the ground. Exchanging the empty Whitworth rifle for another, a breech-loader, I followed after the buck, and found him standing at the bottom of the hollow; but before I could get my aim he bounded off, though only to a short distance, when he again stood and offered a fair broadside chance. I pressed the trigger—click! a bad cartridge, thought I, and cocked the other hammer; click! again, and away trotted the goa. I opened the breech and found nothing but daylight in the barrels: dolt that I was, I had forgotten to put in the cartridges.

As the buck had taken a direction exactly opposite to the one I wished to go, and my Tartar guide said it was a long way to our next camping-place, I abandoned further pursuit, as, even if wounded, the animal might have led me a long and a hungry chase, for I had stupidly neglected to take any provender with me that morning. We therefore returned to pick up the buck I had killed, and the Tartar having shouldered him, we made the best of our way in the direction our yaks had gone, overtaking them in time for a late breakfast, to which I felt quite ready to do ample justice.

In the afternoon, before we could get the tents pitched, we were overtaken by a tremendous storm of thunder and hail. The Major had not turned up, but fortunately he had found shelter by paying a call on some Tartar ladies from Hanlé at their temporary country residence in a black yak's-hair tent, where his urbanity towards these fair dames had also obtained him hospitable entertainment, in the shape of a draught of butter-milk.

After working over this ground from morning to night for two days, seeing only the ubiquitous kiang, a few female goa with their young at foot, and a fine pair of horns attached to the sun-dried remains of a ram which had probably died of starvation in winter, we shifted camp towards the source of the Hanlé river, near the Chinese border. Several more goa were seen on our way there; but all being "hummel," I refrained from shooting at them lest the firing should disturb better game, though I would fain have had some more venison in camp, our Tartars' appetites being voracious.

As this locality was considered a sure find for goa, the Major and I started very early next morning in quest of them. He took the right and I the left of a fairly wide valley, towards the head of which there was a pass leading over from the Hanlé province, which is under the rule of the Maharajah of Cashmere, into the Chinese-Tibetan territory of Chumurti, we having previously arranged that the first of us to reach the summit of the pass, some seven or eight miles distant, should await the other's arrival there.

The scenery of the upper part of this valley was perhaps of a grander character than any we had as yet seen in Tibet. This was owing to the mountains on both sides looking more rugged, precipitous, and snow-clad than usual, and from there being at the head of this wild glen a confluence of two fine glaciers, from the base of which the Hanlé stream issued, and thence flowed in a broken, tortuous torrent, between banks of bright green turf, down through the otherwise almost verdureless valley. Our pass, however, led over a depression at the top of a high stony acclivity on the left of the glen, where the steep mountain-slopes on either side approached each other more closely, five or six miles short of the glaciers.

Among some broken raviny ground in the valley I found a herd of several goa, and farther on a solitary doe. The former made off without giving me a chance; the latter, although offering an easy shot, I did not molest, for which she afterwards served me a good turn in a rather singular manner.

On nearing the top of the pass I observed several men sitting behind the shelter of a big stone. These, my Tartar companions (one of whom was our interpreter Kurreem) informed me, were "Cheen log" (Chinese people), who were keeping watch and ward there, having probably heard that two Europeans were encamped in the vicinity. As we approached, they retired out of sight; but on arriving at the summit, one of them suddenly reappeared and squatted himself on the ground some distance from us. On getting up to him, a rather animated conversation was commenced between him and my men, who informed me that he was remonstrating against our proceeding any farther. On it being explained to him that we had no intention of invading his country, he seemed satisfied; but on my moving forward a short distance down the gently sloping Chinese side of the pass, in order to obtain a better view of the country beyond it, I fancy his suspicions were aroused, for, although he offered no further remonstrance, he proceeded to tell us, with a view to intimidation I suppose, that some more men would soon be up to join him.

I now sat down to wait until the Major should arrive. A quarter of an hour had scarcely elapsed when the clatter of horses' hoofs, and the jingle of the little bells that are always attached to the Tibetan bridles, were heard coming up the pass, and presently three or four Tartars, mounted on capital ponies (for which Chumurti is famed), hove in sight. One of them, a rather well-dressed corpulent individual, turned out to be the head functionary of the Chumurti province. They galloped by without at first observing us as we sat amongst the rocks and stones; but on suddenly catching sight of us, the stout party, seemingly in a high state of excitement, wheeled round his pony and rode straight towards us, shouting and waving his arm in the air, as if he were leading on his army of Tartars, who had not as yet arrived in sight. Very soon, however, parties of two or three men at a time began to appear in the most marvellous manner, as though they had suddenly arisen out of the ground, like " Clan-Alpine's warriors true," until a small crowd, numbering about forty or fifty, had collected around us. Where they had all come from so quickly it was impossible to conjecture, for the top of the pass was as desolate-looking a spot as a height of, I should say, nearly 18,000 feet could make it. A dirtier or more ill-favoured lot than the generality of them were, I never set eyes on. Had they carried any other weapons than their wool-spindles, and had I not been aware that the resistance offered by these borderers to European travellers or sportsmen attempting to cross the Rubicon of the Chinese Empire in Tibet was usually more of a passive than a forcible kind, I should have felt considerable relief of mind at being reinforced by the Major and his men, who, having crossed the stream below the pass, soon appeared on the scene of action. I took the precaution, nevertheless, to keep my rifles within reach, in case of any attempt being made to appropriate them.

Whilst the Major and I sat there making futile attempts at polite conversation with the stout potentate, who of course could not understand a word we were saying, his myrmidons were gesticulating and clamouring away in an excited manner, quite as unintelligible to us, with one exception, which was a kind of pantomime of the act of binding the hands behind the back. All this, we afterwards learnt, was inveighing against the Hanlé men for taking us up to the pass, and threatening to bind the Major's guide, whom they considered the arch-offender, hand and foot, and drown him, as they put it, for doing so. Their having suggested this mode of disposing of him struck me as being scarcely compatible with the means, considering that, as far as we could see, there was not water enough to drown a flea in nearer than the river far down below. When we arose to depart they all collected around their portly leader, and, as we retired, followed us for a short distance, still vociferating loudly, and finally they saluted us with a parting derisive jeer, evidently under the impression that they had frustrated an attempt on our part to enter their country. At hearing this, such was the Major's ire, that he was for turning back to forcibly resent what he considered an insult, and I had some difficulty in persuading him that, under the circumstances, discretion was the better part of valour.

On our way back to camp, I thought I would again look up the place where I had in the morning seen the solitary doe, as she did not then seem to be at all scared. This time I was determined not to lose another chance if she gave me one, as our supply of animal food was done, and bucks were scarce. I had not much difficulty in finding her again; but now she seemed to have some suspicion of my deadly intent, for on each occasion that I tried to steal a march on her among the broken ground, she would move off just out of range. This sort of thing had happened for the third or fourth time, and I had just topped a rise over which she had gone, when, instead of seeing the doe, up sprang two fine bucks from a hollow in front. As I felt pretty sure that before going far they would stop to look back, I instantly lay down, got my elbows well planted on the ground, and the rifle levelled for a steady shot. Sure enough, they pulled up at about a hundred yards. There was little to choose between them, so I took the one that offered the better mark, and dropped him on the spot. The other trotted on some twenty yards, and then turned to look back for his companion. I had only his chest to aim at, but fortune again favoured me, for he too went down, never to rise again. Great was the astonishment of my Tartar companions when, on coming up, instead of finding, as they expected, that I had shot the doe, or perhaps missed her, I showed them a dead buck, and still greater was it on my pointing out a second lying within twenty yards of him; for their surprise was so great at seeing even one dead buck, that they had never thought of looking for another. But where was the doe? She had vanished, and her having thus been fortuitously the means of my finding two such beautiful bucks, after my forbearance towards her in the morning, was really a curious coincidence; for had I shot at her then, I should never have got them. The Tartars soon shouldered the game, and we bent our steps towards camp rejoicing. Both pairs of horns were just over a foot long.

The Major got back soon after me. He had found no goa, but had seen two black wolves, which unfortunately he was unable to get a shot at. They must have been two I had made out with the telescope from my side of the valley in the morning, when my attention had been attracted towards them by their dismal howling. During our absence it appeared that the camp had been invaded by some of our mounted friends from the pass, at whose unexpected advent, our Indian domestics informed us, the Hanlé yak-drivers seemed much exercised in their minds.

We now returned to Hanlé by a different route to the one we had travelled from it. On our way we made a Sunday halt, which our men devoted to marmot-hunting. A few goa were seen, but nothing was bagged except some hares. It had been our intention to hunt up the big sheep on the ground north of Hanlé; but man proposes, and the *Ovis Ammon* very often disposes, at any rate of itself. We now learnt that this ground had just been hunted over by the two Changchenmo sportsmen unsuccessfully, owing to the *Oves* having this season left it. When too late we had discovered the mistake we had made in not persevering longer in our pursuit of the splendid rams we had seen north of the Indus.

Only remaining one night at Hanlé, we thence took a westerly direction, and after traversing a long level stretch of dreary country, which appeared quite destitute of any sort of animal, and almost so of vegetable life, we camped late in the afternoon on a patch of greensward in a wild gorge east of the Lanak la, which rises between the Hanlé and Rookshu districts. Next day we crossed the pass, which is somewhere about 17,000 feet high; but, as is so often the case with Tibetan passes, the gradient was easy. Some distance down on its western side, among the broken stony slopes, hares were numerous, but generally so wild as to afford better rifle-practice than sport for a shot-gun. Here we found perfect parterres of sweetly-scented, pale-blue flowers, with which our Tartars at once proceeded to deck their caps, after the manner of the Swiss mountaineers with the Alpine roses. Notwithstanding the sterile aspect of the country, the variety of beautiful wild flowers growing in many Tibetan localities would delight the heart of a botanist. On a little isolated patch of green beside the Pangong lake, where we stopped one morning to breakfast by a spring, the ground was covered with a plant having flowers like a small pink geranium. In the sterile wilds of Changchenmo, on damp spots, at an altitude of quite 17,000 feet, I sometimes found whole beds of a kind of polyanthus, with delicate pink flowers, and usually, strange to say, in places where there was scarcely a blade of any other vegetation to be seen. Another curious fact I

TSO MORARI LAKE, 15,000 FEET ABOVE SEA LEVEL.

noticed was, that almost every weed growing on these high wastes had a highly aromatic perfume.

Another day's journey brought us to a spot called Ooti, a few level acres of bright-green turf moistened by the snow-drainage from the neighbouring heights, and thickly besprinkled with flowers, principally of a yellow hue. These poor little Tibetan flowerets have so few places to flourish in, that when they do find a favourable spot they seem to take every advantage of it. Here we found the tents of one of the Changchenmo sportsmen pitched. Their owner returned to them late in the evening, bringing with him a fine buck goa which he had killed on the bare undulating wilderness in the neighbourhood of this little oasis. We clubbed dinners, and sat up till a late hour comparing notes and recounting our respective experiences. He, too, had had little luck with the *Oves Ammon* and wild yaks; but his companion had been most fortunate in finding the latter, as I have already mentioned.

The following morning, as we traversed the desert tract westward towards the Tso Morari, we saw one or two packs of a large kind of pinnated sand-grouse, which, I was told, frequent these bare uplands in considerable numbers at this time of year. They were about the size of the large migratory sand-grouse found on the plains of India in winter, but their plumage more resembled the smaller pinnated variety. I found them very wild, and only got one long shot, which fortunately brought down a bird.

That evening we pitched our camp in a sheltered nook near the southern end of the Tso Morari, which is 15,000 feet above sea-level, and almost, if not quite, the highest of known lakes in the world. Although much smaller than the Pangong tso, being only about 15 miles long by 5 or 6 broad, it has even a grander appearance, from the more precipitous nature of some of the adjacent mountains. It has the same strangely intense blue colour so characteristic of all Tibetan

lakes when rippled by wind, and as its water is not salt, there
is a certain amount of verdure here and there along its margin, and beside the streams that flow into it, which gives a
pleasing variety to its otherwise barren scenery. The surrounding mountainous country is desolate to a degree, there
not being a human habitation within a radius of at least 40
miles of it, except the miserable little hamlet of Karzok, with
its small monastery situated on its western shore. The water,
to me, seemed perfectly good, although rather flat, so to speak,
to the taste; but the Tartars have an objection to drinking
it. Although there is a large amount of drainage into the
lake, there is no visible outlet from it. This is a remarkable
fact; and evaporation alone, one would suppose, could hardly
account for the disappearance of the constant and abundant
supply of water from the great quantity of melted snow
draining into it off the neighbouring mountains.

On our way to Karzok along the shore of the lake, we got
numerous shots at wild geese of the bar-headed kind, and
as they had young goslings with them, I concluded they
bred in the vicinity. Fortunately the strong wind was blowing shorewards, as most of them dropped on the water and
we had no dog to retrieve them. The old birds were dreadfully tough, and even our Warren's cooking-pot failed to
extract much flavour from them when made into soup; but
the goslings were much more palatable.

Whilst at Karzok, we were surprised, late one evening, by
the advent of a solitary sportsman who had just come over
the Parang la into Tibet, with the intention, late in the season
as it was, of hunting in Changchenmo. He seemed to have
suffered pretty severely from the combined effects of cold,
wind, and sun on the pass, as his face was in rather a sorry
plight, being something like a raw beefsteak, and the deep
cracks on his lips and nose were profusely patched with bits
of sticking-plaster. The account he gave us of some hunting-
ground for nāpoo, on the south side of the Parang la, was so

seducing as to cause us to alter our intended return-route over the Baralacha pass into Lahoul, for that across the Parang la, and thence through Spiti. In course of conversation he told us that we should get lots of "fees" at some of the halting-places on the south side of the Parang la. Not wishing to expose our ignorance as to the sort of game, or whatever else "fees" might be, nor to seem impolite by suggesting that he could possibly mean anything in the pecuniary line, we made mental note of the information, and adroitly changed the subject. It afterwards struck us that he had meant the vegetable pea, which we were rejoiced to find growing in abundance about the villages where we happened to camp in Spiti. His poor lips were so cracked and sore that he had substituted an *f* for a *p*, as being less painful to pronounce. We gave him what information we could, and after exchanging a few creature-comforts and good wishes, saw him off on his way next morning.

There now only remained about a fortnight before we should have to commence retracing our steps across the Himalayas. This I resolved to devote to a final search for *Ovis Ammon* in the vicinity of the Tso Kar, better known as the Salt Lake, three or four days' journey to the north-west of Karzok.

Leaving the Major at Karzok, where he preferred to remain shooting wild geese and trying his luck on the ground about the Tso Morari, the second evening found my camp pitched on the east side of the Kazura la, at an elevation of about 17,500 feet, calculated by boiling. In the grey of the following morning I was very loath to turn out into a temperature of twelve degrees below freezing (and this in the month of August), although my sleep had not been either of the soundest or most comfortable kind, from my being unable to respirate freely in a recumbent position at such a height. The cold, too, was dreadful, as the wind blew through the thin canvas of the little tent, which I had exchanged for my own blanket-lined one with my two Indian domestics, who felt the severity of the climate much more than I did. I must confess, however, that this was not done out of pure philanthropy: there was a certain amount of selfishness in it, as one's own comfort on a trip of this kind so much depends on keeping one's servants in health and good-humour.

A skull and massive pair of ram's horns lying bleaching in the sun showed us we were once more among the haunts of the big sheep. About two hours' slow walking—for I was now afoot again, having sent back the pony from the Indus with Changter—took us to the top of the pass, on the farther side of which the Karzok men had told us we should find an encampment of Rookshu people, where a guide for the locality could be procured. On and on we trudged over the bare hard ground, under the glaring sun, and against the everlasting cutting wind, for hour after hour, not meeting with a sign of life except a few marmots, and the cheerless relics of a Tartar camp in the shape of smoke-blackened stones and dilapidated "pullas,"[1]—all was silent solitude.

Towards the afternoon we topped another rise, from whence we got a fine view of the Tso Kar lying far away below. Situated in the middle of an extensive barren valley, surrounded by arid brown hills, the Tso Kar is, I think, the least interesting, as far as appearance goes, of any of the larger lakes of this part of Tibet; and to increase its dreary aspect, the shore, for some distance from its crooked margin, is covered with a white saline efflorescence, from which a most abominable glare is reflected. It is curious that, in the same valley, and only about a mile or so from this salt lake, there is a smaller sheet of fresh water, bordered to a certain extent with green turf, presenting a remarkable contrast to its salt neighbour. On

---

[1] A "pulla" is a low wall built of loose stones, which the Tibetans build round the bottom of their tents, or more frequently in the open, as a protection from the wind; for these hardy nomads seem to care little for any shelter except from the cruel biting blast. We always piled large stones, of which there was never any lack, round our little tents, if only to keep them from being almost blown away.

the fresh-water lake numbers of wild-fowl congregate, affording some sport for a shot-gun. The mountains in the vicinity hold both *Ovis Ammon* and nāpoo, and the valley, I believe, a few goa, if one has the luck to find them there.

After a gentle descent for some distance, a strange scene suddenly presented itself. Instead of a small encampment, as I had expected to find, there appeared a perfect city of black blanket-tents, pitched on either side of a rivulet that flowed through a long, narrow, comparatively low-lying valley, the bottom of which was carpeted with bright greensward. There must have been considerably over a hundred tents. It seemed as though the whole nomadic population of Rookshu were collected on this meadow-like spot. Vast herds of sheep, goats, and yaks were scattered over the neighbouring heights, where the wild yodling kind of hulloo of the Tartar herdsmen and the barking of their dogs was heard on every side.

This did not look much like a locality near which to find such wary game as *Ovis Ammon*, and I could not but feel that I had been regularly humbugged by the Karzok men. Of one fact I was now more than ever convinced, that as a rule, to which there may be occasional exceptions, the sportsman, in this part of Tibet at any rate, must undergo the vexations and disappointments of a first season's personal experience in that country to ensure success on a second visit.

Unpropitious as matters looked, I was nevertheless determined to give the ground a trial; but after several days of severe work, during which I must have sometimes been considerably over 19,000 feet, I saw nothing but a flock of nāpoo, a few *Ovis Ammon* ewes with lambs, and one or two young males, at which latter I did not attempt to shoot lest I should disturb better ones. Kiangs were numerous as usual, but of course were never molested. The Tartars, however, being hippophagous, did not seem at all to appreciate my thus abstaining from horse-butchery. One evening I came suddenly on a brood of snow-pheasants, large game-looking birds of a

general light-grey colour, with a whitish head and breast.[1]
They were at first unwilling to rise, but made such good use
of their legs that I had to put my best foot foremost for some
distance to overtake them before I could get a shot. At such
a height this exertion, slight as it was, so completely pumped
the breath out of me that I was only just able to loose off both
barrels into the "brown" of the covey as it rose. I had not
another yard left in me to secure the runners; but my Tartar
attendants, who had wisely followed more leisurely, gathered
the old hen and three well-grown chicks. The old one proved
rather dry and tough, even after many days' keeping; but the
chicks were as tender and well-flavoured birds as I ever tasted.

It was now time to return to Karzok, as I had promised to
meet the Major there on a certain date. The cold, too, at the
great heights I had camped during the last few days, had become unpleasantly intense, owing to frequent snowstorms and
to the sun having been obscured by clouds. There was, however, no lack of sunshine on the day I started for Karzok by
a short cut across the mountains, where the ground was completely covered with new-fallen snow, off which the glare was
almost intolerable. For several miles our way led gently
upward through a narrow glen, which wound along between
rolling rounded hills. The crisp snow, that at first merely
crunched under our feet, became deeper and more laborious to
trudge through as we gradually ascended. Not a vestige of
any living thing was visible in this white solitude, save here
and there a tailless kind of rat,[2] that, scared at our approach,

---

[1] This bird, although generally termed a pheasant, is really a partridge,
sometimes called the "gigantic chuckor." There are two kinds, that found
on the southern slopes of the Himalayas being a good deal smaller than the
Tibetan variety. They are found only at very high elevations, far above the
limit of forest.

[2] Colonel E. Smyth, an excellent authority on Himalayan fauna, considers
this little animal, which is about the size of an ordinary rat, and of a dirty
white or light fawn colour, to be a kind of rabbit. He says they are inquisitive little creatures, and by no means addicted to shyness, as the following
experience of his concerning them will show:—

would dart away over the snow, and, with a shrill eerie
chirp, suddenly vanish; and one little bird, something like a
robin, that followed us for a long way, flitting and hopping
from stone to stone in the ice-bound brook beside us, as if
courting our companionship. So profound and deathlike was
the solemn hush that brooded over mother earth as she lay
wrapped in her snowy shroud, that one was almost startled
at the slight rustling noise caused by the slipping of melted
snow from off some neighbouring rock; for, in the still frozen
air of that high silent region, fancy almost led one to imagine
the sound resembled the mysterious whisperings of invisible
beings whose sanctuary we were invading. Even on emerging from this dismal glen upon more open ground, nothing
met the weary aching eye but a vast lone wilderness of white
undulating hills, and, more distant, domes and pyramids of
snow. At last we reached the culminating point, and began
to descend, when it was quite a relief to look down on a bit
of dark-blue water of the Tso Morari, some 2000 feet below
us, cold and cheerless though it appeared as it lay amidst
mountains which were now draped in virgin snow almost to
its margin.

The Major's luck with the rifle had been no better than
mine. To tell the truth, we were both getting a little tired
of toiling after game day after day from morning to night
over these desolate regions to so little purpose; so next
morning we were not sorry to retrace our steps along the
shore of the lake, en route for the verdant and forest-clad
slopes of the Himalayas. One or two more geese were
bagged; but they had now become very wary from having

"I was once resting myself on a cairn at the top of the Niti pass. Everywhere around the ground was covered with snow, except on this cairn. One
or two of these little things soon appeared from among the stones; and as I
sat perfectly still to watch them, they came up to me and began nibbling at
my boots."

The Niti pass, I may remark, is nearly 17,000 feet high, and well above the
limit of any visible sort of vegetation.

been potted at so freely, and generally kept well away from
the shore. On a marshy bit of ground, or what I once heard
an old gamekeeper describe as a "stanky sort o' place," near
the end of the lake, I killed two specimens of the ruff. Another British bird that we frequently saw up here was the
common magpie; also that cosmopolitan bird, the hoopoe.

Next morning we forded the Parang, a turbid broken flood
of melted snow, which, as is usual with these capricious snow-
fed torrents of Tibet, was only passable at an early hour. For
three days we trudged up the valley of the Parang, a seemingly endless narrow glen, totally destitute of vegetation, and
closely hemmed in by steep stony landslips and precipices of
a brownish-yellow hue, rising stark and gaunt one above
another to a stupendous height, like gigantic stair-steps, save
where the V-shaped cleft of some lateral gorge disclosed the
broken termination of a glacier, or a towering white mountain-
summit.

The Parang la, with its glaciers and perpetual snow, is quite
in keeping with the wild approaches to it on either side. It
is perhaps as savagely grand as any of the passes that are
ordinarily used as highways for crossing the "divide" or
backbone, as it were, of the Himalayan range into Tibet, as
well as being one of the highest and most arduous to traverse.
And certainly, from my experience of it in September, when
its difficulties are supposed to be at their minimum, I can
quite imagine it to be the latter. Its height is about 18,600
feet, and it is seldom, if ever, open before June, and generally
becomes again impracticable to cross about the beginning of
October. On our arrival at Leh in June, we found several
Indian servants of some travellers who had just come over
this pass, laid up there in a pitiable plight from frost-bite;
one of them had lost many of his toes, and his companions
were little better off.

The evening previous to our crossing, we camped a short
distance below the foot of the glacier that extends down

almost from the summit of the pass for some four or five miles on its northern side. Snow began to fall thickly just before dark, and continued to do so, more or less, during the night. In the morning the weather at first looked rather promising, but the tents were frozen as stiff as boards, and were so incrusted with hard snow that we had to delay our departure until the sun, of which we only got an occasional glimpse, should thaw them a little. After our breakfast, which we managed to cook over a smoky little fire made of the few remaining scraps of wet fuel which, with considerable difficulty, we had coaxed into burning, we loaded the yaks and started just as it again began snowing more thickly than ever. The limited supply of fuel we had brought up with us was done, and the poor yaks had already been fasting for two days or more; besides this there was some fear, if the snow-storm continued, that the pass might become permanently closed for the winter: we therefore determined, under any circumstances, to make an effort and push over it at once into Spiti.

For more than six weary hours did we toil up against the almost blinding snow and piercing wind that chilled us to the very marrow, although the distance to the summit was only six or seven miles. It was truly wonderful to see the way in which the yaks struggled through the deep snow, and scrambled over places which were often difficult, and some-times dangerous to traverse. Nothing could have exceeded the powers of endurance evinced by these animals, which were game to the backbone and as sure-footed as goats. One of them, notwithstanding, lost its footing on a steep slope of *névé*, and went rolling and sliding down until it was fortu-nately stopped by a friendly rock, otherwise it must have disappeared for ever under the glacier, and with it my dear old Whitworth rifle, which, among other things, it was carrying. On regaining its feet the creature merely shook itself, and on being disentangled from its load soon clambered up again.

For the last three miles of the ascent our way was over the glacier, where we waded and floundered through the soft fresh-fallen snow, with an occasional dive into it up to the middle, as we followed in the steps of our Tartar leader, who, in order to avoid hidden crevasses, cautiously sounded the way with his long mountain-pole. Here we experienced a regular _tourmente_, for, besides the falling flakes, the dry drifting snow was whirled up into our eyes and nostrils by the freezing blast, causing a suffocating sensation which was most trying, and the cold was so intense that my beard, from my breath on it, became a mass of ice, and was frozen hard to my coat.[1] Whilst on the glacier all the marks we had to indicate the right track were the giant outlines of the white eminences rearing up on either side, and these only occasionally loomed dimly through the driving snow. Never shall I forget the ludicrous picture of utter misery presented by my Hindustani cook as he sat resting himself on a bank of snow, his head closely enveloped in a black blanket, and his beard covered with icicles. Blank despair was depicted on his face as he gazed ruefully, through a pair of green goggles, on the bewildering scene around him. Right glad were we all to at last reach the top, where we sat down for a short time to rest our weary limbs and to admire the grand landscape before us; for the snowstorm had passed over, and the blue mountains of Spiti were gradually becoming disclosed to view through the broken masses of cloud and mist that came rolling up from below.

But our day's work was not to end here, for the descent on the Spiti side of the pass was so steep and rough, that even

---

[1] With reference to what I have already said concerning the effects produced by rarefied air under different conditions, I may here mention that when crossing this high pass, which is approached from the south by a very steep ascent, and is flanked on both sides by high eminences, neither my companion nor myself felt any of the more disagreeable sensations, such as headache and nausea, even under such circumstances as might have been expected to induce them.

after we got clear of the snow the track was almost worse than if covered with it. As the Major remarked, "it was macadamised with a vengeance." Such a howling wilderness of sharp pinnacles of rock, and bare, rugged, perpendicular cliffs, piled tier upon tier to an appalling height, as flanked the stupendous cañon down which our route lay, I never beheld.[1] Some of the lofty fantastic-shaped summits bore a striking resemblance to ruins of gigantic towers and turrets. As the last rays of the sun, sinking behind the mountain-tops, shed a parting gleam of golden radiance on these aerial castles, rock-spires, and snow-crowned peaks, leaving the profound depths of the abyss beneath wrapped in gloomy shade, the effect was truly magnificent; — scenery altogether so sublimely wild, so awe-inspiring, and on so vast a scale as to be quite beyond description, and almost beyond conception. Dame Nature must indeed have been in a terrible mood when she fashioned such awful works.

When darkness compelled us to call a halt, we were still several miles short of the usual camping-place; and as there was not a blade of grass in the vicinity, the poor yaks had to fast another night. Fortunately we found sufficient fuel for cooking purposes.

A short but very stiff walk on the following morning up through another wild gorge, brought us to our next camping-ground, on the heights above which was the locality for nāpoo, recommended by the sportsman we had met at Karzok. Some of our Tartars were half-blind from the effects of the previous day's snow on the pass, notwithstanding their having improvised kind of goggles of wisps of black hair pulled from their yaks' tails, and tied loosely over their eyes,

---

[1] The Grand Cañon of the Yellowstone, in Wyoming, with its fantastic features and profound depth, is the nearest approach to it in appearance I know, though the American cañon falls far short of it in magnitude and savage magnificence of surroundings. And doubtless there are many other such gorges in the higher Himalayas that quite equal, if they do not surpass, this one in savage grandeur.

none of them having brought the woven yak's-hair spectacles they often use on such occasions with them. I found one man sitting by the wayside endeavouring to extract blood from his nostrils with the point of his knife, at which surgical operation he implored me to assist him, at the same time handing me the knife. A good punch on his proboscis would, I thought, have been much less dangerous, and just as effectual, as regarded relief to his eyes. Our Indian servants had not suffered so much, owing to their having been provided with green goggles. There was plenty of grass here for the famished yaks—and how they did pitch into it! Never have I seen animals making such good use of their time and teeth. But, to use a much hackneyed, but in this case a rather appropriate phrase, *revenons à nos moutons.*

Although the wild sheep here called nāpoo are numerous in many parts of Tibet, I have hitherto made but little mention of them, as I seldom hunted expressly for them, owing to my time having been fully occupied in searching for other game not found on the south side of the Himalayan chain, specimens of which I was then more anxious to secure. Stalking burrell, as these animals are called in the Himalayas, is really splendid sport on ground where they are fairly plentiful.

A full-grown male nāpoo or burrell (*Ovis nahura*) stands about 33 inches at the shoulder usually, but its size seems to vary in different localities. The thick arching horns, which spread laterally and curve downwards, and slightly backwards near their points, occasionally attain a length of 30 inches, or even more, and are about a foot in girth. The beautiful skin, with its thick elastic pile, is of a bluish-grey, bordered with distinct jet-black and pure-white markings. In winter it is handsomest, when the colour becomes more decidedly slate-blue. The ewes are rather smaller than the rams, and their horns are much thinner and shorter, their colour paler, and the black and white bordering less distinctly defined. They usually produce two lambs in spring. To-

wards autumn burrell often assemble in very large flocks, but
in spring and summer they are generally found in much
smaller batches, sometimes only two or three together, the
large rams, as a rule, herding separately. The flesh of a young
male or ewe is, in autumn, as fat, tender, and better flavoured
than domestic mutton. Although the favourite haunts of the
burrell are open and comparatively gentle slopes of short
grass just under the snow-line, these sheep are quite as sure-
footed and agile as the wild-goat tribe on precipitous rocky
ground, which is never very far distant from the slopes where
they feed, and to this they usually resort when scared. They
have the most acute sense of smell, so it is always necessary
to take this into account before arranging a stalk. If burrell
have sighted you, it is generally useless to follow them.
They at once commence moving off, slowly and deliberately
at first, feeding as they walk, leading on an inexperienced
sportsman for miles, until they have fooled him sufficiently,
when they gallop away, and seldom stop before they are lost
to view among the eternal snows and glaciers. When disturbed the burrell gives a shrill double whistle, which alarms
every other animal within sound of it; and you will seldom,
if ever, get a shot after hearing it. Early in summer the
best of burrell-shooting can be got on the upper ranges of the
mountain provinces of Kumaon and Gurhwal, without having
to cross the passes into Tibet for it.

As the ground for nāpoo in this vicinity was so limited
as only to admit of one of us shooting over it, and a few days'
journey farther on there was a similar bit of country for
ibex, the Major and I arranged that I should have a turn
at the nāpoo, and he at the ibex, which he was more anxious
to get.

Having bundled up a few requisites for a night's absence
from our camp, I started upwards about noon next day, and
after a long and stiff pull of several hours, reached a huge
sort of corrie where my Spiti guides expected we should find

2 A

our game. On our way we passed through the village of Kiwar, situated at an elevation of 13,400 feet. Although at such a high altitude, it is a fairly large, well-to-do village, and several kinds of grain are raised there (chiefly buckwheat and barley) entirely by irrigation, for the climate of Spiti is extremely dry and almost rainless. As the village lies on the south side of the mountains, it is tolerably warm.

After a careful scrutiny of the ground with the glass, I discerned a flock of about fifteen nāpoo nearly a mile off. As none of them appeared to be old rams, and we were not very far from where we intended to pass the night, I remained watching them, in the hope that bigger fellows might show themselves as evening drew on. However, as no others put in an appearance, and the sun was getting low, I commenced a stalk after those in sight, with a view to supplying our empty camp-larder with good venison. We got within easy range of them rather unexpectedly, as they had fed quickly down towards us whilst hidden from view during our stalk, when the excited behaviour of my two men, on suddenly seeing the beasts so near us, was very ludicrous. Whilst one of them snatched my cap off, the other seized me under the arms and tried to lift my head over the top of some rocks, behind the cover of which we had been stealing towards the animals, he being under the impression that I could not see them. After shaking one fellow off at the risk of the burrell detecting us, and recovering my cap from the other, I was able to shoot, and took down two right and left with the old Whitworth, much to the delight of my excited companions. After securing the beasts, and dragging them to a convenient spot for leaving them until next morning, we made the best of our way to the place we intended passing the night, under the lee of a rock. The cold was bitter lying out at night, as there was keen frost and a high wind.

We were afoot early next morning over fresh ground, and soon descried a large flock with two fine rams in it. But our attempts to approach them were fruitless, as they were in a very open position, and proved too crafty for us. Nothing more was seen except a brood of snow-pheasants which we flushed on our way down to the tents.

A few days' travelling brought us to the ibex ground, where the Major had an unsuccessful hunt, whilst I took a good rest in camp.

Any attempt of mine to describe the glacier scenery of the Spiti and Lahoul mountains, through which our way led for several days, would be quite inadequate to convey the slightest idea of its wild grandeur. Suffice it to say that the longest of Alpine glaciers, the Aletsch, which is some twenty miles in length, cannot be compared in size with many of those in the Himalayas, the largest of which are found in the Karakorum range, far to the north-west of Cashmere and Ladak. Colonel Godwin-Austen, the greatest authority on Himalayan glaciers, gives the length of the Biafo glacier as 64 miles of continuous ice; the Baltoro as 35 miles, up to K 2 (now named Mount Godwin - Austen), the second - highest known peak in the world: but this glacier took him some 55 miles of walking, and then he had not reached the watershed. One morning we traversed the lower part of the Shigri glacier in Spiti, but it was there so covered over with dirt and stones, that, until we had repeatedly probed it with our iron-shod sticks, it was difficult to believe we were walking for miles over solid ice.

The ponies bred in Spiti are much more celebrated for their comeliness than are its human inhabitants, more especially the womankind. And justly so, if I may judge from the personal appearance of a batch of sturdy-limbed females who one day, after depositing the heavy loads they had carried on their backs for ten miles or more, treated us to a terpsichorean performance, accompanied by their unmelodious voices. They are, however, as cheery and almost as unsophisticated a set of people as the Tibetans. Here, where the inhabitants are Buddhists, even the clerical members of the community are not too proud to earn a trifle by carrying your baggage, and after depositing their loads, these holy Lamas may be seen receiving the obeisances of the villagers, and distributing blessings with outstretched hands.

After quitting the snow and ice on the top of the Hampta pass between the districts of Spiti and Kulu, how changed was the aspect of the mountains on its southern side, from the barren dreary solitudes amongst which we had been roaming during the past four months! With what keen delight did we hail the first glimpse of the green slopes, birch-woods, and pine-clad hills of Kulu—a country as famed for the romantic beauty of its scenery as for its bonny lasses! Of these latter, we met two very pretty specimens as we were descending the track from the pass. One of them in particular was a perfect model of rustic beauty, as, with her long glossy tresses falling dishevelled about her shoulders, and the olive complexion of her face all flushed from climbing up the hill, she stopped to take breath, her large brown eyes wide open with half-startled amazement at thus unexpectedly meeting with two such wild-looking figures as the Major and I presented, with our red sun-cracked faces and old travel-worn clothes. Most of these Kulu belles endeavour to heighten their natural charms by wearing, in addition to their own hair, a long thick plait of black worsted coiled round a little cap of some bright colour jauntily set on the crown of the head. They are very fond of adorning themselves with flowers, with which we noticed most of the women we met had tastefully decked their chignons. The men also had generally a flower or two stuck in their caps or behind their ears.

On reaching Sultanpore, the chief town of Kulu, we put up in a house and procured some fresh vegetables—luxuries we had not indulged in for months, the afore-mentioned "fees" in Spiti excepted. A newspaper many weeks old, that had been left there by some former occupant, was greedily pounced

upon. From it I learned that my regiment was to form part
of a force about to proceed on active service. There was no
time to lose; so we hurried through the beautiful Kangra
valley, with its numerous tea-plantations, to Dhurrumsala,
the nearest military station. Here I bade good-bye to the
Major, who was bound for the Punjab.

Irrespective of the ground worked over in hunting, we had
covered, during this my first trip beyond the Himalayas, a
good 1300 miles of regular mountain travel, about a thousand
of which were in Tibet, at an elevation, on an average, of
nearly 15,000 feet—almost as high as the top of Mont Blanc,
though not quite so snowy. But my pleasure in looking back
to these wanderings is mingled with sorrow, when I think that
my boon companion throughout them has since then gone on
another long journey, and this time to the "happy hunting-
grounds" whence there is no returning.

CHAPTER XXI.

IT might naturally be supposed that, after the experiences
of one visit to trans-Himalayan regions, nobody would be in
a hurry to return to those cold and desolate steppes. It is
not so, however, with such as are imbued with a taste for
wandering among Nature's wild and wonderful works. What-

ever trials and difficulties they may have undergone are soon forgotten in their ardent longing for fresh adventure or sport. Even the dangers to which the mountain-hunter is so often exposed have a sort of alluring fascination about them. I have no doubt many a Himalayan sportsman, when traversing some terribly awkward bit, where a slip might launch him into eternity, will, like myself, have inwardly declared he would never again be enticed into such a position, but only the very next day to find himself perhaps in a worse one.

Whether I am right or not in these surmises, I, at any rate, found myself ere long preparing for another trip to the wild land beyond the Himalayas. I shall not, however, ask the reader to follow our old trail there, but offer to conduct him in quite a different direction—towards Nari-Khorsum, better known as Hundés (pronounced Hoondace), the Chinese-Tibetan territory situated across the high mountain-passes of the provinces of Gurhwal and Kumaon.

On the 20th of April I set out from Dehra Doon, and as I did not expect the Niti ghat (pass), which I intended to cross into Hundés, would be practicable before the beginning of June, there would be plenty of time for a turn over the Himalayan haunts of the burrell, to which I alluded when describing this wild sheep, known as nāpoo in Tibet.

Here I need say little about the middle Himalayan ranges through which I travelled for about a fortnight. On Sirkanda-devi—a grand hill rising 10,000 feet—on the route between the sanitarium of Mussoorie and Tehree, the chief town of (foreign) Gurhwal, I killed a buck gooral close to the rude little temple built on its summit. Being my first shot on this trip, I regarded its success as a good omen.

At Tehree, five days out, I paid my respects to the rajah, Pertab Sing, who had been kind enough to send some of his officials to assist me in obtaining supplies, &c., whilst passing through his State. On the evening of my arrival there he sent his gold and silver sticks-in-waiting to usher me into his august presence. He seemed an intelligent youth, and fond of sport. Three days more took me beyond the confines of his territory, to Srinuggur, the capital of British Gurhwal.

One evening, when encamped in a low warm valley between these two places, I witnessed a most extraordinary display of fireflies. A corn-field just below where my tent was pitched looked literally alive with them, as they glanced to and fro in myriads, like a waving sheet of fire over the tops of the corn.[1] The straggling town of Srinuggur, situated in the low-lying valley of the Alaknanda—a tributary of the sacred river Ganges—although showing evidences of former importance in its numerous old ruins, seems now only famous for intense heat and scorpions. In this neighbourhood the latter are said to be such a pest as in some instances even to interfere with the tilling of the stony soil; in one particular locality so much so that it had to be abandoned by the barefooted natives, according to whose account every stone there hid a scorpion. The only one I chanced to see in those parts had got rolled up in one of the loads of baggage, and stung the man who was carrying it.

For several days on from here the villages along our route looked desolate and forlorn, their inhabitants having temporarily deserted them to escape the ravages of a disease called by the natives "māhāmurree" or "gola,"[2] which was then rife in this part of the district. In its symptoms this dreadful malady much resembles the plague of Western Asia, and it is quite as deadly. It is endemic in the provinces of Gurhwal and Kumaon, and sometimes takes a virulent epidemic form. It is supposed to originate from the excessively dirty mode of living of the villagers, who usually have

---

[1] There are usually spring and autumn harvests in India, the former chiefly of wheat, the latter of rice, &c.

[2] "Māhāmurree," being interpreted, means the great sickness; "gola" means ball, probably so called from the glandular swellings which are among the symptoms of this malignant disease.

their cattle housed on their ground-floors, which they never
think of cleaning out. On a village being attacked by this
plague, the terror-stricken inhabitants at once flee to the
jungles, leaving the unfortunate victims to their fate.
Strange to say, it is generally preceded by the rats being
found dead about the village it attacks. But the villagers
are often so apathetic as not to accept this warning until
too late; consequently the infection is carried with them to
the jungles, where cold and exposure only aggravate the
disease, and they die there like rotten sheep, for those
attacked seldom recover.

All honour is due to the memory of the late Dr F. Pearson
for his voluntary and perilous labours in attempting to discover the cause and stay the progress of this fell disease.
Many an anecdote of his dreadful experiences have I heard
from himself. He and his coadjutor, Dr Francis, had themselves often to remove the decomposing bodies from the
deserted houses for their *post-mortem* examinations, as nothing would induce the terrified natives to touch them. One
little episode was very characteristic of the people they had
to deal with. At a place where Dr Pearson had been rigor-
ously carrying out his sanitary measures—by burning houses
that contained putrid corpses, having the cattle removed from
the villages, whitewashing, and suchlike—the inhabitants sent
a petition to the commissioner of the province, imploring him
to take away the doctor sahib, as they said they would rather
have the mahamurree amongst them than him with all his
worry. These Gurhwal villagers usually grow, close about
their houses, a quantity of hemp, which they weave into cloth
during the winter months. The combined odours of this tall
rank plant and the village ordure are sometimes truly abominable. No wonder the villages are hotbeds of disease. This
horrible pestilence seems to confine itself entirely to the
natives of the country. Even the pilgrims who yearly pass
through this province by thousands, on their way to and

from the Hindoo shrines of Badrinath and Kedarnath, are
seldom, if ever, infected with it.

At one of our halting-places I met a dear old friend and
quondam companion on many a shikar trip—Colonel Fisher,
the assistant commissioner of the province, who was out on
his circuit. At his camp I found Puddoo, a Bhōtia of Niti,
my shikaree and guide on a former visit to the upper ranges
of Gurhwal, who had come down to meet me.

The Bhōtias[1] of Kumaon and Gurhwal are a half-Tibetan,
half-Himalayan people, inhabiting the highest villages on the
upper ranges of those provinces. They are more pastoral
than agricultural in their habits, and their manners and
customs are more Tartar than Hindoo, although they profess
to be of the latter persuasion. They occupy their villages
for a few months only during the summer, migrating to
the middle ranges in winter, during which they lead a
nomadic life. While the passes into Tibet are open (from
about the middle of June until the end of October) they are
constantly on the move, crossing and recrossing them with
their sheep, goats, and other beasts of burden, all and sundry
laden with grain, ghee (clarified butter), English manufactured
goods—chiefly broadcloth, which they barter with the Tibetans
for borax, salt, and wool; trading in Tibet being almost entirely done by barter, money seldom changing hands. During
winter they carry their commodities from their camps on the
middle ranges down to the large towns and fairs in the
plains. Their religion is decidedly peculiar. They are
Hindoos in name, but are not recognised as such by the strict
Hindoos of the lower country, who will not intermarry with
them. While in Tibet they throw off Hindooism and become
Buddhists.

[1] "Bhōt" is the term applied by the lower countrymen in general to the
snowy ranges. The Bhōtias themselves, when they talk of Bhōt, invariably
mean what the lower hill-men call Hundés—the district of Tibet beyond the
Gurhwal and Kumaon mountain-passes.

At Kurrunpryag, the junction of the Pindar river with the Alaknanda, I tried for a mahseer unsuccessfully, although the last time I had been there on my way to "the snows," I had not been fishing a quarter of an hour before I was hard and fast in a 30-pounder, which ran me for nearly an hour ere I landed him, and I afterwards lost another the same evening that must have been nearly as big. A day further on, however, at Nandpryag, where the Nandakni flows into the Alaknanda, I had good sport during the few hours I fished there in the evening, killing three nice fish with spoon-bait, the largest weighing 12 lb. In one of the pools here I saw a monster mahseer. He really looked as long as myself as he lay motionless as a log in the deep water, but nothing would tempt him. As the fish were evidently taking well, I would fain have remained here for a day or two had not the heat beside the river been so terrible and the flies a perfect pest.

In three more days I reached the village of Joshimutt, the winter residence of the Raol or high priest of the Temple of Badrinath, a sort of Hindoo Pope who gives absolution to thousands of "jatrees," as the pilgrims are here called, who flock there yearly from every part of Hindustan. As the temple was only about eighteen miles distant up towards the glacier sources of the Alaknanda and I had time to spare, I thought some of it might be spent to advantage in visiting this Ultima Thule of Hindoo sanctity.

The road leading to it was not of the best. After a very steep descent to where the river Doulee (which here joins the Alaknanda) is crossed by a "sanga" bridge,[1] the path leads

---

[1] A sanga bridge has its piers constructed of long beams or logs projecting from both banks over the stream in layers slanting upwards, each layer supporting the next above it—which projects beyond it—on transverse logs ; the uppermost layers, therefore, being the longest. The space left over the stream, between the outer ends of the uppermost layer on each pier, is spanned by stout planks or poles for crossing on. The inner or shore ends of the pier-beams are firmly embedded among heavy lumps of rock or boulders.

up the Alaknanda for a mile or so to where it also is spanned by another sanga. Thence it proceeds along the western side of the latter river. There were flights of rudely built steps to ascend and descend on the steep acclivities, often nearly overhanging the river rushing and chafing along its rocky bed below. In such places the narrow track sometimes became quite choked with the unceasing stream of pilgrims, which in the distance resembled a string of ants creeping tortuously to and fro on the face of a wall. There

Temple of Badrinath.

were lame and blind, decrepit and infirm, old and young, even to the babe in arms; Hindoo nobles; "jogees" (religious mendicants), with matted locks and orange-coloured sheets,[1] or with their nude bodies looking hideous from the white ashes with which they were smeared over from head to foot, and sometimes doing penance by holding an arm straight upward until it had become permanently stiffened in that

[1] This orange-coloured garment represents the winding-sheet in which the bodies of defunct Hindoos are cremated, and indicates, I suppose, that its wearer is dead to the pomps and vanities of the world.

position, and the nails of the tightly clenched fingers had actually grown through the hand and protruded at its back: all of them jostling or being jostled along the narrow path. A few of the more aged or sick were being carried in baskets on the backs of men, sometimes of women. Occasionally a man might be seen measuring his length flat on the ground, then rising and remeasuring it, thus progressing by a regular succession of these prostrations throughout his whole journey, perhaps for hundreds of miles, to the shrine. How some of the wretched creatures contrived to get over such rough ground was truly astonishing. When performing their religious observances on this arduous mountain-pilgrimage, they seem utterly reckless of all hardship and danger. Many are drowned at the confluence of the Alaknanda and Doulee, a sacred spot (as every junction of large rivers is by Hindoos considered), where they all think it an imperative duty to bathe off a smooth slab of rock jutting out into the deep rapid current of the combined streams. By way of propitiation, some even cast themselves voluntarily into the river. Fifteen had that year been swept away by an avalanche. A poor old man I accosted on the way, carrying a little child in his arms, burst into tears as he told me his sad tale. The child's mother had slipped on a snow-slope on the way between the two mountain-shrines of Kedarnath and Badrinath, its father in attempting to rescue her had also lost his footing, when both had fallen together and disappeared for ever in a torrent far below, and he, its grandfather, was left to return home with the infant alone. One poor wretch had managed to crawl as far as the shrine, and had lain down and died, from sheer exhaustion, on its very threshold, the day I arrived there.

The temple is situated in a wild glen begirt with towering snowy heights, but the summits of some of the higher peaks are invisible from it. Although its sublime surroundings are such fit emblems of the majesty of the Almighty, the temple itself, which is built on the rocks overhanging the river, is small and unimposing, being an adjunct only to the general sanctity of the whole locality as a chief source of "Holy Mother Ganges," and so by Hindoos devoted to the homage of the Supreme Deity.   In its immediate vicinity some rest-houses for the pilgrims, the residences of the officiating Brahmin priests, and a few shops, chiefly occupied by vendors of sweetmeats, are clustered together.   The shrine is dedicated to Vishnu, the divinity of the Hindoo triad who, according to Brahman theology, represents the beneficence of the one Eternal and Omnipotent Being, as Brahma and Siva personate the wisdom and power.   Large quantities of rice are daily cooked within the precincts of the temple by the priests, nominally as an offering to the Deity, but really more for feeding the poorer class of pilgrims who come to do "puja" (worship) there, charity and hospitality being among the chief attributes of the Hindoo religion.   The expense of this is defrayed from the offerings made at the shrine, those of the wealthier pilgrims being often very considerable both in money and jewels; and by the Raol himself, who is the recipient of the rents of certain villages and lands with which the temple is endowed. This divine, who holds such a high ecclesiastical position among Hindoos, is, I believe, always inducted, as Raol or chief priest at Badrinath, from a certain family in which this office is hereditary, residing somewhere in the uttermost parts of the south of Hindustan.

On the evening of my arrival the Raol showed his hospitality by sending me a liberal present of sweetmeats.   Next morning I started to visit Bussoodārā, a consecrated waterfall some five miles farther up the glen, and about 2000 feet higher than the site of the temple, paying a visit *en route* to the high priest.   His holiness, contrary to what I should have expected, had nothing of the ascetic either in his appearance or demeanour.   I found him a pleasant, intelligent man of the world, and his spiritual calling had seemingly not caused him to neglect his temporal interests, as his chief topic of conversation was concerning his worldly possessions. As I had nothing more suitable to offer, at Puddoo's suggestion I presented him with a canister of gunpowder, which he was pleased to accept on account of his son, who, he said, was a great shikaree. He evidently considered me in the light of a pilgrim, as on taking my leave he wound a new white turban about my head, and promised to show me the temple on my return from Bussoodara.

On the way to the waterfall, under Puddoo's guidance, we passed through the Bhōtia village of Mānā, at an elevation of about 12,000 feet. It was empty and desolate, none of its inhabitants having as yet returned to it for the summer. The only living thing I saw there was a chuckor partridge we flushed in its main alley. To reach the fall we crossed a curious natural bridge formed of a gigantic block of stone that had fallen athwart the stream. A truly wild spot it looked, as the glen here suddenly grows very narrow, its rugged sides rising abruptly from the river, and the heavy volume of snow-water rushes down in a roaring cataract through a dark narrow cleft under the overlying rock-bridge. The "dārā," or cascade, is situated up a lateral gorge, and near the confluence of three fine glaciers. It much resembles the Staubbach in Switzerland, as the water, which is precipitated from a height of several hundred feet, is blown into dust-like spray before reaching the rocks below.

On my return the Raol fulfilled his promise of showing me the interior of the temple. The entrance is approached by a steep flight of steps. There are three doors, the outer one of wood, the second of silver, and the inner one of gold— at least so I was informed. I was not, however, permitted to enter beyond the silver one, and therefore had only an indistinct view of the symbolical figure of Vishnu in the gloom of the innermost part of the temple. By the glimmer of a torch which the Raol was good enough to have lighted, I could just discern that the image was profusely adorned with gold and jewels. One of the gems on its forehead, a large diamond, to which my attention was particularly directed, could distinctly be seen sparkling in the torchlight. Although for five or six months in the year the temple has no other guardian than the deep snow under which it then lies buried, such is the religious—some might call it superstitious—veneration with which it is regarded by the natives, that no attempt is ever made to plunder it.   I doubt very much whether any such "heathenish" (?) and "idolatrous" (?) feelings would influence the mind of the enterprising burglar of our own enlightened land. From the shrine I was taken to see the sacred hot spring which issues from the rocks below the temple. The steaming warm water is collected in a large roofed tank, where the pilgrims perform the ablutions which are supposed to purge them of their iniquities, though I had ocular proof that this ceremony is not always infallible as regards their dirt.

Next morning, after a refreshing tub in hot water brought from the spring, I started to return to Joshimutt, much edified by what I had seen of the so-called " heathen" pilgrim at Badrinath.

There is a shorter way of reaching Niti village from Badrinath than that round by Joshimutt, by proceeding up a lateral gorge to the left called Beeundyar, about six miles below the temple. It is a difficult route, over a very high pass, and was at that season quite impracticable. The only European who, to my knowledge, had up to that time ever traversed it, was my old friend Colonel E. Smyth, one of the boldest cragsmen and most experienced mountain-hunters that ever climbed the Himalayas. I give his own graphic and interesting account of his experiences on that occasion:—

" On the 30th October 1862 I had just come from Hundés to Gumsali, and as I had to go to Badrinath and Mana, and as the weather was fine though very cold, I sent off my ser-

vants and baggage to Joshimutt, and merely took two loads
with me—one bedding and clothes, the other a basket containing a few cooking-pots and eatables for five days—and with
seven or eight Bhootiahs, picked men, started to cross this
pass. My two loads were divided equally among the men.
I could only find one man in Gumsali who had ever been
across this pass to Badrinath ('Beea,' pudhan of Gumsali).
I took him as a guide.

"I started about noon of 30th October: the Bhootiahs were,
of course, all drunk, as they always are on starting on any
expedition. We went about ten miles up the Gumsali valley,
and bivouacked in the open at an elevation of 14,000 feet. The
night was clear, and my thermometer next morning showed
about twelve degrees of frost. There was no firewood procurable beyond this place, so we took on a small supply, enough
for breakfast, intending to cross the pass and encamp about
3000 feet down on the other side. Three miles up the valley
took us to the foot of the Gumsali glacier. We then went
three or four miles over the surface of the glacier to where it
is joined by another from the right, and we breakfasted on a
moraine between the two. There is a large lake two or three
miles from this spot, up the glacier to the right, which I had
not time to go and see, as it lay entirely off my road. By all
accounts it must be about half a mile in length. After breakfast we went about eight miles farther over the glacier, when
we came within sight of the top of the pass about two miles
above us.

"Up to this point there had been no difficulty. The ascent
had been easy, though here and there there had been a little
hindrance in the masses of rock and stones that lay piled on
the glacier. From this point, however, to the top of the
glacier, was very steep and very much crevassed. We had to
cut footsteps with axes nearly the whole way. This delayed
us very much, and it was nearly sunset when we reached the
top. Here our guide was at fault. He had only crossed the

pass once before, and that was many years ago, and in the month of July, when the state of the snow was very different to what it was now. He took us too much to the right, and we were brought up by a frightful precipice. We spent half an hour or so trying to find a way down, but night coming on, we had to remain here without firewood, water, or food. My thermometer at this time was at 12°. It must have gone down to zero during the night. We could not find room to lie down. I was comfortable enough myself. I put on all my spare clothes, and wrapped myself up in a postheen,[1] put on my Canadian fur boots, leggings, &c., and gave up my blankets to the Bhootiahs. I had a small flask of rum and some cold meat and biscuits. The meat was frozen hard. I did not feel the cold, and should have slept well but for the anxiety I felt for the men with me, who all suffered very much. The cold affected them in different ways. Some had a violent headache, others were sick all night. The night was beautiful and quite cloudless, and the moon nearly at the full. We looked straight down upon a regular sea of ice 3000 feet below us, at the foot of the precipice on the top of which we were perched. There seemed to be nothing but glacier as far as we could see, and the moonlight gave this *mer de glace* the appearance of being perfectly level. We were probably at an elevation of 18,000 feet, within 200 or 300 feet of the top of the pass, and on one side of us was that peculiar-looking flat-topped mountain 'Goree Purbut,' so distinctly visible from Almora, Paori, and the plains. The top of this mountain could not have been more than three miles from us. We had to remain squatted here until 10 A.M., when the sun made its appearance from behind 'Goree Purbut.' The cold was so intense that we could not touch the rocks with our hands. If the guide had not lost his way we should have met with no difficulty.

"We now used our own judgment. We saw where we had

---

[1] A long kind of leathern cloak lined with fur, made in Afghanistan.

to go, and we commenced climbing down this precipice. In several places we had to let one another down by ropes, and we did not reach the foot of the precipice until 2 or 3 P.M. Here we found a little firewood, enough to cook our breakfast. We then went about four miles farther down the glacier and bivouacked among some rocks at the side. Next morning we went about four miles farther down to where the river issues from the glacier, and we then left the river to our left and ascended the Poonch range. This range we crossed at an elevation of 15,000 feet, descended about 1000 feet the other side, and bivouacked in the open. To-day's march was about twelve miles. Next morning we descended in about eight miles to Amlagarh, where we joined the Joshimutt-Badrinath road, and in the evening went up six miles to Badrinath. From Niti to Badrinath by this route is about fifty miles; by Joshimutt route about sixty-five miles. Two of the Bhootiahs with me arrived at Badrinath with frost-bitten feet, and I had to leave them at the Joshimutt dispensary, but they recovered in about a month."

But let us now proceed to our shikar-ground.

Some nine miles up the valley of the Doulee from Joshimutt, we crossed the river by a narrow wooden bridge below the village of Tapoobun, and ascended the opposite heights, with a view to having a day or two among the tahr. After a long and stiff climb we reached our ground towards evening, and having selected a spot for our camp, proceeded to watch some steep green slopes, to which Puddoo expected the tahr would be likely to descend, from the craggy verdureless heights above, for their evening feed. We had not long to wait before we descried a herd of tehrny (female tahr) on their way down. They descended so rapidly that in the distance they looked like a lot of yellowish-brown balls hopping and rolling down over the crags, until all but two, that remained behind on the rocks, were hidden from view in an intervening grassy hollow. Presently four shaggy old bucks followed them, performing the most eccentric gambols in their descent. These were soon joined by three other old fellows coming from a different direction. At last there were none left in sight but the two tehrny, which still kept their positions like sentinels on the rocks above. We waited patiently for them to move down, until it grew so late that, at the risk of their detecting us, we commenced crawling cautiously on towards the hollow. We had almost reached a spot which commanded it, when up got a chuckor partridge in front of us. This was bad enough, but it was much worse when, a little farther on, the rest of the covey rose with a whirr! and flew right over the hollow. On carefully raising my head to reconnoitre, I could see at a glance that the tahr had taken alarm and were on the alert. One old buck stood within easy range, gazing straight towards me; but before I could cover him, he was galloping away with the rest of the herd down the hollow. I let drive at a big black fellow that was leading, and thought I had hit him, though he still continued his course. We followed up at once, and soon came on our friend as he lay, looking very sick, behind a rock. Another shot sent him off again into some precipitous ground, where we could see him standing rather groggily on a ledge; but it had now grown too dark to follow him farther that evening. Fortunately there was a bright moon to light us back to our camp, which was about two miles off, and some of the footing was not of the best.

That night I witnessed from our camp a remarkably beautiful moonlight effect. As the moon sank towards the irregular ridge of the summit of Trisool,[1] rising 22,300 feet high, away across the misty depths of the Doulee valley far below, the immense snow-fields that lay along its upper slopes glistened

[1] So called by the natives from its irregular summit being supposed to resemble a "trisool" or trident, which is by Hindoos regarded as symbolical of their divine triad—Brahma, the creator; Vishnu, the preserver; Siva, the destroyer.

like broad sheets of burnished silver in the sheen of the moonbeams that played on them, causing the shadowy forms of the adjacent snow-peaks to loom all the more dim and unearthly in their pallid solemnity.

Early next morning we went to look after our wounded tahr.˙ We found him lying dead at the foot of the precipice where he had fallen, evidently from the very ledge on which we had last seen him standing. A shaggy, black old buck he was too, with horns nearly 14 inches long.

Although I saw many more tehrny and young bucks, I had no further sport among the great old tahr during the remainder of the short time I was up here. There were, however, ample and continual sources of delight in the ever-changing views of the grand frozen peaks in the neighbour-hood, as seen from these heights. One charming prospect I especially remember. As the last rays of the setting sun, shooting out from under a cloud-bank of violet, crimson, and gold, shed a ruddy glow on the snowy slopes of Trisool, and the half-naked crest (over 25,600 feet high) of Nandadevi —the wall-like shoulders of which mighty mountain are so nearly vertical as in some places to leave the pale-coloured rock quite bare of snow—the effect was truly magnificent.

On the evening I returned to Tapoobun, some villagers came running to tell me that a bear was in a corn-field close by. On reaching the place, sure enough there I could in-distinctly see a black object among the corn. But thinking, from its being so close to the village, it might possibly be a human being enveloped in a black blanket, I refrained from shooting until the brute hustled off, when I missed my chance at him in the dusky twilight. Good black-partridge shooting might have been got about here, had the birds been in proper season, judging from the number of cocks that were crowing in the vicinity.

Above this the Doulee valley grows much narrower, and its flanking heights more lofty and precipitous—so much so

that, although up here you are in the midst of vast snowy
mountains, the higher white peaks and ridges are only now
and then visible from the bottom of the valley, either through
lateral gaps or when they seem to terminate the glen you are
in. The river, too, now becomes more impetuous, as it leaps
furiously down among huge masses of rock in a succession
of roaring cataracts. Altogether the scenery here begins to
assume a more savagely grand character. Soon after crossing
the Reni bridge over the Rishi gunga (river)—a wild torrent
fed by the snow-fields and glaciers around Nandadevi—where
it flows into the Doulee, the eye is at once attracted by a
remarkable cascade on the north side of the latter river. The
water pours down from a tremendous height, in a narrow
white stream, over a perfectly smooth and nearly perpendicular face of dark rock. It has only one break in its long
descent, where it falls into a deep receding cavity evidently
hollowed out by the constant action of the water behind a
ledge on the cliff; thence it leaps forth and continues its
precipitate course in an unbroken line for many hundred
feet. When in flood, this waterfall, which is called Bingareebeyl, has a singularly fine effect. As we trudged along,
Puddoo beguiled the time with a wonderful legend about
this place, which was, as near as I can translate it, to the
following effect:—

"In the village of Lātā, on the opposite side of the Doulee
to Bingareebeyl, there once lived a big strong fellow named
Deena. From his constant bullying and overbearing ways,
he had made himself so thoroughly objectionable to his
fellow-villagers that they at last resolved to dispose of him.
The difficulty, however, was as to how they should accomplish this, for they all dreaded him; besides which, they did
not wish it to appear as though they had actually committed
murder, until one day the long-wished-for opportunity presented itself.

"Some men who had been hunting among the crags above

the cascade returned to the village with a story of their having killed a big tahr, which they were unable to bring back owing to its having fallen down Bingareebeyl and lodged on the ledge there. On hearing this, Deena, who was as plucky as he was powerful, and prided himself on being a daring climber, volunteered, as was expected, to recover the tahr by clambering down to the ledge on a rope. Having succeeded in reaching the tahr, he cut off its legs, which were each hauled up by his companions above. But instead of letting the rope down again, they shouted to Deena that he might keep the carcass as food for himself, and straightway departed, leaving him to his fate.

"As he sat there pondering hopelessly over his desperate position, a big 'gooroor' (lammergeyer), attracted by the remains of the tahr, came soaring past, when a happy idea struck Deena as to how he might possibly effect his escape. Unwinding the girdle of rope the paharrees usually wear, he tied himself with it to the carcass, under which he contrived to conceal himself. As he expected, the gooroors soon came circling round, and as each one alighted on the carcass he stealthily seized its legs and secured them in nooses, made with bits of unravelled rope he had attached to the ribs, until he had thus caught a sufficient number of the birds for his purpose. He then gave a loud shout, which had the effect of making the affrighted gooroors simultaneously flap their wings and lift him, with the carcass, from the ledge, the result being to deposit him safely on *terra firma* below. On the unexpected and seemingly supernatural reappearance of their enemy among them, the astonished and terrified villagers fled, leaving him in sole occupation of Lātā, though not before he had taken his revenge. They eventually, however, came to terms with him; but he made the place hotter than ever for them on their return to it."

As I happened to breakfast by the wayside near Lātā, on my broaching this subject to some of the villagers who brought me milk, they entertained me with a corroboration of Puddoo's version of the tale, and positively declared " it was all quite true."

Our next halt was at Seraitota, so called from some "serai" (cypress) trees growing in the vicinity. We camped at the foot of a wild gorge, which, on a former visit to these parts, I had explored with Puddoo, who, well as he knew these mountains, had never previous to that time been more than a mile or two up it. As our expedition was not altogether uneventful, I shall here make a digression, and endeavour to briefly relate our experiences.

At first Puddoo had tried to dissuade me from going up this glen by telling me it was held in bad repute by the villagers, who believed it to be the haunt of an evil spirit, and that the tahr there bore charmed lives. The real truth, I suspect, was, that being my first expedition with him, he was doubtful as to what my capabilities might be at mountain work, and therefore wished to avoid the responsibility of having taken me to a place where the ground was reported to be excessively bad, in the event of any accident occurring. However, on returning to Seraitota, after hunting with him farther up the Doulee valley, he made no more objections to our visiting this " enchanted glen." [1]

At the hamlet of Tolma, hard by, we secured the services of the "pādān" (head-man), a queer old character named Ganna, and also of two or three stout fellows to assist the lower-range coolies I had brought with me thus far, who were quite unaccustomed to carrying loads over such ground as they would have to encounter up here. For some distance we had no difficulty in getting along, up beside the torrent, until the gorge took the form of an acute-angled V, where the

---

[1] This wild cañon is, I think, one of those alluded to by Mr Graham in a graphic account, read at a meeting of the Royal Geographical Society in June 1884, of his attempt to reach the summits of the Doonagiri and Nandadevi peaks. Even he, an experienced Alpine climber, remarks, "It is impossible to exaggerate the difficulties of traversing these cañons."

rocks rose so abruptly from the water that we were obliged to take a higher route along the steep hill-face. Each moment the ground became more frightful, until at last it seemed as though further progress were next thing to impossible. Ganna now took the lead as we essayed to cross a terribly steep incline at a height of several hundred feet above the raging rock-bound torrent, where the short slippery grass that partially covered the almost vertical slope served only to make the footing more precarious. There was no way of turning this place, unless perhaps by making a very long round above. For about 150 yards there was often absolutely nothing between this world and the next but the breadth of less than half a footsole, chipped with the iron-shod point of an alpenstock, out of the hard ground, in such places as there happened to be no protruding scraps of rock which might afford better footing. As Puddoo remarked, " For ourselves it was hazardous enough, but for the laden men it would be positively dangerous."

On our reaching more practicable ground we waited for the coolies to come up, as my two companions seemed to have misgivings about the lower-range men being able to proceed any farther with their loads. As we expected, when they got to the bad bit they stopped, and called out to us that they objected to crossing it. But Puddoo shouted jeeringly back, taunting them with being no mountain-men, and telling them that if they were afraid to come on they had better go home and fetch their women to help them, and suchlike banter, until they at last agreed to break up their loads and bring the things over a few at a time. I was much relieved in mind when they all arrived safely at the only possible place we could find near at hand to bivouac on—for camping was out of the question—which they never would have reached with their loads, had it not been for Puddoo's persuasive powers, and the assistance of the Tolma men who were with them. The spot we had selected was a narrow sloping shelf

above the rocky linn, where, by dint of clearing off big stones
and scraping away earth, we managed to get just sufficient
space for sticking up my little tent, after a fashion, against the
face of a high beetling crag, my followers finding the best
shelter they could in holes and crannies among the rocks.

In the afternoon, as I sat scanning the steep ground across
the torrent, I could see several young bucks and some tehrny
on the crags. At last I detected a solitary old tahr almost
hidden among some birch bushes growing on a sloping ledge,
where he was browsing on the young leaves. In the distance
his shaggy coat looked quite black as I caught occasional
glimpses of him through the spy-glass. After planning our
stalk, I started with Puddoo and Ganna to try and circumvent him. With considerable difficulty we clambered down
to the torrent, where it was spanned by a bed of hard snow,
and thence climbed up through a steep wood of tall black
pines until we were nearly level with the tahr. He was still
browsing among the birch bushes, at what I judged to be
about 150 yards distant across a precipitous rocky gully.
After recovering my wind I rested the rifle against a pine-
tree, took a steady aim, and let drive. "He's hit!" exclaimed
Puddoo, as the beast seemed to shoot headlong into the gully
and out of sight. I was congratulating myself on having, as
I thought, secured so fine a specimen, when Puddoo excitedly
whispered, "Look! there he is again," as, to my great surprise, the tahr suddenly reappeared on our side of the gully.
As he stopped short to listen and look about him among some
fallen pine-trunks within easy range directly below us, I again
took a careful shot over a prostrate tree, which offered a convenient rest. "You've surely got him this time!" said Puddoo, as the animal seemed to fall over backwards among the
fallen trees. After reloading the rifle, we moved down in confident expectation of finding him lying dead; but nothing was
there but the marks ploughed up by his hoofs, where he had
evidently galloped headlong down hill. We followed the

track as far as we could do so without risking being benighted on our return over such awful ground, but not a drop of blood was there to be seen on it.

We had recrossed the torrent on our way back, and had reached a narrow and almost perpendicular cleft between a smooth wall of rock and a hard bank of old snow: a very awkward place, which, from being scarcely wider than a man's body, it required considerable exertion both of arms and legs to ascend. Puddoo went first, and reached the top. I followed next, and had elbowed myself half-way up, when, in endeavouring to clutch at a niche above me, I in some manner wrenched my weak shoulder, and instantly felt I had dislocated it. Calling out for assistance, I fortunately managed to support myself with the one arm and my knees until Ganna reached me from below, and Puddoo, who had divested himself of his shoes, had climbed down from above to extricate me from my unpleasant and somewhat critical position. On reaching a spot where there was space enough to lie down, with Puddoo's assistance the joint was soon replaced—for, since my first accident of a similar nature on the Pir Punchal, the experience of several repetitions of it had taught me how to act in such an emergency, and consequently I thought little of it. My companions gravely shook their heads, and I overheard them making sundry mysterious allusions to the evil reputation of the glen. A wild and eerie-looking spot this certainly was, with its frowning precipices, beetling crags, and tall black pines. As the shades of night closed down on our gloomy surroundings, the big owls began their dismal hootings from the dark echoing pine-wood across the torrent, as if deriding our futile attempt on the charmed life of that black old tahr.

During the night I was suddenly startled from a restless and rather feverish sleep—the natural consequence of my little mishap—by the sound of an avalanche of rocks and stones that came rattling down a steep gully some twenty yards from where I lay. This was followed by the occasional fall of a loose pebble on the canvas of my tent, suggesting to my disturbed imagination the idea of impending danger from above, which kept me wakeful until morning. It was therefore not surprising, taking all things into consideration, that next day my nervous system was slightly upset, and that I was quite unfit for mountain work. My cook regarding me, I suppose, in the light of an invalid, had considerately prepared a surprise for me in the shape of some delicious jelly, all duly moulded and flavoured, which he had made from tahr meat. How he had contrived to produce such a delicacy in the little rocky hole he had selected for his kitchen, was a marvel of culinary skill. But the expedients resorted to on a pinch by your Indian Francatelli, and the celerity with which he can in an emergency prepare you an excellent meal, are always marvellous.

Towards dusk Puddoo, in a state of excitement which was quite unusual to his ordinarily rather phlegmatic temperament, came hurrying to tell me he had just seen what he felt sure was the tahr I had shot at the evening before, moving among the birch bushes on the same ledge we had at first descried him. Getting out the telescope, there, sure enough, I could see a big black tahr just disappearing behind the bushes. As he did not again show himself before dark, Puddoo thought he would be unlikely to move far away during the night. That it could be our old friend, I, however, considered highly improbable—though Puddoo positively declared he could recognise in it the same uncanny beast, which had now returned to its favourite haunt to feed there on the birch-sprouts.

Next morning, as soon as it was light enough to see the opposite crags, all eyes were turned towards them—for every one of my followers, even to the cook, seemed to have become imbued with an excited sort of interest in that mysterious old tahr; but not a sign of him could we see. Except for being unable to freely use my left arm, I was now tolerably fit again. I therefore proposed visiting some ground farther up the glen, which Ganna reported as being a pretty sure find for old bucks. We were just about to start, when it struck me that I had better take one more look through the glass towards the birch bushes on the ledge. This time I noticed through an interstice among the branches a dark patch which I had hitherto not observed. After steadily watching it for some time I imagined I saw it move. At last all doubt was dispelled by the branches above it being shaken to and fro. Directing Puddoo's attention to it, I handed him the telescope. After a long look through it he suddenly ejaculated, " It's that —— again !" using an expressive but unmentionable term of native abuse towards the animal.

Our proposed arrangement for the day was now upset, for even if this were not the big tahr I had shot at, it was his exact counterpart; at any rate it was unlikely that a finer would be found elsewhere. This time the whole day was before us, so we resolved to try a stalk from a different direction. Owing to the precipitous nature of the ground, it would necessarily be a very much longer and more difficult business, but would, we thought, bring us much nearer our game. After about two hours' climbing, imagine our disappointment on finding that the animal's position was quite hidden below the spot which, from the other side of the glen, we had supposed would command it within easy range ; and we could discover no other means of approaching it, from this side at any rate, without our being seen by the tahr. The only plan we could now devise was to send Ganna to try and steal round beyond the place from above, on the chance that, by flinging down a stone, he might frighten the animal back towards us. But the crafty beast must have decamped in some other direction than ours, for not a sign did we ever see or hear of him. If an evil genius presided over this glen, I now began myself almost to think that it must have been embodied, for the time being, in that black old buck. For not only did he seem to bear a charmed life himself, but he had effectually succeeded in inveigling us away from other animals we might have found elsewhere. How heartily did I join with my companions in anathematising the brute, as, with only one of my arms to trust to for support, I wearily scrambled back by even a more breakneck, though a much less circuitous, route than the one by which we had come out.

Soon after daybreak next morning we were making the best of a bad way up the side of the glen. We scrambled along for about a mile and a half, and then struck up a lateral gorge, where our work soon became comparatively easy and the ground more open. Here we found many fresh tracks of big tahr, and altogether the place looked a perfect sanctuary for game. We started several musk-deer, for which the nature of the ground was particularly well suited, there being many strips and patches of birch and rhododendron bushes alternating with rocky gullies. I killed one of the little animals which offered an irresistibly tempting chance, a rather unwise proceeding where there was every probability of the shot disturbing the game we were more especially in quest of. Thence we ascended a long steep gully, flanked with rhododendron bushes and birches, in order to prospect the ground on the farther side of a high ridge, from which the gully ran down.

On reaching the crest of the ridge, the superb prospect that suddenly burst in sight was in itself a more than adequate compensation for all the difficulty and trouble undergone to obtain it. Anything more weirdly grand in the shape of a snow-scene it would have been difficult to find. There, facing us, immediately across a wide treeless abyss, stood the pale spectral form of Doonagiri "purbat" (high mountain), its gigantic proportions abruptly rising in vast cliffs and slopes of solid ice and snow until they culminated in a glistening white peak over 23,000 feet high. Although I had become habituated, I may say, to grand mountain-scenery, the effect produced on me by the startling revelation of this mighty frozen pile, and my unexpected proximity to it, was such, that at first it inspired an almost overpowering sensation of mingled wonder and awe, until the shrinking eye gradually became more accustomed to its dazzling magnificence. What an insignificant atom of mortality I felt as I silently contemplated this stupendous immutable work of nature! If any Alpine traveller can imagine himself brought suddenly face to face with the Jungfrau, as viewed from the Mengern Alp, but considerably exaggerated, and with a towering cone of snow piled above it, he may perhaps be able to form some idea of what was before me, and of my feelings whilst I stood regarding it. As the morning wore on, huge masses of snow, detached by the sun's heat, began thundering down with a dull booming sound like salvoes of distant artillery.

Several noonday hours were passed on the ridge resting and watching for game. Towards the afternoon, as we sat under the rhododendrons, where we had been sheltering from a shower of hail, we descried two tahr far up among the craggy ground across the wide hollow we had last ascended from, and almost directly above where I had killed the musk-deer. Three more soon put in an appearance still higher up, and all were fine old fellows. They took some time to make up their minds to descend towards the greener slopes lower down, my shot at the musk-deer having probably made them suspicious of danger below. Once started, however, they lost no time on their way, as they rattled down with the succession of playful skips and bounds by which these wild goats are often wont to seemingly show their glee at the prospect of their evening meal. It was very interesting to observe them through the glass, with their long shaggy hair tossing wildly about in the wind, as they reared up and butted at each other in their gambols, sometimes appearing as though they were knocked headlong, or had even fallen backwards, down from crag to crag. How little did they know they were being watched with deadly intent! At length they all settled quietly down to feed, upon which we at once proceeded to gird up our loins for the business before us. Two men we had brought with us for carrying game were left as markers on the ridge, with directions not to leave it unless the tahr should move off before we could get within range of them. As we left the ridge I turned a parting look towards Doona-giri, where the bluish-grey shadows were now growing longer and deeper, and the declining sun was beginning to tinge the western slopes of the mighty frozen pile with a beautiful golden light.

The long narrow gully we had ascended to the ridge was unfortunately in full view of the tahr, and there was no other way of getting down, but we trusted to being able to descend it unobserved by keeping as much as possible under cover of the rhododendrons on either side. An hour's work from the ridge brought us within what we judged must be pretty close under where we had last seen the tahr from below, and as our markers had not left the ridge, we knew the animals had not moved away. But the evil genius of the glen, in the shape of ill-luck, seemed still to dog our footsteps. To our dismay a dense cloud of mist now came whirling round from below and soon hid everything above. The wind, too, which had hitherto been right, suddenly shifted and blew straight up towards the tahr. In vain was all our patient waiting until the mist cleared off, for when it temporarily did so, we saw that our markers had quitted their post, from which we knew that our game was up and gone. They afterwards told us that the tahr were all lying within 150 yards, directly above us, at the time we became enveloped in the mist.

As it was now getting late, our guide proposed that, instead of our returning by the long round below, we should take a shorter way he knew of over the mountain above. Now short cuts are not invariably the easiest or the quickest, and more especially when they have to be made through the clouds. It was all very well for Ganna with his habitually naked feet and toes as prehensile as a monkey's, and for Puddoo, who could without inconvenience go barefooted when he chose; but, for myself with my boots, had I known what I was being let in for, I think that, considering all things, my weak shoulder included, I should have chosen the longer route. We continued our steep ascent until we reached what appeared, through the clouds that enveloped our more distant surroundings, to be a ridge of huge rugged rocks, from whence a dark narrow chasm descended abruptly into infinite misty space below. Black wall-like crags rose on both sides of a narrow strip of hard snow, shooting downward at an angle of something less than 45 degrees. Down this gloomy forbidding-looking abyss our way now led. We commenced the descent by lowering ourselves over an almost perpendicular face of rock for some twenty feet on to the sloping slippery snow-bed, down which we went slowly and carefully, having often to notch the hard snow for foothold. Thus we proceeded over alternate snow and bare rock, with the same clouded emptiness still below us, until we must have descended at least 1000 feet, when the monotony of our precarious and seemingly endless undertaking was varied by a musk-deer starting up close to us. As he stood to look back within twenty-five paces, his dim shadowy form looming large and spectre-like through the mist, I got hold of the rifle from Puddoo, who was carrying it, and rolled him over; but as he contrived to struggle away for a short distance down the rocks, we had some trouble in securing him. This caused considerable delay; consequently, by the time Ganna had shouldered him, the already waning light had almost failed us. Down and still down we scrambled through the murky mist, until at length it grew so dark as to make it next thing to impossible to move a step without danger of missing our footing. Matters were now getting rather serious, for our guide, in reply to my repeated and anxious inquiries as to how far we had yet to descend, had rather unwillingly

2 c

informed me that there was still some "mooskhil" (difficulty) below us. Moreover, I had casually discovered that we were in the very gully down which the avalanche of rocks and stones had fallen two nights before. I was just beginning to realise the disagreeable probability of our having to pass a. cold gruesome night in an upright position on some narrow ledge of rock, when, to my infinite relief of mind, I heard voices below, which were joyously replied to, and ere long the welcome glimmer of a light appeared dimly struggling up through the fog. Our two markers, who were Tolma men, after picking up the musk-deer I had killed in the morning, had returned to our bivouac by the lower route, and knowing the difficulties of the upper one, which they thought it probable Ganna, to save time, would take up the gully, had, on its growing dark, started to meet us, accompanied by my Goorkha servant carrying a lantern. Another half-hour of very ticklish work took us down to the tent, after a direct descent of several thousand feet, a great part of which might, under the circumstances, have fairly been termed rather perilous.

My time being then limited, I was reluctantly obliged next day to quit this excellent though to me unlucky bit of tahr-ground, by the same difficult way we had got at it. But let us now resume our present trip, and in another chapter try a turn at the burrell for a change.

CHAPTER XXII.

DOONAGIRI VILLAGE—A HIMALAYAN GLACIER—BURRELL - GROUND—
KILL TWO RAMS—FEMALE PORTERS—FINE OLD DEODAR - TREES—
BHŌTIA VILLAGES OF KOSA AND MALĀRI — BURGLARIOUS BEARS—
SOLITUDE AND DESOLATION—BHŌTIAS, MALE AND FEMALE—GOOSE-
BERRY AND CURRANT BUSHES—ROCK-SLIPS—PROVIDENTIAL ESCAPES
FROM THEM—NITI VILLAGE—STRANGE COLLECTION OF OLD SHOES—
TIBETAN ENVOY—THE "JOOBOO"—FROM NITI TO GOTING—SUMMER
AVALANCHES—OLD BIRCH-TREES—SNOW-PHEASANTS—BAD WALKING
—A DAY'S SPORT AT GOTING—AN AWKWARD BRIDGE—ALPINE ROSE—
A GRAND OLD RAM—A MISTAKE—A SNOW-LEOPARD SHARES OUR
SPOILS—WILD DEFILE—THE NITI PASS—VIEW OF HUNDÉS FROM ITS
SUMMIT—A NOTEWORTHY WATERSHED — SKETCHING UNDER DIFFI-
CULTIES—A TERRIBLY COLD CAMP—A DEPUTATION FROM THE JONG-
PEN—OUR HOONYA ESCORT.

BELOW the northern slopes of Doonagiri purbat, in the
middle of an immense kind of corrie several miles broad, lies
a Bhōtia hamlet bearing the same name as the mountain, at
an elevation of nearly 12,000 feet. The broken grassy slopes
about the foot of a big glacier which runs down the east side of
the purbat and discharges itself into this huge natural amphitheatre, are, early in the season, a favourite resort of burrell,
before the villagers take their flocks up there for the summer
pasturage. Thither, therefore, I now resolved to direct my
steps.

Crossing the Doulee by a rude wooden bridge, we proceeded
for several miles along its opposite bank, where the rocks
sometimes rose so directly from the river as to necessitate
their being passed on rough loose planks or poles supported

on stakes driven into crevices below them. Blue pigeons,
which were plentiful among the overhanging rocks, afforded
some pretty shooting on the way, and were acceptable for the

A " Sanga," or wooden bridge.

pot. In consideration of their being the latter, I was not too
proud to take a family-shot at them on the ground, if I had
a chance. On one of these occasions I "shot at the pigeon
and hit the crow," not figuratively but actually, when I
unwittingly sacrificed a red-billed specimen of the jackdaw
tribe (Cornish chough) which had the misfortune to be feeding in the line of fire. Recrossing the Doulee next morning
by another very rustic, and in this instance rather rickety
bridge, we struck up a narrow and deep glen, as romantic
and wild as forest and crag could make it, passing the pic-
turesquely-built little wooden chålet of Rwing about a mile
from its foot. After ascending 4000 odd feet from the river,
in a distance of only five or six miles, we reached the afore-
mentioned wide and elevated mountain-basin, and camped
close beside the hamlet, to which the Bhōtia inhabitants had
only just returned from their winter sojourn below. The
village pādān was most attentive and obliging, and willing

to give us all the assistance and information we required regarding game. Up here we were almost above the limit of forest, except for a few birch-trees and rhododendron bushes, which latter were all abloom with pure white and pale lilac blossoms.

As we left the hamlet next morning and took our way up towards the glacier, the snowy heights above were just being tipped with a pale rosy reflection, though the dawning light was still dim and grey below. The crisp frosty air was pinching cold, but an hour's sharp walking warmed us up. On reaching the foot of the glacier, we stopped to take a careful survey of the neighbouring slopes. There were three small flocks of burrell visible, but the spy-glass showed that they contained no old rams; so we let them be, and went on upward along the lateral moraine of the glacier in search of something better. Nothing more, however, being discovered, I got on to the glacier and proceeded up over it, more from curiosity regarding it than with any idea of finding game farther up. The ice was grey and very dirty, with few crevasses, and the surface, though lumpy, irregular, and thickly strewn with large stones, was quite easy to traverse.

I have before mentioned the enormous size of Himalayan glaciers. They do not, however, often present in their lower formation the broken, split-up, and white appearance of Alpine ones. For this you must here ascend to a very high altitude, where the ice and *névé* are as pure as in the Alps. There are very few glaciers in the Himalayas which descend lower than 11,000 feet. The temperature at that elevation is said to be much the same as that of 3000 feet in the Alps. Owing to the heat and melting power of the sun, the lower part of a glacier is here much more covered with stones and dirt than in more northern latitudes. Here you may walk for miles over the lower part of a glacier and not see any ice. Nor do you notice the beautiful azure blue so much in the depths of holes and fissures of Himalayan glaciers; in their lower parts not at all. As the ice-fall in these mountains is much higher and more difficult of access than in the Alps, the ordinary traveller, who here usually sees only the lower and more level portions of glaciers, is apt to imagine them to be totally devoid of the beautiful colouring of Alpine ones. There is just a possibility that, if it is less vivid here, this may be due to the fact of Himalayan glaciers lying at much higher elevations, where the air is thinner, and the refraction of light consequently less: but the probability of such being the case I leave for scientists to determine. The following account of a trip over a high and difficult pass between Pindree and Murtolee, in Kumaon, by Colonel E. Smyth (to whom I am indebted for several interesting and graphic accounts of his mountain adventures, which he has kindly permitted me to insert in these pages), gives an excellent idea of the higher regions of a Himalayan glacier:—

"This pass had only been crossed twice within the memory of man—once about fifty years ago by Mr Traill, and in 1855 or 1856 by one of the Schlagintweits. I crossed it at the end of September 1861. I sent my baggage and servants round to Milum and Murtolee by the regular road, and merely took one load of bedding and clothes with me, and accompanied a friend as far as Pindree. Next morning my friend went with me, and we breakfasted on the glacier and then parted. He agreed to remain at Pindree until he could be certain that I had crossed safely. I took eight or nine Danpore villagers with me. My guide was old Ram Sing, so well known to all travellers to Pindree. He was one of the finest-made hill-men I ever knew, and though more than sixty, I found he had more pluck and endurance than all the rest. He had crossed this pass on the two occasions I have mentioned.

"My road lay up the right bank of the glacier for seven or eight miles, and I bivouacked in a cave at an elevation of 15,000 feet, overlooking the Pindree glacier. In this seven or eight miles, I had to cross two or three small side-glaciers.

On this occasion I had left Almora in the middle of September, about the worst season of the year for travelling, and my road to Pindree lay up the valley of the Surjoo, a particularly hot and unhealthy valley; and all this had not been a very good preparation for crossing a very high and difficult pass. We had had a great deal of rain on the way up, and the leeches had been very troublesome. I lay awake all this night with a very bad toothache, and in the morning felt anything but fit for a hard day's work. All these Danpoorees, on the contrary, seemed as gay as larks, and were playing each other practical jokes. We breakfasted before daybreak, and ascended the hillside about 2000 feet, when we reached the top of a range and descended 200 or 300 feet on to a glacier, which we never left for the rest of the day. Our way lay over this glacier for about five miles. The slope was very gentle, and there was no difficulty whatever in this part of our journey, beyond meeting, now and then, broad crevasses; but we managed to turn them all. We then reached the crest of the pass (at an elevation of about 18,000 feet), which is a depression in the ridge that connects Nundadevi (25,700 feet) with Nunda-kote (24,000 feet). Up to this the sun had been very bright, and the glare so painful that I had not been able to look about me. For the last five miles I had seen nothing but snow and glacier, both singularly pure and free from *débris* and rocks, and the glacier broken up into chasms and pinnacles of pure ice of most fantastic shape, and of colours varying from deep blue to deep green, according to the light thrown on them.

" On arrival at the crest of the pass, I found before me a descent of about 2000 feet, over snow much too steep to descend. At first we thought of tying ourselves together and sliding down. This we should have done if it had not been for some broad ugly-looking crevasses down below, that appeared open-mouthed ready to receive us. I sent men to the right and left to see if there were any better place to commence the descent from, but they returned unsuccessful. It was now about 2 P.M., the clouds had come up, and it began to snow and hail. The wind at the same time arose, and the snow was flying about up our noses and into our eyes, ears, &c. These coolies who had been so lively but a few hours before began to give in ; some lay down to go to sleep. There was a ledge of rocks that seemed to run up from below to within a quarter of a mile of where we were. Ram Sing and another man took the two axes and commenced to cut steps towards these rocks along this steep slope of snow. I employed myself in keeping these wretched coolies from going to sleep until Ram Sing and his companion had proceeded about 100 yards. I then made them all get up and follow. We kept along the same level, and the slope was so steep that while standing upright our left hands were buried in the snow as we proceeded. It took us two hours to go over this quarter of a mile. A false step would have sent any one of us 2000 feet down the snow, probably into a crevasse below. My left hand soon became quite benumbed from cold, and I did not quite recover from its effects for several months. We reached the ledge of rocks safely, and climbed down to the glacier below, and then went four or five miles over the glacier to an empty kurruck (or shieling) below. Next morning seven or eight miles took me to Murtolee. Tradition says that this pass used to be in common use ages ago, but has been blocked up by glacier.

" Two or three of my Danpoorees were snow-blind for a day or two after this trip."

People in India have not yet taken to attempting ascents of the highest mountains. Of late years the few members of the Alpine Club who have come to the Himalayas for that purpose, have found the native shikarees and guides, who are unequalled as cragsmen, to be quite useless as ice-men. The fact is, they seldom have any occasion to cross glaciers. Very few of the passes usually traversed lead over them, and in the pursuit of game glaciers are avoided, as no game is found near their higher regions. Another reason why these "paharees" are so helpless on ice is, that they are so badly shod. Boots are unknown among them, and many of them only wear shoes on festive occasions. Moreover, every high snow-peak is regarded by these mountaineers, who are mostly Hindoos, with superstitious awe, as the abode of one or other of their deities, whom they fear to offend. Himalayan guides will doubtless improve at ice work ere long, if their services are in demand for that purpose. The Cashmere mountaineers, who are chiefly Mahomedans, and who have their lower extremities protected by sandals and bandages, are much more at home on steep snow-slopes and ice.

After going up one of the Doonagiri glaciers—for there are two which unite—a considerable distance, I got such a racking headache, probably from the combined effects of the intense heat of the sun on the glacier and the cutting wind that came sweeping over it, that I was forced to return. The evening was spent watching, with the spy-glass, the movements of two or three small lots of burrell that were feeding on a rugged, partially grass-clad slope away across a deep and wide treeless hollow, down which ran the broken torrent that drained the glacier. As there were several good-looking heads in one of the flocks, I resolved to be after them on the morrow.

Not caring to ford the deep rapid snow-stream the first thing in the morning, we took a longer way to cross it dry-footed, up over the bottom of the glacier; consequently we were a considerable time reaching our ground, close as it appeared in a direct line. At the early hour we had set out, it was too dark to take a look with the glass across the hollow, but on nearing the place where, the evening before, I had last seen the burrell, we descried a flock with rams in it away down below. Whilst attempting to approach these, another lot we had not noticed above, and which evidently contained the bigger-horned fellows we wanted to find, got intelligence of us and betook themselves far up the slope, until they apparently thought they were well out of danger, as after a time they all lay down. A misty drizzling shower of rain now began to fall, which, as the footing was easy and the ground somewhat open, rather favoured our movements than otherwise; consequently we had little difficulty in reaching a spot within eighty yards or so of where we had seen the animals lie down. On reconnoitring them from behind a rock, I saw they had risen and were slowly moving off, as if they had just got wind of us. There was no time to lose, so I let the biggest fellow have it, when down he went, rolling over and over among the rocks. The rest sped on, but as the ground they had to get over was rough and steep, I was able to get a chance at another ram before they all disappeared in succession round a sort of ledge overhanging a deep drop.

As we could see that the first ram was safely disposed of, we followed up as quickly as possible in order to mark the flock, for both Puddoo and I thought the second shot had also told. We had got round the ledge and were making our way over the crags beyond it, when Puddoo, who was tracking ahead, stopped short, and gazing downward, remarked, "There's no need to go farther, for look there!" The steep rocks below were smeared with blood, from which, and other unmistakable signs, it was evident that the wounded ram had toppled over and slid down them, though, from the drop beneath being so abrupt, we were unable to see how far he had gone. We now turned back and got down to where the first ram had fallen. He was a good beast, with thick horns about two feet long. After cutting off his head and cleaning him, we hid his carcass with stones from the soaring carrion-feeders, and then proceeded round below to look for the other animal. We found him lying quite dead, and considerably smashed by his tremendous fall among the rocks. Luckily his head, which was nearly as good as that of the first I had shot, was little injured. Well satisfied with our forenoon's sport, we made

straight for camp, which, by fording the stream, we reached
in a much shorter time than we had taken in coming out.

It was now the end of May, and as the Niti ghat was
several days' journey from here, I concluded it would be practicable for crossing by the time we got there. We therefore
struck our camp next day. Six buxom Bhōtia lasses assisted
in carrying our traps down as far as Rwing, where we camped
that evening. At first they were timid and shy, but soon
became more confident and communicative as they trudged
merrily along with their loads, laughing and joking as they
went. From here we easily reached the village of Malāri in
a day. The wild beauty of the Doulee valley below Malāri
is much added to by grand deodar cedars and cypress-trees
(*Cupressus torulosa*), which are scattered over the lofty overhanging crags. You see great old trees, some of them many
feet in diameter,[1] clinging by their gnarled roots to narrow
ledges or clefts on the faces of almost vertical precipices, and
you wonder how on earth they can stand and flourish there
as they do, with nothing apparently but the naked rock to
sustain them. On the opposite (north) side of the river, situated at the entrance of a narrow gap, through the vista of
which you can see a fine glacier rising white and broken, the
village of Kosa stands perched among the rocks, having, with
its projecting eaves and weather-stained timbers, all the picturesque look of a Swiss châlet. Up this gorge towards the
glacier is good ground for tahr. In fact all the lateral gorges
of the Doulee valley are, in their upper regions, the resorts of
either tahr or burrell; but in some of them the difficult
nature of the ground is such that I do not think I overrate it
when I affirm that unless one is tolerably free from the feeling of apprehension commonly termed "giddiness," hunting

---

[1] These two beautiful trees, which are the pride and ornament of the Himalayas, grow to a height of considerably over 200 feet, and in girth are
frequently met with 38 to 40 feet, at 4 or 5 feet from the ground. The timber
of both is excellent.

there is always more or less attended with risk. Indeed a great many of the native mountaineers themselves lose their lives in the pursuit of tahr.

The village of Malāri, consisting of about eighty houses, is situated, almost overhanging the river, in an open kind of basin, where the tolerably level ground is, in the summer months, taken every advantage of by the inhabitants for the cultivation of buckwheat (here called " phaper ") and barley. The Bhōtias having just reoccupied the place, it presented a much more cheerful aspect than it did on a former visit I had made to it earlier in the spring, when it was all silent and deserted, with the wooden roofs here and there torn up, where the bears had during the winter effected a burglarious entrance after the stores of grain. I found the burrell at that time low down on the slopes in the immediate neighbour-hood, and shot a ram there. The track upward to Niti had, in many places where it almost overhangs the river, been carried clean away by avalanches, or was blocked by huge pine-trees, rocks and *débris* lying over it, that had been swept down by them. In short, all above this was at that season solitude and desolation. Now the road had been cleared and repaired by the Bhōtias, with parties of whom, male and female, moving up with their goods and herds by easy stages to the higher villages, we found it thronged. The men wore long, light, drab-coloured woollen tunics, and continuations of the same material. The women were more gaily attired in coloured skirts and bodices, with a brown blanket tastefully and ingeniously wrapped about their upper persons so as to leave the arms free. A white cotton cloth was thrown over the head, drawn tight above the brows, fastened back behind the ears, and allowed to hang loosely down the back. Most of them sported jewellery in the shape of ear-rings, nose-rings, and necklaces. The men were stout and sturdy, and some of the young girls, with their olive complexions and ruddy cheeks, were pleasing and bright-looking, if not actually pretty.

This is the only place in the Himalayas where I noticed the real old British gooseberry. Here it grows wild, as well as the currant, which is common in many parts, both black and red. On my return here from Hundés, the gooseberries were well formed, although scarcely large enough at the time for a tart. They never ripen sufficiently to eat raw. Excellent wild rhubarb, too, is often to be found on the southern slopes of all the higher ranges, where it commences shooting up from its roots just after the winter snow melts off the ground. It is called " dolu " by the Bhōtias, and is the same as the Turkey rhubarb. Another kind called "taturee" is found on the northern slopes of the Himalayas and all over Tibet, in a cold dry climate.

After passing the Bhōtia hamlets of Bumpa and Gumsali, the path enters a narrow gorge, where the scenery for about a mile is magnificently wild. The raging river is flanked on each side by bare black cliffs and crags rising from the water to a stupendous height. Colonel E. Smyth, whose experience of this country extended over many years, and whose mountaineering exploits are so often quoted in these pages, tells me that in 1859 he found the road at this spot quite impassable. In fact, for a quarter of a mile he said it was quite obliterated. A landslip had commenced the year before from the overhanging heights. Every two or three minutes, day and night, great stones came thundering down. This state of things went on without intermission for about two years, when it stopped quite suddenly. The road was then remade, and has never since been interrupted. In his many wanderings among the higher ranges, Colonel Smyth had two very narrow escapes from these rock-slips, of which the following are the short but thrilling narratives he has kindly favoured me with :—

" Twenty-two years ago I was very fond of exploring, and I determined to cross from Ralum, in the Johar valley of Kumaon, into the Darma valley, by a pass which had long been disused. The people in Ralum endeavoured to dissuade me. They told me it was three long days' journey over glaciers and snow-peaks, that no one then alive had traversed it, that the difficulties were insuperable, &c., &c. Natives are very much inclined to talk in this way when they don't want you to go to some place you wish to see, so I was determined to go. However, in this instance I found they spoke the truth. The first day's journey lay mostly over glaciers, but there was no great difficulty, except that at the end of the day's journey I had to pitch my tent in the middle of a large glacier, on a great stone, at an elevation of 15,000 feet.

"Our next day's journey lay for about three hours over this glacier to the foot of the range we had to cross. The top of the range was concealed in a thick black cloud, and it was several hours before we discovered the cairn which had been built on the top of the pass ages ago. The top of the pass was nearly 19,000 feet above the sea. We descended the other side about 3000 feet, when we were brought up by a deep broad valley which descended from the snowy mountains on our left. Long before we reached the edge of this valley, our attention had been attracted to constant loud reports like cannon, which we soon discovered the cause of. The valley was about half a mile broad, and the sides and bottom of it were worn and polished quite smooth by constant avalanches of rocks and stones which have been falling for years and years from the mountains above. Night was coming on, and it was absolutely necessary for us to cross this somehow. Behind us was nothing but snow and glacier, in front of us this terrible valley, and rocks and stones falling in every direction while we were holding a consultation on the edge of it. To retreat would have been death from cold and starvation to some of my men; so we determined to run the gauntlet.

"There was a large overhanging rock in the centre of the valley, which looked as if it would afford shelter to two or three people, not more, from falling stones; so I despatched two men first, with directions to make their way as fast as possible to this shelter, take breath there for five minutes, and then run across to the other side. It was about a quarter of a mile to this shelter, and we all sat down and watched this forlorn hope with breathless suspense. They had gone about half-way when I saw a huge rock bounding down towards them. It seemed to strike one of them and then bound away again into the abyss below, and the man rolled over. But immediately he got up again, to our intense relief, and both of them reached the other side in safety. Presently afterwards the whole valley was alive with rocks and stones, and the noise was deafening. When this had nearly subsided, I started with two other men in the same way. There were many hair-breadth escapes from rocks, some of which whizzed close past us. I was struck on the arm by a small stone, but not much hurt. The rest of our party came over in twos and threes without accident, and I was never more thankful in my life than when the last man arrived safe on the other side. By dark we reached a place where were a few bushes and some running water, where we could encamp comfortably at an elevation of about 16,000 feet. Next morning we descended to Siboo, the highest village in Darma (13,000 feet) without difficulty.

" I was told that this landslip had been going on for thirty years or more. It may stop suddenly some day, like the smaller one between the villages of Gumsali and Niti, and the road may be opened again."

The other escape was equally providential :—

" It is now thirty-six years ago that I paid my first visit to Milum, and crossed the Oontadhura pass from Milum into Tibet. My first camp was Shelong, seven or eight miles from Milum. On arrival there I saw three ram Ovis burrell feeding on the hill 1500 feet above. These were the first burrell I had ever seen, and the stalk was successful. I rolled over the largest one with the first shot. The ground was very steep and difficult, composed of crumbling slate. The burrell rolled some 300 feet down a kind of water-course, and we followed, and after a good deal of clamber-ing, we reached the place where the burrell lay. My two men were beginning to gralloch him, and I had placed my two guns on the ground close to me and was standing by admiring the beast, when I heard a deafening noise up above, and looking up I saw the ravine we had just descended full of stones and rocks which were thundering down towards us. There was no time to avoid them; in an instant they were whizzing past us in every direction. I just remember that I was looking at one huge rock coming towards us, which I thought perhaps I might be able to avoid, when I heard a deafening noise close to me; another rock which I had not seen had fallen upon the stocks of my two guns, smashing them to pieces. The guns flew up into the air six or seven feet with the force of the blow, and one of the barrels exploded. I did not distinguish the noise of the explosion, and only knew it afterwards by finding the end of the gun-cover (which I had put on, as it was snowing at the time) all burnt. The force of the blow was such that the barrels of both guns were quite bent. The rock had only struck the stocks, so that the barrels were not flattened, or even dented. All four nipples were broken off flush with the barrel. The stocks were in splinters : one hammer of one of the guns was broken into three pieces. I picked up most of the pieces afterwards, until my men hurried me away, as another land-slip was so likely to follow. Most providentially none of us were struck."

Beyond the gorge above Gumsali the valley widens into an open space, where on a sloping spur lies the village of Niti, the highest in the valley, at an elevation of nearly 12,000 feet. A mile or so before reaching the village, a track branches off to the right, leading over the Chor Hōti pass. Although a shorter route into Hundés, it is considerably

higher than that over the Niti pass, and therefore not practicable as early in summer. The heights above the village,
where not too steep for anything to grow on, are thickly clad
with a kind of gorse, which, when covered with its pale golden
bloom, gives them quite a gorgeous appearance. A curious
thing that attracted my attention here was an extraordinary
collection of old cast-off shoes that were strewn over a flat
space immediately below the village. There must have been
several hundred, all looking black and shrivelled up from having probably lain buried there under the snows of many a
winter.

Here I learnt that the pass had been declared open by the
Tibetan vakeel (envoy), who, with his small retinue, had
arrived at Niti village after crossing it. The Niti pass,
which is only 16,600 feet, is often practicable earlier than
this, but then at the risk of falling avalanches and other
dangers, and only for pedestrians, the snow being too deep,
and on steep slopes too unstable, for baggage - animals to
travel over. The Hoonyas,[1] moreover, object to its being
crossed, even by the Bhōtias, before sending their vakeel
over to Niti to arrange matters of business with them
respecting the pass, which here separates the British and
Tibetan dominions. The " boss " of the party, a fine-looking
Tartar, paid me a visit at my tent. As he was to leave Niti
on his return homewards next day, I sent a polite message by
him to the " Jongpen," or governor of the district beyond the
pass, requesting his permission to hunt there. But few of the
Bhōtias having as yet returned to the village, I was delayed
here a day or two whilst " jooboos "[2] for carriage, and supplies
for our sojourn in Hundés, where nothing of the kind could be
procured, were being fetched from the Bhōtia encampments
lower down.

[1] The Tibetan inhabitants of Hundés are called Hoonyas.
[2] The " jooboo " is a cross between the yak and the ordinary horned cattle of
the Himalayas.

2 D

All arrangements being completed, I started on 6th June with fifteen laden jooboos, and eight Bhōtias to look after them. This may seem rather heavy marching-order for a sportsman's requirements; but having to carry with us an extra tent for the Bhōtia followers, a month's food for about a dozen people, and the baggage-animals having, moreover, to be lightly laden for getting over the snow-beds, which would still be lying deep along portions of our route, will account for it. The summit of the pass is about 25 miles from Niti village, beyond which the mountains, except for a few birch-trees, become bare and desolate. The first day we proceeded up the valley of the Doulee—here called the Niti —to a spot called Goting. Soon after leaving the village the way leads for some eight miles, in a succession of tiresome ups and downs where it crosses deep precipitous gullies, along a bare stony hill-face with so sharp a slope that you cannot see the river, although you can hear it roaring sullenly down its narrow rocky channel some 2000 feet, on an average, below. The track, which had not as yet been repaired by the Bhōtias, was narrow and broken, and in many parts had been carried clear away by slips of earth and snow, and broad beds of snow still lay hard, smooth, and terribly steep in some of the gullies we crossed. In such places we had ourselves to make it passable for the jooboos, with tools we carried with us for the purpose. As we went along we could sometimes see the summer avalanches — which are quite different from the more destructive ones of the early spring — coming tumbling down the rocky gullies on the steep mountain-face across the river; the streams of falling snow appearing in the distance to descend quite slowly, though they were really thundering down at a fearful rate. At one point we reached an elevation of nearly 15,000 feet, just before descending to Goting, which is about 13,000 feet. These altitudes I ascertained by my mountain aneroid, which I had had corrected at the headquarters of the great Trigono-

metrical Survey of India, at Dehra Doon, before starting.
Few aneroids, however, if any, are to be much depended on
above 15,000 feet at most.   Up to that height I found mine
wonderfully accurate at altitudes marked on the Survey
maps.   Above this it played all kinds of jinks, making the
summit of the Niti pass, for instance, which is well under
17,000 feet, to be over 20,000 feet; but on again descending
below 15,000 feet it resumed its normal good behaviour.

The camping-place of Goting is a small flat of green turf,
almost surrounded with abrupt scarps of earth overhanging
the river.   A solitary clump of birch-trees growing on a
slope hard by afforded a plentiful supply of fuel for our camp-
fire.   Some of these gaunt old specimens, with their gnarled
and crooked limbs, must have weathered the storms of cen-
turies.   One or two grey old giants I measured in this neighbourhood were nearly 15 feet in girth.   These were the last
trees we saw beyond Niti.   Before the snow melts off the
neighbouring heights, the slopes about Goting are good for
several days' burrell-shooting, and there, on a former visit, I
got the biggest horned ram of the kind I ever killed.   As he
afforded me a capital day's sport, I shall here devote a page
or two to his memory.

As I had no intention of crossing the pass that season, I
reached Niti much earlier in the year.   The village then
looked tristful and forlorn in its emptiness.   The snow still
lay in broad patches on the heights close above it, and the
burrell were all low down.   As we left the village for Goting
in the grey of early morning, the only living sound that broke
the still frosty air was the wild whistling call of the "heoon-
wal" (snow-pheasants), as they sat on bare knolls among the
gorse bushes, their long-drawn mournful notes according well
with the lonesome scene around.   They did not seem very
shy, but as they were generally in pairs I refrained from
going after them.   The track to Goting was often, for long
distances, quite buried in snow.   In some places where it

had just melted off, and the hard steep ground was glazed over with a slippery coating of ice, which had at times to be chipped for foothold, a glance down towards the hidden depth far below sent a cold creepy thrill through the nerves that was anything but pleasant.

A few miles below Goting we descried across the valley a flock of twelve burrell, and with the glass I could distinguish two grand old rams in it. They were on a small sloping patch of green grass above the precipitous rocks rising directly from the river, having evidently descended to feed there from the heights above, the upper regions of which were covered with snow, and the steep declivities below, where it had only recently melted off, were, for a long way down, still quite destitute of verdure. There was no means of crossing the river nearer than Goting, where Puddoo said we should find a natural bridge of snow. It was too late, however, when we reached there to go after the burrell that day; but as nothing was likely to disturb them, and there was then no food for them above, we should have every chance of finding them still on or near the same ground in the morning. As we were pitching the camp, one of the men who had gone to fetch water came and told me he had seen some burrell feeding farther down our side of the river; so Puddoo and I at once started to look after them. There was one good ram in the flock, which was a small one; but our attempt at a stalk was a failure, as the wary creatures got wind of us and made off.

Early next morning we clambered down the steep scarp of frost-rotted earth to the natural bridge which was formed of hard old snow jammed up between huge fragments of rock that had fallen from above, almost across the river, where it rushed through a narrow chasm. It was an awkward place to cross, and after getting over, there was an abominably steep bit to be surmounted, where the ground was smooth and friable, before we could proceed down the valley, along the rocks that overhung the river raging along its narrow bed. Thence we got on pretty easily for a mile or two, keeping a sharp look-out upward before crossing each steep gully we came to, lest an avalanche of snow, or loose rocks and stones, which at any moment might be expected, should come down upon us. At last we neared the place where, from the opposite side, we had seen the flock of burrell. We had just rounded a corner, when a lot of ewes, which started up from a ravine just beyond it, went scampering away, and almost immediately after we saw the flock containing the two big rams also moving quickly upward from the very place where we had at first sighted it, having evidently taken alarm at the flight of the ewes. This was very annoying; but as the second flock had not actually seen us, there was still a chance of getting a crack at the rams before evening. Up and still up the beasts continued slowly to ascend, until, after watching them for an hour or more, we finally lost sight of them among the snow-fields above. As they would be pretty sure to descend again in the evening to their feeding-ground, we moved upward for some distance towards a commanding spot from whence we could more easily watch their movements. We were skirting a small coppice of birch and rhododendron bushes, when a fine little buck musk-deer jumped up close to us. As he stopped to look back I sent a bullet through him, but had to follow up and give him a second shot before securing him. After relieving him of his musk-bag (which ought always to be done at once), and hiding him from the birds of prey, we continued our ascent to the spot where we intended to wait for the burrell.

Here I discussed my breakfast, and then commenced a careful search with the telescope for our friends above. At length I made them out, reposing on some bare rocks among the snow-fields; and with the glass I could discern the arching horns of one of the big fellows, standing out in relief against a snow-bed, as he lay on a slab of stone below it. For hours we waited there, every now and then taking a look through the spy-glass at the burrell, lest we should lose sight of them if they moved, until, as the afternoon wore on, they rose. At first they came downward very slowly; but hunger, I suppose, soon made them quicken their movements, till they got below the snow-fields, when they stopped from time to time to nibble the dry withered leaves of the dwarf rhododendron plants,[1] the only vegetation apparently up there. After making pretty sure of their intentions, we commenced a stalk up to meet them, for it was now drawing towards evening, and we were a considerable distance from our camp. It was a long and steep climb, and all the more difficult from our having sometimes to scramble round, over awkward bits, in order to keep out of view of the animals.

At length we reached a point where some big rocks projected over the side of a wide gully, into which we knew the burrell must have descended, though they were now hidden from our sight. Puddoo, who had climbed on to the rocks to reconnoitre, at once beckoned me to come up beside him. On slowly raising my head to look over, I beheld, within 150 yards, and almost on a level with us, a big ram standing on an isolated crag above a deep drop. What a beauty he looked as he stood there motionless as a statue, gazing intently downward! But I had little time for admiring him, as his companions were moving on. Owing to the ram's position, and the shape of the rocks we were on, it so happened that shooting from the right shoulder was difficult. I, however, managed to screw myself round into an awkward attitude, and taking as steady an aim as, under such circumstances, I was able, fired my shot. The ram tottered for a second, and then fell headlong down some 150 feet. The rest of the flock at once huddled together and commenced retracing their steps slowly upwards, but after going a short distance they stood

[1] The bloom of these little shrubs is here a pale yellow; in other respects they are exactly similar to the Alpen rosen. I was told that the red-flowered kind also grows here, though I never saw it myself.

"AS HE STOOD THERE MOTIONLESS AS A STATUE."

again, with all their heads turned towards us. Singling out the other big fellow, I sent the contents of the second barrel at him, and saw him, as I imagined, go tumbling down after his companion. "Quick!" whispered Puddoo, "now take the other big one," as he handed me my spare rifle. To my surprise, I now saw the big fellow I had just shot at continuing his ascent with the rest of the flock. But, alas! I had missed my chance, as the other rifle was only a little ·360 bore, for an accurate shot with which the ram was now too far out. The second bullet had gone just over the big fellow's shoulder, and had brought down a ewe that had been standing immediately above and behind him. Had it struck an inch or two lower, it would in all probability have killed them both.

It was disappointing to have thus killed the wrong animal by mistake, but on getting down to the beasts I had shot, it was consoling to find that the ram had perfect horns, 27 inches long. As it was now getting late, there was no time to gralloch them, so we merely cut slits in their paunches to let out the foul gas, and taking off the big fellow's head, made the best of our way back to camp, which we reached just before dark.

Next day the men sent to fetch the dead burrell found an "ounce," or as it is more commonly called, a snow-leopard, at work on them. If the stupids had only had sense enough to leave one of the carcasses as a bait, the beast would certainly have returned to it, and in all probability I should have got a shot at a rather rare animal I was most anxious to kill. During that visit to Goting I had two more days on other good beats; but as I have said quite enough about burrell-hunting for the present, we will now resume our journey towards Hundés.

A few miles above Goting the valley suddenly contracts into a deep and narrow defile. Just before entering it, I shot a ram out of a flock of burrell that unexpectedly showed themselves above some high rocks overhanging the track.

The animals had evidently come down to a salt-lick there is here close by the wayside. The beast I had killed had most conveniently fallen down on to the track, where we left him for the men following with the jooboos to pick up. Throughout the defile, which is several miles long, the river was then covered over with a hard bed of snow, which made our progress there much easier than on our return, after the snow-bed had disappeared, when the baggage-animals had to scramble along the rocky steeps rising abruptly from the river. We had some trouble, however, in circumventing one or two awkward places where the snow had already fallen in and left yawning holes disclosing the dark gurgling water tearing along below. We stopped for that day at the head of the defile, where the stony ground was clear of snow, and the cold blast that blew down the gorge as if through a funnel raised the dust in clouds and made it difficult to keep our tents standing. Beyond this, for the ten or twelve miles before reaching the summit of the pass, there is no difficulty to speak of, and the scenery is grand though somewhat dreary and monotonous. Across the river, on the south side, several flocks of burrell containing some good rams were seen on the steep slopes. We camped just below the short but pretty stiff final ascent to the top of the ghat, in order to get over it in the early morning before the snow became softened by the heat of the sun.

Starting very early, the crest was reached soon after sunrise. The view you get from it of Hundés is more striking than beautiful. In the glaring picture before you there is an absence of what a painter would call chiaro-oscuro; not in its literal sense by any means, for there is certainly no want of light and shade, but in the harmonious blending of these effects, which is, I think, the technical acceptation of the term. The aerial perspective, too, looks almost unnatural in its clearness. That mighty object of Hindoo veneration, the Kailás peak, rising 22,000 odd feet, about a hundred miles away eastward, close above the great holy lake of Mansora-war—which latter, though invisible from the pass, I knew to be quite that distance as the crow flies—did not seem more than half as far off. In vain do you here look for the beautiful sunrise or sunset effects of more dense and humid atmospheres, for the sun shines through the thin air of these high Tibetan regions with the same garish-white glare when on the horizon as when on the meridian. Perhaps I might have viewed the prospect before me in a different light under more agreeable circumstances, but the high wind that blew the dry drifting snow off the neighbouring mountain-tops in long pennon-like clouds chilled one to the very marrow, and I had a dreadful headache to boot.

The watershed here deserves notice. Speaking figuratively, if, when standing beside the cairn on the pass, you throw a snowball towards the west, it melts into a tributary of the Ganges, and so into the Bay of Bengal. If you fling another towards the east, it will melt into the Sutlej—here flowing almost northward beyond the pass—be carried back by that river westward through the Himalayan chain, and so find its way eventually down the Indus into the Arabian Sea.

After getting half-frozen whilst attempting to make a hurried sketch, with my fingers so benumbed that I could scarcely hold the pencil, it was almost a relief to be plodding on again knee-deep through the snow, down towards where we camped for the night, four or five miles farther on, after a descent, for the most part over deep snow, of some 2000 feet.

The cold here at night was terrible. All the wraps I possessed failed to keep out the piercing wind, so we waited until the rising sun warmed us up before we set out next day. We only went four or five miles, chiefly along the stony bed of the Sakchu—a stream of snow-water, which had to be forded several times—to a spot where there was some grazing for the poor jooboos, which had been fasting for two days. Here we were interviewed by a deputation of Hoonyas, sent by the Jongpen from his residence at Dāpā, about twenty miles off, to arrange about the period he was to permit us to remain in Tibetan territory. At first these emissaries would hear of nothing more than eight days; but after a good deal of persuasion from Puddoo, and their hearts had been softened by a bottle of whisky, they eventually agreed to fifteen, beyond which they said it was impossible to extend the permission without the sanction of the Jongpen. To this functionary I therefore sent by them a present of a revolver, accompanied by a request that, as I had come so far to hunt there, he would do me the favour to extend the privilege to a month. Before taking their departure, however, they asked me to sign an agreement to the effect that I would not attempt to cross the river Sutlej, and that I should return over the pass by the appointed time, pending a reference to the Jongpen. They also left two queer-looking old fellows of their number behind them, to see that we did not trespass beyond the prescribed limits. They were quite open to a little trade, and sold me a large thick woollen rug called a " chookta," which, after drowning its inhabitants by soaking it for several hours in the stream, made a most comfortable and requisite addition to my wraps at night.

A sudden snowstorm delayed our departure until rather late next morning, when we started in the direction of a good locality for *Ovis Ammon*, known as Tāzāng, with our escort of Hoonya cavalry, mounted on yaks as their chargers, following at some distance behind us.

CHAPTER XXIII.

IMPRESSIONS OF HUNDÉS—WARY OLD RAMS—KIANGS IN THE WAY—THE
JONGPEN'S MESSENGERS RETURN—SIGNING A CONTRACT—HOONYA
SHEEP-SHEARING—AN OVIS AMMON WITH BRONCHITIS—GREY WOLVES
—DONGPU—A TARTAR HAMLET—LARGE TROOPS OF KIANG—THEIR
MANŒUVRES—THE SUTLEJ—THE LĀL DĀKĀ—VENISON FOR CAMP—HOW
WE CAUGHT A DISH OF FISH—A STUDY IN ENTOMOLOGY—EMBARRAS
DES RICHESSES—THE DUKKA HILLS—MISFORTUNES WILL HAPPEN—
THEY NEVER COME SINGLE—A CRUELLY COLD MORNING IN JUNE—
LARGE FLOCK OF BIG RAMS—IN THE NICK OF TIME—A MOST ENJOY-
ABLE SMOKE—AFTER A WOUNDED RAM—INTRUDERS ON THE SCENE
—JUST TOO LATE—A BEWILDERED FLOCK—A TANTALISING OPPOR-
TUNITY—A TIRESOME TRUDGE—WELCOME REST.

WE were now well out on the undulating uplands of Hundés,
and traversing ground where we might expect to find the big
wild sheep. A strange weird-looking land, to all appearance
a desert, stretching far and wide before us towards distant
ranges of barren undulating mountains, tinted with every
shade of red, yellow, purple, and blue, rising tier beyond tier,
and culminating in snow-clad ridges and peaks—all their
features looking marvellously distinct through the clear rare
atmosphere. Broad table-lands, averaging about 15,000 feet
above the sea-level, bare, brown, and monotonous, sloping
gradually down from the foot of the great snowy chain of the
Himalayas behind us, and intersected by huge ravines, growing deeper and wider as they all trend northwards towards
the river Sutlej, here called the Satroodra, flowing (from east
to west), hidden among their mighty labyrinths, far away
below us. The solemn waste here and there diversified by

low arid hills of a brick-red hue. In the dark sapphire-blue firmament, a blazing sun shedding a cheerless dazzling glare on all around us. Not a sound but the wailing of the wind to break the dead depressing silence, save perhaps the hoarse croak of a solitary big raven, or the snorting of a troop of kiang, as the startled animals stand for a few seconds to gaze inquiringly at the intruders on their wild domain, ere they wheel simultaneously about and gallop madly away over the rolling wind-swept slopes of shingle and sun-baked earth, leaving a drifting cloud of dust to mark their track.

Here, in small flocks, few and far between, roams the ponderous-horned *Ovis*, ever watchful and wary, suspecting danger in each gust of the icy blast that comes fitfully sweeping over this bleak howling wilderness. A wolf may occasionally be detected slinking stealthily off. Sometimes a shy hare starts from the cover of a scrubby tussock of the stunted herbage that is sparsely scattered over the stony soil; or a grey marmot may be seen sitting erect on some sandy knoll, disturbing nature's silent repose with its shrill chirping whistle ere it vanishes into its burrow hard by. Even the Tartar hamlets, which very rarely occur in these dreary inhospitable wilds, have a dilapidated, decayed, and forlorn look about them that is quite in keeping with their desolate dream-like surroundings. Such were my general impressions of the country we were now in.

As we were trudging along some distance ahead of the jooboos, a small flock of ewe *Oves Ammon* was descried in the distance. Kiangs were feeding here and there among the few bunchy tufts of herbage on the stony plain. We also saw a fine reddish-coloured fox. Our camp was pitched in the best shelter from the wind we could find in a ravine, where some strips of greensward along the banks of a small stream afforded food for the jooboos, but there was no fuel except the thick roots of the "debsing" grass. The boortze of more northern Tibetan regions is here called "debsing."

Here we decided to remain for a day or two, to hunt in the vicinity. We found one flock of five splendid old rams, and made several attempts to get at them; but the ground they were on was so flat and bare, and the beasts were so wary, that it was impossible to get within measurable distance of them: we might just as well have tried to stalk the moon. The innumerable kiangs too, here grazing about in every direction, were a great nuisance, their startled movements being always calculated to put the *Oves* on the alert. For even when you may think you are quite safe from detection by an *Ovis Ammon* as regards sight and scent, no animal has a keener perception of danger from any suspicious sign or movement on the part of other living beings within range of his vision, however far distant from him they may be.

Whilst camped here the messengers from Dāpā again turned up, bringing with them a present from the Jongpen of some yaks' tails, and an answer to the effect that twenty-one days was the utmost time he could possibly allow me, owing, he said, to pressure put on him in such matters from Lhasa. So the contract was signed, sealed, and delivered, and I was of course in honour bound to abide by it. This limited period precluded any chance I might have had of getting a shot at the wild yaks (here called " bunchowr "), which, though very numerous on the other (north) side of the Sutlej, are only sometimes to be met with on this side, and generally so far eastward from here that I should not have time to reach their haunts.[1]   I might have adopted the arbitrary plan of refusing to sign any agreement, but the passive resistance to all my further proceedings in the country which might probably have been the only consequence of my doing so, would have been quite as detrimental to my chances

[1] Tibetan antelopes—here called "tso"—and "goa," Tibetan gazelles, are also to be found in Hundés, but only, I believe, well northward of the Sutlej, or farther eastward beyond the Mansorawar lake.

of sport there as a more active and forcible one. I therefore
determined to make the best use of the time allowed.

Next morning the cattle were packed and sent off to a spot
where there was feeding for them a few miles from here, in
the direction of the Sutlej, whilst Puddoo and I made a circuit over the table-land and through the ravines more eastward. We made out a flock of *Oves* miles away, up towards
the Himalayan slopes ; but as, even with the aid of the spy-
glass, we were doubtful whether they were ewes or young
males with small horns, and they were also in a direction
opposite to the one we wished to take, we paid them no further attention. Towards the afternoon we found two burrell
rams, which we stalked without much difficulty, and one
of them was killed. I noticed on this occasion, and many
others, on these high undulating uplands, that a shot had a
peculiarly dull and flat sound, which was probably due to
atmospheric influence. There was none of the usual ring or
reverberation in the thin air of this high region. Nor was
there an echo to the report of a gun even under conditions of
ground where it might ordinarily have been expected. Had
it not been for the usual recoil, I might have supposed that
the rifle was loaded with an insufficient charge of powder.
On our way back we came across a Hoonya encampment, the
occupants of which were busily engaged sheep-shearing.
They were using a knife in place of shears for removing the
fleeces, which I noticed were very fine and long.

Herds, consisting sometimes of thousands of sheep, goats,
and yaks, may be seen about a Hoonya camp, all of them as
wild as deer, and it is interesting to observe the way in which
they are tended. The sheep and goats are picketed at night
in troops, exactly like the horses of a cavalry regiment. Two
long ropes are stretched along the ground and made fast
about a yard apart, with nooses on each rope about two feet
apart. In the evening the sheep and goats are collected, and
surrounded by the men, women, and children in a circle, who

all continue singing, which appears to have the effect of quiet-ing the animals. This circle is gradually contracted around the ropes, and in a marvellously short space of time all the animals' heads are tied in these nooses, heads inwards, facing each other. The women then go round with pails, singing all the time, and milk them. Eight or ten women follow each other, each operating on every sheep and goat, but not spend-ing more than a quarter of a minute over each. Sheep and goats are tied up indiscriminately, and the milk is of course mixed.

From here we next day took a beat northward, over the same description of ground, and soon discovered two good *Oves Ammon* rams. Although they were not much more than half a mile from us, we had to make a round of what appeared to me several miles, to try and approach them—and all on account of there being only some fifty yards of the interven-ing ground to cross exposed to their watchful eyes, which difficulty it was impossible otherwise to circumvent. And after all our trouble, the animals seemed to have spirited themselves away, for not a trace of them could we find on the hard gravelly ground to indicate what direction they had taken. It was now noon, and we had brought no food with us, having that morning intended to return early to camp; but the two rams had upset this arrangement, so we sent back our spare man to fetch something to eat, and con-tinued our search for them. We had not gone far when we espied a solitary ram, carrying fairly good horns. After moving restlessly about for some time, he lay down on an exposed eminence, where there was no possible way of ap-proaching him nearer than about 400 yards. We therefore lay down and waited, in the hope that he might move on to more suitable ground for a stalk. He seemed to be suffering from an attack of bronchitis, for, as I watched him through the glass, I distinctly saw that he was constantly coughing. After we had lain there about two hours, exposed to the hard wind and baking sun, waiting for the beast to rise, hunger began to assert itself, which caused us to grow impatient. We therefore decided to try and shorten the intervening distance by creeping towards him in the open, under the delusion that his seeming indisposition would perhaps make him reluctant to bestir himself. Strange to say, he allowed us to get well within 300 yards before he rose, which unusual negligence on the part of an *Ovis Ammon* we could only attribute to his ailment. He moved off very slowly, so I hastened his departure with a bullet; and as on examining the place where I had shot at him we found a good-sized tuft of his hair on the ground, I must have shaved him pretty closely. We now made for the spot where Puddoo had arranged for the provinder to be brought to, and after appeasing our hunger, proceeded to try fresh ground. No game was found on it, however, which was not surprising, as we detected poachers there in the shape of two grey wolves (here called "chanko"), one of which I sent limping away with a broken hind-leg. By the time we got back to camp in the evening, I felt as if I had done perhaps a little more than enough work since early morning.

Our camp was moved next day to Dongpu, the first inhabited place we had met with since leaving the village of Niti. A Tartar hamlet and small gompa (monastery) — the latter coloured red—perched along the crest of a pale-yellowish low ridge, of which the crumbling half-dilapidated houses seemed to form a part. A rapid turbid stream of melted snow (the Sakchu) wound along below it, and some terraced fields in the vicinity looked so arid and stony that it was difficult to conceive how anything could ever grow there. The village looked utterly dreary and forsaken,—a few decrepit old men and wizened hags being its sole inhabitants, the rest being absent in their camps, grazing their flocks in the wilderness around. Altogether, the place and its surroundings looked so dreamy and unreal in the quivering reflected heat and dazzling white glare of noon, that it seemed almost as though it belonged to some other and less beautiful world.

From here we worked over ground where Puddoo had made certain of finding *Oves Ammon*, but unfortunately we found it occupied by flocks of Oves Tartar and goats instead. Out on a big plateau we saw two unusually large troops of kiang— one of some fifty, and the other of about thirty animals. The serried cavalcades would trot up towards us, and suddenly halt within 150 yards or so, and after standing there snorting and gazing wistfully at us for a few moments, wheel about, as if by word of command, and careering round in a wide circle, return again and again to perform the same manœuvre, ere galloping away for good and disappearing over some neighbouring rise.

Next day being Sunday, we were glad of a much-needed rest, not only for our weary limbs, but for relief to my face and hands, which were almost raw from the combined effects of biting wind and scorching sun. When that abominable blast happened not to be blowing, which was seldom, the climate at this place was simply perfect in the shade, although the cold at night was bitter as usual. Watching the proceedings of a colony of grey marmots (here called " pheea "), not far from my tent, was quite an interesting pastime.

From Dongpu we had a long and weary tramp among the broken ground and deep ravines lying between it and the Sutlej. The one satisfaction I derived from going there was a good view of that river from the heights immediately above it—here a rapid flood of muddy snow-water, rolling along a desolate and verdureless valley between stony undulating hills. Almost directly below us I could see, spanning the stream, a wooden bridge, which only made me more fully realise the disappointing fact of my being debarred from so easily visiting the country beyond it, where bunchowr (wild yak) and other Tibetan game were said to abound. The wild

2 E

camel, too, is found on some of the wide plateaux beyond the Kuen Lún range, farther north—though, even could one reach its haunts, it is not the kind of animal a sportsman would care to pull trigger on.

This was an utterly blank day. Not a living thing, either biped or quadruped, was to be seen. As we toiled slowly and wearily over those boundless shingly slopes and high table-lands, breathless from their rarefied air, and buffeted by the ever-blowing blast, how often did I ask myself whether the game was really worth all the time and trouble entailed by its pursuit, until, late in the evening, we got back to camp, tired out and dejected. Even the stolid but usually good-tempered Puddoo showed evident symptoms of ill-humour at our fruit-less work.

Some distance to the eastward of Dongpu lies a low range of rounded hills, known as the Lāl Dākā (red hills), so called from the brick-red colour pervading them. These hills are generally considered to be a favourite resort of *Oves Ammon*. The range is pretty extensive, but there is only one spot there nearer than the Shipchillum stream, at its eastern extremity, where water is to be found. Thither we now decided to proceed. Several hares, and some coveys of the Hodgsonian partridge, were put up on the way. As we neared our camping-place, on turning a corner in a winding ravine we came suddenly on four ewe *Oves*, one of which I shot to provide meat. The little stream that ran past the tents was full of diminutive dark-coloured fish, which were easily caught by dragging the water with a sheet, and proved excellent for eating. Hares were numerous in this vicinity, though, strange to say, very wild, but I did not care to disturb the ground by shooting at them.

The first morning we tried the western part of the range, but saw no fresh sign of large rams. Nothing could we find there except three ewes—probably the same lot I had shot one out of the day before: we therefore proceeded more east-ward. About noon we made out four big-horned fellows about two miles off. Whilst working towards these we descried another flock of seven, and most of them good rams too, not far from the first lot. As usual, they were in an open and unapproachable position. Both lots, however, appeared to be feeding up towards the brow of a rise above them; so, after getting as near as we could, which was still over a mile from them, we lay down to watch their movements, in the hope that they would soon put the brow of the hill between them and us. As we lay motionless there, getting half roasted by the blazing sun, I was much entertained by a curious little entomological study that chanced to come under my observation. I noticed innumerable small grey grasshoppers—I should call them crickets, as there was very little grass for them to hop on—which showed a strange amount of curiosity respecting our persons. They came creeping towards us over the stones from all sides, even crawling and hopping over us, and paying particular attention to the oil on the guns, the flavour of which seemed to be very attractive to them. They were so fearless as even to greedily devour the ends of atoms of dry grass softened between my teeth and held close to their mouths.

As soon as the last of the rams had disappeared over the brow, we made for it as fast as we were able, in order to get there, if possible, before they were out of range beyond it; but on reaching it, not a vestige of the animals was to be seen. Soon, however, we descried two fine rams in another direction, and whilst deliberating as to the best way of approaching them, six more came over a rise on to the same ground. It was truly a case of *embarras des richesses* this time, for the relative positions of the two lots were such that it was impossible to stalk one without our being detected by the other. As it was now growing late, and we were at least six miles from our camp, we reluctantly had to abandon further pursuit that evening, in the hope of finding the animals in the same vicinity next day.

As all the game appeared to be more eastward on the Lāl
Dākā, the following morning our camp was shifted to a
locality about seven miles off called Dukka, where there was
grass for the jooboos, and a stream of water, among some low
rounded hills near the foot of the Himalayan slopes. These
hills also were considered a favourite resort of *Ores Ammon*,
and our camp there would be within reach for a long beat
over the eastern end of the Lāl Dākā range, which was
separated from them by a level expanse some six miles wide.
After packing off the jooboos, I started with Puddoo and a
spare man to look after our friends of the previous evening.
They were still near where we had last seen them, the two
rams having apparently joined company with the flock of six.
We contrived to get within 150 yards of them, but the shot
was so downward that I had only the width of their backs to
aim at. The first bullet went clean over a big fellow, upon
which they all started off, but, after going a few yards, stood
to look about them. Again my shot went high and missed,
and this time they departed for good. We watched the retreating animals with silent disappointment until they were
out of sight; but as such things will happen, there was no
use grieving over my misfortune, so I sat down and consoled
myself with my breakfast and a pipe, hoping for better luck
next time. I had probably forgotten to allow for the flight
of a bullet being less acted upon by the rarefied air at such
an altitude, and so had used too high a sight.

After resting for a short while, we moved on eastward
along the range, and had not gone far when Puddoo, who had
been searching about with the telescope, discovered a magnificent old ram, lying alone, within half a mile of us; and,
for a wonder, the ground was most favourable for circumventing him. When Puddoo got really excited over a stalk, he
had a habit of slowly lifting the corners of his long woollen
coat-tails and carefully tucking them one by one into his belt.
By the time he had tucked all four corners up, we had got

within 100 yards of the ram as he lay close to the edge of a small projecting slope below us, stretched out at full length on his side, with his back towards us, and his ponderous horns resting on the ground. For once I had caught an *Ovis Ammon* napping! A slight noise, unfortunately made in some manner, betrayed our presence, and caused the animal to suddenly lift his head and look about him. Fearing lest he might spring to his feet and disappear over the edge of the slope before I should have time to get my aim on him, I foolishly, and against Puddoo's advice, fired without waiting, as I certainly ought to have done, until he rose. Starting to his feet, he stood for a second broadside on; but as I was covering his shoulder for a second shot, he turned sharp round and dashed off downwards, just as I pressed the trigger, and was out of sight in an instant. *Eheu mihi!* I had missed him clean with both barrels! Words cannot express my feelings as I watched him going away after he reappeared. Puddoo, however, expressed his sentiments at the time pretty freely in his native dialect; and could I have understood what he was saying, I might doubtless have heard some rather uncomplimentary remarks respecting my duffer-like performance. We followed the animal's tracks for a long way, on the slight chance of the first bullet having hit him with a ricochet, as we noticed it had knocked up the dust on our side of him, but not a drop of blood could we find; so we sorrowfully turned our steps campwards. How I imprecated the cutting wind as we trudged wearily over the six long miles of flat ground between the Lāl Dākā and our camp. As we skirted along the base of the Dukka hills, we saw another big flock of *Ovis Ammon* away up on the sloping heights to our left; but we were both of us too done up and down-hearted to think of going after them that evening, even had there been time.

So hard was the frost here at night in the month of June, that the stream close to our camp, which we had forded nearly

knee-deep the evening before, was until mid-day quite dry.
Nothing was for the time left of it but a hollow crust of ice,
below which the water had ceased to flow. Having to depend
on this stream for water, we had, whilst here, to collect a
sufficient supply overnight to last until it began to flow again
next day at noon. It can therefore be imagined what bitter
cold work it was starting forth in the dawn to look after the
animals we had seen on the neighbouring hills the evening
before. About eight o'clock Puddoo spied out with the glass
a flock of five *Oves*, but none of them were big rams. Whilst
he was watching them through the telescope, I chanced to
notice a large group of animals, which I took to be kiangs,
suddenly appear away up on the sky-line of a rounded
eminence nearly a mile off. Drawing Puddoo's attention
to them, he turned the glass in their direction and instantly
pronounced them to be "nian" (*Oves Ammon*). There were
eleven in sight, and all of them were rams carrying fine
horns. Presently they lay down on the very brow of the
hill, where we could distinctly see their splendid heads
in relief against the sky. As they completely overlooked
our position, and were quite unapproachable from any other
quarter, even could we have dared to move, there was nothing
for it but to wait patiently there until they again rose and
shifted their ground. The wind had now sprung up, which,
combined with the keen frost, made the cold during the hour
or more we had to lie there like stones, about as cruel as
I have ever felt. My hands and feet got so benumbed that
I began to think, if we remained there inactive much longer,
they would be frozen. At last the animals rose, and after
pottering restlessly about for some time, retired quickly
beyond the brow towards the same direction they had come
from.

On this occasion I fully appreciated the advantage of
having a man with me who knew every feature of the ground
as well as the habits of its wild denizens. Puddoo at once

concludes that the animals will be likely to make for a wide ravine, where there is more or less grazing for them, some distance beyond and to the left of the brow they so hastily quitted, and that by our quickly making a circuit below, we may possibly be able to reach the foot of it in time to intercept them. Off we start as fast as we can shuffle along, for running is next thing to impossible in such trying atmosphere. In less than an hour we have almost reached the foot of the ravine. As we cautiously approach it round the shoulder of a spur, I can judge by the unwonted haste with which Puddoo not only lifts his coat-tails, but this time winds them tightly round his waist, that his excitement is unusually intense. On gaining the cover of some rocks, which he says will command the lower part of the ravine where he hopes to find the flock, we slowly raise our heads to reconnoitre. We are just in the nick of time, as five or six of the animals, which are evidently still on the move, have reached the foot of the ravine, and one or two have commenced ascending an opposite slope at, as near as I can hastily judge, about 180 yards off. Quickly adjusting the sight, I let drive at a grand fellow as he stands for a second or two at the bottom of the slope; but from being rather shaky after our hurried stalk, I hit him in the haunch instead of the shoulder. Off they all speed, but again stop a short way up on the slope to look back, giving me ample time for a shot at another good beast, which rolls over to rise no more. Away they start again at a gallop, with the exception of a big old ram—not the wounded one—that lags slowly behind. I have now only my miniature ·360-bore Rigby rifle left to use, and although many a black buck and cheetal stag, and once even a full-grown stag jurrow, have fallen to it, I hardly expect it to do for a big *Ovis Ammon* at quite 200 yards: but luck is on my side this time. The little expanding bullet chances to hit, and so hard that the old ram merely moves on a few faltering steps and once more stands stock-still. Meanwhile the rest of the flock have reached the top of the rise, and after standing clustered there for a few moments as if irresolute about their further movements, they finally disappear beyond it, with the first fellow I had shot at limping after them. Reloading the Whitworth as quickly as possible, I give the laggard I had wounded with the little bullet another shot, which at first I am not sure has struck him, but after tottering for a few seconds he falls over on his side dead.

Had the Whitworth rifle been a breechloader I should probably have accounted for at least one more of the animals, for, as they stood on the brow, they were not more than 250 yards off, and an *Ovis Ammon* is a good-sized mark to shoot at though he is sometimes so easily missed. Now the sporting reader will at once ask, "Why hadn't you a breechloader?" Well, it was my misfortune, not my fault, that I had not, for a new Express rifle I had ordered especially for this trip was then lying useless at Dehra Doon, owing to the transmitting agents carelessly neglecting to forward it in time to take with me. However, I had little reason to repine in this instance, as two splendid old rams were down, and a third had gone off so badly wounded that I had great hopes of eventually securing him as well.

On moving across to the brow, which commanded an uninterrupted view of the wide flat between these hills and the Lāl Dākā, we could easily trace the course the animals were steering, and with the telescope I could distinguish the wounded one, now limping along ahead of the flock. At length we saw him lie down, whilst his companions slowly continued their course towards the Lāl Dākā. By this time it was getting late in the forenoon, so we had our breakfast, keeping an eye on the wounded ram whilst we were quickly disposing of it. The spare man was now despatched to camp to fetch jooboos for carrying the spoils, and also for my pipe, which I had purposely left behind under the impression that my egregious misses of the previous day might possibly have been due to my indulging too freely in tobacco. After watching the wounded ram for a long time, it being impossible to approach him where he lay, we at length saw him rise and hobble onward, stopping now and again, until he reached the Lāl Dākā, where with the glass I could see he once more lay down on an open slope. It had now grown too late to follow him that afternoon, so we proceeded to gralloch the dead beasts. On the arrival of the jooboos, I sat down and thoroughly enjoyed a smoke whilst they were being packed with the spoils. On our return to camp, a dram of whisky was served out to all hands for celebrating this red-letter day among the big sheep. I weighed one of the rams with a portable machine I had brought with me—a Yankee "notion," which was "calculated" to weigh correctly up to 360 lb. The figures were as follows: Weight, "clean," 350 lb. odd, or about 18 stone. Of this, the head alone (as cut off for stuffing) was upwards of 50 lb., and perhaps 2 stone might be added for the gralloch, making a total of, say, 20 stone. Not a bad weight for a sheep! The horns were good average specimens of their kind. The larger pair would have measured quite 3½ feet round the curve had not the tips been slightly broken. The other pair were a few inches shorter, but equally thick (18 inches) and their tips uninjured.

The following day we were not long in again finding the wounded ram, on a slope of the Lāl Dākā above the Ship-chillum stream, and with the spy-glass I could distinctly see his blood-stained haunch. He was slowly moving up-wards, but ere long he lay down on an exposed ridge high up on the range, from whence he evidently kept a sharp look-out on all sides, as we noticed that his head was being continually turned suspiciously about. It was necessary to use the ut-most caution in approaching him, for any wounded wild animal is always hard to get near when not quite disabled, let alone an *Ovis Ammon.* After making a round of quite two miles, we had almost reached a spot which we had judged to be within 200 yards of him, when, suddenly taking alarm, he sprang to his feet. From the alacrity with which he at once sped upward and disappeared over the top of the range, it was evident that, although his haunch was badly wounded, no bone was broken; and having detected us on his track, he would most likely go a very long distance without stopping, as a wounded beast on being alarmed often will do. At any rate, this was the last we ever saw of him, though possibly he fell to the rifle of another sportsman, who, when hunting on this ground shortly after us, killed a big ram there which had a recently-made wound in its haunch.

On our way out in the early morning, several lots of small-horned rams and ewes had been seen, and during our stalk after the wounded animal, we had noticed five rams move over the top of the range. We had also descried in the distance what we thought to be the eight remaining rams of the flock I had thinned the day before; but as they would now, most probably, be well on the alert, we turned our attention to the five fresh ones, three of which carried grand horns. We came upon them where they had stopped to graze in a ravine on the north side of the range, and we had just reached a spot from which, in another minute, I should have got an easy chance within 150 yards, when three other rams suddenly appeared, coming over the rise on the far side of the ravine, and instantly catching sight of us, turned tail and made off. Before I could get ready to shoot at the rams in the ravine, they also, taking alarm at the flight of the three intruders, started off at a gallop, and put a good 300 yards between us and them before they pulled up on the crest of a sloping spur, beyond another ravine running down on our right into the one they had just quitted. The first shot, sent at the big lord of the flock, knocked up the dust several yards short of him. From not having seen us, and being far out, the animals seemed only startled, so I had time for

another chance. Again the bullet fell short, but this time
so close to the big fellow's feet that it must have sent up
the gravelly ground against him. The beasts now got so
bewildered that, instead of at once disappearing behind the
spur, as might ordinarily have been expected, they galloped
straight up along it, and again stood broadside on within
200 yards, and level with us across the ravine to our right,
in the most tantalising manner. Oh for a good breechloader
then, for I had only the "pea-shooter" left to depend on!
Whether the big fellow carried away the contents of the
latter I never found out, for though his tracks were followed
far beyond the spur, nothing more of either him or his
companions did we ever see again. There were eight or nine
long miles to trudge over before getting back to camp, and I
could have wished no fitter penalty for the delinquents
who had so disappointed me about my Express rifle, than
to have had them grinding breathlessly alongside me that
afternoon, with the cold cutting wind blowing right in
their teeth, and the glaring sun scorching the skin off their
faces and cracked lips.

Next day was Sunday, and never did I more welcome
a rest.

Tibetan wooden Cup and Tobacco-pipe.

CHAPTER XXIV.

SUDDEN CHANGE OF TEMPERATURE—AN UNEXPECTED EVENT—A BROTHER
SPORTSMAN TURNS UP—"IT NEVER RAINS BUT IT POURS"—WE TRY A
LITTLE FISH-POACHING—A WELCOME POST-BAG—BURRELL AGAIN—
WAITING FOR A RAM TO RISE—"HABET"—A NURSERY OF WILD SHEEP
—A LONG CHASE—A LUCKY FLUKE—AN AGED RAM—OUR HOONYA
ESCORT DEPARTS—BED OF FOSSILS—TIBETAN DOUANE—AFTERNOON
TEA—THE WAY IT WAS MADE—DICE-THROWING—A TOKEN OF GOOD-
WILL FROM THE JONGPEN—TIBETAN METHOD OF CURING BUTTER—
A TRYING JOB—RECROSS NITI PASS—BHŌTIA WHISKY—PUDDOO IMBIBES
RATHER FREELY—A BIT OF ADVICE—A CHANGE FOR THE BETTER—
PUDDOO AND CO. CELEBRATE THEIR RETURN HOME—A TRANSFORMA-
TION-SCENE IN THE THEATRE OF NATURE—A REVERIE—RAMNEE—
FAREWELL TO THE GRAND OLD HIMALAYAS.

THE time was now drawing nigh when, according to my contract with the Jongpen, I should have to quit Tibetan territory; and the Niti pass, over which I intended to return, was three or four days' journey from here. These few days I resolved to devote to hunting burrell, which Puddoo said were fairly plentiful in certain localities where there was some scanty vegetation,[1] below the snow-line, on the Himalayan northern slopes, along the foot of which our way led towards the pass. There would also be a chance left of finding *Ovis Ammon* as well, though the ground was not considered so good for old rams as that which we had been over.

Our camp now presented the appearance of a "flesher's"

[1] The limit of vegetation in these trans-Himalayan regions is at an altitude of about 17,000 feet.

shop, every available tent-rope being hung with long strips of raw meat drying in the sun. Cooking, too, was going on at a great rate, there being an unusual amount of fuel about here suitable for the purpose in the shape of a scrubby bush called dāmā. Indeed the table-lands lying between here and the Lāl Dākā were more scattered over with a scrubby sort of vegetation than any other locality I had visited in Hundés. Towards evening the sky, which had been cloudless since the slight snowstorm we had experienced at Tāzāng, became over-cast, and a shower of rain fell, which raised the temperature in a most sudden and remarkable manner—so much so that I could dispense with many of my warm wraps at night. Just after I had turned in to bed, a messenger arrived with a note —a surprising event in these inhospitable wilds. The epistle was from a son of the late Mr F. Wilson (of Himalayan hunting celebrity), intimating that he had just come over the Chor Hōti pass, and that his baggage-animals being unable to get as far as my camp that night, he (in a true sportsman-like spirit) had therefore sent on a messenger to ask me the direc-tion of my beat next day, in order that he might not interfere by hunting over it. In reply, I told him I was leaving this ground next morning, but hoped to see him at breakfast before I started. Another note, however, arrived in his stead, telling me that as the Tibetans had allowed him only seven days in their territory, he was making the most of his short time in hunting, and so was unable to come. My time would in all probability have been equally limited had it not been for the revolver I had presented to the Jongpen of Dāpā, and the whisky with which I had propitiated his messengers.

As we intended hunting over the ground along our daily stages towards the pass, they were necessarily made rather short. The first day no game was seen, but a shot heard on the ground we had left told of Wilson having found some-thing there. Our camp was reached just in time to escape a tremendous storm of hail, accompanied by much thunder and lightning. From here we despatched two men with some jooboos to Niti for a fresh stock of supplies, our present one being rather low. Late in the evening I received another note, this time from a sportsman camped in the neighbourhood, with whom, it turned out, I was acquainted. As I had not talked a word of my native language for more than six weeks, except to my dog Ranger, I was very glad that an opportunity was thus offered of meeting with a brother sportsman, and an acquaintance to boot. For the wanderer in these dreary Tibetan solitudes is apt to get tired of his own society alone, and after a long spell of it, begins to fully realise the fact of his being naturally as gregarious in his habits as the wild animals he hunts there. Your native followers are capital fellows in their way; but, from the difference of their ideas and their mode of life, they cannot be your boon companions. You are in the same relative position to them as a burrell would be among a herd of tahr. No; Nature never intended that white men and black should amalgamate a whit more than the burrell and the tahr, when she gave them each a skin of a different colour, whatever may be argued to the contrary. I therefore decided to remain here for a day, and asked my compatriot over to breakfast next morning. He had just come over the Niti pass, and had so far found no big rams; but as he was accompanied by an excellent Bhōtia shikaree, and was *en route* for the Lāl Dākā, his work was still before him. After hearing from him how the busy world had been wagging during the past two months, and giving him in return all the information I thought might be useful, of this quiet and remote corner of it, not forgetting to describe the whereabouts of the big wounded ram, I wished him good luck as he continued his way towards the Dukka hills.

In the evening I took a murderous advantage of a large flock of blue Tibetan pigeons that came and settled to feed near the camp. A raking pot-shot on the ground, followed up with the second barrel as they rose, floored a baker's dozen of them, which, with eight I had secured the previous evening in the same ignoble manner, kept me in pigeon-pies for a week or more. The adage, " it never rains but it pours," was exemplified when again I was aroused from my slumbers by a messenger with yet another note. This one had been sent by an officer of the great Trigonometrical Survey of India, who with his party had arrived at our last camping-place, after crossing the Üntadhura pass from the province of Kumaon. He was on his way, he told me, to fix his survey stations on the highest points of the Lāl Dākā, with a view to making observations from them of more distant, and, to Europeans, almost unknown regions beyond the Sut-lej. His letter contained a message respecting his progress thus far, which he asked me to convey to his chief—Colonel J. T. Walker, R.E., at Dehra Doon. I congratulated myself on having finished my hunting operations on the Lāl Dākā before he and his party commenced their scientific ones, which, valuable as they most assuredly would be to geo-graphical interests, were not likely to be conducive to those of sport.

Next day we sent our camp on a few miles, whilst Puddoo and I took a beat over the broken slopes above, which turned out blank. In the evening, however, we did some successful fish-poaching—at which my Goorkha servant proved an adept —in a stream that ran past the camp, by constructing a dam to divert the course of the water above a shallow pool, the result being about a dozen fish left high and dry. They averaged five or six inches in length, and were coarse-headed, and to all appearance scaleless, of a greyish colour above, silvery below, and profusely covered with dark-grey spots. Some of the streams in Tibet contain a prodigious number of fish, and all, I believe, are good eating. Many of the streams lose themselves in the sand, and appear again at intervals, sometimes only in little pools of clear water.

These pools often teem with little fish about the size of small minnows. The glacier streams that flow from the north side of the Himalayan range, though perfectly clear until noon, are in the afternoon far more muddy and thick than those that flow from the south side. The fish in these northward-flowing streams ascend the clear little brooks that run into them, often in shoals, when quantities of them can sometimes easily be captured up to a pound or more in weight.

Here we found some Niti Bhōtias encamped, and amongst them one of Puddoo's brothers. From him we learnt that the Niti pādān, who was travelling by another route, had brought up a lot of letters and newspapers for me; so I at once despatched a messenger to overhaul him, the arrival of a post-bag being as welcome and exciting an event as it was an unusual one in this remote region.

The ground now became more tiresome to traverse; the sides of the deep ravines we had to cross in our next day's work along the base of the Himalayan slopes being very abrupt, and the earth of which they were composed rotten and friable from constant frosts. The elevation, too, being considerably higher than that of the table-lands below, we consequently had " bellows to mend " pretty often, owing to the constant succession of ups and downs. Away up on the steep slopes above where we intended to camp, we made out with the telescope a flock of some twenty *Oves Ammon*, but all of them were ewes and lambs. Five or six burrell rams were also descried lower down, and to these we at once devoted our energies. We had managed to get round well above them, as we thought, when Puddoo, who was leading, suddenly caught sight of a single ram that was still slightly above us, at what looked to be well over 200 yards off. By great good luck he did not detect us from the commanding position he occupied, before we had made ourselves as flat as possible behind a hummock. As a burrell is not so big a mark as an *Ovis*

Ammon, and there was such a gale of wind blowing as to make accurate shooting almost impossible, I refrained from attempting to take him at so great a disadvantage, hoping that we might eventually get nearer, until presently he lay down where he was. The sun had now sunk behind the snowy Himalayan summits, and still the burrell did not move. At long-last he rose, and as it had grown too late for us to wait until he thought proper to shift his ground, I decided to risk a long shot. He was standing broadside on, with the upper half of his body showing against the sky, and the strong wind was blowing from directly behind him; so taking as steady an aim as rude Boreas would permit, I let drive at his haunch, trusting that the deflected bullet might catch him somewhere about the shoulder. "*Habet!*" Away he goes with that reckless headlong speed which an animal, when struck in the region of the heart, so often puts forth for a short distance ere he falls lifeless; and almost immediately we lose sight of him behind a neighbouring brow. As I had distinctly heard the unmistakable "tell" of the bullet, we at once followed up, and soon found him lying stone-dead, about 150 yards beyond where he had disappeared, with the bullet-hole just behind his shoulder. His head, which was a fairly good one, was cut off, and leaving his carcass to be fetched next morning, we were soon "making tracks" towards camp. On our way down we disturbed a large flock of burrell, our attention having first been drawn towards them by the clatter of stones and shingle dislodged, in their rapid flight, on the steep hill-face they were ascending. As far as we could see in the dusky light, they were ewes and little lambs. We were evidently in a nursery of both *Ovis Ammon* and burrell in this locality, for we had seen no small lambs of either kind elsewhere.

Previous to our descent we had noticed that the companions of the ram I had killed, which turned out to be seven in number, had, after their first scare from the shot, resumed

2 F

their composure and recommenced feeding considerably higher
up among the slopes, owing probably to their not having
actually seen us. We therefore decided to remain here a
day, with a view to again attempting to circumvent them;
besides, the dead beast had to be fetched down.

By reason of the manner in which nature so often assimilates the colour of wild animals to their surroundings, it is
sometimes difficult to detect them at a distance with the
naked eye, unless they are in motion; and the burrell exhibits
a marked instance of this. With the aid of the telescope,
however, we soon discovered the rams again next morning,
though they had shifted their ground to where it entailed a
long circuit above to approach them. At length we arrived
within 180 yards or so of their position, which was as near
as we could possibly manage to get. It was not only a long
shot, but also a nasty downward one, for which your sight
elevation is always most difficult to judge correctly, even when
you have not got rarefied air to take into account as well;
consequently the first bullet went clean over the big ram I
fired at. The report of the rifle, from being so far above
them, I suppose, had luckily only the effect of startling the
animals without putting them to flight. My first shot had
given me a clue to the proper sighting, so the second was
aimed about a yard short of the same fellow's stern as he
stood end on with his head from me. Away they all scam-
pered this time, but we could see that the one I had shot at,
which had taken a separate line of his own, carried his off
hind-leg dangling loosely about, though he still held on until
we lost sight of him behind a ridge. We followed as quickly
as possible to a commanding spot on the ridge, whence he
was again viewed, now moving more slowly over a high tract
of bare undulating ground, sloping gently up towards the
snow-fields above, for which he was evidently steering. We
watched him with the glass as he continued to hobble on,
sometimes standing for a few moments to rest, until we be-

gan to despair of his ever lying down, as we hoped he would
do. So I had my breakfast, and by the time it was finished
the burrell must have been about two miles off. He now,
however, began to show signs of a more permanent stoppage,
for all above him was a steep bed of snow, which he evidently
did not care to ascend with a broken leg, for he altered his
course and moved slowly out of sight in a neighbouring ravine.

After watching for some time without seeing the beast
emerge from the ravine, we concluded he must have at last
lain down there, so we set off as fast as the lead-like weight
of our " stumps " and the power of our " bellows " at such an
altitude would admit of, until at length we neared the ravine.
Cautiously we stole towards it, as if treading on eggs; but on
peering into it, not a sign of our burrell could we see. Thinking he must have gone down the ravine, we moved carefully
onward with a view to searching for his tracks, and had not
proceeded many yards when we heard a clatter behind us.
To our surprise we saw that the beast had jumped up from
where he had been lying hidden behind the cover of a rock
just below where we had at first looked over into the shallow
ravine. As he made off upward, along its wide and gently
sloping bed, I lay down and got my elbows well planted for
the steady pot-shot I each moment expected he would offer if
he chanced to stop, as I did not care to risk missing him with
a snap running one, which might have scared him away for
good. At last he pulled up and turned broadside on to look
back. I hesitate to mention the distance that I judged lay
between us and him; suffice it to say, I thought it necessary
to raise the sight that was marked 300 yards. Everything,
however, was in my favour except the distance. The day
was less windy than usual, the ground was fairly level, and
my position was as steady as if I had been aiming at a target.
Nevertheless I was as much astonished as delighted at seeing
the ram fall flat on his side without even a struggle. On
examining him we had some difficulty in finding the mark

of the bullet that had floored him, until at last we discovered it in his neck, close behind the ears, which accounted for his having dropped so stone-dead. It was a lucky fluke. His horns were very prettily arched and 25 inches long. We were now a long way from camp, and as we proposed striking our tents early on the morrow, it was necessary to have the burrell fetched down that day; so we merely covered him up with stones as a protection from the wolves and birds, and after planting a stick with a handkerchief attached to attract attention towards the cairn, descended as quickly as possible. On our way down we descried in the distance a large flock of *Oves Ammon*, ewes and lambs, which we took to be the same we had seen on the previous evening.

Between this camp and the next, the slopes above the Tāzāng table-lands were worked over, but nothing better was seen than some ewe *Oves Ammon* and a flock of young males, which soon showed us the white of their sterns as they went scouring away in the distance. It was here that my friend Colonel E. Smyth many years before shot the largest ram *Ovis Ammon* of the many he has killed. It was lying on open exposed ground, but to his surprise he managed easily to approach it within 100 yards, and rolled it over with his first shot. He found it to be a ram of the largest size, with immense horns, but very old and toothless, and nothing but skin and bone. It was so thin that even the Hoonyas, who will eat kiang, dog, fox, or any animal they can find, would have nothing to say to it. Colonel Smyth said he considered himself very fortunate in having secured such a fine specimen, as he thought the animal could not possibly have lived through the winter.

A very troublesome mile or so had to be traversed before reaching our camp, through a deep abrupt-scarped ravine filled with huge detached blocks of rock and masses of hard old snow, over which we had to clamber. Our jooboos had been brought round by a lower and easier route. The Tartar

7. Tibetan Gazelle.
8. Do, skin.
9. Wild Yak, cow.
10. Shappoo.
11. Burrell.
12. Wild Yak's skin.
13. Tibetan Gazelle skin.
14. Do. Antelope skin.
15. Burrell skin.
16. Wild Yak's tail.

1. Wild Yak, bull.
   This bull, a particularly fine specimen, was killed by Major J. Leith Ross, Scottish Borderers.

2. Tibetan Antelope.
3. Tibetan Antelope.
4. Ovis Ammon.
5. Ovis Ammon.
6. Tibetan Gazelle.

TIBETAN GAME

escort here bade me farewell, and took their way homeward mounted on their bovine chargers, trusting to my good behaviour during the remainder of my short sojourn in their territory. They departed rejoicing greatly in a " bucksheesh " with which I presented them; and being Lamas, let us hope they gave their little prayer-wheels an extra twirl on my behalf, as a parting benediction.

The following morning broke with rain, which was still drizzling when we packed up and started about noon. It had been our intention to cross the pass that day, but it was now too late to attempt to get farther than its foot. In a bed of black-looking soil we passed on our way I found numerous fossils — ammonites and belemnites — which my Bhōtia companions called " shalgram " stones. About a mile short of the spot where we proposed passing the night we took shelter from the rain, until the jooboos came up, in a blanket-tent—the *douane* of the pass. Two of its five or six occupants were squatted on the ground throwing dice, whilst the rest were lolling lazily about, either dozing or smoking their little brass-bowled pipes. The manners of these Tartar excisemen were bluff and independent, but quite civil. On our entering the tent, a small wooden cup was ladled full of tea from a dirty metal pot on the fire, and offered to each of us in turn. The tea[1] was made, as is the custom in Tibet, with butter and salt. It was greasy uninviting stuff, but I swallowed a cup of it in good-fellowship. This rite of Tibetan hospitality being over, the play was resumed. The ostensible stakes were pebbles, though they doubtless represented something more valuable. The dice were cast from the little wooden cups of the players, each time with a short exclamation like " put." Although I watched the game intently for some time, I failed to follow the intricate score. On rising to leave the tent I was

[1] The Tibetans import their tea from China in the form of solid lumps known as "brick-tea."

presented with a token of goodwill from the Jongpen, in the shape of some more yaks' tails, and two round lumps of butter sewn up in raw sheep's-hide as tight and hard as a cricket-ball. Puddoo told me that yak-milk butter thus prepared keeps good for a very long time in the dry cold climate of Tibet, and that these balls were probably more than a year old. Whatever was their age, the butter they contained was tolerably palatable.

The rain had now become sleet, and the icy wind blowing down off the snow-fields had increased to a gale, which made pitching the tents, with our hands benumbed with cold, a rather trying job. As the scant amount of grass-root fuel we could collect was wet, and refused to emit anything but smoke, I served out grog all round to my shivering companions, and after a hastily despatched meal, turned in under my blankets to try and keep warm. In the morning there were two inches of snow on the tents, it was still snowing, and the pass was enveloped in mist. About eleven o'clock the sun shone forth again, so we commenced the ascent. The jooboos had a rough time of it ploughing up through the fresh-fallen snow, which was also most trying to our eyes. On the summit of the pass we met the men and jooboos returning from Niti with the supplies. A leathern flask of native spirit they had brought with them was produced and freely imbibed from by my Bhōtia followers, who had not had a big drink for a month. The liquor was weak mawkish-tasted stuff like bad whisky. It was potent enough, however, to make Puddoo very drunk, so I left him to the tender mercies of his companions. When he turned up towards evening at the tents, he had got sufficiently sober to look sheepish and ashamed of himself. And here I may offer a bit of advice: never touch spirits on a cold high pass, where their effects are as rapid as they are disagreeable, and your head often aches badly enough there without them.

The road between the pass and Niti had been repaired by the Bhōtias. Even in the narrow defile above Goting, where the snow-bed had now disappeared and the track lay over the steep stony scarps rising from the river, the jooboos had not much difficulty in getting along, although in some places, on landslips, it was like walking over loose broken bricks. And below Goting, where the steep snow-slopes had been so troublesome, you might almost have cantered a pony. About Niti, too, what a change had come over the scene! The village was busy with life, and the neighbouring heights, which only about a month before had been cold, bare, and desolate, were now cheerful with the yodling of herdsmen tending their flocks on the green slopes, and tuneful with the cuckoo's notes in the leafy birch-brakes.

As Puddoo and Co. had been celebrating their return home by a drunken debauch overnight, I had considerable difficulty in getting the jooboos collected and loaded to start at a late hour next morning. At Malāri women took the place of the jooboos as baggage-carriers, the village being almost destitute of men, most of whom had gone off with their droves of laden sheep and goats to Hundés to trade with the Hoonyas. Here I bade farewell to my worthy friend Puddoo and his Bhōtia companions, who were all about to set out again for Hundés on business of their own.

At Tapoobun I left the low hot route by which I had travelled up, and returned over the middle ranges by a higher and more beautiful one. An ascent of about 5000 feet from the river, partly through a forest of large hazel trees—not bushes—brought us to a small green flat near the ridge of a spur of Trisool, where wild-flowers and wild-strawberries vied with each other in their abundance.

During the day the clouds had been dull and lowering, veiling the mountain-tops deeply in mist, but towards evening they began to lift and disperse, and never in my wanderings over many parts of the globe have I seen anything to equal the marvellously grand and expansive panorama which the rising curtain of sun-illumined, rose-tinted vapour gradually disclosed to view. It was indeed a splendid final transformation-scene, so to speak, in this vast theatre of nature I was leaving, and will ever remain deeply engraved on my memory. Eastward, to the right, over a rugged foreground of huge fragments of grey rock, and the irregular line of pointed plumes of the dark-green pines shooting up, tall and straight, from the mountain-side below, rose the noble snow-cone of Doonagiri in bold relief against an intensely blue firmament; whilst the more distant crest of Kāmet (25,400 feet) reared itself among a medley of frozen peaks, glaciers, and vast untrodden snow - fields lying in dreamy magnificence away northward. Nearer, and more westward, across the profound hazy depth of the intervening valley of the Doulee, mighty phalanxes of rock-panoplied giants, mantled in violet, purple, and blue, and helmeted with eternal snow, stood resplendent in the golden glory of sunset, keeping watch, as it were, around the sacred precincts of the Badrinath shrine lying latent in one of the deep dark gorges below them.

When contemplating the sublime grandeur of those majestic snow-crowned peaks, standing there as they have done for unknown time, and, for aught we know, as they will do for countless ages, unchanged in their wan solemnity, it seemed to me that nowhere could a place in which to hold communion with the great Creator of the universe have been more fitly chosen than there, among His own mighty and wonderful works. What is the basilica of St Peter at Rome, with its vast and perfect proportions and gorgeous interior; or the Duomo at Milan, with its forest of elaborately wrought pinnacles; or the mosque of Sta Sophia at Istamboul, with its precious marbles, jasper, and porphyry, its huge cupola and graceful minarets; or our own St Paul's Cathedral, with its more solemn style of architecture; or any other grand fane fashioned by human art,—when compared with the awful magnitude and natural beauty of the creations around this hallowed spot? For hallowed it may certainly be termed, as every place which is dedicated by any creed whatsoever to the service of the one Supreme Being whom all acknowledge ought to be. Yet, sad to say, there are some—let us hope they are few—who ignore the sanctity of a Hindoo place of pilgrimage, and who preach nothing but damnation for the lame, the blind, and the poor infirm old devotee who, to show his faith in the tenets of a religion in which he has been brought up to believe, and to whom they have been rendered venerable by the observances of ages,[1] trudges his weary way from the uttermost parts of Hindustan, often barefooted and enduring the most cruel hardships, all in the earnest hope of being able to wash away his sins in the, to him, holy hot-spring at Badrinath. Surely this faithful, though in many respects misguided, pilgrim may, through the infinite mercy of the Almighty, hope for salvation as much as the uncharitable individual, calling himself a Christian, who presumes to condemn him as a "heathen." Does such an one ever think, when fulfilling his mission to make converts to a better religion, that many professing it have but the form and little of the real unselfish religious feeling which is so fully manifested by many a poor Hindoo?

Some such thoughts as these filled my mind whilst I sat enraptured with the glorious scene before me. Not a sound was there to disturb my reverie but the wild call of the moonal pheasant echoing among the neighbouring crags, as I watched the cold grey shade creeping slowly on, gradually darkening each successive sunlit mountain tier, until it stole over the highest peaks of eternal snow, leaving them weird-looking and unearthly in their stern frozen dignity, their

[1] The Vedas—the sacred books of the Hindoos—are said to have been written more than 1000 B.C.

pallid lineaments each moment growing more dim in the deepening gloom.

The chilly night wind that came whispering through the pine-trees, wafting an alluring odour from the culinary department, and a voice at my elbow murmuring " Khana tyar " (dinner is ready), soon recalled me from the ideal to the real ; and I was very hungry.

In two days from here I reached Ramnee—a charming locality as regards scenery and climate, and a capital centre for sport, there being excellent ground for jurrow, gooral, and other middle-range game, in its almost immediate vicinity, and both burrell and tahr were plentiful on the higher ranges within a few days' reach of it. But the rainy season had now set in, and the horns of the jurrow stags were still in velvet; so I proceeded on my way, and in about ten more days had rejoined my regiment.

This was my last expedition to the higher regions of those grand old mountains, whose memories are so dear to me, and which, alas, I shall never see again !

Tartar tent.

CHAPTER XXV.

CONTAINING A FEW HINTS CONCERNING KIT, CAMP-EQUIPAGE, ETC., FOR
A HIMALAYAN HUNTING-TRIP, WHICH, TO THE YOUNG HAND, MAY
BE USEFUL.

BEFORE taking leave of the kind reader, I would crave his
patience for a moment or two longer whilst I add a few concluding remarks, some of which may be of use to the inexperienced, whereas others I should perhaps call apologies for
my shortcomings.

To those who are not disciples of St Hubert, should they
have cared to open such a volume, the fact of its being
almost entirely devoted to subjects connected with wild sport
will, I fear, have made it dull and unavoidably egotistical;
and the brief descriptions of animals will, I daresay, have
been as uninteresting as they are imperfect. These latter are
mere notes of my own observations. They are given more
for the benefit of those who, being unacquainted with the
Himalayan *feræ naturæ*, may naturally, when reading of their
pursuit, wish to know something about their general appearance[1] and habits, than with the idea of adding anything to
natural history beyond that which is well known.

The tyro, I venture to hope, may not have found this book
altogether uninteresting, and some of the hints it contains
may possibly be of some service to him.

[1] The two groups of heads, from photographs by Mr R. Milne of Aboyne,
have been given with the same intention.

To any old Himalayan sportsman who may have perused it, most of its contents will doubtless have proved stale. Still, I trust that it will have served to while away a few leisure hours by recalling to his mind some of the scenes and incidents of his own experiences.

To such as consider competition in scoring a big bag more than the beauties of nature, combined with real wild sport, my sentiments have perhaps been rather freely expressed. But in giving vent to them I feel sure I only echo the voice of the majority; for it behoves every one who has the interests of sport truly at heart, to strive as far as possible to discourage cruel, useless, and indiscriminate destruction of game at all seasons in a country where there are no strictly enforced laws for its protection.

One object at any rate will have been attained, if the unvarnished sketches of wild Himalayan life and sport I have endeavoured to portray may, in conjunction with other works on the same subject, offer an incitement for young hands going to India to spend some of their spare time there profitably for both mind and body, in visiting these grand and inexhaustible hunting-grounds. But those who hope to be successful in Himalayan sport must be prepared to undergo a good deal of trouble, toil, and frequent disappointment, and to have a fair stock of those cardinal virtues in all manly sports—namely, patience, endurance, and perseverance. For no one ought to start with the idea that game will always be found wherever it is sought after, be the ground ever so good.

By the inexperienced in rough mountain work, it may perhaps be expected that I should offer a few suggestions respecting the kit which ought to be taken on a hunting-trip to the Himalayas. Well, to those I say, take nothing from your own country beyond the requirements of an ordinary traveller, except your battery,—a double 500-bore Express rifle, and a 12-bore gun,[1] will, I think, be ample; its ammunition; a good

---

[1] A Lancaster's "Colindian" would perhaps be the best.

telescope with large field; and, if you be disciples of the immortal Izaak, your fishing-tackle. To these may be added a couple of pairs of strong shooting-boots well shod with square-headed nails, and a few pairs of very thick double-heeled and double-toed worsted stockings. Tents and all other requisites, even to a Warren's cooking-pot, can easily be procured in India, and most of them will be more suitable for the purpose they are intended than the things you may spare yourselves the trouble of carrying so far with you.

The tent I have always used, and which, I think, will be found comfortable and portable, as well as suitable for pitching on a limited space, is of the following description. Material, the common cotton cloth of India called "dosootee" —as being light and easily dried—lined with coarse white (as being more cheerful than the ordinary black) native blanket. Width of tent, 9½ feet; length from pole to pole, 7½ feet; height 6½ feet, with small hanging walls at the sides 9 inches deep. Four short ropes of thin but strong cord, for making fast to pegs on each side; and a stay-rope for each upright pole, of the same material. The ridge and upright poles to be of thin strong male bamboo. Front end of tent to open from top to bottom, but made so as to overlap well when closed either with strings or leather buttons. Back end to open in like manner, but made to lace up, with a flap to button over the lacing in order to keep out the wind. By this means the tent can be thrown wide open at both ends for a free current of air during hot weather. In order to resist the wear and tear of stones, which in Tibet are often piled round the bottom of the tent, it should be edged all round with coarse thick tape called "newar," four inches wide. Such a kind of little tent, or "shuldarree" as in India it is called, can be carried by one man, and the poles used as walking-staves by the coolies. A second tent of a similar description will be required for your servants. In the Himalayas, tent-pegs can generally be cut near at hand; but for Tibet, where wood is not procurable, about two dozen light iron ones will be necessary, and made so that when not in use they can be chained together and secured with a padlock, otherwise they are apt to stick to "light-fingered" hands like needles to a magnet.

The best kind of camp-bed is that made like the native's common "charpai" (bedstead, literally meaning four legs), constructed so that the side and end poles can be removed from the holes made for them in the legs. A piece of strong "durrie" (coarse Indian canvas) is laced tightly to one of the end and one of the side poles, the other two having first been passed through loops made to receive them by doubling over the canvas, thereby saving time and trouble in lacing. The great advantage of such a bed is its simplicity, as, if a pole is broken, it can easily be replaced with a stick from the nearest wood; besides its convenience of transport.

For whatever else in the way of travelling equipments the sportsman may deem necessary, I may refer him to 'Galton's Art of Travel' and 'Hints to Travellers,' published by the Royal Geographical Society. But the less he takes with him, beyond what is absolutely required, the better, more especially on the higher ranges, where carriage for his traps and his trophies is often difficult to obtain.

The following will be found a good way of dealing with large-horned heads, as rendering them more portable. When skinning a head, which should be cut off as near the trunk as possible without disfiguring the rest of the skin, commence by slitting up the skin on the *top* of the neck towards the nape, almost as far as the space between the burrs. From thence cut a short lateral slit to the base of each horn. Then peel off the skin bodily from the neck and head, severing the cartilages of the ears from the head as they are reached. After the skull has been thoroughly cleaned, and the lower jaw removed from it, saw it in two down the centre. When required to be set up, the divided skull is refastened together and the lower jaw replaced. The skin of the head should be well rubbed, more especially about the roots of the ears and the lips, with salt and wood-ashes, or arsenical soap, then partially dried in the sun and packed separately. Thus there is no chance of the hair being rubbed off in transport. Moreover, the unsightly mark of a join on the gullet is obviated when the head is eventually stuffed. I may further suggest that when your shikarees, should they be Mahomedans, perform the "hullal," they should be strictly warned not to bleed the animal close behind the jaws, as is invariably their custom, thereby disfiguring the throat; but to do so far back, where the head is to be severed from the trunk, as a bit of the neck adds so much to the appearance of a specimen when set up.

It has been suggested to me that a sketch-map should be attached to this book. But with such excellent topographical and route maps as are published at the office of the Surveyor-General of India, at Calcutta, to refer to, anything less perfect would be worse than superfluous. And with the landmarks, together with the habitats of different game given throughout these pages, the sportsman can have little difficulty in finding his way to many of the best hunting-grounds.

The means of communication with India are now so rapid and easy, that a trip to the Himalayas is nothing to any one accustomed to travel. The very name of India, which carries with it, and truly to a certain extent, the idea of heat, sickness, and discomfort, deters many from going there, except, perhaps, for a few winter months, when some of its grandest attractions are lost to the sportsman or tourist, owing to the higher Himalayan ranges being then almost impracticable from snow. But it must be borne in mind that a "gentleman at large" in India differs vastly, in his position there, from a servant of Government. The latter has, of course, to put up with whatever inconveniences may fall to his lot, and is dependent for his shikar expeditions on the limited periods of leave he may be able to obtain, and these at times of year which are not always the best either for travel or sport; whereas the former, who is tied neither to time nor to place, can suit his taste as to season and climate, and indulge his sporting or wandering proclivities to his heart's content, amidst romantic scenery which rivals, if it does not surpass, that of any other part of the known world.

Horns of Goen (swamp deer), killed in the Oude Terai.

PRINTED BY WILLIAM BLACKWOOD AND SONS.

cf.

d H.

CPSIA information can be obtained at www.ICGtesting.com
Printed in the USA
LVOW13*0842090614

389202LV00010B/57/P